EFFORTLESS ACTION

Effortless Action

Wu-wei as Conceptual Metaphor and
Spiritual Ideal in Early China

Edward Slingerland

OXFORD
UNIVERSITY PRESS

2003

OXFORD
UNIVERSITY PRESS

Oxford   New York
Auckland   Bangkok   Buenos Aires   Cape Town   Chennai
Dar es Salaam   Delhi   Hong Kong   Istanbul   Karachi   Kolkata
Kuala Lumpur   Madrid   Melbourne   Mexico City   Mumbai   Nairobi
São Paulo   Shanghai   Taipei   Tokyo   Toronto

Copyright © 2003 by Oxford University Press, Inc.

Published by Oxford University Press, Inc.
198 Madison Avenue, New York, New York 10016

www.oup.com

Oxford is a registered trademark of Oxford University Press

Library of Congress Cataloging-in-Publication Data
Slingerland, Edward G. (Edward Gilman)
Effortless action : Wu-wei as conceptual metaphor and spiritual ideal in early China /
Edward Slingerland.
   p. cm.
Includes bibliographical references and index.
ISBN 0-19-513899-6
1. Philosophy, Chinese—to 221 B.C. 2. Nothing (Philosophy). I. Title.
B126 .S645 2003
181'.11—dc21   2002071518

9 8 7 6 5 4 3 2 1

Printed in the United States of America
on acid-free paper

For
Nana Person,
who taught me how to fish like a Daoist,

and
Pop Person,
who continues to teach me the joys of being a Confucian

Preface

This book attempts to accomplish two primary tasks, one related to subject matter and the other methodological in nature. With regard to subject matter, the goal is to present a systematic account of the role of the personal spiritual ideal of wu-wei or "effortless action" in Warring States Chinese thought, showing how it serves as a common ideal for both Daoists and Confucians, and also contains within itself a conceptual tension that motivates the development of Warring States thought. Methodologically, this book represents a preliminary attempt to apply the contemporary theory of conceptual metaphor to the study of early Chinese thought. Although this book focuses on Warring States China, both the subject matter and methodology have implications that go beyond the study of early China. The subject of wu-wei, it will be argued, is relevant to anyone interested in later East Asian religious thought or the so-called virtue-ethics tradition in the West, while the technique of conceptual metaphor analysis—along with the principle of "embodied realism" upon which it is based—provides an exciting new theoretical framework and methodological tool for the study of comparative thought, and even the humanities in general. Part of the purpose of this work is thus to help introduce scholars in the humanities and social sciences to this methodology, and provide an example of how it may be applied to a particular specialty such as religious thought.

Because of the broader implications of this project, I have attempted to make it accessible to scholars beyond the narrow field of Chinese thought by including background material that sinologists may find unnecessary, but that will hopefully allow scholars from a broad range of humanities disciplines to follow the discussion. I have also attempted to keep to a minimum technical discussions concerning textual issues or debates in my particular subfield, and whenever such material has proved necessary I have tried to relegate it to appendices. Specialists in the field of Chinese thought will find more in-depth discussion of technical matters in the dissertation upon which this book is based (Slingerland 1998). It is never easy to address adequately the interests and needs of a broad academic audience, and I can only hope that I will be able to hold the interest of my intended target audience without completely alienating any particular subgroup.

Wu-wei as spiritual ideal was the subject of my Ph.D. dissertation, which represents approximately half of this current work. I would like to acknowledge again the help of my dissertation committee members Lee Yearley and Carl Bielefeldt, and most of all my committee chair, Philip J. Ivanhoe, who mentored me throughout graduate school and beyond, and without whose painstaking attention and carefully considered comments the dissertation and this book would never have come into being. The methodological approach is entirely new, and my dissertation advisors at Stanford are in no way to be held responsible for any errors introduced or other scholarly crimes committed during the extensive rewrite process. The field of contemporary metaphor theory is quite young, and as a relative neophyte I have been very grateful for the guidance and feedback provided by George Lakoff and Mark Johnson, as well as the other participants in the workshop on metaphor theory and the humanities held at the University of Southern California in October 2000 under the aegis of The Ahmanson Initiative. During the rewrite process I have benefited greatly from the comments and criticisms of Philip J. Ivanhoe, Joel Sahleen, Mark Johnson, and George Lakoff. Most of all, I would like to thank Eric Hutton—an academic Bodhisattva, ever generous with his time and energy—who heroically agreed to review in detail the entire manuscript, helped me to correct some of the more egregious faults, and did his best to get me to make this work more palatable to philosophers. The fact that he was probably not entirely successful is attributable to my own stubbornness rather than to any lack of effort or sensitivity on his part, and I apologize to him in advance. Thanks are due to Cynthia Read at OUP for her basic faith in this project and the patient extensions granted to me as the rewrite grew in magnitude, to Theo Calderara, and to Bob Milks and his OUP editorial team. Finally, the monumental and brutal task of converting this manuscript into FrameMaker, typesetting it, and inputting copyedits was undertaken by Mary Behshid—friend, FrameMaker Goddess, and general all-around wonderful person—who somehow managed to pull it off with unfailing good cheer and grace. My heartfelt thanks to her, as well as my apologies to Farshid, Aram, Iman, and Rosemary for taking up so much of her time.

Contents

Conventions

Unless otherwise noted, all translations (whether from classical Chinese primary sources or modern Asian and European scholarship) are my own. Textual references for the *Analects*, *Laozi*, and *Mencius* refer to the standard textual divisions as reflected in the following English translations:

Analects: Lau 1979
Laozi: Lau 1963
Mencius: Lau 1970

Ode numbers for *Book of Odes* references refer to the standard Mao edition as reflected in Karlgren 1950. With regard to the two texts that lack widely accepted textual divisions small enough for convenient reference—the *Zhuangzi* and *Xunzi*—reference is made to the page number in the standard English translation and the standard critical editions of the Chinese text published by Zhonghua Shuju 中華書局, formatted as follows:

Zhuangzi: Wxxx/Gxxx, where (W) refers to the page number in Watson 1968, and (G) refers to the page number in Guo Qingfan 1961; and
Xunzi: KI-III: xxx/Wxxx, where (K) refers to the page number in Knoblock (1988–1994), the roman numeral refers to the volume (I–III) number in Knoblock, and (W) refers to the page number in Wang Xianqian 1988.

For the sake of convenience, the names, "Confucius," "Laozi," and so on, will be used to refer to the author(s) of the books that bear these names. Details of the textual problems and problems of authorship will be discussed in the appendices.

Some use will be made of traditional Chinese commentaries. While it is true that traditional Chinese commentators are less concerned than modern scholars with preventing anachronistic assumptions from being introduced to the classics, it would be foolish to ignore the insight that is provided by scholars who have spent their lives immersed in the classical tradition. When using traditional commentaries, I have made an attempt to avoid allowing post-classical metaphysical schemes (e.g., the neo-Confucian metaphysics of "principle" and "material force") to creep into my interpretation of pre-Qin texts.

Readers might note that I have followed the colloquial practice of using "them" or "their" in such sentences as, "Every person has the capacity to realize their true nature." Although this practice is often condemned as grammatically incorrect, the linguist Steven Pinker has observed (Pinker 1994: 378–379) that this condemnation is based upon a logical confusion. In a sentence such as "Everyone returned to their seats," "their" is not functioning as a referential possessive pronoun that must agree in number with its antecedent, but is rather functioning as what linguists refer to as a "bound variable" referring to an earlier "quantifier"; the sentence thus means, "For all X, X returned to X's seat." Since "X" does not refer to any particular person, the "their" in this sentence actually refers to no one at all, and is merely a homonym of the more familiar referential pronoun. Pinker suggests that anyone who doubts this try to "correct" the sentence: "Mary saw everyone before John saw them." The use of the plural pronoun in such cases, Pinker concludes (and I concur), "has the advantage of embracing both sexes and feeling right in a wider variety of sentences" (Pinker 1994: 379).

The pinyin method of romanization will be adopted throughout, except in citations that employ Wade-Giles or in the case of Chinese scholars who use different spellings for their own names.

A convention in the study of conceptual metaphor is to indicate metaphor schemas by means of small caps, as well as to use "schemas" (rather than the proper but awkward "schemata") as the plural of schema. It is also a practice in this field to refer to "entailments" of given metaphor schema, in which usage "entailment" has a rather looser meaning than it does as a technical term in the study of logic.

EFFORTLESS ACTION

Introduction

> Students of Chinese philosophy have usually seen their subjects as a succession of people who lived, acted, taught and died, rather than a weaving of strands, any one of which may be a subtle dialectic of question and answer.
>
> —David Nivison, *The Ways of Confucianism*

Western scholars have in recent years grown justifiably reluctant to make sweeping generalizations about the character of Chinese or Eastern thought. Not only is most of the history of Chinese thought complicated by the presence of such "alien" traditions as Buddhism, but the pre-Buddhist tradition has shown itself to be much more complicated and multifaceted than once was thought. For example, the reconstruction of previously lost works such as the later Mohist canons has made less convincing the often-heard claim that "the Chinese" were not interested in problems of logic or language, while the renewed interest in the thought of Xunzi has shown the classical Confucian tradition to be much more complicated than the received, neo-Confucian account of Mencius as the sole orthodox successor to Confucius would have it. Nonetheless, our increasingly sophisticated conception of early Chinese thought allows us to continue to maintain some generalizations, paramount among which is the claim that Chinese thinkers were interested primarily in *practical* rather than *theoretical* questions. While there was a certain amount of debate between various schools concerning such theoretical questions as, for instance, what the good life for humans might be, the primary focus of early Chinese thinkers remained the problem of how to *become* good. The sort of knowledge that was therefore valued was not abstract knowledge *that* the good was to be defined in a certain way, but concrete knowledge concerning *how* to act in a way that was good, [1] and the various schools customarily defended their positions not by theoretical argument but by pointing to exemplars who personified their values or by focusing on the practical implications of their own and others' theories. Similarly, with regard to ethical standards, these thinkers appeal not to a set of maxims or abstract principles but rather to something resembling Aristotle's "good person" criterion[2]—that is, the concrete model provided by teachers or exemplars from the past.

The religious exemplars that we find in early Chinese texts are thus admired more for the sort of practical skill knowledge they display in their actions than the sort of arguments that they could marshall in defense of their particular way of life. In his article, "Pensée occidentale et pensée chinoise: le regard et l'acte,"

Jean-François Billeter has formulated this distinction between theoretical and practical forms of knowledge in terms of a contrast between ocular and action-based metaphors for true knowledge. "The 'ocular metaphor' is conspicuous in Chinese texts through its absence," he observes, "and the epistemological problematiques that developed from this metaphor in the West are therefore also unknown" (1984: 34). This observation is exaggerated—ocular metaphors are in fact found throughout the early Chinese corpus[3]—but its basic thrust is still quite valid. For these mainstream early Chinese thinkers, true understanding is not an abstract gaze that—as for Plato or even the neo-Confucians—sees *through* concrete reality in order to acquire a theoretical grasp of some sort of underlying (and ultimately more real) order. Rather, true "clarity" is an illumination of the actual landscape before one's eyes that serves to guide one through it, and is thus always intimately and inextricably tied to action. Thus, in place of the representational model of knowledge exemplified by the "gaze" of a subject acquiring theoretical knowledge of an eternal order behind the phenomenal world, the Chinese instead emphasize a sort of knowledge appropriate to a subject already engaged in the world through the medium of "the act." This is the import of David Hall and Roger Ames's well-known contention that thinking (*si* 思) in the *Analects* is "not to be understood as a process of abstract reasoning, but is fundamentally *performative* in that it is an activity whose immediate consequence is the achievement of a practical result."[4]

Several scholars have suggested that this form of practical, engaged knowledge be understood as a sort of "skill-knowledge."[5] That is, in understanding what early Chinese thinkers thought of as knowledge, we should see it in terms of mastery of a set of practices that restructure both one's perceptions and values. The theme of skill- or practice-knowledge has been explored in some detail by contemporary Western thinkers such as Michael Polanyi 1966 and Alasdair MacIntyre 1984, 1990, both of whom employ their concepts of "tacit knowledge" or practice mastery as foils to critique the representational theories of knowledge so dominant in recent Western thought. Most central to the organization of this work is the fact that this alternate model of knowledge inevitably brings with it a correspondingly alternate ideal of perfection: an ideal of perfectly skilled action rather than comprehensive theoretical knowledge. For the early Chinese thinkers I will be discussing, the culmination of knowledge is understood not in terms of a grasp of abstract principles but rather as an ability to move through the world and human society in a manner that is completely spontaneous and yet still fully in harmony with the normative order of the natural and human worlds—the *Dao* 道 or "*Way*." While this ideal (along with the alternate model of knowledge upon which it is based) allows these thinkers to avoid the various epistemological dilemmas involved in, for instance, the Cartesian ideal of an isolated subject somehow obtaining perfect knowledge of an external objective realm,[6] Jean-François Billeter notes that such a model of perfection (which he refers to as "l'idée de l'act parfait") must inevitably bring with it its own unique set of conflicts:

The idea of perfected action seems to us a sort of central insight that, in China, exercises a stronger pull upon the mind than any other, and toward which speculative thought is constantly drawn. . . . In Chinese texts, this idea is most commonly present only in an implicit form, because it is expressed in and lies beneath all of the various forms to which we must refer. The passage from the *Zhuangzi* that has served as our point of departure [the story of Cook Ding cutting up the ox] seems to us to possess a paradigmatic value, although this value remains as yet to be firmly established. In any case, our idea will continue to rest upon a relatively arbitrary edifice in so far as it has yet to prove its hermeneutic value in contact with multiple texts. Before it can be accorded some degree of importance, it must be put to the test in a different fashion: by rendering more intelligible not just a single isolated passage, but rather *an entire philosophical problematique as well as its historical development*; and by revealing more clearly the coherence and the power—as well as the tensions, contradictions and the aporias—of Chinese philosophy, or, better, Chinese philosophies. In short, it must perform a service with regard to the Chinese context comparable to that which it seems one can expect [in the West] from the notion of the "ocular metaphor." (1984: 50; emphasis added)

Although this project was conceived and begun before I became aware of Billeter's work, it can be seen as in many ways answering his call to arms. My purpose in this book is to demonstrate that the attainment of *wu-wei* 無為 — "effortless action" or action that is spontaneous and yet nonetheless accords in every particular with the normative order of the cosmos—serves as a central spiritual ideal and philosophical problematique of a particular group of pre-Qin Chinese religious thinkers who represent the core of what (following Donald Munro) I shall refer to as "mainstream" Chinese thought: Confucius, Laozi, Mencius, Zhuangzi, and Xunzi.[7] I will also attempt to show how the ideal of wu-wei has built into it precisely the sort of tension mentioned by Billeter—a tension that I will be referring to as the "paradox of wu-wei"—and how this tension can be seen as a motivating force in the historical development of Warring States Chinese thought.

The concept of wu-wei has played an extremely important role in the development of Chinese religion, but has been rather neglected by scholars in both China and the West. In an article entitled "A Brief Discussion of the Concept of 'Wu-wei' in the Pre-Qin Period," Li Shenglong notes that:

"Wu-wei" is an extremely rich concept, including within itself views concerning nature (*ziran*), government and human existence. It has never ceased to develop, grow increasingly complex and rich, and become increasingly perfected. The scholarly world, however, has yet to systematically address either its content or course of development. (Li 1986: 7)

In the time since this comment was written, there has been at least one major work devoted to the theme of wu-wei: Roger Ames's *The Art of Rulership* (Ames 1994), which is a careful study of the development of wu-wei as a principle of government in Confucianism, Daoism, Legalism, and the syncretist text the *Huainanzi*. Ames's interest in wu-wei reflects the dominant approach toward the subject; that is, while the personal spiritual dimensions of wu-wei have not gone unnoticed, wu-wei as an ideal of government or technique of social control has been the primary focus.[8] This can be partially attributed to the fact that the term "wu-wei" itself *is* used most commonly and prominently to refer to an ideal form of government, and an approach that focuses upon the term alone and not its larger conceptual structure will thus inevitably confine itself mostly to the political context. An additional factor is that, in the later Legalist and Syncretist writings where wu-wei plays such a prominent role, it is used exclusively in the sense of a principle of government—its function as a spiritual ideal having been lost.[9] One of the purposes of this work is to invert this received approach to wu-wei. That is, I will argue that it is the personal spiritual ideal of wu-wei that is most basic to the group of "mainstream" Chinese thinkers I will discuss, and that wu-wei as a governmental ideal is parasitic upon this more fundamental conception.

In addition, my task will be to show that this common spiritual ideal of effortless or perfected action not only serves as a powerful lens through which we can view these early texts but also that, as a concept, it contains within itself a productive tension that motivates certain developments in pre-Qin religious thought. This tension arises from the fact that the state of effortless, perfected action represented by wu-wei is portrayed as a state that needs to be achieved: we are currently *not* practicing wu-wei, and the thinkers I will discuss propose various soteriological paths designed to bring us from our current state of "effortfull" action into this ideal state of effortless action. The question that inevitably arises is this: how is it possible to *try* not to try? How can a program of spiritual striving result in a state that lies beyond striving? It would seem that the very act of striving would inevitably "contaminate" the end-state.

Many scholars have noted the existence of this tension,[10] but to my knowledge it is only David Nivison who has perceived its *productive* quality. In a series of essays found in Nivison 1997, Nivison explores the tension that he refers to as the "paradox of Virtue (*de* 德)"[11] in early Confucian thought. Structurally equivalent to the paradox of wu-wei, the paradox of Virtue centers upon the fact that Virtue can only be acquired by someone who is not consciously trying to acquire it—that is, performing a virtuous act while at the same time being self-conscious of its virtuousness makes it, paradoxically, not fully virtuous. Confucius himself did not directly address this problem, but Nivison attempts to demonstrate that one of the motivating forces in the development of the Mencian and Xunzian secondary theories about human nature is a desire to resolve this paradox.[12] One of the main purposes of this work is not only to expand upon Nivison's observations concerning the productive role of this paradox in early Confucian thought but also to bring both Laozi and Zhuangzi into this discussion—to demonstrate that they too have parts to play in the "subtle dialectic of question and answer" revolving around the paradox of wu-wei.

The implications of this dialectic extend far beyond its contribution to our understanding of early Chinese thought. Arguably, the tensions produced by the paradox of wu-wei resurface in Chan Buddhism in the form of the debate between the "sudden" (*dun* 頓) and "gradual" (*jian* 漸) schools (and between the Rinzai and Soto schools of Japanese Zen),[13] and yet again in the conflict between the Lu-Wang and Cheng-Zhu branches of neo-Confucianism.[14] Indeed, one of the tasks of this work is to provide for the first time an account of the pre-Buddhist antecedents to these debates.[15] In addition, tensions resembling the paradox of wu-wei can also be identified in non-Asian forms of religious thought. For instance, David Nivison has noted some of the parallels between the Confucian paradox of Virtue and the problem in Plato that "to be taught, one must recognize the thing taught as something to be learned" (*Meno*, 80d ff.) or the puzzle raised by Aristotle that "to become just we must first do just actions and to become temperate we must first do temperate actions,"[16] and the significance of Aristotle's paradox and the so-called Meno problem for the development of virtue ethical theories in the West has been a theme explored at some length by Alasdair MacIntyre.[17] We might thus be justified in seeing the dialectic of question and answer circling about the paradox of wu-wei as having significance not only for early Chinese thinkers but also for any thinker concerned with the problem of self-cultivation—that is, with the problem of not merely winning from the individual rational assent to a set of principles but actually *transforming* that individual into a new type of person.

The Concept of Wu-wei

"Wu-wei" literally means "in the absence of/without doing exertion," and is often translated as "doing nothing" or "non-action." It is important to realize, however, that wu-wei properly refers not to what is actually happening (or not happening) in the realm of observable action but rather to the state of mind of the actor. That is, it refers not to what is or is not being done but to the phenomenological state of the doer. As Pang Pu notes in his discussion of wu-wei, the term denotes "not a basic form of action, but the mental state of the actor—the spiritual state (*jing-shen zhuangtai*) that obtains at the very moment of action" (1994: 15). It describes a state of personal harmony in which actions flow freely and instantly from one's spontaneous inclinations—without the need for extended deliberation or inner struggle—and yet nonetheless accord perfectly with the dictates of the situation at hand, display an almost supernatural efficacy, and (in the Confucian context at least) harmonize with the demands of conventional morality. As Jean-François Billeter describes it, wu-wei—what he refers to as "l'idée de l'activité parfaite"—represents a state of "perfect knowledge of the reality of the situation, perfect efficaciousness and the realization of a perfect economy of energy" (1984: 50). It represents not a transitory state but rather a set of dispositions that has been so thoroughly transformed as to conform with the normative order. This state of wu-wei harmony is even reflected in the agent's physical bearing and thus can be perceived by others.

For a person in wu-wei, proper conduct follows as instantly and spontaneously as the nose responds to a bad smell, and with the same sense of unconscious ease and joy with which the body gives in to the seductive rhythm of a song. This is not to say, however, that wu-wei actions are automatic, completely unconscious, or purely physiological.[18] The more extended phenomenological accounts of wu-wei found in such texts as the *Zhuangzi* and *Xunzi* make it clear that this state of harmony contains complex cognitive as well as somatic elements, involving as it does the integrated training of the body, the emotions, and the mind. The individual still makes choices—and may even at times pause to weigh various options or consider the situation ahead—but even such deliberations are performed with a sort of effortless ease. As Butcher Ding explains to Lord Wen Hui,

> [in cutting up an ox] whenever I come to a knot, I perceive the difficulties, adopt an attitude of careful awareness, focus my vision, slow down my movements, and move the blade with the greatest subtlety, so that [the ox] just falls apart effortlessly, like a clump of earth falling to the ground. (W51/G119)

Unlike instinctual or merely habitual forms of actions, then, wu-wei calls for some degree of awareness on the part of the agent, and allows for a considerable amount of flexibility of response.[19] Although it does not involve abstract reflection or calculation, it is not to be viewed as "mindless" behavior[20] but should rather be seen as springing from what we might call the "embodied mind."

In addition to portraying wu-wei as being characterized by a feeling of spontaneous ease and graceful effortlessness, all of the "mainstream"[21] Chinese thinkers I will discuss link this personal state of mind to an observable, almost supernatural efficacy in the world. It is this efficacy that allows the sage-king Shun to order the world merely by taking the proper ritual position, the Laozian sage to attain personal immunity from harm and be able to cause the entire world to return to simplicity, and Butcher Ding to cut up oxen for nineteen years without ever dulling his blade. As several scholars have pointed out, whereas spontaneity in the West is typically associated with subjectivity, the opposite may be said of the sort of spontaneity evinced in wu-wei: it represents the highest degree of objectivity, for it is only in wu-wei that one's embodied mind conforms to the something larger than the individual—the will of Heaven or the order represented by the Way. This is why the state of wu-wei should be seen as a *religious* ideal,[22] for it is only by attaining it that the individual realizes his or her proper place in the cosmos.

Recognition of the religious nature of wu-wei should make us cautious concerning the models we might use for understanding it. It is clear that understanding wu-wei and the sort of knowledge it involves in terms of skill-mastery is a powerful and illuminating way to portray the early Chinese thinkers I will discuss, and is indeed a metaphor that they themselves often employ. However, this model is also potentially misleading if not situated in its proper religious context.

The skill-knowledge valued by these thinkers is not to be understood on the analogy of skill in a limited practice (such as piano playing or carpentry), for we can imagine someone being a skilled pianist, for instance, and yet still an atrocious human being in other aspects of his or her life. What wu-wei represents is a perfection of a unique and ultimate skill: the skill of becoming a fully realized human being and embodying the Way in the full range of one's actions. This is why Confucius is rather contemptuous of any practice more limited than the "master-craft"[23] of becoming fully human (*ren* 仁),[24] and why Butcher Ding's magnificent performance in cutting up an ox in the *Zhuangzi* is understood by Lord Wen Hui in a metaphorical sense ("Excellent!" he exclaims at the conclusion of this story. "I have heard the words of Butcher Ding and learned the secret of caring for life"). As the formulation of this ideal in the early Chinese context involved relating the individual to a larger normative cosmic order—as well as presenting an at least implicit picture of human nature as it relates to this order—we must not lose sight of wu-wei's role as first and foremost a *spiritual* ideal. All five of the thinkers discussed share a religious worldview that has its roots in archaic Chinese religion, in which Heaven, the Way, wu-wei, and Virtue are intimately linked to one another.

Part of the problem with past treatments of the ideal of perfect skill mastery by scholars such as Robert Eno or Chad Hansen is that the place of wu-wei within this worldview has been ignored or misrepresented, which opens the way to mere conventionalism or even moral relativism. Such conventionalism or relativism has no place in the early Chinese mainstream worldview. For each of the early thinkers discussed, the "proof" that their specific way to establish contact with the Way is correct is provided by the phenomena of Virtue. Conceived of in the earliest texts of the Chinese religious tradition as a reward granted by Heaven to a person who accords with its will—as well as a power that enables that person to realize this will on earth—the manifestation of Virtue by the exemplars of their tradition served in each thinker's view as perceptible evidence that their soteriological path would lead to success. Therefore, though it can be viewed as a form of skill-mastery, wu-wei avoids the possible relativistic implications of this model by being explicitly linked to both a normative, metaphysical order and a charismatic power that was thought to be clearly apparent to believers and nonbelievers alike. "If there was a ruler who achieved order through wu-wei, was it not Shun?" we read in *Analects* 15.5. "He did nothing but make himself reverent and face South [the proper position for an emperor], that is all." For the author of this passage, the fact that Shun had achieved a state of wu-wei and thus unified and ordered the entire world solely through the power of his Virtue was a historical fact that proved the viability and superiority of the Confucian way.

Wu-wei as a spiritual ideal is thus coupled with a strong sense of realism. As Alasdair MacIntyre has noted, the model of skill-mastery in any form provides one with access to a unique type of realism that differs significantly from—and lacks some of the weaknesses of—the sort of realism found in Cartesian or Kantian representational theories of knowledge:

It is a central feature of all crafts, of furniture making and fishing and farming, as much as of philosophy, that they require the minds of those who engage in the craft to come to terms with and to make themselves adequate to the existence and properties of some set of objects conceived to exist independently of those minds. The embodied mind, in and through its activities, has to become receptive to forms [*eide*] of what is other than itself and in being constituted by those formal objects becomes, in the appropriate way, them. It is therefore not judgements which primarily correspond or conform to those realities about which they are uttered; it is the embodied mind which conforms adequately or inadequately to the objects, the *res*, the subject matter, and which evidences this adequacy or inadequacy in a number of ways, one of which is the truth or falsity of its judgements. It is in becoming adequate to its objects that the embodied mind actualizes its potentialities and becomes what its object and its own activity conjointly have been able to make it. (1990: 68)

The realism that governs the skill of cabinet making, for instance, is reflected in the fact that cabinets can be made well or poorly, and the difference between these two types of cabinets is observable in the material realm. A cabinet that cannot fulfill its intended use because its doors do not close properly or because it falls apart after a short period of use can be said to have been made by a *bad* cabinet maker. When we realize that the object of the skill-knowledge being cultivated by both Confucians and Daoists in early China was the Way—a normative order existing independently of the minds of the practitioners —and that one's embodied mind becoming "adequate" to this object was thought to be evinced by an apparent ease of action (wu-wei) and the possession of a sort of numinous power with observable effects (Virtue), it becomes apparent why the ideal of skill-knowledge did not lead to relativistic consequences for the Chinese. Although they disagreed with each other, each of the thinkers felt quite confident that their way was the only Way to be wu-wei.

Wu-wei as Conceptual Metaphor

Appropriating the term "wu-wei" to denote the state of effortless, perfected action that serves as both a Daoist and Confucian ideal—as well as in referring to the tension contained within this ideal as the "paradox of wu-wei"—involves an anachronism. As a term of art, wu-wei does not appear at all in one of the texts I will examine (the *Mencius*), and is found only once in another (the *Analects*)—in a chapter that is arguably of quite late provenance.[25] In the absence of a common use of "wu-wei" as a technical term, one might ask how we are to justify treating the seemingly different ideals in these texts as common expressions of "the" wu-wei ideal. This is where the conceptual metaphor approach can prove most helpful to the scholar of religious thought.[26] The fact that wu-wei is not to be understood as literal "non-doing" but rather refers to the phenomenological state of the actor (who is, in fact, quite active), suggests that we should understand the term metaphorically.[27] In what follows, I will argue that the term "wu-wei" refers to a metaphorically conceived situation where a "subject"[28] is no longer having to exert effort in order to act. As will be discussed in some detail in chapter 1, "wu-wei" was adopted as the general technical term for the state of effortless action because it represents the most general of a whole set of families of conceptual metaphors that convey a sense of effortlessness and unself-consciousness. These metaphor families include those of "following" (*cong* 從) or "flowing along with" (*shun* 順), being physically "at ease" (*an* 安), enjoying a perfect "fit" (*yi* 宜) with the world, and "forgetting" (*wang* 忘) the self—the last quality also often being expressed literally as unself-consciousness (*buzhi* 不知) or the forgetfulness that comes from strong emotions such as joy (*le* 樂).

The recognition of wu-wei as a deeper conceptual structure expressed by a variety of specific metaphorical or literal phrases allows us to avoid confusing the existence of a concept with the presence of a specific term of art. It is precisely this sort of confusion that has led some scholars to such absurd conclusions that, for instance, the early Chinese had no conception of "truth" because they lacked a single, specific term for it.[29] Many previous studies of wu-wei in both the West and in Asia have thus been hampered by what we might call a concordance-fixation: in order to understand a concept such as wu-wei, the approach is simply to wade through the concordances of the classics, pulling out passages that contain the term "wu-wei" and using these as the data for one's study. It is precisely this sort of approach that led Herrlee Creel—to mention one prominent example—to the conclusion that wu-wei is a concept that actually originated with the Legalist thinker Shen Buhai (1970: 59–60). While few scholars today find Creel's proposed chronology entirely convincing,[30] most continue to follow his lead in confining their treatments of the concept to passages in which the term of art itself appears. Ironically, Creel himself, in his treatment of the concept of "forms and names" (*xingming* 形名) in the *Shenzi,* acknowledges that this is an overly confining approach to the study of thought: "The *Shen Tzu* fragments do, I think, contain the idea denoted by *hsing-ming*," he explains, "but *the term itself does not occur once in them*" (1970: 62, n. 76 [emphasis in the original]). Creel fails to apply this insight to his treatment of wu-wei, which in turn prevents him from seeing the role that wu-wei plays as both a personal and governmental ideal in the early texts of Confucianism.

Once the term "wu-wei" itself is recognized as the linguistic sign of a deeper conceptual structure we can begin to establish a connection between such apparently diverse ideals of perfected action as the effortless, spontaneous mastery of morality displayed by Confucius at age seventy, described in *Analects* 2.4; the state in which virtue is so completely harmonized with one's inclinations that, as we read in *Mencius* 4:A:27, one "begins unconsciously to dance it with one's feet and wave one's arms in time with it"; and the sort of spiritual efficacy displayed by Butcher Ding in the *Zhuangzi*. While such connections have always been intuitively apparent to traditional commentators and Western students of these texts,[31] I will attempt to show that the contemporary theory of metaphor gives us a concrete and theoretically coherent methodology for describing the conceptual structure of metaphors such as wu-wei and documenting the connections between the various members of the wu-wei "families" of metaphors. This in turn allows us to trace the development of the *concept* of wu-wei through a diverse collection of texts in order to illustrate its central importance as a problematique in Warring States thought—an importance that is severely obscured when we focus solely upon the term "wu-wei" itself.

Overview of the Argument

Chapter 1 begins with an introduction to the contemporary theory of metaphor, followed by a brief overview of the various families of metaphors found in Warring States texts that relate to the concept of wu-wei. With this blueprint of the conceptual structure of wu-wei in place, I will then use the appearance of some of these metaphors in portions of the *Book of Odes* and *Book of History* to discuss the pre-Confucian roots of wu-wei as a spiritual ideal. Chapters 2 through 7 trace the development of this wu-wei ideal—as marked by the presence of the wu-wei families of metaphors—over the course of the Warring States period. Despite common metaphorical formulations of the wu-wei ideal, each of the texts I will examine presents its own particular soteriological strategy for realizing wu-wei in practice, and these soteriological strategies are themselves formulated in terms of conceptual metaphor. For each text, I will demonstrate how the "paradox of wu-wei" appears in a new form, manifesting itself in terms of metaphoric incommensurability with regard to soteriological strategies designed to produce wu-wei. I will argue that it is partly in response to such incommensurability that subsequent texts adopt new strategies for attaining wu-wei intended to resolve the conceptual difficulties characteristic of earlier attempts.

The attempted "solutions" to the paradox can be generally be characterized in terms of a split between self-cultivation internalism and self-cultivation externalism.[32] Each response merely chooses a horn of the dilemma upon which to impale itself. The self-cultivation internalists answer the question of how one can try not to try to be good by gravitating toward the "not trying" horn: at some level, they claim, we already *are* good, and we merely need to allow this virtuous potential to realize itself. Zhuangzi, Laozi, and Mencius fall into this camp. The self-cultivation externalists, exemplified by Xunzi (and most likely including the author(s) of the *Analects* as well), maintain, on the contrary, that it is essential that we *try* not to try. That is, they claim that we do *not* possess the resources to attain wu-wei on our own and that wu-wei is a state acquired only after a long and intensive regime of training in traditional, external forms. Toward this end they formulate a rigorous training regime designed to gradually lead us from our original state of ignorance to the pinnacle of spiritual perfection. Unfortunately neither of these responses to the paradox proves entirely satisfactory or even internally consistent, and both are plagued by various sorts of difficulties.

My first extended analysis of wu-wei will concern the *Analects*, supposedly the record of the teachings of the historical Confucius and the subject of chapter 2. Wu-wei appears in the *Analects* as a kind of fusion of two pre-Confucian ideals: the effortlessly skilled, martial aristocrat and the unself-consciously virtuous ruler. Confucius himself represents this wu-wei ideal, which in the text is portrayed as a kind of unself-conscious, effortless mastery of ritual and other Confucian practices attained through a lifetime of rigorous training in traditional cultural forms. One who has in this way mastered the Confucian Way comes to love it for its own sake, and takes a kind of spontaneous joy in its practice. The paradox of wu-wei as it appears in the *Analects* involves the problem of how one can be trained to spontaneously, unself-consciously *love* the Way if one does not love it already. If one is born already loving the Way (as is apparently the case with the disciple Yan Hui or the sage-king Shun), it would seem that the Confucian soteriological project is unnecessary. If such a feeling needs to be instilled through training, however, we have the problem of how one can try not to try: how one can force oneself to love something one does not already love.

This conceptual paradox is concretely manifested in terms of a tension between two incommensurable soteriological metaphors, the more internalist SELF-CULTIVATION AS ADORNMENT and the more externalist SELF-CULTIVATION AS CRAFT REFORMATION. The text tends to emphasize the more externalist craft model of self-cultivation as the arduous reformation of an inherently flawed or rough material, or the more effort-oriented metaphor of SELF-CULTIVATION AS LONG JOURNEY, where wu-wei is conceptualized as the destination at the end of a long, difficult journey. The problem, however, is that the author(s) of the text seem to feel that the successful cultivation of wu-wei virtue requires the proper internal motivation—metaphorically, that successful carving requires sound material or that the successful completion of a journey requires inner determination. In the absence of this inner component, the arduous course of training involved in Confucian self-cultivation would produce a hollow hypocrite, the "village worthy" who simply goes through the motions of virtuous behavior without genuinely embodying virtue. It is in response to this need for proper inner motivation that the SELF-CULTIVATION AS ADORNMENT schema—where self-cultivation is conceptualized as merely the metaphorical adornment of a previously existing, already well-formed substrate—finds its way into the text. The problem with this set of metaphors is that the idea of an already well-formed substrate merely awaiting adornment undermines the need for effort and hard work in attaining wu-wei—important entailments of both the SELF-CULTIVATION AS CRAFT REFORMATION and SELF-CULTIVATION AS LONG JOURNEY schemas that the authors of the text do not want to see compromised. Both the adornment and craft metaphors for self-cultivation seem to serve important functions in compensating for the shortcomings of the other, but the two sets of metaphors do not themselves seem to be compatible.

It is in response to this tension that the *Laozi*, the subject of chapter 3, turns to the celebration of internalist and no-effort metaphors. Whereas the *Analects* urges us to adorn the self by submitting to the culture (*wen* 文 ; lit. patterns, designs) of the Zhou, Laozi demands that we exhibit the "unadorned." Against the Confucian metaphor of carving the self like a piece of jade, Laozi famously advocates becoming like "uncarved wood." And while the Confucian soteriological process is portrayed as a sort of grueling, lifelong journey, Laozi warns us to put a halt to this misguided trip—to turn back and return home to our primordial Mother, to our origins or roots. Most generally, Laozi advocates "no-doing" (wu-wei) and a reliance upon the effortless, spontaneous "so-of-itself" (ziran) to defuse the tension between the more-effort and less-effort found in the *Analects*: we already *are* good, and will only realize this fact when we stop *trying* to be good and exert no effort at all. Both carving and adornment accomplish nothing but the destruction of our inborn, pristine nature.

Here, though, Laozi runs into his own conceptual problem. If, in fact, we are naturally good in a "so-of-itself," no-effort fashion, why are we not good already? If the Laozian soteriological path is so effortless and spontaneous, why do we have to be *told* to pursue it? Concretely, this tension manifests itself through the appearance of effort metaphors for self-cultivation that take their place uneasily alongside the dominant no-effort metaphors in the text. Laozi urges us to behaviorally "do wu-wei" (weiwuwei) and to cognitively "grasp oneness," while at the same time he systematically condemns doing and grasping. He urges us personally to reduce our desires and politically to reduce the size of the state, while at the same time warning us that human nature is a piece of uncarved wood that should not be touched and that the state is a "sacred vessel" that should not be handled. The paradox of wu-wei as manifested in the *Laozi* reveals perhaps most strikingly the conceptual difficulty involved in trying not to try.

Cryptic references to meditative practices found in the *Laozi* point in the direction of an interesting strategy of circumventing at least one aspect of the effort/no-effort tension by means of the body. That is to say, one way of dealing with the conceptual paradox of "trying not to try" is turn away from the cognitive and toward the behavioral: for instance, toward a regimen of meditative or breathing practices designed to bring about psycho-physiological changes in the self. Faced by the problem of how to desire not to desire, then, one solution might be a purely physical set of exercises that alter the *qi* (vital energy) in such a way that desire is eventually nipped in the bud at the physiological level. This is perhaps the motivation behind what appear to be meditative and breathing techniques that we find described in such texts as the "Inner Training" (neiye 內業) and "Techniques of the Heart/Mind" (xinshu 心術) chapters of the *Guanzi*, and in the recently discovered medical texts from Mawangdui. In the "Inner Training," the primary focus of chapter 4, we find passages that seem to suggest that simply taking up a particular physical posture is enough to attain wu-wei: "Simply align your four limbs / And the blood and *qi* will be stilled."

Unfortunately, wu-wei is apparently not that simple. The line quoted is thus immediately followed by the injunction: "Unify your awareness and concentrate your mind / And then your ears and eyes will not overflow." It thus seems that even in texts such as the "Inner Training" a combination of physical and mental discipline is required to achieve wu-wei, and the "Inner Training" soteriological path therefore seems, like that of the *Laozi*, to have both behavioral and cognitive components. On the one hand, it is necessary to "clean out" the "lodging place" of the spirit through physical hygiene and posture, while, on the other, one must also "still one's mind" and stop *worrying* about attaining the quintessential *qi* or spiritual power. Of course, the question is then, how one can pursue goal-directed activity without being consciously goal-directed? Despite the suggestion of a new technique for circumventing the paradox of wu-wei by means of the body, then, the author(s) of the "Inner Training" still see a need for physical austerities to be accompanied by a kind of cognitive transformation, and thus do not escape the grasp of the paradox as we saw it in the *Laozi*: the problem of how one could try not to try. Nonetheless, they do manage to introduce to Warring States thought a new "technology of the self"—perhaps derived from medical and other naturalistic theory, but from this point on available to the elite philosophers as well—which posits the existence of *qi*, the "quintessential," and the spirit as active forces within the body that can be accessed and activated through physical and cognitive means. This suggestion that physiological forces within the self can be harnessed and allowed to do much of the work of wu-wei is a powerful one, and will be adopted in different ways by all of the thinkers that follow.

The first of these post–"Inner Training" thinkers we consider is Mencius, the subject of chapter 5. Mencius attempts to circumvent the paradox of wu-wei as it appears in the *Laozi* by drawing upon a set of metaphors from the realm of agriculture. The metaphor schema, SELF-CULTIVATION AS AGRICULTURE, is a very powerful and productive one, providing Mencius with a model of how nature and nurture (non-effort and effort) might be harmonized: we already are wu-wei in the sense that we contain the potentialities for wu-wei within us, but these potentialities—like fragile sprouts of grain—need to be tended to and nourished if they are to grow and realize their telos. Confucian morality, then, is "natural," but natural in a special way that requires attention, time, and effort. In this way Mencius is able to associate Confucian morality with the "natural" (*ziran*) model of wu-wei championed by the *Laozi*, while also starkly distinguishing his soteriological path from anything that might be championed by the sort of self-preservationists and primitivists who compiled the *Laozi*.[33] In place of Laozi's inert block of "uncarved wood," Mencius's primary metaphor is the dynamic "sprout," which has a natural direction and motive force of its own. In this way Mencius can portray the achievement of Confucian culture (*wen* 文)—rejected outright by the Laozian primitivists as unnatural—as the proper and unforced culmination of human nature. In other words, we can get the cultural "grain" without having to "tug on the sprouts," to borrow a metaphor from *Mencius* 2:A:2. The natural world is not static but has its own direction, and it is therefore no more "unnatural" for us to practice the Confucian rites than it is for wheat plants to produce a crop—in fact, it is precisely the Laozian/primitivist call for "return" that is truly unnatural and therefore against the will of Heaven. These agricultural metaphors also allow Mencius to deal with the Laozian tension of why one needs to *try* to be natural: "nature" for Mencius is not what the modern Chinese call "the natural world" (*da ziran* 大自然) (i.e., untrammeled by human beings), but *domesticated* nature. Domesticated plants thus represent for Mencius the perfect marriage of human effort with natural tendencies, and thereby serve as the ideal metaphor for the "cultivation" of wu-wei moral tendencies.

Mencius supplements his agricultural metaphors with a separate, equally evocative water-based family of metaphors, according to which one can find the "source" (*yuan* 源) of morality in order to access the "flood-like" (*haoran* 浩然) *qi*, allowing moral behavior to follow as inevitably and irresistibly as a spring breaking through the ground or water bursting through a dike. This water family of metaphors also allows Mencius to link his project with the new physiological concern with *qi*, thereby giving him access to a range of liquid metaphors for wu-wei—such as "flowing" (*liu* 流) or "going along with the flow" (*shun* 順)—and providing him with a new conceptual schema for understanding the power of Virtue. These are the most prominent of the "wild nature" metaphors that provide Mencius with very useful entailments, such as the idea that Confucian morality is spontaneous, unstoppable, and effortless.

We can identify at least two tensions that still plague this seemingly elegant solution to the paradox of wu-wei, each of which serves as a point of attack for the two thinkers that follow Mencius in my account. Let us begin with the first tension that exists between the domesticated and wild nature metaphors in the text. A potential criticism of the agricultural metaphor as a model for natural morality is that domesticated plants are not *really* natural, and that this is why they require so much care if they are not to wither or be choked out by weeds. Projecting this criticism onto the realm of self-cultivation, if the Confucian Way is so natural for us as human beings, why do we have to work so hard to concentrate upon it? If it were truly natural, it should be completely effortless—natural in the way that weeds grow or water flows downhill. Mencius seems to sense at some level this criticism, and this is why he seasons his more "effort-full" domesticated nature metaphors with a liberal sprinkling of the effortless "wild nature" metaphors just mentioned: the drive toward morality is as powerful and irresistible as floodwater breaking through a dike or water flowing downhill. The problem, of course, is that these two conceptualizations of nature do not sit well with one another. To take the most obvious example, while congratulating himself on possessing a "flood-like" *qi* or praising the sage-king Shun for having unleashed a moral power like water breaking through a dike, Mencius in other passages holds up the flood-taming Yao as an exemplar of moral perfection. Yao was great, Mencius says, precisely because he knew how to exert effort in order to *tame* and channel the otherwise dangerous and destructive power of wild nature, and Yao's taming of the floods is to serve as a metaphor for how aspiring Confucian gentlemen are to restrain and rechannel their natures.

It is tension, I will argue, that is the target of Zhuangzi's valorization of wild nature and the "weeds" of humanity—the cripples, the criminals, the ugly—who have been driven out of the carefully tended Confucian fields.[34] Domesticated nature is not natural, and if we wish to achieve true naturalness we have to abandon all hoeing and watering and let the weeds flourish. Zhuangzi, as I discuss in chapter 6, thus rejects the self-conscious approach of Confucians such as Mencius, who employ the heart/mind in order to force the rest of the self to be "spontaneous." Any sort of mind-dominated, goal-directed, "effort-full" activity is, in Zhuangzi's view, anathema to wu-wei. His soteriological path, like Laozi's, thus attempts to eschew effort metaphors. Zhuangzi advocates a kind of paring away or undoing of Confucian effort: "forgetting" morality, "losing" the self, and making the heart/mind empty in order allow access to previously suppressed powers within the Self—clearing a space for the "entry" into the Self of the normative order, portrayed metaphorically as a physical substance or human guest. Once the damage inflicted by society and heart/mind has been undone, the individual can enjoy a wonderful lack of exertion through "lodging" (*yu* 寓), "fitting" (*shi* 適), or "properly dwelling" (*yi* 宜) in the Way, conceived of as a kind of river or moving force able to simply carry the Subject along for a ride.

The problem here, not surprisingly, is similar to the problem we found in the *Laozi*: how do you try not to try? More specifically, how can one use the heart/mind in order to eliminate the heart/mind or render it vacuous? The fact that we are not already tenuous or open to the Way means that we need to somehow render ourselves receptive, and Zhuangzi is thus forced to supplement his effortlessness and unself-consciousness metaphors with references to hard work and training, as in the story of the marvelous Butcher Ding, who apparently had to train for years and pass through several levels of attainment before he was finally able to follow his spiritual desires. We see Zhuangzi here playing the same game as Mencius, but from a different side: whereas Mencius feels the need to spice up his dominant metaphors of cultivation or effort with a few piquant pinches of "wild nature" abandon, Zhuangzi's celebration of "wild nature" is muted by an apparently recognized need for cultivation. The manner in which this tension plays itself in terms of Zhuangzi's metaphors is also quite similar to the *Mencius*: we have a dominant set of metaphors representing sudden transformation or release—"forgetting," "losing," "wandering," "release/undoing" (*jie* 解)—uneasily coexisting with a small contingent of such "effort" metaphors as "cultivating" (*yang* 養) life or "getting rid of" (*qu* 去) knowledge.

The second of the Mencian tensions—related to the first, but slightly different—is between internalist and externalist metaphors for self-cultivation. The dominant metaphors for self-cultivation in the *Mencius* can be characterized as internalist, such as the telos-containing "sprouts," which exist inside the mind from birth and include an innate sense of rightness that "is not welded on from the outside." However, the entailments of these internalist metaphors somewhat go against the intuition that living a moral life involves some kind of commitment to external norms, as well as the potential for tension between these external norms and inner inclination. That Mencius shared this intuition is apparent from the fact that he feels the need to supplement his dominant internalist metaphors with such externalist metaphors as the carpenter's square or compass (*guiju* 規矩)—external standards that are used to correct one's intuitive perception of straightness or roundness. Such metaphors are relatively rare in the text, but the fact that they found their way in at all suggests that the compilers of the text were aware of the potential shortcomings of their internalist metaphors.

This internalist-externalist tension serves as the main focus of Xunzi's explicit criticism of Mencius as discussed in chapter 7. Against Mencius's internalist, naturalistic agricultural metaphors, Xunzi returns to Confucius's SELF-CULTIVATION AS CRAFT REFORMATION and SELF-CULTIVATION AS LONG JOURNEY schemas with a vengeance. In the *Xunzi*, as in the *Analects*, wu-wei is portrayed as the "destination" at the end of a long, arduous trip, or as the respite or "ease" (*an* 安) enjoyed after a lifetime of bitter training and submission to external forms of behavior and thought. Xunzi's metaphors are much more explicit in their externalism than anything seen in the *Analects*, however, with our inborn nature conceptualized as a recalcitrant raw material in need of violent re-shaping so that it might be "transformed" (*hua* 化) into a shape dictated by external standards or measuring tools: the carpenter's square and ruler (*guiju* 規矩), the inked marking line (*shengmo* 繩墨), or the balance scale (*chong* 衡). Becoming wu-wei is, in Xunzi's view, profoundly *unnatural*, and his emphasis upon the arduousness of self-cultivation is thus targeted against both Mencius's and Zhuangzi's celebration of effortlessness and faith in the "natural" or Heavenly. The sort of unconscious ease that characterizes Xunzi's gentleman comes only after a lifetime of rigorous training and submission to external cultural norms.

Probably the most basic manifestation of the paradox of wu-wei in Xunzi's thought involves a problem with his use of craft reformation as a metaphor for moral self-cultivation. As Aristotle was careful to point out, there is a crucial disanalogy between craft production and virtue: craft production can be judged solely on the basis of its product, without any reference made to how the craftsperson was feeling when he or she created the product, whereas moral or virtuous acts are from the very beginning inextricably tied up with the *internal* state of the actor. If it turns out that I gave money to the poor in order to make myself look good or merely to win a tax break for myself, this fatally tarnishes the act itself—a "generous" action performed in the absence of genuinely generous motivations is merely a semblance of generosity. Xunzi shows himself to be in agreement with Aristotle on this point when he repeatedly emphasizes that truly virtuous acts must be accompanied by "sincerity" (*cheng* 誠) if they are not to be dismissed as mere semblances of virtue. The implication that Aristotle drew from this disanalogy between craft and virtue is that a person who is not already generous to some degree cannot be *made* generous through external instruction or training, and therefore he could accept as students only proper Athenians who already had the beginnings of virtue instilled in them from childhood. We see Xunzi attempting a similar type of solution to this problem by invoking "soaking" or "infusion" metaphors: potential gentlemen come to the task of self-cultivation already endowed with the beginnings of virtue because they have been "soaked" in a proper environment.

The problem with this attempted solution is that, in Xunzi's view, the proper "soaking medium" (one's social environment) must be *chosen* by the aspiring student, who is unfortunately surrounded by hypocrites and imposters and must therefore successfully pick out the "excellent friends" and "worthy teachers" from among this motley collection of poseurs. How, though, does someone completely devoid of moral resources distinguish true morality from its counterfeit? This question is similar to the one Xunzi faces concerning the origin of morality itself: human beings in the chaotic state of nature were driven to morality, he says, by fear. Why, though, would inherently chaotic beings fear chaos rather than simply revel in it? It is in response to these tensions that Xunzi finds himself moved to import occasional internalist metaphors such as an inborn "taste" for morality or a natural "response" or attraction to goodness—metaphors that do not, of course, sit at all well with his dominant externalist metaphors. Just as with the *Analects*, then, tensions surrounding the paradox of wu-wei give rise in the *Xunzi* to a tension between incompatible externalist and internalist metaphors for self-cultivation.

My discussion will thus suggest that the early Chinese tradition was never able to formulate a fully consistent or entirely satisfying solution (whether internalist or externalist) to the tensions created by its central spiritual ideal. Historically, the tensions inherent in the early Chinese spiritual ideal of wu-wei were subsequently transmitted to later East Asian schools of thought that inherited wu-wei as an ideal. The continued, stubborn reemergence of this split—ultimately related to a failure to produce an entirely consistent or satisfying internalist or externalist position—suggests that the paradox of wu-wei is a *genuine* paradox and that any "solution" to the problem it presents will therefore necessarily be plagued by the sort of superficial and structural difficulties described earlier. We might thus be justified in seeing the "subtle dialectic of question and answer" circling about the paradox of wu-wei as having significance not only for early Chinese thinkers but also for any thinker concerned with the problem of self-cultivation—that is, with the problem of not merely winning from the individual rational assent to a system of principles but actually *transforming* him or her into a new type of person.

Chapter 1

無為
Wu-wei as Conceptual Metaphor

Before elucidating the conceptual structure of wu-wei as metaphor, I will first explain what is meant by "conceptual metaphor," and this will require a brief introduction to a subfield of cognitive linguistics[1] concerned with metaphor theory.

The Contemporary Theory of Metaphor

Contemporary metaphor theory is perhaps most familiar to the general academic public through the works of George Lakoff and Mark Johnson, who see themselves as being engaged in a kind of "descriptive or empirical phenomenology" aimed at sketching out a "geography of human experience" (Johnson 1987: xxx–viii).[2] One of the basic tenets of the contemporary approach to metaphor is that human cognition—the production, communication, and processing of meaning—is heavily dependent upon mappings between domains, with "mapping" understood as "a correspondence between two sets that assigns to each element in the first a counterpart in the second" (Fauconnier 1997:1) Another tenet is that the process of human cognition is independent of language, and that linguistic manifestations of cross-domain mappings are merely manifestations of deeper cognitive processes.[3] These mappings take several forms, but perhaps the most dramatic form—and the form I will be primarily concerned with here—is what Fauconnier refers to as "projection mappings" (1997: 9), where part of the structure of a more concrete or clearly organized domain (the *source* domain) is used to understand and talk about another, usually more abstract or less clearly structured, domain (the *target* domain). It is this sort of projective mapping that I will refer to as "metaphor," which—understood in this way—encompasses simile and analogy as well as metaphor in the more specific, literary sense.

Our primary and most highly structured experience is with the physical realm, and the patterns that we encounter and develop through the interaction of our bodies with the physical environment therefore serve as our most basic source domains. These source domains are then called upon to provide structure when our attention turns to the abstract realm. Probably the most crucial claim of cognitive linguistics is thus that sensorimotor structures play a crucial role in shaping

21

our concepts and modes of reasoning.[4] The most basic of these structures are referred to as "primary schemas"—"dynamic analog representations of spatial relations and movements in space" (Gibbs and Colston 1995: 349)—that come to be associated with abstract target domains through experiential correlation, resulting in a set of "primary metaphors." Lakoff and Johnson 1999: 50–54 provide a short list of representative primary metaphors (derived from Grady 1997) such as AFFECTION IS WARMTH,[5] IMPORTANT IS BIG, MORE IS UP, and so on, specifying their sensorimotor source domains and the primary experience correlations that give rise to them. Two examples that I will invoke are as follows:

1. PURPOSES ARE DESTINATIONS
Subjective Judgement: achieving a purpose
Sensorimotor Experience: reaching a destination
Example: "He'll ultimately be successful, but he isn't *there* yet."
Primary Experience: reaching a destination in everyday life and thereby achieving a purpose (e.g., if you want a drink, you need to go to the water cooler)

2. ACTIONS ARE SELF-PROPELLED MOTIONS
Subjective Judgement: action
Sensorimotor Experience: moving one's body through space
Example: "I'm *moving* right along on the project"
Primary Experience: common action of moving oneself through space (Lakoff and Johnson 1999: 52–53).

It is important to note that schemas understood in this way are based upon experiential correlation, rather than pre-existing similarity,[6] and that they represent analog or image "irreducible gestalt structures" (Johnson 1987: 44)—including entities, properties, and relations—rather than propositions. Thus, the phrase PURPOSES ARE DESTINATIONS should be seen as a shorthand way to refer to "the complex web of connections in our experience and understanding formed by this mapping across domains of experience" (Johnson 1987: 7) rather than a propositional statement; "the metaphor itself is not reducible to the proposition we use to name it" (Johnson 1987: 7).

Traditional theories of metaphor usually portray it as a relatively rare and somewhat "deviant" mode of communication thrown in to add rhetorical spice, but fully reducible to some equivalent literal paraphrase. Metaphor understood in this way is thus a purely optional linguistic device. An important claim of the cognitive approach to metaphor is that metaphor is, in fact, primarily a matter of *thought*, not language, and that conceptual metaphor is ubiquitous and unavoidable for creatures like us.[7] Conceptual metaphor, it is claimed, serves as one of our primary tools for reasoning about ourselves and the world—especially about relatively abstract or unstructured domains. While abstract concepts such as "time" or "death" may have a skeleton structure that is directly (i.e., non-metaphorically) represented conceptually, in most cases this structure is not rich or detailed enough to allow us to make useful inferences. Therefore, when we attempt to conceptualize and reason about abstract or relatively unstructured realms, this skeleton structure is fleshed out (usually automatically and uncon-sciously) with additional structure provided by the primary metaphors derived from basic bodily experience, often invoked in combination with other primary schemas to form complex metaphors or conceptual blends.[8] When primary or complex source domains are activated in such cases and mapped onto the target domain, most aspects of the source domain conceptual topology—that is, infer-ence patterns, imagistic reasoning pattern, salient entities, and so forth—are pre-served, thereby importing a high degree of structure into the target domain.[9] Lakoff has referred to this as the "invariance principle" (Lakoff 1990).

To give an illustration of this process, consider the question of how we are to comprehend and reason about something as abstract, for instance, as "life." Lakoff and Johnson (1999: 60–62) note that, when reasoning or talking about life, English speakers often invoke the complex metaphor, PURPOSEFUL LIFE AS JOURNEY, which provides them with a schema drawn from embodied experience that helps them to reason about this abstract concept. This schema derives from a folk belief[10] that it is important to have a purpose in life, and is based upon the two primary metaphors mentioned above, PURPOSES ARE DESTINATIONS and ACTIONS ARE SELF-PROPELLED MOTIONS—two schemas that have become a part of our conceptual "toolbox" through experiential correlation. When these two pri-mary metaphors are combined with the simple fact (derived from our common knowledge of the world) that a long trip to a series of destinations constitutes a journey, we have the complex metaphor schema, PURPOSEFUL LIFE AS JOURNEY, which Lakoff and Johnson map as follows:

Journey   ⟶   Purposeful Life

Traveler   ⟶   Person Living a Life

Destinations ⟶   Life Goals

Itinerary   ⟶   Life Plan

The PURPOSEFUL LIFE AS JOURNEY metaphor thus arises out of our basic embod-ied experience and gives us a way to think and reason about this abstract "entity,"[11] which "in itself" is fairly unstructured and therefore difficult to reason about. As Lakoff and Johnson note, the full practical import of a metaphor such as this lies in its entailments: that is, the fact that the metaphoric link between abstract life and a concrete journey allows us to draw upon our large stock of commonplace knowledge about journeys and apply this knowledge to "life."[12] So, to return to their example, we have in our stock of experience concerning lit-eral journeys some of the following pieces of knowledge:

A journey requires planning a route to a destination.
Journeys may have obstacles, and you should try to anticipate them.
You should provide yourself with what you need for your journey.
As a prudent traveler, you should have an itinerary indicating where you
    are supposed to be at what times and where to go to next.

> You should always know where you are and where you are going next,
> and how to get to your next destination. (62)

Mapping this knowledge and set of inference patterns onto the abstract realm of "life," we get the following entailments:

> A purposeful life requires planning a means for achieving your purposes.
> Purposeful lives may have difficulties, and you should try to anticipate them.
> You should provide yourself with what you need to pursue a purposeful life.
> As a prudent person with life goals, you should have an overall life plan indicating what goals you are supposed to achieve at what times and what goal to seek to achieve next.
> You should always know what you have achieved so far and what you are going to achieve next, and how to go about achieving these goals. (62)

We thus unconsciously assume that life, like a physical journey, requires planning if one is to reach one's "destination," that difficulties will be "encountered" "along the way," that one should avoid being "sidetracked" or "bogged down," and so on. Having become convinced that I have become "side-tracked," for instance, I unconsciously import reasoning structures from the source domain and project them on the target domain: exerting more effort (traveling farther) in my current endeavor (path) will only make things worse (lead me father astray); if I wish things to improve (get back on track), it will be necessary to first radically change my current manner of doing things (backtrack, reverse) until they resemble the manner in which I used to do things at some particular time in the past (get back to the "point" where I went astray), and then begin making effort again (begin moving forward) in a very different manner than I am doing now (in a new direction). We can thus see how a single complex metaphor can have profound practical implications, influencing decision making and providing us with normative guidance. In addition, the sheer awkwardness of the (mostly) literal paraphrases just given illustrate how deeply the PURPOSEFUL LIFE AS JOURNEY schema penetrates our consciousness: it takes a great deal of effort to avoid invoking it in some way when discussing life-decisions.

As we can see from this example, a single complex, conceptual metaphor structure can inform a whole series of specific linguistic expressions, such as being "lost" in life, working at a "dead-end" job, or "going nowhere." These "families" of specific metaphorical expressions (whether linguistic or material) are not random or unrelated but are rather all motivated by a common conceptual schema. This, indeed, is a crucial proposition of cognitive linguistics: that metaphorical expressions are not simply fixed, linguistic conventions but rather represent the surface manifestations of deeper, active, and largely unconscious *conceptual* structures. This means that a metaphoric structure such as PURPOSEFUL LIFE AS JOURNEY exists independently of any specific metaphoric expression of it, and can thus continuously generate new and unforeseen expressions. Anyone familiar with the PURPOSEFUL LIFE AS JOURNEY schema can instantly grasp the sense of such metaphors as "dead-end job" or "going nowhere" upon hearing them for the first time, and can also draw upon the conceptual schema to create related but entirely novel metaphoric expressions. When the novel expression "living in the fast lane" was introduced into American culture, it was immediately comprehensible because it is based upon the PURPOSEFUL LIFE AS JOURNEY schema, and became popular because it allowed Americans to draw upon a wealth of reasoning patterns about a concrete source domain (driving in the fast lane of the freeway, which is exciting but potentially dangerous) and use them to reason about life (your friend who is "living in the fast lane" may be having a good time at the moment, but there is a potential for disaster, so maybe she should "slow down" before she "crashes and burns").

Scholars studying metaphor from a cognitive perspective cite several types of phenomena as evidence that metaphors in fact represent conceptually active, dynamic structures. The expression "living in the fast lane" is an example of "novel-case generalization" evidence: the fact that entirely novel linguistic expressions can be generated that are nonetheless instantly comprehended by a competent speaker, because they draw upon a shared conceptual structure. Related evidence includes polysemy (the fact that we find systematically related meanings for single words or expressions such as "dead end" or "lost") and inference patterns—that is, the fact that reasoning patterns from well-structured source domains (physical travel, for instance) are commonly used to draw conclusions about abstract target domains (e.g., life). In addition to such linguistic evidence, a growing body of psychological experiments have demonstrated the cognitive reality of metaphor schemas as manifested in such processes as sensory perception,[13] and several studies have provided evidence that cognitive mappings are actually physiologically instantiated in the brain.[14] All of this convergent evidence suggests that conceptual metaphor is not only a very real phenomenon but is an inevitable part of embodied human cognition.

This leads us to the "experiential realist" or "embodied realist" stance that informs the cognitive linguistic approach. Conceptual metaphors "are interactive . . . structured modes of understanding" that arise as a result of our embodied mind having to adapt to "our physical, cultural, and interpersonal environments" (Fesmire 1994: 152). Because human bodies are quite similar the world over, and the types of environments human beings face are also shared in most important respects, one would expect to find a high degree of similarity with regard to conceptual metaphors across human cultures and languages, especially with regard to primary metaphor. For instance, it is not unreasonable to claim that all human beings—regardless of culture, language, or period in history—have had the experience of needing to move from point A to point B in order realize some purpose, and we should thus not be surprised if the primary metaphor PURPOSES ARE DESTINATIONS is universal or near-universal among human cultures. In other words, since human experience involves a huge number of shared, embodied gestalt structures, we should expect these shared structures—as a result of projective mapping—to be reflected at the level of abstract thought as well.

Of course, since these gestalt patterns arise through the interactions of our embodied minds with our environment, we would also expect that dramatic changes in environment would be reflected in the creation of novel conceptual metaphors. To a certain degree we see this happen with the development of important technologies that have an impact on daily life; to cite only a more recent example, the advent of widespread computer use over the past decades gave rise to important and influential new metaphors for the brain and for language processing (Boyd 1993: 486–87; Lakoff and Johnson 1999: 251–52). Phenomena such as the Internet are also generating new modes of human interaction, which will presumably result in the formation of new metaphor schemas. Although long-term human habitation of space is still in the realm of science fiction speculation, it would be interesting to imagine what would happen if it became a reality and there were generations of children raised in a zero-gravity environment. Would they continue to make use of older "gravity-based" schemas out of linguistic or cultural conservatism, or would they eventually toss these metaphors aside and develop their own entirely new—and to us, quite alien and perhaps incomprehensible—sets of conceptual metaphors?

In any case, despite the great strides in technology that have been made over the centuries and the large impact these technologies have had on our lives, the basic shared human environment has remained remarkably stable. We still have to physically move in order to get something that we want, still obtain most of our information about the world through our sense of sight (the experiential basis of the common primary metaphor, KNOWING IS SEEING), and overall the basic repertoire of motions and physical interactions possessed by a modern American is not terribly different from that possessed by, say, a Chinese person in the fourth century B.C. Despite the advent of electricity, moveable type, computers, and the Internet, then, the basic stability of the human body and the environment with which it is forced to interact across cultures and time would lead us to expect a high degree of universality in basic metaphor schemas. As we shall see as we begin to apply the methods of cognitive linguistics to classical Chinese texts, the degree of similarity we will find between modern English and ancient Chinese conceptual metaphors is quite striking, even when it comes to quite abstract and presumably culturally contingent domains. While this might seem surprising or unlikely from the perspective of neo-Cartesian postmodern theory—where linguistic-cultural systems are conceived of (metaphorically!) as sui generis, autonomous structures—it is rather to be expected from the standpoint of the cognitive theory of metaphor.

In the chapters that follow I will use the method of metaphor analysis to discover conceptual links between thinkers in a more or less shared linguistic and cultural environment. As I will discuss again in the conclusion, though, the analysis of conceptual metaphor also represents an exciting new methodology for scholars interested in cross-cultural comparison work, and the principle of experiential realism upon which this methodology is based provides a theoretical grounding for comparative work in general. The exploration of the conceptual "deep grammar" (to invoke a Chomskyan metaphor) that underlies linguistic signs such as metaphor effectively gets us out of the postmodern "prison house of language," allowing us to use the body and bodily experience as a bridge to the "other." At the same time, the recognition that shared conceptual structures are contingent upon bodies and physical environment, that no set of conceptual schemas provides unmediated access to the "things in themselves," and that some degree of cultural variation in schemas is to be expected allows us to avoid the sort of rigid universalism that characterizes Enlightenment-inspired approaches to the study of thought and culture. The method of conceptual metaphor analysis might be presented as a sort of "middle way" between more traditional approaches to comparative work that focus more exclusively upon, respectively, specific technical terms (linguistic signs) or general philosophical theories. My hope is that this book will help to popularize this approach among scholars in the humanities and social sciences.

Applying Metaphor Theory to Classical Chinese: Wu-wei as Conceptual Metaphor

In the following sections I will attempt to show how the theory of conceptual metaphor can help us to elucidate the concept of "wu-wei" or "effortless action." As we shall see, the metaphor of wu-wei is strongly tied up with metaphoric conceptions of the self and agency that are shared cross-culturally, a fact that will help us greatly in exploring its cognitive structure. Therefore, before I can discuss the metaphoric structure of wu-wei, I must first discuss the schemas commonly used to conceptualize the self.

Conceptualizing the "Self"

Perhaps one of the most common abstractions we need to conceptualize and deal with in everyday decision making is ourselves (our "selves"). Lakoff and Johnson have mapped out some of the basic schemas we employ in English to conceptualize and reason about the Self, and—as we will see later—almost all of these schemas are found as well in Warring States classical Chinese.

With regard to conceptions of the self in modern American English, Lakoff and Johnson note that there is no single monolithic way that speakers of English invoke in order to conceptualize inner life. We rely upon a variety of metaphoric conceptions to understand ourselves. These various metaphors do, however, draw upon a fairly small number of source domains such as space, object possession, exertion of physical force, and social relationships (1999: 267). Although these various schemas are at times literally contradictory, they are generally not incompatible—that is, they serve to supplement one another and thereby fit together to form a coherent conception of self. In elucidating the structure of the wu-wei metaphor, we will have reason to discuss several of these schemas.

To begin with, it is necessary to examine the most general metaphoric structure for conceptualizing the self, first identified by Andrew Lakoff and Miles

Becker 1992 and elaborated in Lakoff and Johnson 1999: 268–70: the SUBJECT-SELF schema. After examining a wide variety of metaphors for the self in modern American English, Lakoff and Becker concluded that English speakers fundamentally experience themselves in terms of a metaphoric split between a Subject and one or more Selves. In this SUBJECT-SELF schema, the Subject is always conceived of as person-like and with an existence independent from the Self or Selves; it is the locus of consciousness, subjective experience, and our "essence"—everything that makes us who we are. The Self encompasses everything else about the individual, and can be represented by a person, object, location, faculty, physical organ, body, emotion, social role, personal history, and so on. The basic SUBJECT-SELF schema can be mapped as follows:

A Person	$\longrightarrow$	The Subject
A Person, Thing, or Place	$\longrightarrow$	The Self
A Relationship	$\longrightarrow$	The Subject-Self Relationship

Consider, for example, the expression, "I had to force myself to do it." What Lakoff and Becker are arguing is that this phrase is based upon a conceptual split between a metaphoric Subject ("I")—the ever-present locus of consciousness—and a separate Self ("myself") that has to be "forced" to do what the Subject wants it to do. This is the Subject-Self split at its most basic. In an expression such as, "My fear overwhelmed me," the Self is an emotion ("my fear"), distinct from the Subject ("me") and conceptualized as a physical force not under the Subject's control, whereas in the phrase "I was able to step outside of myself," the Self is conceptualized as a metaphoric location (a kind of container) where the Subject normally resides, but which the Subject can leave when it needs to "observe itself." What makes all of these expressions metaphoric is the fact that 1) they are not literally true (e.g., there is no "me" that is literally separate from an "I" that can be physically "forced" to do something), and 2) (as I will explain shortly) they draw upon concrete source domains—object relations, physical forces, physical locations or containers—in order to describe and reason about the abstract realm of "the self."

Many of the metaphors for self I will describe are merely special cases of this single general metaphor system.[15] Phenomenologically, this is very significant; as Lakoff and Johnson note, "this schema reveals not only something deep about our conceptual systems but also something deep about our inner experience, mainly that we experience ourselves as a split" (269). The precise manner in which this split is conceptualized, as well as the specifics of the "Relationship" element mentioned in the mapping, then, depends upon the concrete source domain that is invoked. Some of the more common source domains—and the more specified versions of the SUBJECT-SELF metaphor that go along with them—will be described as I relate the generic SUBJECT-SELF schema to the metaphor of wu-wei.

Manipulating physical objects is one of the first things we learn how to do and is also something we continue to do frequently throughout our lives. We should thus not be surprised that object manipulation serves as the source domain for many of the SUBJECT-SELF metaphors, including that of wu-wei itself. The basic schema is SELF-CONTROL IS OBJECT CONTROL, and since the most common way to control an object is to exert force upon it, this schema is often formulated as SELF-CONTROL IS THE FORCED MOVEMENT OF AN OBJECT, which can be mapped as follows:

SELF-CONTROL IS THE FORCED MOVEMENT OF AN OBJECT

A Person	$\longrightarrow$ The Subject
A Physical Object	$\longrightarrow$ The Self
Forced Movement	$\longrightarrow$ Control of Self by Subject
Lack of Forced Movement	$\longrightarrow$ Noncontrol of Self by Subject

Examples from English given by Lakoff and Johnson include:

> I *lifted* my arm. The yogi *bent* his body into a pretzel. I *dragged* myself out of bed. I *held* myself *back* from hitting him. (1999: 271)

As we shall see, this schema of self-control and object movement informs the most basic metaphorical conception of wu-wei, that of "effortlessness."

Primary Wu-wei Metaphor: Lack of Exertion

Generally, control of the object Self by the Subject is desirable, but even in English we sometimes speak of noncontrol of the Self in a positive sense, as when a person who—perhaps after much effort and no progress in learning how to dance—at last succeeds and explains, "I was finally able to *let* myself *go*." This is the sense in which we are to understand the basic metaphor of wu-wei: literally meaning "no doing/effort/exertion," it refers metaphorically to a state in which action is occurring even though the Subject is no longer exerting force. "Wu-wei" itself thus serves as the most general metaphoric expression of the concept of effortlessness or lack of exertion. Sharing its conceptual schema structure are two main "families" of metaphoric expressions, both of which fall under this rubric of "effortlessness" but differ from each other slightly in conceptual structure.

The "Following" Family   The schema upon which metaphors in this family are based is that of the Subject surrendering control and physical impetus to the Self. The most common of these are as follows:

following (*cong* 從)
following/adapting to (*yin* 因)
leaning on (*yi* 依)
flowing along with (*shun* 順)

In these metaphoric expressions, the Subject is able to be free of exertion because the Self is allowed to do all of the work. Perhaps the earliest and most famous example of such a metaphor is Confucius at age seventy as described in *Analects* 2.4, able to "follow [*cong*] [his] heart's desires without transgressing the bounds." Here Confucius, after a lifetime of exertion, is able to relax and allow an aspect of the Self—the desires of his heart—to take over the initiation of action, with the Subject merely following along behind.

The "At Ease" Family   An alternate family of metaphors expresses the same concept of effortlessness, but in a slightly different form. The structure of the "at ease" metaphors is focused solely upon a unitary Subject, who is portrayed as simply resting or not exerting force, with no mention of the Self. Metaphors in this family include the following:

> at ease/at rest (*an* 安)
> relaxed (*jian* 簡; *shu* 舒)
> still (*jing* 靜)
> at rest (*xi* 息; *she* 舍; *xiu* 休)
> wandering/rambling (*xiaoyao* 逍遙, *fanghuang* 彷徨)
> playing/wandering (*you* 遊)

Here there is no explicit inclusion of the Self as an agent of action, although of course it would be a logical entailment—based upon our knowledge of physical objects and movement—that the Subject is able to "rest" only because someone or something else has taken over. This entailment is actually spelled out explicitly in a set of idiosyncratic metaphors found in the *Zhuangzi*, where the unitary Subject can "rest," passively be "housed" or "lodged," or be able to simply "go for a ride," because the normative order is doing the work:

> resting [*xiu* 休] on the Potter's Wheel of Heaven [*tianjun* 天鈞] (W41/ G70)
> housed [*zhai* 宅] in oneness and lodging [*yu* 寓] in what cannot be stopped [*budeyi* 不得已] (W58/G148)
> riding [*cheng* 乘] the rightness of Heaven and Earth and taking the reigns [*yu* 御] of the discriminations of the six forms of *qi* (W32/ G17)

Conceptually, then, the difference in structure between the "following" and "at ease" families is slight. We will see that, as a consequence, the "following" and "at ease" metaphors are often used in combination and in a more or less interchangeable fashion.

These two families of metaphors, both having to do with lack of exertion or effortlessness, form the core of the wu-wei constellation and determine its basic conceptual structure. In turn, though, the entailments of this basic structure motivate other sets of conceptually related metaphors.

Secondary Wu-wei Metaphor: Unself-consciousness

Object manipulation is not the only way to conceptualize self-control. Another common way, found in English (Lakoff and Johnson 1999: 272–73) as well as classical Chinese, is in terms of object possession, which can be mapped as follows:

SELF-CONTROL IS OBJECT POSSESSION

A Person	⟶ The Subject
A Physical Object	⟶ The Self
Possession	⟶ Control of Self
Loss of Possession	⟶ Loss of Control of Self

Examples from English include "losing yourself" or "getting carried away," and this is generally understood in a negative sense. We find such negative portrayals of loss of object possession in classical Chinese as well. In the *Zhuangzi*, for instance, we read of the second-rate shaman who is confronted with a true Daoist master that "before he [i.e., the shaman] had even fully come to a halt he lost himself [*zishi* 自失; i.e., lost his nerve] and ran away" (W96/G304).

Nonetheless, this phenomenon is not always given a negative valuation, for "losing oneself" in the enjoyment of a book or work of art, for instance, is a desirable and pleasurable experience. In cases such as this, the ordinary state of metaphorically "possessing" the self is conceived of as a restriction or burden, and the elimination of possession understood as a kind of release. We might therefore remap the schema in the following way to reflect this alternate valuation of object possession:

SUBJECT ESCAPES CONTROL OF SELF THROUGH OBJECT LOSS

A Person	⟶ The Subject
A Physical Object	⟶ The Self
Possession	⟶ Control of Subject by Self
Loss of Possession	⟶ Subject Freed from Control by Self

Applying the SUBJECT-SELF and OBJECT POSSESSION schemas to Warring States texts such as the *Zhuangzi* allows us to understand more clearly such stories as that of Zi Qi of Southwall, who—after making his body like dead wood and his mind like dead ashes through some sort of meditative technique—declares that "I have lost myself" (*wu sang wo* 吾喪我) (W36/G45). Much has been made of this passage by scholars such as Wu Guangming and David Hall, who see it as evidence of two different types of self in the *Zhuangzi*: the *wu*-self and the *wo*-self (Wu 1990; Hall 1994). As Paul Kjellberg has noted, however, the phrase *wu sang wo* is simply proper classical Chinese, *wu* being the standard first-person subject pronoun and *wo* usually serving as the first-person object pronoun (Kjellberg 1993a).[16] In this respect, the sense of *wu sang wo* could have equally been expressed with interchangeable first-person reflexive pronouns (as in *wu sang ji*

吾喪己 or *wu zisang* 吾自喪), and the phrase itself is neither more nor less freighted with philosophical significance than the English phrase, "I lost myself." As we have noted, however, even this English expression is significant in that it gives expression to the SUBJECT-SELF and OBJECT POSSESSION conceptual schemas, and this is no less true of classical Chinese. Metaphorically, then, Zi Qi's meditative technique has allowed him (the Subject) to escape the control of the Self—which, as we shall see, is a common way to understand Zhuangzian wu-wei.

Although the literal structure of the OBJECT LOSS schema can be distinguished from the "effortless" metaphors described above, the two schemas are closely linked conceptually as a result of our experience of the world. That is, since physical effort requires concentration and focus, an entailment of effortlessness—one that follows quite naturally for anyone familiar with the domain of physical exertion—is an accompanying state of unself-consciousness. It is thus not surprising that the two schemas are often associated with one another in English. We see this phenomenon, for example, in the conceptual equivalence of the concepts of "letting yourself go [in enjoying an activity]" and "losing/forgetting yourself [in an activity]." Here, the Subject ceasing to exert force on the Self ("letting yourself go") is conceptually equivalent to the Subject "losing" or "forgetting" (i.e., losing from consciousness) the Self.[17] To choose some examples from the *Zhuangzi* (our richest source for wu-wei metaphors), we can see forgetting/losing linked to effortlessness in several passages:

> [He] forgets [*wang*] his liver and spleen, forgets/loses [*yi* 遺] his ears and eyes, and unself-consciously [*mangran* 芒然] roams [*fanghuang* 彷徨] outside the dusty realm, wandering easily [*xiaoyao* 逍遙] in the service of wu-wei. (W207/G663)

> Harmonize [right and wrong] with Heavenly equality and follow along with [*yin* 因] them by means of vastness, and in this way live out your years. Forget [*wang*] the years and forget rightness, and leap into the boundless. (W49/G108)

A basic entailment of "forgetting" is that, once you have forgotten something, you no longer know it. This entailment allows us to bring the common literal expression of unself-consciousness, *buzhi* 不知 ("unaware"), into the losing/forgetting family. Another association is provided by the fact that the experience of strong emotions often induces a kind of unself-consciousness, as the Subject is overwhelmed by the Self (in the form of an emotion). We thus find strong emotion being linked to the losing/forgetting family throughout Warring States texts, as in the example cited from the *Zhuangzi* above, where powerful fear causes the second-rate shaman to "lose himself" and run away. The strong emotion can also be a positive one, though, as in the case of Confucian "joy" (*le* 樂). In *Analects* 7.19 we see the conceptual link between joy, forgetting, and literal unself-consciousness very elegantly illustrated in a single line where Confucius describes himself as "the type of person who becomes so absorbed in his studies that he forgets [*wang*] to eat, whose joy [*le* 樂] renders him free of worries, and who grows old without being aware [*buzhi*] of the passage of the years."

The "Forgetting" Family   We can thus classify all of these metaphors or literal expressions as being members of what we will call the "forgetting" family:

> forgetting (*wang* 忘)
> losing (*shi* 失; yi 遺; *sang* 喪)
> not knowing/unaware (*buzhi* 不知)
> joy (*le* 樂) or other overpowering emotion.

Understood metaphorically in terms of the OBJECT LOSS schema, unself-consciousness is thus closely linked to the LACK OF EXERTION schema as one of its entailments, and is expressed throughout the texts we will be examining by means of the "forgetting" family of metaphors and literal expressions. Together, effortlessness and unself-consciousness represent the two conceptual, metaphorical hallmarks of what we will be calling "wu-wei" activity.

Related Metaphors

I cannot conclude my discussion of the metaphoric structure of wu-wei, however, without mentioning some other families of metaphors that are often associated in Warring States texts with effortlessness and unself-consciousness. These metaphors work together with the primary and secondary wu-wei metaphors to help clarify them or spell out more clearly their entailments.

The "Emptiness" Family   The metaphor of emptiness or tenuousness (*xu* 虛) is often associated with wu-wei in writings that might be identified as "Daoist," as well as in the writings of Xunzi, and serves to supplement the "forgetting" family of metaphors in conveying the idea of unself-consciousness. It is based upon an alternate schema for conceiving of the Subject-Self relationship, that of the SELF AS CONTAINER. This schema derives from our interactions with bounded spaces and containers,[18] and can be mapped as follows:

SELF AS CONTAINER

A Person	$\longrightarrow$ The Subject
A Container	$\longrightarrow$ The Self
Objects in Container	$\longrightarrow$ Qualities of the Self

Virtues, vices, tendencies, character traits, and knowledge of various sorts are understood, through a basic ontological metaphor, as substances that can be "put into" or "taken out of" the container of the Self. The CONTAINER SELF can be the Self in the most general sense, or merely a part of the self, such as the heart/mind (*xin* 心) or the *qi* 氣 ("vital essence").

In texts such as the *Laozi* or *Zhuangzi*, the container of the Self being rendered empty or tenuous (*xu*) allows the Subject to enjoy a state of effortlessness and unself-consciousness. An interesting example of this is found in the "fasting of the mind" passage from chapter 4 of the *Zhuangzi*, where the mind is likened to a stomach that can be made empty through metaphorical fasting. Once the fasting is complete, the only thing left "inside" is the *qi*, which is described as being so tenuous a substance that it has space to "receive things" and serve as a reservoir where the Way will naturally gather. The result of this psychic purge of the container of the mind is said to be a Subject who can "play" (*you* 遊) in a previously dangerous cage and "lodge" itself in "what cannot be stopped" (*budeyi*) (W58/G147)—thus linking the emptiness metaphor with metaphors from the effortlessness family.

Inner-Outer Family   The metaphors in this family are based upon the SELF AS CONTAINER schema but combine this schema with another metaphor, that of the ESSENTIAL SELF. As described in Lakoff and Johnson (1999: 282–84), the ESSENTIAL SELF metaphor is based upon what they call the "folk theory of essences": that is, the idea that every object has "within it" an essence that makes it the kind of thing it is and that this essence is the causal source of every object's "natural" behavior (1999: 214–15). Applied to human beings, our "essence" is usually vaguely associated with the Subject. There are, however, situations when "our concept of who we are essentially . . . is incompatible with what we actually do" (1999: 282), and such situations are explained by invoking the ESSENTIAL SELF metaphor

ESSENTIAL SELF

Person 1	⟶	The Subject, with the Essence
Person 2	⟶	Self 1, the Real Self (Fits the Essence)
Person or Thing 3	⟶	Self 2, Not the Real Self (Does Not Fit the Essence)

Consider the phrase, "I am not myself today." As an apology or explanation for undesirable behavior, this metaphor posits a desirable relationship—the Subject ("I") being coterminous with Self 1 (the "real" self)—that has failed or been disrupted. In this expression, Self 2 is not mentioned explicitly, but this is presumably "who" the Subject "was" when the undesirable behavior was going on. Self 2 is, however, mentioned explicitly in such similar phrases as, "That wasn't the real me talking." Here, Self 2 has taken over control of the Subject, with the existence of Self 1 being implied: the existence of a self that is not the "real" me presumes the existence of self that *is* the real me, who has presumably taken control now that the Subject is apologizing.

Lakoff and Johnson note three different special cases of this metaphor, but the one that is the most relevant for my project is the metaphor of the INNER SELF, which involves combining the ESSENTIAL SELF metaphor with the SELF AS CONTAINER schema:

ESSENTIAL SELF + SELF AS CONTAINER

Inside of Container	⟶ Self 1 (Fits Subject/Essence)
Outside Surface of Container	⟶ Self 2 (Does Not Fit Subject/Essence)

This is a very common and immediately comprehensible metaphor in both modern English and classical Chinese. "She seems friendly," we might say, "but that is just a façade [concealing her real (i.e., internal) self]." Similarly, Yan Hui explains a scheme in chapter 4 of the *Zhuangzi* where he intends to be "inwardly straight [*zhi* 直] while outwardly bending [*qu* 曲 —lit. crooked]"[19] (W56–57/ G143)—that is, seeming on the (false) outside to be agreeing with a wicked ruler while (really) on the inside maintaining his correctness.

The combination of ESSENTIAL SELF + SELF AS CONTAINER becomes crucial for our understanding of wu-wei when it is adopted as the structural basis for a metaphor popularized by the *Laozi*: that of the "natural" (*ziran* 自然). Meaning literally "so-of-itself," *ziran* refers to the way a thing is when it follows its own internal Essence. Metaphorically, the image evoked by the term *ziran* is of actions emerging "naturally" out of the container of the Self—an example of the NATURAL CAUSATION IS MOTION OUT metaphor noted by Lakoff and Johnson (1999: 214) in their discussion of events and causes.[20] We will see that this *ziran* metaphor is associated throughout Daoist texts with both effortlessness and unself-consciousness.

The "Fitting" Family   This family of metaphors concerns the unitary Subject's relationship to the world, with both Subject and World conceived of as physical objects. It can be mapped as follows:

The Subject	⟶ Object A
The World	⟶ Object B

Proper Relation	
Between Subject and World	⟶ Object A physically fitting or matching up with Object B

Conceptual metaphors in this family include the following:

yi 宜 (fitting, appropriate)
he 合 (fitting, matching)
he 和 (harmonizing)
dang 當 (appropriate, matching)
shi 適 (appropriate, fitting)
pei 配 (accompanying, fitting together)

An extension of this metaphor gives us the popular metaphors of "timely" (*shi* 時), where the Subject's actions are conceived of as somehow "matching up" with the situation, and "responsiveness" (*ying* 應), where the Subject is conceptualized as a thing being stimulated or moved (*gan* 感) by the WORLD AS OBJECT. All of these metaphors are related to effortlessness and unself-consciousness through our shared experience of the world—that is, our knowledge that no exertion or conscious struggle is necessary when parts fit, clothes fit, the seasons come on time, or one is provoked by an appropriate stimulus. This conceptual connection is nicely illustrated by a passage from the *Zhuangzi*, where we see the "fitting" metaphor woven together with metaphors from both the "forgetting" and "inner-outer" families:

> You forget your feet when the shoe fits [*shi* 適], and forget your waist when the belt fits. [Similarly], you forget right and wrong when the mind fits, and remain unwavering on the inside and unmoved by the outside when events come together in a fitting fashion. You begin with what is fitting and never experience what is not fitting when you experience the comfort [*shi* 適] of forgetting what is comfortable. (W206–7/G662)

Metaphorical Coherence

One might note at this point that the various metaphor schemas are in many cases mutually inconsistent at the literal level. For instance, it is difficult to reconcile the fact that the Subject is alternately conceptualized as a unitary object (as in the "fitting" or "at ease" metaphors) or as divided in terms of the Subject-Self split. As Lakoff and Johnson have noted, however, literal consistency is not something that we require of our metaphors, as long as they work together in a coherent fashion. Lakoff and Johnson (1980: 87–105) describe the manner in which mutually inconsistent metaphors for such abstractions as an argument (ARGUMENT AS WAR, ARGUMENT AS JOURNEY, ARGUMENT AS CONTAINER) work together to form a coherent metaphorical conception of argument. Basically, since no one metaphorical image is sufficient to generate all of the entailments necessary to conceptualize and deal with the complex, abstract phenomenon of "argument," different schemas are invoked in various situations to highlight the entailments relevant to that situation. What makes these literally inconsistent schemas cohere conceptually is the fact that, although each has its own set of unique entailments, these entailments partially overlap and supplement one another.[21]

We will see that this is the case as well with the metaphors having to do with wu-wei and the attainment of wu-wei.[22] A good example of multiple-structurings of single concepts is the set of metaphors used to conceptualize *xing* 性 (human nature) that are invoked by Xunzi in his essay entitled "Human Nature Is Bad" (KIII: 150–62/W434–49). The metaphor schemas invoked are literally inconsistent, but nonetheless conceptually coherent, because each of them targets a particular entailment:

1. Human nature is an internal force that we can follow (*cong*) or flow along with (*shun*).

   Targeted entailment: do not let this force carry the Subject away.

2. Human nature is a physical location, like the starting point of a journey, that we leave (*li* 離) and to which do not return (*gui* 歸).

   Targeted entailment: what we have at birth is only the starting point for the long "journey" of self-cultivation; we would be "regressing" if we wished to return to our inborn state.

3. Human nature is an object we lose (*shi* 失 , *sang* 喪) and cannot recover.

   Targeted entailment: our inborn nature is something quickly grown out of; we cannot attain this state again, even if it were desirable to do so.

4. Human nature is a warped material to which we must apply external force if we wish it to be straight.

   Targeted entailment: self-cultivation (making our Self "straight") requires a great deal of effort and fundamental reformation.

5. Human nature is a thing shared with others.

   Targeted entailment: we are all equal at birth, and thus all equally capable of becoming sages.

The fact that some of these metaphoric schemas are literally inconsistent does not present a problem for Xunzi or the reader because they are conceptually coherent by virtue of their similar or complementary entailments. For instance, whether our inborn nature is a "place" that we leave and to which we do not return or a "thing" that we lose and cannot recover, the basic entailment is the same: that, as we might say in English, "there is no going back." Similarly, although the portrayal of human nature as a substance always shared by everyone contradicts the metaphor of its being something that we irrevocably lose, these schemas do not come into direct conceptual conflict because they have very different targets (equal opportunity vs. cannot regress), which means that none of their entailments directly contradict each other. That is, we could understand human nature as something shared at birth while still realizing that it is "lost" as we mature. In this sense, the HUMAN NATURE AS SHARED MATERIAL metaphor makes explicit an entailment that is at least consistent with, and perhaps implied by, some of the other metaphors: we all "leave" from the same place or have the same "raw material" to work with.

With this said, we must also note that not all literally inconsistent metaphors are necessarily conceptually coherent. As we shall see, some of the metaphor schemas related to wu-wei in Warring States thought—particularly metaphors having to do with self-cultivation aimed at producing wu-wei—possess central entailments that are mutually contradictory. To return to the Xunzian example, we find in the "Human Nature Is Bad" chapter a further metaphoric characterization of human nature that does not sit well conceptually with the five already discussed:

6. Human nature is a human agent that is bad, and we know that it is bad because it desires (*yu* 欲) or wishes (*yuan* 願) to be good.

   Targeted entailment: human nature is bad

   Problematic side-entailment: human nature has internal *tendencies* toward being good, precisely because it is bad.

As we shall see in chapter 7, this is an example of the sort of internalist element that creeps into the *Xunzi* from time to time and serves as a seed of conceptual dissonance. We shall see many such examples throughout the texts. In the *Analects*, for instance, there is a conceptual tension between the two primary metaphors for self-cultivation, SELF-CULTIVATION AS ADORNMENT and SELF-CULTIVATION AS CRAFT REFORMATION. An important entailment of the first schema is that a suitable substrate must be present if adornment is to take place, while the second schema involves a complete reformation of the original material—its original structure being more or less irrelevant. Similarly, we see a tension in the Mencius between the SELF-CULTIVATION AS AGRICULTURE metaphor—an entailment of which is the need for external effort over a long period of time in order to guide and help nourish one's innate endowment—and a schema whereby one's nature is conceived of as a wild force (such as a flood or stampede of animals) that can simply be released in an instant.

Indeed, part of the point of this project is to show that *all* of the metaphoric portrayals of self-cultivation aimed at producing wu-wei found in the mainstream Warring States texts involve schemas within the same text that are both literally incompatible and conceptually incoherent because they contain contradictory (or at least competing) entailments.[23] These instances of conceptual dissonance will be particularly interesting to us, because they serve as the most visible symptoms of the tension built into the goal of mainstream Warring States self-cultivation: the so-called "paradox of wu-wei" mentioned in the introduction. Generally speaking, what we will find is that all of the thinkers examined employ a mix of externalist and internalist metaphors for self-cultivation, which engenders a tension with regard to entailments between "trying" and "not trying." That is, if self-cultivation requires the fundamental reformation of the "stuff" of one's nature or the fasting away of some inborn "essence" (as in the *Zhuangzi*), an entailment is that we must try rather hard not to try. On the other hand, if self-cultivation is conceived of metaphorically as the simple release of some innate force or superficial adornment of some innate quality, the entailment is that we do not really have to try too hard not to try—wu-wei will happen, as a Laozian metaphor would have it, "so-of-itself" (*ziran*).

The continuing tension between these two basic types of metaphors is quite significant phenomenologically. The religious goal of the thinkers I will discuss later is to achieve the ease of wu-wei, and therefore the idea of "no effort" needs to be metaphorically conveyed. At the same time, wu-wei is understood as an *achieved* state, and each thinker therefore has to specify some sort of effort-ful program for attaining this state. What we will see in the development of pre-Qin thought is a kind of movement back and forth between an emphasis on external or internal metaphors for self-cultivation, with each thinker being characterized by which side he chooses to emphasize. No matter which side is dominant, however, we shall see that the opposing type of metaphor—bringing along with it all of its incompatible entailments—still manages to creep back in somehow, setting up a field of conceptual dissonance. What follows in the next chapters is an attempt to portray the development of pre-Qin thought as a continuing effort to invoke new sorts of metaphors for the self and self-cultivation—drawn from the domains of human technology or the functioning of the natural world—in an attempt to resolve this conceptual dissonance. As we shall see, none of these attempts proves entirely successful, and this failure itself (as I will discuss in the conclusion) has significant phenomenological implications.

Wu-wei in the Pre-Confucian Tradition

Although the term wu-wei itself does not come into widespread use until fairly late in the Warring States period, the metaphoric ideal that it describes—acting effortlessly and unself-consciously in perfect harmony with the cosmos, and thereby acquiring an almost magical efficacy in moving through the world and attracting people to oneself—can be identified as a central theme in Chinese religious thought in texts as early as the *Book of Odes* (*Shijing* 詩經) and the *Book of History* (*Shujing* 書經).[24] These texts are relatively vague and not nearly as conceptually developed as "writings of the masters" we will be looking at, but even here one can see instances of metaphors that will later become central to the Warring States conceptualization of wu-wei.

The theme of personal perfection being reflected in both harmonious, efficacious action and in one's physical appearance can be found throughout the *Book of Odes*.[25] The aristocratic lord or gentleman (*junzi* 君子)[26] is often described as embodying the martial and social virtues that become his station with an effortless ease that reveals itself in his efficacious skill as much as his personal bearing. Metaphorically, this is understood as a kind of "fitting" (*yi* 宜) with the world. Consider, for instance, the description by an admiring poetess of the object of her affection in ode 214:

> Magnificent are the flowers, gorgeous their yellow;
> I have seen this young one,
> And how glorious he is!
> How glorious he is!
> This is why he enjoys good fortune. . . .
> Magnificent are the flowers, their yellow, their white;
> I have seen this young one,
> Driving white horses with black manes,
> Four white horses with black manes,
> And six reins all glossy.
> He rides to the left, to the left,
> My lord does it fittingly [*yi* 宜];
> He rides to the right, the right,

My lord has the knack [*youzhi* 有之].
And because he has the knack,
it shows in his deportment [*sizhi* 似之].[27]

A similar picture of consummate mastery and effortless accordance with what is "proper" or what "fits" the situation is rendered in ode 106:

Lo! How splendid he is!
How grand and tall.
How fine the brow,
His lovely eyes so bright.
He runs agilely, moving in a stately way;
When he shoots, he is skilled.
Lo! How illustrious he is!
The beautiful eyes so clear,
Perfect in propriety [*yi* 儀],
Can shoot all day at a target,
And never miss the mark [*bu chu zheng* 不出正].
Truly a proper kinsman of mine!
Lo! How handsome he is!
His clear brow well-rounded,
When he dances, he is in perfect step,[28]
When he shoots, always piercing the target.
His four arrows all find their mark,[29]
In this way he guards against disorder [*luan* 亂].[30]

The idea of being able to shoot all day while "never missing the mark" has definite metaphorical, moral overtones—*zheng* 正 signifying "proper" or morally "upright" as well as the central mark of a target—and it is in this sense that this ode has been read by later commentators. Nonetheless, the wu-wei "lord" or gentleman in the odes primarily represents a martial, aristocratic ideal—the handsome and physically powerful warrior.

A more explicitly moral ideal of wu-wei is to be found displayed by another exemplary type in the *Odes*: the virtuous sage-ruler of old. Here both effortlessness and unself-consciousness are emphasized. In ode 241, for instance, we find the Lord on High (*shangdi* 上帝) praising King Wen:

I cherish your bright Virtue;
Despite your great reknown, you do not flaunt it,
Despite your enduring prominence, it remains unchanged.
Without recognizing or being conscious of it [*bushibuzhi* 不識不知]
You go along with [*shun* 順] my model.[31]

King Wen is able to effortlessly "flow along with" the normative standard embodied by the Lord on High in a completely unself-conscious manner. Although this accordance with the cosmos endows him with a powerful moral Virtue, King Wen does not dwell upon it or parade it in front of others, nor allow it to become corrupted by arrogance or pride. He enjoys his Virtue naturally and unself-consciously. The description of the perfectly tuned moral skill of King Xuan in ode 304 is similar:

> King Xuan martially established order:
> When he received a small state, it prospered,
> When he received a large state, it prospered;
> He followed in the footsteps [of his ancestors] [*shuailü* 率履] without
>   straying/transgressing [*yue* 越],[32]
> And everywhere he gazed [*suishi* 遂視; lit. following his gaze] the stan-
>   dards were realized. . . .
> He received the blessing [*xiu* 休; lit. ease, rest] of Heaven.
> He was not forceful, not pressing,
> Not hard, nor soft;
> He spread his government in gentle harmony,
> And all the blessings [of Heaven] he combined in his person.[33]

Here King Xuan's effortlessness is portrayed as a consequence of allowing him- self to be simply drawn along by the example of his ancestors ("following in their footsteps"), with the result being a kind of spontaneous efficacy—a sign that Xuan possesses Heavenly "ease" (*xiu* 休). We also see a reference to this kind of ease in the description of the great sage-king Yao that is part of the opening pas- sage of the *Book of History*: "He was reverent, intelligent, cultured and thought- ful, all with a gracious ease [*an'an* 安安]" (Legge 1991b: 15). As we shall see, this metaphor of being "at ease" (*an*) will become a favorite Confucian expres- sion for wu-wei.

We noted above that the effortless moral skill possessed by King Xuan in ode 304 is portrayed as a result of a special relationship to Heaven. This is also the case with the other sage-ruler exemplars that we find in the *Odes*.[34] Consider, for example, the link between effortless "fitting" (*yi* 宜) and the favor of Heaven that is described in ode 166:

> Heaven protects and settles you,
> It causes your grain to flourish
> So that there is nothing that is not proper/fitting [*yi*].
> You receive from Heaven the hundred emoluments;
> It sends down to you enduring good fortune.
> Only the days are not sufficient (to hold so much blessing).

In this ode, this fortunate ruler is said also to have accumulated a powerful Virtue by means of "auspicious and pure" offerings and flawless ritual behavior. This concept of Virtue provides another (albeit indirect) link between Heaven and wu- wei. Recall that, in the description of the noble archer in ode 106, it is said that his harmonized skill is the result of having "perfected propriety," and that his effortless ability to hit the mark (*zheng* 正) serves to guard against "disorder." Virtue is portrayed throughout the *Odes* as a sort of charismatic power that accrues to those who are ritually correct—that is, those who accord with Heaven's order. Attaining a state of wu-wei harmony with Heaven's order, they are thus rewarded with a power that not only brings them personal benefit but also allows them to more effectively realize Heaven's will in the world.[35] The idea of Virtue as a power granted by Heaven to one who accords with its will is not only found throughout the *Odes*[36] *and History* but is also one of the earliest identifiable religious themes in China, being traceable to the most ancient written records in China, the Shang oracle bones and Zhou bronze inscriptions.[37]

We can even find in the *Odes* prefigurements of the idea that conventional morality as expressed in the rites and the classics not only has its origin in Heaven but is also something grounded in the affective and biological nature of human beings themselves. In ode 260, we read that Heaven has created people in such a way that they respond instinctively to Virtue:

> In giving birth to the multitude of the common people,
> Heaven created things and created models [*ze* 則].
> That the people hold to the norms
> Is because they love this beautiful Virtue.[38]

In ode 239, the "joyous and pleased lord" is described as taking great pleasure in his virtuous, ritually correct action—feeling as at home and at ease with the demands of ritual as "a hawk soaring through the skies or a fish leaping in the deep"; in ode 252, we even find a similar "joyous and pleased lord" enjoying a state of wu-wei ease and social virtue that is explicitly linked to the fulfillment of his *xing* 性 or "natural course of development":

> There is a curving slope,
> The whirlwind comes from the south;
> The joyous and pleased lord
> Comes to play [*you* 遊], comes to sing,
> And so inspires my song:
> "Relaxed is your play,
> Pleasant and easy is your rest [*xiu* 休].
> Joyous and pleased lord
> May you fulfill your *xing* 性,
> And like the former princes (your ancestors) bring it to completion.

As we shall see in the chapters that follow, this connection between wu-wei, Virtue, human nature, and the normative order is inherited by later mainstream Chinese thinkers.

Chapter 2

安
At Ease in Virtue:
Wu-wei in the *Analects*

Although the term wu-wei itself appears only once in the *Analects*[1]—in a relatively late passage, 15.5, that is discussed later—we find instances of the wu-wei family of metaphors throughout the text. Perhaps most well-known is the account of Confucius at age seventy in 2.4, where he is said to be able to "follow [his] heart's desires without overstepping the bounds [of propriety]." Here we have a classic example of the first hallmark of wu-wei, lack of exertion by the Subject (Confucius), who surrenders control and follows (*cong* 從) the promptings of the Self (the desires of his heart). Most commonly, however, the *Analects* expresses the idea of lack of exertion through the "at ease" (*an* 安) family of metaphors, often in combination with metaphors for the second hallmark of wu-wei, unself-consciousness. While the text at times employs the more common metaphors for "loss of self"—"forgetting" (*wang* 忘) and "not knowing" (*buzhi* 不知)—its favorite metaphorical expression of this aspect of wu-wei is spontaneous "joy" (*le* 樂): a state of completely unself-conscious enjoyment of one's activities. The graphic pun between "joy" (樂 AC: *lak*) and "music" (樂 AC: *ngåk*) also sets up a quite elegant link between joy/unself-consciousness and musical performance and dance, a metaphor for wu-wei that makes its debut in the *Analects* but becomes a favorite among later Confucians.

In the *Analects*, however, this wu-wei family of metaphors coexists alongside quite contradictory metaphors implying hard work, extreme effort, and even doing violence to the natural tendencies of a material. Below we will explore the relationship between the various metaphoric conceptualizations of wu-wei, as well as the manner in which the "effortless" metaphors are linked to the "effort" metaphors by means of Confucius's soteriological strategy.

The Soteriological Mission

"Would that I did not have to speak!" Confucius sighs in 17.19. His stubbornly obtuse disciple Zigong is puzzled. "If the Master did not speak," he asks, "then how would we little ones receive guidance?" Confucius's response is brief, poetic, and tinged with a trace of bitterness: "What does Heaven ever say? Yet the four seasons go round and find their impetus there, and the myriad creatures are born from it. What does Heaven ever say?"

We see here the invocation of a social metaphor that has venerable pre-Confucian roots: HEAVEN AS RULER, here with the natural world being portrayed as the ruled.[2] Heaven governs the natural world in an effortless fashion, without having to issue orders. The seasons go round, the myriad creatures are born and grow to maturity, and all these phenomena find their source in Heaven. The counterpart to Heaven in the social world is the sage-king of old, someone like Shun:

> Was not Shun one who ruled by means of wu-wei? What did he do? He made himself reverent [*gongji* 恭己] and took his [ritual] position facing South, that is all. (15.5)

In the ideal state of harmony between Heaven and humans that obtained in ancient times, the ruler had no need to act or to speak. He simply rectified his person and took up the ritual position befitting a ruler, and the world became ordered of its own accord. This is the way of the true king: ruling through the power of Virtue.

The analogy between this manner of ordering the human world and the spontaneous harmony effected by Heaven in the natural realm is made clear in 2.1:

> The Master said, "One who rules through the power of Virtue [*de*] might be compared to the Pole Star, which simply remains in its place while receiving the homage of the myriad lesser stars."

Here we see the social metaphor being applied to the natural world (POLE STAR AS RULER), which then allows the qualities of the natural world to be mapped back onto the social. Like the natural world, then, a properly ordered human society functions silently, inevitably and unself-consciously. People in ancient times simply performed their ritual duties, embodied the Way in all of their actions, and the world became ordered of itself. This is why Confucius finds the need to "speak"—that is, to teach, cajole, admonish—so distasteful, and is so contemptuous of the glib and "clever of tongue":[3] ideally, the human world should function in the same effortless, wu-wei fashion as the natural world. It is only because in Confucius's own age the Way has long been lost that he has been summoned to speak, to bring the world back into the state of wordless harmony from which it has fallen. Confucius's own speaking—the "categorized conversations" that constitute the *Lunyu*—is a necessary evil, a wake-up call sent from Heaven to a fallen world. Such is the opinion of the border official of Yi, who perceives quite clearly the sacred nature of Confucius's mission.[4] After being presented to Confucius, he has some comforting and prophetic words for the disciples:

> You disciples, why should you be concerned about your Master's loss of office?[5] It has been too long that the world has been without the Way, and Heaven intends to use your Master like a wooden-tongued bell. (3.24)

The wooden-tongued metal bell (*muduo* 木鐸) was traditionally used by official heralds to summon the people to listen as they made their rounds, proclaiming governmental regulations and announcing admonitions.[6] Here we see the metaphor of HEAVEN AS RULER combined with a new metaphor, SUBJECT AS TOOL, in a manner that nicely suggests lack of exertion: Confucius is merely a tool being wielded by the normally silent ruler, who has broken this silence because he has need to admonish the people.[7]

We can thus see the soteriological thrust of Confucius's project: to serve as the warning bell of Heaven in order to rouse the world from its fallen slumber and summon it back to the state of sacred, wu-wei harmony that prevailed in the Golden Age of the Zhou. It is for this reason alone that the book we call the *Analects* came to be; if the Way were actually realized in Confucius's time, there would be no need for him to speak, and certainly no need for a compendium of "classified sayings." Understanding the nature of this task helps us to understand how the "effort" metaphors in the *Analects* are to be reconciled with the "effortless" metaphors: just as Heaven must break its customary silence and employ the summoning bell, effort is necessary for human beings because we exist in a state of fallenness. This effort, though, has as its goal the transcendence of effort: the state of wu-wei that comes naturally once human beings are once again in harmony with Heaven. In the following sections, I shall explore the various elements of the task at hand: Confucius's diagnosis of the causes of the fallenness of his age; the specific soteriological path he proposes; the nature of the ideal state that lies at the end of this path; and the religio-political implications of this ideal.

Fallenness

Contemplating the world around him, Confucius was appalled by the sorry state of his contemporaries. In 8.20, he reflects wistfully upon the relative wealth of talented officials who served the ancient sage-kings Yao and Shun, and notes that this flourishing of Virtue reached its peak in the Zhou Dynasty. "The Virtue of the Zhou—now this can be called the highest attainment of Virtue!" Infused with this powerful Virtue, the ritual practice of the Zhou was of the highest efficacy and brought order throughout the world. Asked about the *di* 禘 sacrifice (the performance of which became the prerogative of the duke of Zhou) in 3.11, Confucius answers: "I do not fully comprehend it; one who truly understood it could handle the world as if he had it right here," pointing to his palm. By his time, however, the performance of the *di*—continued by the nominal successors of the duke of Zhou in his native state of Lu—had degenerated to the point where Confucius could no longer bear to look upon it (3.10). This degeneration in ritual performance was accompanied by a similar decline in the quality of men participating in public life. After having explained the various grades of worthiness in 13.20, Confucius is asked, "How about those who today are involved in the government?" His answer is dismissive: "Oh! Those petty bean counters are not even worth considering." Even in their faults and excesses the men of ancient times were superior to those of Confucius's own day (17.16).

The general state of decline that followed the demise of the Zhou is metaphorically summed up by the disciple Zengzi in 19.19: "For a long time now the rulers have lost the Way, and the common people have been without direction [*san* 散 ; lit. scattered]." We see here the invocation of a schema employed throughout the Warring States corpus, LIFE AS JOURNEY, with the "Way" (*dao* 道) as the proper, bounded "path" along which to take this journey. The Way is "followed" (*you* 由), one can collapse partway down the road (6.10), and moral achievement is usually described as "reaching" or "arriving" (*da* 達 or *zhi* 至)— that is, completing a physical journey. Although there is only one Way along which to travel properly, people seem to have an uncanny and perverse tendency to disregard it. "Who can leave a room without using the door?" Confucius asks rhetorically in 6.17, adding with some exasperation: "Why, then, does no one follow this Way?"

What, in Confucius's view, are the causes of this moral "disorientation"? At least two factors can be distinguished. The first is the familiar panoply of basic human weaknesses: lust, greed, sloth, and so on. These vices are portrayed as barriers that all people aspiring to the moral life must struggle to overcome. Although the treatment of the psycho-physiological barriers to spiritual realization is not as developed or systematic in the *Analects* as it is in the post–"Inner Training" world,[8] this theme is not entirely ignored. For instance, in a later stratum passage (16.7) we see various vices—lust, bellicosity, and greed—being associated with variations in the blood and *qi* as a result of age. This passage is interesting because it is the only place in the *Analects* where human vices are explicitly linked to psycho-physiological factors.[9] A similar type of point is made more obliquely in passages such as 9.18, where Confucius notes that he "has yet to meet a man who is as fond of Virtue as he is of the pleasures of the flesh." [10] In 8.12, we find that greed is not a vice confined merely to old age but is rather the engine driving the majority of young aspirants to official appointments in Confucius's day: "It is not easy to find someone who is able to study for even the space of three years without the inducement of an official salary."

Certain of these character flaws seem to have been conceived of as congenital and irremedial. In 5.10, for instance, the SELF-CULTIVATION AS CRAFT metaphor (discussed in more detail later) is invoked to explain the slothful nature of a certain disciple named Zai Yu, whose habit of sleeping late into the day earns for him the sharp rebuke from Confucius that "rotten wood cannot be carved, and a wall of dung cannot be troweled." As I will discuss in more detail later, Confucius conceived of human character metaphorically as a combination of "native stuff" (*zhi* 質) and cultural "adornment" (*wen* 文), and—although it is possible that in 5.10 Confucius is merely exaggerating for effect and did not really believe Zai Yu to be a piece of "rotten wood"—the metaphor suggests the possibility that a person's "native stuff" could be inherently flawed.

Such inherent flaws in the basic "stuff" of human beings would seem to be a fairly universal and eternal problem, and one presumably encountered even in the Golden Age of the Zhou. Of relatively more timely concern to Confucius is the second causative factor in human fallenness: the skill of the metaphorical "wood carver" or "cosmetician"—that is, the quality of the tradition into which individuals are acculturated. A crucial entailment of the craft and adornment metaphors used by Confucius to describe self-cultivation is that inherited systems of ritual practice, music, and linguistic conventions play a primary role in shaping the "stuff" of human character. It is clear that by the time of Confucius the Zhou cultural tradition had been severely corrupted and that this corrupted tradition was in turn responsible for leading the vast majority of people "astray." What *caused* the Zhou tradition to decline is never adequately explained in the *Analects*, but it is quite clear that natural flaws in the stuff of human beings are only magnified under the rule of a corrupted tradition, making the reestablishment of harmony between humans and the cosmos very difficult indeed. In his only recorded comment explicitly concerning human nature in the *Analects*, Confucius seems to emphasize the influence of social forms over that of inborn human nature: "By nature [*xing* 性] people are similar; they diverge as the result of practice [*xi* 習]" (17.2).[11] Although there is some commentarial debate concerning its meaning, the comment in 12.8 that "shorn of their pelts, tigers and leopards look no different from dogs or sheep" seems to have a similar import: beneath the refinement of culture (*wen*) we can find a degree of commonality in native substance (*zhi*).

The view that prevails in the *Analects* seems to be that the imperfections inherent in human beings are not too great a problem for a tradition in good order—one that has the resources to trim, guide, and reform one's raw nature in such a way that a state of harmony between both the individual and society and the social order and the cosmos as a whole can be attained. The culture of the Zhou in its heyday was just such a tradition. It is only in the absence of such a tradition—or in the presence of a corrupted or decadent tradition—that these imperfections in human nature are allowed to go uncorrected.

We have seen this portrayed metaphorically as a kind of moral "disorientation" caused by losing the true Way. We also see it expressed as a matter of disorientation with regard to what is to be properly emphasized: things within the self or things outside of the self. For instance, even though the greediness of his contemporaries for official emoluments might find its source in some general human tendency toward acquisitiveness, it could flourish only in a society that has completely ignored the Way because of its obsession with "externalities." Confucius's complaint in 14.24, "In ancient times scholars worked for their own improvement [*weiji* 為己]; nowadays they seek only to win the approval of others [*weiren* 為人]," is echoed in 15.21: "The gentleman looks for it within himself; the petty person looks for it from others." What pertains to one's ESSENTIAL SELF (as opposed to the false appearance one may present to others) is one's own moral qualities and level of self-cultivation, and although in a good society a high degree of internal cultivation should be accompanied by external recognition, this recognition does not always follow. Hence 4.14:

> The Master said, "Do not be concerned that you lack an official position, but rather concern yourself with the means by which you might take

your stand. Do not be concerned that no one has heard of you, but rather strive to become a person worthy of being known."

The sentiment expressed here is similar to one found in 12.1, where we read that *ren* 仁, the virtue of being "truly human," comes from (*you* 由) the self (*ji* 己), not others (*ren* 人).

This self-other dichotomy is often coordinated with the SELF AS CONTAINER + ESSENTIAL SELF metaphors, in that the "true" state of the Subject is to be found by looking to the "inside" (*nei* 內).[12] In 12.4 we read that the gentleman is "free of vexations or concerns" because he can "examine himself internally and find nothing there to fault [*neixing bujiu* 內省不疚]"; in 4.17, the aspiring gentleman is encouraged to "examine himself inwardly" (*neizixing* 內自省) when presented with unworthy behavior; and in 5.27 we are told that a person, perceiving a fault in himself, should then "take himself to task inwardly [*neizisong* 內自訟]." With regard to this "inner-outer" language, it is not always clear what the identity of the container self is. In passages such as 12.1, the self (*ji* 己) is portrayed as a kind of space from which *ren* can emerge—a space distinct from the realm of "others" (*ren* 人). In this schema, it seems that the "inside" of the CONTAINER SELF merely delineates a fairly broad sphere of concern that is associated with the ESSENTIAL SELF. On the other hand, in the description in 17.12 of the people who "assume stern and dignified countenances, though on the inside they are weak [*seli er neiren* 色厲而內荏]," it is clear that the CONTAINER SELF is the physical body. As we shall see, the SELF AS CONTAINER metaphor with the physical body as the container will become standard after the "Inner Training," but we might not necessarily be justified in reading this back into the *Analects*. In any case, the characterization throughout the text of what is properly internal (*nei* 內) and external (*wai* 外) is fairly consistent, no matter how the container involved is specifically conceived:

PROPERLY INTERNAL	PROPERLY EXTERNAL
the self (*ji* 己)	other people (*ren* 人)
the intention or ambition (*zhi* 志)	salary, material comfort
state of self-cultivation	social honor
The Confucian Way (rites, study)	official position
ren 仁	glibness (*ning* 佞), verbal skill

The problem with the contemporary world, in Confucius's view, is that the prevailing ethos emphasizes the obtainment of external goods, causing people to lose sight of the goods internal to Confucian moral self-cultivation. People of his day mechanically fulfill the outward forms of the rites and engage in study as if they were true seekers after the Way, but their activities amount to nothing more than empty show. Even the most intimate and personally significant of the rites—one's filial duties toward one's parents—have in Confucius's view been rendered hollow and meaningless:

Nowadays "filial" is used to refer to anyone who is merely able to provide their parents with nourishment. But even dogs and horses are provided with nourishment. If you do not treat your parents with reverence, wherein lies the difference? (2.7)

For Confucius, the emptiness and superficiality of his age is typified by the famous "village worthy" (*xiangyuan* 鄉愿), who carefully observes all of the outward practices dictated by convention and so attains a measure of social respect, but who lacks the inward commitment to the Way that characterizes the true Confucian gentleman. Confucius refers to the village worthy as the "thief of Virtue" because from the outside he *seems* to be a gentleman and so lays a false claim to Virtue. This is no doubt the sentiment informing 17.18 as well:

The Master said, "I hate it that purple is usurping the place of vermillion,[13] that the tunes of Zheng are being confused with classical music, and that the clever of tongue [*likou* 利口] are undermining both state and clan."

Just as the debased people of his time use the mixed color of purple in place of pure vermillion and confuse the decadent music of Zheng with true music, they mistake village worthies and glib talkers for true gentlemen.[14] The prevalence of these counterfeiters of Virtue and the popularity of decadent music are mirrored by the corruption of ritual practice among the political and social elite. I have already noted that, in Confucius's native state of Lu, the practice of the *di* 禘 sacrifice had degenerated to the point that Confucius could not bear to look upon it. Similarly, the overweening pride of the so-called "Three Families" who ruled Lu in Confucius's time caused them to usurp the ritual privileges properly accorded only to the Zhou kings—a transgression against the very structure of the cosmos that appalled and saddened Confucius (see 3.1, 3.2 and 3.6)

The direction of the causality involved in this state of affairs is not entirely clear. That is, it is hard to say whether the rise of hypocrisy and degeneration of ritual practice—most publicly and egregiously evinced by the three ruling families of Lu—are to be seen as the root cause of the fallenness of Confucius's age or merely as a symptoms of it. However, just as an unusual prevalence of shoddy woodcarving or ugly people would suggest a failure on the part of the local woodcarvers and cosmeticians, Confucius seems to give etiological priority to the state of cultural practice. Were there a Shun reigning respectfully in his ritual position facing South, we imagine that not only would the Three Families never dare to transgress their ritual privileges but that the virtuous suasive power of a ritually correct king would have transformed them into the kind of people who would not even consider such an arrogant display. Similarly, the ritually improper behavior of the Three Families can be seen as a prime factor encouraging the "wildly ambitious" and "unpruned" character of the young men of Lu (see 5.22), and the general loss of ritual correctness among the rulers of Confucius's time can no doubt be largely blamed for the mercenariness and superficiality of the lesser public officials. The priority given to the power of cultural forms will become even more clear when we look at Confucius's proposed soteriological path, for the emphasis there is upon the proper instantiation of traditional forms rather than upon techniques of psycho-physiological purification. Of course, the two are interdependent to a certain degree: proper performance of the rites brings about transformations in inner psychic state, and these rites themselves must be approached in the proper state of mind and by someone with basically whole-some "native stuff." The emphasis, though, is primarily upon the *cultural* forms without which the aspiring gentleman will never find the Way.

Soteriological Path: The Adornment and Shaping of the Self

The primary metaphor for self-cultivation in the *Analects* is that of adornment. The SELF-CULTIVATION AS ADORNMENT schema informs the metaphor pair of "native stuff" (*zhi* 質) and "cultural refinement" (*wen* 文 ; lit. lines, strokes), as well as the most common term for self-cultivation itself, *xiu* 修 —literally, deco-rating or adorning a surface.[15] This primary metaphor is often supplemented by and mixed with a related metaphor, SELF-CULTIVATION AS CRAFT, where the pro-cess of education is understood as an actual reshaping of the "stuff" of the Self rather than the adornment of a surface. In either case, the process of adornment or refashioning is guided by ideal models from a time before the world became cor-rupted—that is, from a time when a harmony between human beings and Heaven was perfectly realized in the sage rulers and ritual practices of the Zhou. Were the scholars of Confucius's age able to remake their own persons in order to accord with the ideals embodied in the Zhou cultural heroes and institutions, they would be able to transcend the fallenness of their own age and attain the status of "gen-tlemen" or even "sages," and the suasive power of their Virtue would be able to transform the common people and lead them back to the "Mean."

Moral adornment or reshaping is accomplished by means of the two primary Confucian practices, ritual practice (*li* 禮) and learning (*xue* 學), both of which involve a form of model emulation.[16] By perfecting ritual practice, the student internalizes ideal models of behavior in various life-situations, and through inten-sive learning he masters model literary forms and modes of thinking from the deeds and words of ancient exemplars. The constitutive role played by these cul-tural forms is neatly summed up in the famous line that makes up 8.8: "Find inspiration [*xing* 興] in the *Odes*, take your stand [*li* 立] through ritual, and be perfected [*cheng* 成] by music." There has been a great deal of commentarial dis-agreement over what it might mean for one to be inspired by the *Odes*,[17] but per-haps the most plausible explanation is suggested by later, more elaborate passages. In 16.13, Confucius's son and disciple Boyu is asked if he has been taught anything out of the ordinary.[18] He answers in the negative, but goes on to describe in language obviously derived from 8.8 the "ordinary" instruction he has received:

Once my father was standing by himself in the courtyard and, as I hurried by with quickened steps, he asked, "Have you studied the *Odes*?" I replied that I had not. He said, "Unless you study the *Odes*, you will be unable to speak." I retired to my room and studied the *Odes*.

On another day my father was again standing by himself in the courtyard and, as I hurried by with quickened steps, he asked, "Have you studied the *Rites*?" I replied that I had not. He said, "Unless you study the *Rites*, you will be unable to take your stand." I retired to my room and studied the *Rites*.

These two things are what I have been taught.

The function of the *Odes* is here made a bit clearer: it is to provide one with the resources to speak. This theme is elaborated in 17.9, where Confucius explains the value of the *Odes* for guiding both speech and action to his assembled disciples after rebuking them for their neglect of this aspect of their education:

The Master said, "Little Ones, why do you not study the *Odes*? The *Odes* can be a source of inspiration and can broaden your perspective; they can be used to bring you together with others as well as to give vent to vexations and complaints. In the domestic sphere, they articulate the proper manner to serve your father, and in public life they describe the proper manner to serve your ruler. They also acquaint you with the names for a wide variety of birds and beasts, plants and trees."

As Zhu Xi notes in his commentary on this passage, "with regard to the Way of human relationships, there are none which are not contained in the *Odes*. These two [i.e., serving one's father and one's lord] are cited because of their importance." At perhaps the opposite end of the spectrum of importance, the *Odes* broadens one's scope of knowledge by acquainting one with various proper names for animals and plants with which the student would not normally come into contact. The *Odes* thus plays a broad role in fostering in the individual the ability to speak and interact socially, providing the student with everything from quotations and turns-of-phrase useful in social situations to exemplary models of the most important role-specific duties. Seen in this light, the Master's rebuke of Boyu in 17.10 (which echoes 16.13) is quite understandable: The Master said to Boyu, "Have you begun learning the 'South of Zhou' and the 'South of Shao' sections of the *Odes*?[19] To be a man and not apply yourself to 'South of Zhou' and 'South of Shao' would be like standing with your face to the wall, would it not?"[20]

The passage in 16.13 does not provide any elaboration of what it means for the rites to enable one to "take one's stand," but the metaphor evokes the image of taking one's place among others in society. The traditional commentaries are helpful in this respect. In the elaboration of this story in the commentary by Huang Kan, Confucius's response when Boyu admits that he has not yet studied the rites is as follows:

> The rites are the root of establishing one's self [*lishenzhiben* 立身之本]
> by means of reverence, frugality, gravity, and respectfulness. With the
> rites, one can be at ease [*an* 安]; without the rites, one will be in danger
> [*wei* 危]. (Cheng Shude: 1170)

The student is to take his stand on the rites in the sense that the rites provide the model for every element of his behavior. In 12.1, the Master advises Yan Yuan, "Do not look unless it is in accordance with the rites; do not listen unless it is in accordance with the rites; do not speak unless it is in accordance with the rites; do not move unless it is in accordance with the rites." Confucius himself was of course famous for his strict adherence to the rites; in 10.10, we read that "he did not sit, unless his mat was properly arranged."

The constitutive role of tradition extends even to the cognitive realm. Just as the *Odes* gives one a model for personal expression and the rites provide the form for one's behavior, the accumulated wisdom of the classics is to form the very basis of one's thinking (*si* 思).[21] Herbert Fingarette—responding to A. C. Graham's emphasis on the role of spontaneous responsiveness to reality in Confucian thought (Graham 1985)—notes that for Confucius, consciousness of reality is not unmediated, but is rather conditioned by culture and ritual: "The *li* help determine how we will become aware, and of what" (Fingarette 1991: 220). Thinking outside the context of study might be compared to randomly banging on a piano in ignorance of the conventions of music: a million monkeys given a million years might produce something recognizable as a musical composition, but it is better to start with the classics. "I once engaged in thought [*si*] for an entire day without eating and an entire night without sleeping, but it did no good," the Master confides in 15.31. "It would have been better for me to have spent that time in study [*xue*]." This accounts for Confucius's avid devotion to learning ("In any town of ten households you will be certain to find someone who is as dutiful (*zhong* 忠) or trustworthy as I am, but you will not find anyone who matches my love for learning"—5.28),[22] as well as the meticulousness with which he pursued this endeavor: "The Master used the classical pronunciation when reading from the *Odes*, the *History*, and when conducting ritual. In all of these cases, he used the classical pronunciation" (7.18).

As mentioned earlier, the primary metaphors for this process of character formation are adornment and crafting. A phrase that appears several times in the *Analects* is that of "broadening" (*bo* 博) the student through learning or culture and "restraining" (*yue* 約) him by means of ritual. We read in 6.27, for instance, that "A gentleman who is broadly learned with regard to culture (*wen* 文) and who has been restrained by the rites can perhaps rely upon this training to avoid going against the Way."[23] Understood in terms of the craft metaphor, the purpose of ritual training is to restrain or regulate (*jie* 節) the inherent emotional "stuff" of human beings, which would tend toward excess if left to develop on its own:

> The Master said, "If you are respectful but lack ritual training you will
> become exasperating; if you are careful but lack ritual training you will
> become timid; if you are courageous but lack ritual training you will

become unruly; and if you are upright [*zhi* 直] but lack ritual training you will become inflexible." (8.2)[24]

We saw the craft metaphor above in the characterization of a certain disciple as a piece of "rotten wood" or a "dung wall" that cannot be made into something beautiful, and it appears systematically throughout the text. In 15.10 an aspiring gentleman's seeking out of virtuous company is compared to a craftsman's (*gong* 工) sharpening his tools, and in 19.7 Zixia compares the learning of the gentleman to the work of the "hundred craftsmen" in their shops.

Relying as it does upon our experience with literal crafts, the SELF-CULTIVATION AS CRAFT metaphor contains several important entailments. To begin with, in order for the raw material to be fashioned into something beautiful or properly formed, it will be necessary for external force to be applied, and this application of force will result in a sometimes violent reshaping of the original material. A fair amount of energy and exertion will also be required to perform such a difficult task. We see the reshaping entailment appear in 5.21, where the "wild" youth of Confucius's home state are described as lacking the means by which to "trim" (*cai* 裁) themselves,[25] as well as in 12.22, where something resembling the "press-frame" metaphor that becomes so prominent in the *Xunzi* is invoked: "By raising up the straight [*zhi* 直] and applying it to the crooked [*wang* 枉], the crooked can be made straight." The metaphor of "straightness" is a common one, referring sometimes to a specific virtue (often rendered as "uprightness") but also, as in 12.22, to general moral "straightness."[26] Another metaphor that becomes a favorite of Xunzi's is that of carving and polishing jade, an extremely difficult and time-consuming material to work. In 1.15, Zilu quotes the lines from ode 55, "As if cut [*qie* 切], as if polished [*cuo* 磋]; as if carved [*zhuo* 琢], as if ground [*mo* 磨]," to describe the perfected person, and is consequently praised by Confucius. In 9.19, self-cultivation is compared to building up a mountain or leveling ground, both grueling tasks that allow no respite [*zhi* 止; lit. stopping], and in 9.17 Confucius praises the indefatigability of the flowing river, which "does not rest day or night."

That a slacking off of effort can be metaphorically conceptualized as "stopping" or "resting" indicates a conceptual link between the craft metaphor and the schema SELF-CULTIVATION AS LONG JOURNEY.[27] In 8.7, the process of becoming a gentleman possessing the virtue of *ren* is likened by the disciple Zengzi to a difficult, lifelong journey:

> The burden is heavy [*renzhong* 任重] and the Way is far [*yuan* 遠]. *Ren* must be borne by the self [*ji* 己]—is this not heavy? One comes to a stop only after death—is this not far?

The two schemas are combined in 9.11, where Yan Hui laments the arduousness of the task of self-cultivation:

> The more I look up, the higher it is. The more I drill into [*zuan* 鑽] it, the harder it is. I discern it there ahead of me, but then suddenly it is behind my back. . . . Although I want to follow [*cong* 從] it, I can find no means of passage [*you* 由].

The coordination of the craft metaphor with the journey metaphor serves to reinforce and supplement the entailments discussed earlier. Since the journey is long and difficult, one cannot expect instant results. This is why Confucius criticizes those who want "quick success" (*sucheng* 速成) (14.44), and notes that "a person who wishes to go quickly [*su* 速] will never reach their destination [*da* 達]" (13.17). Like a road, the task of self-cultivation has a definite beginning and a clear end (19.12), and one must forge ahead in a determined manner and avoid distractions or "byways." "Although the byways [*xiaodao* 小道] no doubt have their own interesting sights to see, one who wishes to reach a distant destination [*zhiyuan* 致遠] fears becoming mired [*ni* 泥]," Zixia notes in 19.4 concluding: "This is why the gentleman avoids the byways."

As mentioned earlier, the most common general term for self-cultivation is a metaphor referring to the adornment of a surface, *xiu* 修 , and self-cultivation is also often conceptualized in terms of some cultural "adornment" (*wen* 文) being applied to preexisting "native stuff" (*zhi* 質). The SELF-CULTIVATION AS ADORN-MENT schema possesses many of the entailments discussed earlier—the need for time, for instance, and the external application of effort—but also possesses its own unique and somewhat contradictory entailment. Since painting and adorning do not—like craft reformation (carving, bending)—actually alter the "stuff" upon which they are applied, it is a prerequisite of these processes that a suitable surface or substrate be present. This entailment is clearly expressed in an exchange between Zixia and Confucius in 3.8:

> Zixia asked, "[The lines from the *Odes*]
>
> 'Her artful smile, with its alluring dimples,
> Her beautiful eyes, so clear,
> The unadorned upon which to paint.'[28]
>
> What does this mean?"
>
> The Master said, "The task of applying colors comes only after a suitable unadorned background is present."
>
> Zixia said, "So it is the rites that come after?"
>
> The Master said, "Zixia, you are truly one who can anticipate my thoughts! It is only with someone like you that I can begin to discuss the *Odes*."

Ritual training is here portrayed metaphorically as applying cosmetics to an otherwise unadorned face. Just as all of the cosmetics in the world are of no avail if the basic lines of the face are not pleasing, so is the refinement provided by ritual practice of no help to one lacking in good native substance. It is this entailment that explains both Confucius's concern that cultural adornment be firmly rooted in its native substrate and his preference to err on the side of simplicity:

> Lin Fang asked about the roots of ritual practice [*lizhiben* 禮之本]. The Master exclaimed, "Noble indeed are you to ask such a question! When it comes to ritual, it is better to be frugal than extravagant. When it

comes to mourning, it is better to be overwhelmed with grief than overly composed." (3.4)[29]

The "native stuff" of the basic emotions are the "root" of the ritual forms, and it is important that these forms never lose touch with their organic origins. Unlike the craft metaphor, then, the adornment metaphor involves a substrate material that is not a shapeless mass to be cut or trimmed, but that instead helps to determine the final shape of the "product." We will see that this point of tension between the two metaphorical models forms the basis of my discussion of the paradox of wu-wei as it appears in the *Analects*.

The End-Product: The Mean (*zhong* 中) and Completion (*cheng* 成)

The Mean

Regardless of which metaphor schema is invoked to conceptualize self-cultivation, the end-goal is the same: harmony and perfection. The rites, for instance, rein in the emotions and allow the attainment of social "harmony" (*he* 和):

> Youzi said, "In the application of ritual, it is harmony [*he* 和] that is to be valued. It is precisely such harmony that makes the Way of the Former Kings so beautiful. If you merely stick rigidly to ritual in all matters, great and small, there will remain that which you cannot accomplish. Yet if you know enough to value harmonious ease but try to attain it without being regulated [*jie* 節] by the rites, this will not work either."

As with the English "harmony," one of the primary references of *he* 和 is to the realm of music. What is valued in the "application of ritual," then, is the kind of pleasing balance one finds in harmonious music.[30] As with music, though, such harmony cannot be achieved through the exercise of one's natural dispositions alone, but requires "regulation" (*jie* 節) through traditional forms. Throughout the *Analects*, the restraining function of traditional forms is portrayed as being crucial to the development of true, balanced virtue.

> The Master said, "Zilu! Have you heard about the six [virtuous] teachings and the six corresponding vices?"
>
> Zilu replied, "I have not."
>
> "Sit! I will tell you about them. Loving *ren* without loving learning will result in the vice of foolishness. Loving knowledge without loving learning will result in the vice of deviant thought. Loving trustworthiness without loving learning will result in the vice of harmful rigidity. Loving uprightness without loving learning will result in the vice of

intolerance. Loving courage without loving learning will result in the vice of unruliness. Loving resoluteness without loving learning will result in the vice of willfulness."

This description of the "six [virtuous] teachings" and their attendant faults (*bi* 蔽 ; lit. obscurations) is reminiscent of Aristotle's discussion of the virtues and their excesses and deficiencies. Aristotle describes his virtues as the mean (*mesotes*) point between two extremes: truthfulness or straightforwardness, for instance, is the mean between the vice of excess (boastfulness) and the vice of deficiency (self-deprecation).[31] Although Confucius generally discusses his virtues in pairs (the virtue and its excess when not restrained by the rites) rather than triads (the virtues and its excess and deficiency), this difference probably has more to do with the fact that Confucius was not interested in providing the sort of theoretical account of the virtues that we find in the *Nicomachean Ethics* than with any substantial difference in conceptualization. The basic conceptual structure of the "mean" is very similar, based as it is upon the metaphor of a physical continuum with two ends and a desirable mid-point.

The counterpart to Aristotle's *mesotes* is the Chinese *zhong* 中 : "center" or (by extension) "midpoint." In 6.29 Confucius declares:

Acquiring Virtue through use of the mean [*zhong* 中]—is this not best? And yet for some time now such Virtue has been quite hard to find among the people.

A fragment from some Confucian-related text that makes up 20.1 portrays Yao as advocating "holding fast to the center" (執其中), and in 13.21 Confucius mentions the "middle path" (*zhongxing* 中行) between recklessness and fastidiousness.[32] The original graph for *zhong* depicts an arrow at the center of an archery target, and this is its primary metaphorical reference: the center of a bounded space. In this respect, it belongs primarily to the schema MORALITY AS BOUNDED SPACE, and is thereby related to the family of metaphors for moral "error" that all have to do with the physical transgression of boundary lines. The most common of these is the metaphor of "crossing" or "exceeding [a limit]" (*guo* 過), which is perhaps the most common way to conceptualize moral error in Warring States thought. We see a similar metaphor in the famous passage 2.4, where we are told that Confucius could act in a spontaneous manner without "overstepping the [bounds of] the carpenter's square" (*yuju* 踰矩). In 19.11, we are warned not to "overstep the fence" (*yuxian* 踰閑) when it comes to serious matters, but are assured that, with regard to minor matters, it is acceptable to "go out and enter" (*churu* 出入)—that is, "cross the line" from time to time.[33] The schema of MORALITY AS BOUNDED SPACE is also employed in an interesting manner in 13.3 (the famous "correction of names" passage), where Confucius notes that "when language does not accord [*shun* 順], then punishments and sanctions will not hit the mark [*zhong* 中] . . . if punishments and sanctions do not hit the mark, the common people will have no place [*suo* 所] to put their hands and feet." Here a properly arranged system of names is conceived of as setting up a bounded space within which the common people can act. The bounded space schema also informs the metaphor for balance we find in 3.20, where the Master praises the lyrics and music[34] that make up the first ode in the *Book of Odes*, the *Guanju* 關 雎: "The Master said, 'The *Guanju* is joyful without going to wanton excess [*yin* 淫], and sorrowful without falling into self-flagellation" (3.20). The term *yin* refers literally to the spilling-over of flood waters and is a common early metaphor for "wanton excess" or "licentiousness." Here, proper moral behavior is understood as a kind of bounded container, with immoral behavior portrayed as a liquid that "overflows" the sides of the container.

Despite its primary "home" in the MORALITY AS BOUNDED SPACE schema, we also see a suggestion that *zhong* can function conceptually as the midpoint on a linear spectrum in Confucius's cryptic admonition in 2.16 not to try "working on [self-cultivation] from the wrong ends [*yiduan* 異端]," or in the common use of *zhong* to represent the center point or state between the "highest" (*shang* 上) and "lowest" (*xia* 下). Another way of conceiving metaphorically of the "mean" is found in 11.16, where we see the state of self-perfection conceptualized as a kind of physical goal-line that needs to be reached but not crossed, with Confucius remarking that it is equally bad to "fall short of" (*buji* 不及 ; lit. not reach up to) or to "cross" (*guo* 過) the metaphorical "line" of virtue. An additional schema for conceptualizing the "mean" of virtue relies upon a social metaphor, as in the discussion of "native stuff" and "cultural adornment" in 6.18:

> The Master said, "When native stuff defeats [*sheng* 勝] cultural adornment, the result is a crude rustic. When cultural adornment defeats native stuff, the result is a foppish pedant [*shi* 史]. Only when adornment and stuff do not defeat one another do you have a gentleman."

Here the mean state of virtue is portrayed metaphorically as the failure of either one of a pair of opposed social forces to defeat the other.

Perfection/Completion   My discussion of the constitutive quality of traditional forms has gotten us only two-thirds of the way through 8.8: we have seen how the aspiring gentleman is "stimulated" by the *Odes* and takes a stand in society by molding his actions in accordance with the rites. What remains to be discussed is the final stage of being "perfected through music." The concept of perfection/ completion (*cheng* 成) is related to the craft schema: the perfected person is a "completed product." Perhaps the best way to explore this image is through a discussion of the virtue of *ren* 仁.

Up to this point I have left *ren* untranslated and unexplained. There has been some disagreement over how precisely to translate this term, which has often been rendered as "benevolence" or "humanity." This is apparently its sense in later Confucian texts, but most scholars today are in agreement that in the *Analects* it refers not merely to a limited, specific virtue such as "benevolence," but in most contexts has the general sense of the highest of Confucian virtues. It is cognate with (in both modern Mandarin and ancient Chinese) the word for "human being" (*ren* 人), and we might thus best render *ren* as something like "true humanity" or "true humanness."[35] *Ren* represents the general Confucian virtue, defined in terms of the perfection or completion of the lesser virtues. In 13.19,

Fan Chi asks Confucius about *ren*, and the Master explains it in terms of three lesser virtues:

> When relaxing at home remain reverent; when undertaking affairs, be respectful; when associating with other people, fulfill your role dutifully [*zhong* 忠]. These are virtues that cannot be neglected, even if you went and lived among the Yi or Di barbarian tribes.

In 13.27, the Master says that one who possesses the virtues of firmness, resoluteness, simple honesty, and caution in speech is close to *ren*; in 14.4 it is explained that *ren* encompasses the virtue of courage, but that one who is courageous is not necessarily *ren*;[36] and in 17.6 Confucius declares that anyone who is capable of practicing the five virtues of reverence, tolerance, trustworthiness, diligence, and generosity is worthy of being called *ren*.

The *ren* person is usually referred to as the "gentleman" (*junzi* 君子), but is sometimes also referred to as the "complete person" (*chengren* 成人)—that is, an individual who possesses all of the other virtues and properly balances them through being fully trained in Confucian practice. In 14.12 Confucius implicitly invokes the native substance/cultural adornment metaphor in describing the "complete person" as the product of native virtues that have been refined by means of the Confucian cultural practices:

> The Master said, "Take a person as wise as Zang Wuzhong, as free of desire as Gongzhuo, as courageous as Zhuangzi of Bian[37] and as accomplished in the arts [*yi* 藝] as Ran Qiu, and then adorn [*wen* 文] him with ritual and music—such a man might be called a complete person."

The gentleman is thus one who has embodied the various Confucian virtues in his personal "stuff," properly adorned them, and thereby brought them to completion:

> The Master said, "The gentleman takes rightness as his stuff [*zhi*], and then puts this stuff into practice by means of ritual, gives it expression through modesty, and perfects it by being trustworthy. Now that is a gentleman!" (15.18)

At Ease in Virtue (*anren* 安仁): Confucian Wu-Wei

For a concise summary of the Confucian soteriological path as I have traced it so far, I can do no better than to turn to Confucius's spiritual autobiography, which is recorded in *Analects* 2.4:

> The Master said, "At age fifteen I set my intention upon learning; at thirty I took my stand; at forty I became free from doubts; at fifty I understood the Heavenly Mandate; at sixty my ear could simply go

along [*ershun* 耳順]; and at seventy I could follow my heart's desire without overstepping the bounds [*ju* 矩; lit. carpenter's square]."

We can see this spiritual evolution as encompassing three pairs of stages. In the first pair (stages one and two), the aspiring gentleman commits himself to the Confucian Way, submitting to the rigors of study and ritual practice until these traditional forms have been internalized to the point that he is able to "take his stand" among others. In the second pair, the practitioner begins to feel truly at ease with this new manner of being, and is able to understand how the Confucian Way fits into the order of things and complies with the will of Heaven.[38] The clarity and sense of ease this brings with it leads to the final two stages, where one's dispositions have been so thoroughly harmonized with the dictates of normative culture that one accords with them spontaneously. As Zhu Xi glosses the description of Confucius at age seventy, "Being able to follow one's heart's desires without transgressing normative standards means that one acts with ease [*an* 安], hitting the mean without effort [*bumian er zhong* 不勉而中]."[39]

Effortlessness

We see in this commentary the first of the two main hallmarks of wu-wei, effortlessness, being conceptualized in terms of both the "following" (*cong* 從) and (in Zhu Xi's commentary) the "ease" (安) families of metaphors. In 2.4, the Subject (Confucius) is able to relinquish control and simply "follow" the Self (his heart's desires) without being led outside of the bounded space of morality, and one aspect of the Self (the ear) is described as merely "going along with the flow" (*shun* 順). There has been some commentarial controversy concerning what it means for one's ear to be able to "flow along," but most interpretations take it to mean that Confucius at this point immediately apprehends the teachings he hears[40] or that there is no conflict between his dispositions and the teachings of the sages—thereby more clearly linking it with the stage that follows. The Jin Dynasty commentator Li Chong combines both explanations:

> What it means for Confucius to say that his "ear flowed along" is that upon hearing teachings concerning the models of the former kings, he immediately comprehended their Virtuous manners. He could follow [*cong*] the models handed down by the Lord [*di* 帝] without any aspect of them going against [*ni* 逆] his heart. His heart and ear were perfectly in sync [*xiangcong* 相從; lit. followed one another], and this is why he says that his "ear flowed along." [Cheng Shude: 75].

At this stage, one takes joy in the teachings of the ancients, and so accords with them in a state of effortless release. This joy and sense of ease in turn serves to further strengthen the feeling of certainty derived from understanding the Mandate of Heaven, which in turn fosters resoluteness and further liberates one from both doubts and external distractions.[41]

Metaphors from the "following" and "ease" families abound in the text. In 7.6 the Master describes the ideal way of being in the world as follows: "Set your intention upon the Way, rely upon [*ju* 據] Virtue, lean upon [*yi* 依] *ren*, and explore at ease [*you* 游; lit. wander in] the cultural arts." Similarly, the "complete" person—one who genuinely possesses the virtue of *ren*—feels "at ease in *ren*" (*anren* 安仁), unself-consciously embodying it in his every action. Yan Hui was apparently very close to this stage, and in any case far ahead of his fellow students. As Confucius says of him in 6.7, "Ah, Yan Hui! For three months at a time his heart did not go against *ren*. The rest of them could only achieve such a state by fits and starts." That the Master himself transcended even this state is discernible not only from 2.4 but is also suggested in passages such as 5.26:

> Yan Hui and Zilu were in attendance. The Master said to them, "Why don't each of you speak to me of your aspirations [*zhi* 志]?"
>
> Zilu said, "I would like to be able to share my carts and horses, clothing and fur with my friends, and not become resentful if they are returned damaged."
>
> Yan Hui said, "I would like to avoid being boastful about my own abilities or exaggerating my accomplishments."
>
> Zilu said, "I would like to hear of the Master's aspirations."
>
> The Master said, "To bring ease [*an* 安] to the aged, to have trust in my friends, and to cherish the youth."

What we have here is clearly a progression in nobleness of aspiration or intention. Zilu is overly focused on externalities and what might be called the outer branches (*mo* 末) of the tree of virtue (rather than the roots). Yan Hui is clearly a cut above this: he shows a settled aversion to actions that would violate *ren*, and so has internalized this virtue to a certain extent. Confucius, however, reveals his superiority to even Yan Hui by casting his commitment in positive terms: to bring peace, to trust, and to cherish. I think that Zhu Xi—who explicitly links this passage to 6.7—is correct in summing up the differences between the three answers in this way: "The Master felt at ease in *ren*, Yan Hui did not violate *ren*, and Zigong actively pursued [*qiu* 求] *ren*."

The implication, of course, is that if you have to actively pursue it you just do not truly get it—the genuinely cultivated person does not *have* to try.[42] The Confucian Way should effortlessly permeate every aspect of one's life, which is why even in moments of leisure Confucius appears "proper and serious [*shenshen* 申申] and yet fully at ease [*yaoyao* 夭夭]" (7.4),[43] and why he begins to worry about himself only when the Way of the Zhou no longer penetrates even into his dream-life: "How seriously I have declined! It has been so long since I have dreamt of the Duke of Zhou" (7.5).

Unself-consciousness   In 6.11, Confucius praises his favorite student, Yan Hui, because his dire economic situation does not detract from his joy (*le* 樂) in the Way, and in 7.16, the Master rhapsodizes upon his own freedom from luxuries or external comforts:

Eating plain rice and drinking water, having only your bent arm as a pil-
low—there is certainly joy to be found in this! Wealth and fame attained
improperly [*bu yi* 不義] concern me no more than the floating clouds.

This sort of joy arises spontaneously once the dispositions have been harmonized
with the demands of practice, and allows the experience of a genuine sense of satisfaction in one's activity. We see such joy manifested when the Master hears the
music of the great sage-king Shun and is so enraptured that for three months he
"did not even notice [*buzhi* 不知 ; lit. did not know] the taste of meat."[44] We see
here an association between music, joy, and forgetfulness that is also echoed by
the graphic pun between the words for "joy" and "music" in ancient Chinese,
which are both represented by the character 樂.[45] The joyous rapture inspired by
sublimely beautiful music—involving as it does a kind of unself-conscious ease
and a loss of a sense of self—thus serves as a powerful metaphor for wu-wei perfection.

We see a similar association of joy and forgetfulness in 7.19, where a local
ruler asks the disciple Zilu about Confucius. Confucius advises him:

Why not just say something like this: "He is the type of person who
becomes so absorbed in his studies that he forgets [*wang* 忘] to eat,
whose joy renders him free of worries, and who grows old without being
aware [*buzhi* 不知] of the passage of the years."

Here we see all three of the main metaphors for Confucian unself-consciousness
nicely combined in one passage: forgetting, joy, and "not knowing" or "not being
conscious of." It is precisely this joyful unself-consciousness that distinguishes a
true practitioner from one who has not yet seen the Way. In 6.20 Confucius
describes the progression of affective states that a Confucian practitioner must
experience: "One who knows it[46] is not the equal of one who loves it, and one
who loves it is not the equal of one who takes joy in it." That is, it is not enough to
have a merely intellectual or practical understanding of the meanings of the rites
and the contents of the canon (the Way), and even loving (*hao* 好) the Way
involves too much conscious focus upon the object. The goal is to become so
immersed in the practice that all distinction between self and object is forgotten.
This is how we are to understand 11.26:[47]

Zilu, Zengxi, Ranyou, and Zihua were seated in attendance. The Master
said to them, "I am older than any of you, but do not feel reluctant to
speak your minds on that account. You are all in the habit of complain-
ing, 'I am not appreciated.' Well, if someone *were* to appreciate your talents [and give you employment], how would you then go about things?"

Zilu spoke up immediately. "If I were given charge of a state of a thousand chariots—even one hemmed in between powerful states, suffering
from armed invasions and afflicted by famine—before three years were
up I could infuse it with courage and a sense of what is right."

The Master smiled at him, and then turned to Ranyou. "You, Ranyou!"
he said. "What would you do?"

Ranyou answered, "If I were given charge of a state of sixty or seventy—or at least fifty or sixty—square *li* in area, before three years were up I could see that it was materially prosperous. As for instructing the people in ritual practice and music, this is a task that would have to await the arrival of a gentleman."

The Master then turned to Zihua. "You, Zihua! What would you do?"

Zihua answered, "It is not that I am saying that I would actually be able to do so, but my wish, at least, would be to devote myself to study. I would like, perhaps, to serve as a minor functionary—properly clad in ceremonial cap and gown—in charge of ancestral temple events or diplomatic gatherings."

The Master then turned to Zengxi. "You, Zengxi! What would you do?"

Zengxi stopped strumming upon the zither, and as the last notes faded away he set the instrument aside and rose to his feet. "I would choose to do something quite different from any of the other three."

"What harm is there in that?" the Master said. "Each of you is merely expressing your own aspirations."

Zengxi then said, "In the third month of Spring, once the Spring garments have been completed, I should like to assemble a company of five or six young men and six or seven boys to go bathe in the Yi river and enjoy the breeze upon the Rain Altar,[48] and then return singing to the Master's house."

The Master sighed deeply, saying, "I am with Zengxi!"

Here we have all of the elements of Confucian wu-wei. Zengxi's musical sensitivity, combined with the unself-conscious ease with which he casually responds to the Master's question, contrasts strikingly with the strained, painfully self-conscious responses of the other disciples. His evocative image of effortless joy in the Way can only elicit a sigh of wistful admiration from the Master.

This emphasis on spontaneity and joy is the reason that Confucius is reluctant to pronounce others *ren* based only upon accounts of their exploits. Virtuous deeds can be faked, but true virtue is a stable disposition that endures over time and shines forth in the subtlest details of one's everyday life. The virtue of the truly accomplished Confucian sage—subtle in its detail, and flowing forth as it does so effortlessly—is a mysterious thing that is sometimes invisible to the common person. The Confucian sage is thus at times in the *Analects* described in terms that, in their apparently paradoxical juxtaposition of opposites, call to mind the ideal of the Daoist sage:

Zengzi said, "Having ability, and yet asking for advice from those who are not able. Possessing much, and yet asking for advice from those who have little. Having, yet appearing to lack; full, and yet appearing empty;[49] transgressed against and yet unconcerned. I once had a friend[50] who used to pursue such an ideal." (8.5)

As we shall see, although the paradoxical character of the Confucian sage will be echoed in texts such as the *Laozi* and *Zhuangzi*, the metaphorical valuations will be quite different, with the Daoists trying to *empty* the CONTAINER SELF rather than fill it. Nevertheless, we cannot help but see an affinity between the perfected Confucian and Daoist sages, sharing as they do this sort of unconscious ease and accordance with others. Consider, for example, 14.13, where a certain Gongshu Wenzi is rumored to have never spoken, laughed, or taken anything. His disciple explains that this is not literally the case, but that the rumor has arisen because of the utter genuineness and spontaneity of his master's actions:

> My master only spoke when the time was right [*shiran* 時然], and so people never grew impatient listening to him. He only laughed when he was genuinely full of joy, and so people never tired of hearing him laugh. He only took what was rightfully his, and so people never resented his taking things.

We see here a new term: *shi* 時 or *shiran* 時然 ("timely"). The metaphor concerns the Subject's relationship to the world, portraying the Subject's actions as "fitting" circumstances. I will conclude my discussion of Confucian wu-wei with an examination of this metaphor.

Timeliness and Flexibility   We have seen that the "completed" Confucian gentleman is portrayed as having struck a balance or achieved a kind of harmony between his natural dispositions (his "native stuff") and external cultural forms ("adornment"). This balance allows him follow his spontaneous impulses while still remaining within the bounds of morality. Because the moral action of the gentleman arises effortlessly out of the Self, the Subject is able to display a level of autonomy and flexibility impossible for one who is merely "going by the book." Indeed, one cannot be said to be perfected or completed until one knows how to apply traditional forms skillfully and in a context-sensitive manner. As Confucius notes in 13.5:

> Imagine a person who can recite the three hundred Odes by heart but, when delegated a governmental task, is unable to carry it out or, when sent out into the field as a diplomat, is unable to use his own initiative. No matter how many Odes he might have memorized, what good are they to him?

The goal is to develop a *sense* for traditional culture, and not to focus too exclusively on its formal qualities. Similarly, clinging too rigidly to codes of moral conduct will cause one to lose sight of morality itself; it is better to hold fast to a developed sense for what is right [*yi* 義] and respond with flexibility to the situations that present themselves. "Acting in the world, the gentleman has no predispositions for or against anything" Confucius explains in 4.10. "He merely seeks to be on the side of what is right."[51] Having over the course of a long process of self-cultivation internalized the rules and conventions that define such practices

as the rites, a gentleman such as Confucius is able to display a degree of autonomy in applying—or even potentially evaluating, criticizing, or altering—them.
Hence we have the famous passage, *Analects* 9.3, where Confucius accedes to a
modification in the rites:

> The Master said, "A cap made of hemp is prescribed by the rites, but
> nowadays people use silk. This is frugal, and I follow the majority. To
> bow before ascending the stairs is what is prescribed by the rites, but
> nowadays people bow after ascending. This is arrogant, and—though it
> goes against the majority—I continue to bow before ascending."

It is certainly possible to exaggerate the iconoclastic character of this passage.[52]
Nevertheless, we can appreciate the sense of it without ignoring Confucius's profound conservatism: rites are expressive of a certain sense or feeling, and thus an
alteration in the actual rite is permissible if it will not—in the opinion of one who
has fully mastered the rites and thus internalized it—alter its essential meaning.

In addition to *yi*, a discussion of flexibility and autonomy in Confucian practice must also encompass the virtue of *shu* 恕, which seems to serve an analogous
counterbalancing function in the *Analects*. The importance of *shu* in Confucius's
thought is quite clear. In 4.14, coupled with *zhong* 忠 (role-specific duty) it is
described by a disciple as the "single thread" tying together all that Confucius
taught (*dao* 道). In 15.24, it is described as the "one teaching that can serve as a
guide for one's entire life" and is defined by Confucius as "Do not impose on others what you yourself do not desire." The similar idea of being able to take what
is near at hand (i.e., oneself and what one does and does not desire) as an analogy
is described in 6.30 as the "method of *ren*," and in 5.12 Zigong explains that he
aspires to what is no doubt a paraphrase of *shu*: "What I do not wish others to do
unto me, I also wish not to do unto others."[53] Understanding what is entailed in
shu is therefore quite clearly essential if one is to comprehend Confucius's soteriological vision, and 4.14 makes it apparent that any understanding of *shu* will
involve explicating its relationship to *zhong*. The definition of these two concepts
has been a source of a great deal of controversy among modern scholars, but the
definitive position seems to me to be that of David Nivison, as modified by P. J.
Ivanhoe.[54] In this interpretation, *zhong* is understood as the virtue of properly fulfilling one's ritually dictated duties in service to others, whereas *shu* is seen as the
complementary virtue[55] that "humanizes" *zhong*. *Shu* involves the ability to
amend or suspend the dictates of *zhong*—or to apply them flexibly—when holding to them rigidly would involve "imposing on others what you yourself do not
desire." Understood in this manner, it might be rendered as something like "sympathetic understanding." This interpretation is supported by 12.2, where (as Ivanhoe has suggested)[56] we can see another implicit pairing of *zhong* and *shu* by
Confucius in response to a question about *ren*:

> Zhong Gong asked about *ren*.
>
> The Master said, "When in public, comport yourself as if you were
> receiving an important guest; in your management of the common peo-
> ple, behave as if you were overseeing a great sacrifice. Do not impose

upon others what you yourself do not desire. In this way, you will encounter no resentment in your state or in your family."

The first two injunctions refer to fulfilling role-specific duties and are apparently to be supplemented by the injunction that serves as the definition of *shu* in 15.24. The "sympathetic understanding" of *shu* thus seems to be an indispensable complement to role-specific dutifulness, as well as an essential aspect of the overall virtue of *ren*.[57]

Representing as it does a type of situation-specific disposition rather than a maxim or rule, *shu* cannot be characterized formally, but must rather be illustrated by means of role models or exemplars from the past. This is part of Confucius's function in the *Analects*, for he serves throughout the text as an exemplar of this sort of context-sensitivity. Indeed, the entirety of book 10—an extended account of Confucius's ritual behavior—can be seen as a model of how the true sage flexibly adapts the principles of ritual to concrete situations. While this chapter is often skipped over in embarrassment by Western scholars sympathetic to Confucianism but nonetheless appalled by the seemingly pointless detail and apparent rigidity of behavior ("Under a black jacket, he wore lambskin; under an undyed jacket, he wore fawnskin; under a yellow jacket, he wore fox fur. His informal fur coat was long but with a short right sleeve"—10.6).[58] This discomfort is based upon a fundamental misunderstanding. While the scope and detail of Confucian ritual certainly (and quite rightly) seems alien to a modern Westerner, it is important to understand that what is being emphasized in this chapter is the ease and grace with which the Master embodies the spirit of the rites in every aspect of his life—no matter how trivial—and accords with this spirit in adapting the rites to new and necessarily unforeseeable circumstances.

That Confucius's flexibility in applying the rite is the theme of book 10 is made clear in the last passage, 10.27:

> Startled by their arrival, the bird arose and circled several times before alighting upon a branch. [The Master] said, "This pheasant upon the mountain bridge—how timely [*shi*] it is! How timely it is!" Zilu bowed to the bird, and then it cried out three times before flying away.

This poetic, somewhat cryptic passage[59] seems like a non sequitur at the end of a chapter devoted to short, prosaic descriptions of ritual behavior—unless, that is, it is seen as a thematic summary of the chapter as a whole. "Timeliness" is Confucius's particular forte, and indeed he is known to posterity (through the efforts of Mencius) as the "timely sage"—the one whose ritual responses were always appropriate to circumstances. As Mencius explains in 5:B:1:

> When Confucius decided to leave Qi, he emptied the rice from the pot before it was even done and set out immediately. When he decided to leave Lu he said, "I will take my time, for this is the way to leave the state of one's parents." Moving quickly when it was appropriate to hurry, moving slowly when it was appropriate to linger, remaining in a state or taking office when the situation allowed—this is how Confucius was. . . . Confucius was the sage whose actions were timely.

Universal Salvation through Personal Transformation: Wu-wei and Rule by Virtue

Most treatments of the role of wu-wei in Confucian thought have focused upon its political function.[60] As we have seen thus far, however, to interpret Confucian wu-wei in such a manner is to obscure its function as first and foremost an *individual* spiritual ideal. The bulk of the *Analects* is concerned, not with matters of government, but with the cultivation of the self and the attainment of a state of spiritual development where one's dispositions are perfectly harmonized with the dictates of ancient normative culture—that is, with the overcoming of fallenness through personal effort. This being noted, I should now discuss the fact that Confucius's vision does not end with the salvation of the individual, but goes on to portray this individual attainment as the key to the eventual salvation of the world from its state of corruption. It is in this way that the individual soteriological goal of wu-wei is connected to the effortless political ordering of the world.

The theme of the gentleman rectifying himself in order to rectify (in a concentrically expanding circle) the family, the state, and eventually the entire world becomes a prominent theme in such later Confucian texts as the "Great Learning" (*daxue* 大學), and its roots can be found in the *Analects*:

> Zilu asked about the gentleman. The Master said, "He cultivates himself and thereby achieves respectfulness."
>
> "Is that all?"
>
> "He cultivates himself and thereby brings ease [*an* 安] to others."
>
> "Is that all?"
>
> "He cultivates himself and thereby brings ease to the common people. Even [someone like] Yao and Shun would find such a task difficult." (14.42)

Many early commentaries explicitly link this ideal of "bringing ease to others" with rule by wu-wei, linking it to the example of Shun in 15.5, who simply made himself ritually correct and thereby brought order to the entire world. It is thus quite clear that the project of personal self-cultivation advocated by Confucius, while not always explicitly related to the ordering of the world at large, is intended to have ramifications that extend far beyond the individual himself. This individual—the Confucian gentleman—serves ultimately as the key to the salvation of the world as a whole, and is thus responsible for the salvation of the mass of common people who are incapable of achieving salvation through their own efforts. Although Confucius was quite radical in ethicizing and to a certain extent democratizing the early Zhou worldview by making the attainment of "gentleman" status and the ability to establish a Virtue-relationship with Heaven goals within the reach of any man[61] who chose to apply himself, it is quite clear that the possession of true *ren* is a rarefied achievement quite beyond the grasp of most people. Indeed, there are indications that even the ability to understand the Confucian Way is something confined to a spiritual elite. As Confucius remarks in 8.9, "The common people can be led [*shi* 使] along a path, but cannot be made to understand it." I believe Confucian commentators are correct in rejecting more sinister interpretations of this sentiment,[62] for it certainly does not refer to the sage ruler tricking the people into following the Way. Rather, it refers to rule by means of Virtue.[63] The power of Virtue is the medium through which individual salvation is transformed into universal salvation.

The attractive quality of Virtue in the Confucian scheme, noted in chapter 1, is expressed quite clearly in such passages as 4.25, where we read that "Virtue is never alone; it always has neighbors." Perhaps more important, though, is Virtue's power to *transform*. The ability of a fully cultivated gentleman to raise almost magically the standard of cultivation of those around him through the power of his Virtue is so great that even barbarians are susceptible to its influence:

> The Master expressed a desire to go and live among the Nine Barbarian tribes. Someone asked him, "How could you bear their uncouthness?"

> The Master replied, "If a gentleman were to dwell among them, what uncouthness would there be?" (9.14)

The implication is that even among a chaotic, warlike people such as the Eastern barbarians, the mere presence of a gentleman would bring peace and order, and not just *any* sort of peace and order, but the kind of cultured (*wen* 文) order that is the opposite of "uncouthness" (*lou* 陋)—that is, the kind of order that can be uniquely supplied by the rites and other practices of the Zhou, or by the suasive influence of one who has mastered them. The connection between the ability to sway the people through Virtue and the Zhou rites is made explicit in 14.41 ("When the rulers love the rites, the people will be easy to manage [*shi* 使]")[64] and in 1.9, where the disciple Zengzi says, "Be meticulous in observing the passing of those close to you and do not fail to continue the sacrifices to your distant ancestors. This will be enough to cause the Virtue of the common people to return to fullness."

Here the Virtue acquired through proper ritual behavior on the part of the gentleman is described as evoking a return to Virtue on the part of the common people. The manner in which the Virtue is manifested on the two different levels is clearly different, however. In 13.4, in Confucius's response to someone who wants to be taught something "practical" such as agricultural techniques, we read how the cultivation of the virtues proper to those in officialdom causes the common people to return spontaneously to virtue in their own activities as well, but the virtues actually displayed and the activities engaged in are those proper to the two different stations in life:

> Fan Chi asked to learn agricultural techniques [from Confucius].

> The Master said, "When it comes to that, any old farmer would be a better teacher than I."

He asked to learn gardening.

The Master said, "When it comes to that, any old gardener would be a better teacher than I."

Fan Chi then left. The Master remarked, "What a petty man that Fan Chi is! When the ruler loves ritual propriety, then none among the common people will dare to be disrespectful. When the ruler loves rightness, then none among the common people will dare not to obey. When the ruler loves trustworthiness, then none among the common people will dare not to be honest. The mere existence of such a ruler would cause the common people throughout the world to bundle their children on their backs and seek him out. Why, then, concern yourself with agricultural techniques?"[65]

This is the sentiment behind 12.11, where the ideally governed world is described in terms of everyone fulfilling their role-specific duties:

Duke Jing of Qi asked Confucius about governing.

Confucius responded, "Let the lord act as a true lord, the ministers as true ministers, the fathers as true fathers, and the sons as true sons."[66]

The Duke replied, "Well put! Certainly if the lord is not a true lord, the ministers not true ministers, the fathers not true fathers, and the sons not true sons, even if there is sufficient grain, will I ever get to eat it?"

We can thus see that since Heaven is the source of both the specific patterns of Zhou culture and the Virtue that resides in the person of the gentleman, the attractive and transforming power of Virtue functions in a similarly specific manner: it attracts people away from the corrupt practices that characterize barbarianism (whether that of actual non-Chinese barbarians on the borders or the fallen Chinese people of Confucius's own day) and back to *the* Way—the Way that once prevailed in the Zhou.[67]

The key to saving the world does not involve actively engaging in government in the sense of promulgating laws or raising armies. Confucius had a very dim view of the ability of legal manipulation or managerial techniques to have an effect on the hearts and minds (*xin* 心) of the people,[68] and was very dubious about the effectiveness of force in bringing the fallen world back to the Way.[69] His faith lay in the suasive and transformative power of Virtue:

Ji Kangzi asked Confucius about government, saying, "What would you think if, in order to move closer to those who possess the Way, I were to kill those who do not follow the Way?"

Confucius answered, "In administering your government, what need is there for you to kill? Just desire the good yourself and the common people will be good. The Virtue of the gentleman is like the wind; the Virtue of the small man is like the grass. Let the wind blow over the grass and it is sure to bend." (12.19)

Here Virtue is portrayed metaphorically as a force of nature, which reinforces its connection to the natural order of Heaven. We see a similar theme in 2.1, cited earlier, where the virtuous individual occupying the place of the ruler functions as the proxy of Heaven on earth, receiving the spontaneous and yet pre-ordered homage of the world, just as Heaven commands the orderly progression of the seasons and the timely arrival of rains, and just as the Pole Star rules over the fixed constellations in the nighttime sky. The multitude of stars do not crowd together at random, trying to get as close to the Pole Star as possible. Rather, they all remain situated in their proper, predefined places, which in turn are ultimately oriented toward and held together by the central attractive power of the Pole Star. The Virtue-infused ruler thus brings the order of Heaven—which can be observed in the processes of the natural world—back into the human world. This analogy between the sage ruler and Heaven is made even more explicitly in 8.19, where Yao, modeling himself on the wu-wei manner of Heaven, is described as having caused the people to follow the Way without their being able to describe or articulate how he does it:

> How magnificent was Yao's manner of ruling! How majestic! It is only Heaven that is great, and only Yao who modeled himself after Heaven. How vast and pervasive! Among the common people there were none who were able to put a name to it.[70] How majestic were his successes, how glorious his cultural splendor [*wenzhang* 文章]!

Once a ruler possessing Virtue takes his ritual place facing south, the people will be "caused" to follow the Way in the unself-conscious, noncoercive manner of wu-wei: they will simply be drawn spontaneously to take their proper place in the ordered Way, without knowing why or how. Thus, the best way to govern the world is to not govern it: rectify yourself, Confucius says, and the world will follow.[71] This is his answer to someone who questions why—with the world in such a sorry state—he spends all of his time and effort in the pursuit of such apparently trivial practices as ritual and music, when presumably he should be out "doing something" to save the world:

> Someone asked Confucius, "Why is it that you are not participating in government [*weizheng* 為政 (lit. doing government)]?"[72]
>
> The Master answered, "We read in the *History*:
>
> 'Filial, oh so filial as a son,
> A friend to one's brothers, both younger and elder;
> [In this way] exerting an influence upon the government.'
>
> Thus, in being a filial son and good brother one is already taking part in government. What need is there, then, to speak of 'participating in government'?" (2.21)

The best way to "do governing," then, is to "not do" it: to be wu-wei. In the ideal state of universal wu-wei, names correctly delineate moral space, the rites and other traditional practices are in proper order, and everyone knows how to act without the need for excessive deliberation or uncertainty.

The Paradox of Wu-Wei in the *Analects*

As we have seen from the preceding discussion of Confucian wu-wei on both a personal and universal scale, Confucius places a great deal of emphasis upon the importance of "naturalness" in the moral life. One who has to force morally acceptable behavior is not, in the Confucian view, a truly moral person: a truly moral person dwells in morality as comfortably as in his own home, and the genuinely *ren* person can thus follow the spontaneous promptings of the heart/mind without overstepping the bounds. The fact that there is something of a paradox involved in this vision—submitting to a lifetime of ritual training in order to reach a state where one can finally act "naturally"—has not escaped the notice of scholars of Chinese thought. Joel Kupperman, for instance, asks of Confucius's program of self-cultivation: "How can highly ritualized behavior, which requires much training, practice and self-control, be said to involve 'naturalness'?"[73] He approaches the problem by noting that "naturalness" or "natural" can have more than one sense, and exploits this ambiguity in proposing a solution to the paradox of wu-wei as he sees it in the *Analects*. "Naturalness" for Confucius, he argues, is not to be understood as following the "nature" one is born with; rather, the sort of "naturalness" advocated by Confucius is an *artificial* naturalness produced by a complete transformation of our original emotions, dispositions, and sensitivities:

> It may seem paradoxical to speak of naturalness in a sense in which "nature is art." The paradox disappears, however, once we stop thinking of education as merely placing a *veneer* over our original "nature." Once we realize that education can *transform* what a person is, we realize that it can in a sense transform people's natures. What comes naturally is very much a product of training and habit. (Kupperman 1968: 180; emphasis added)

I would argue that what Kupperman is sensing here in this contrast between two models of education is the tension between the adornment and craft metaphors for Confucian self-cultivation that we noted briefly above. Despite Kupperman's dismissal of the first model of education, Confucius *does* at times portray cultural refinement as a veneer laid on top of a well-shaped substrate, and it is in this tension between the EDUCATION AS VENEER and EDUCATION AS PHYSICAL REFOR-MATION that we can best see the paradox of wu-wei as it manifests itself in the *Analects*.

The Adornment and "Root" Metaphors

David Nivison has identified a tension in Confucian thought that he refers to as the "paradox of Virtue." As I noted in chapter 1, in pre-Confucian times Virtue was something given by Heaven as a reward to a sage ruler—that is, one who displayed perfect, wu-wei ritual behavior, which in turn required infusing ritual practice with genuine generosity, self-restraint, self-sacrifice, and humility. At the same time, the attractive power conferred by Virtue was perceived as something necessary for the ruler to have if he is to function effectively as a ruler. The paradox here, as Nivison sees it, is that Virtue is something that cannot be strategically *sought* after by an aspiring ruler, since if he is performing "good" acts merely with an eye toward obtaining Virtue, these acts are then not really good. Truly virtuous acts must be done for their own sake, not with an eye toward strategic gain. This means that true Virtue—like that of King Wen in ode 241—can only be embodied in a completely unself-conscious manner, which engenders a paradox: it seems that one must already be virtuous in order to acquire Virtue. If King Wen were not from the beginning already following the principles (*ze* 則) of the Lord on High, how would one get him to change his behavior? Were one to point out to him that it would be to his advantage to do so, this would hardly be conducive to achieving the sort of unself-conscious accordance—"without knowledge or wisdom [*bushibuzhi* 不識不知]"—that is required to win the favor of the Lord on High.

This paradox of Virtue is inherited by Confucius, in the sense that the virtue of *ren*, as well as the Virtue that comes with it, can be realized only by one who truly *loves* the Way for its own sake. If, however, one already truly *does* love virtue or the Way, then one already has them. As Confucius declares in 7.30, "Is *ren* really so far away? No sooner do I desire *ren* than it is here." Nivison likens this tension to the paradox of learning discussed in the *Meno*:[74]

> *Wanting* to be moral—being disposed or being sufficiently disposed to perform the role that you and everyone else knows you should perform—is the essential part of *being* moral. But if the teacher is to teach this disposition, to impart it, the student must already be disposed to accept the instruction, and so, apparently, must already have it. The problem is structured like Socrates's paradox of learning in the *Meno* (to be taught, one must recognize the thing taught as something to be learned, and this requires that in some sense one already know it); but in the Chinese moral education form it is far more convincingly and distressingly real. (Nivison 1996: 80)

We might thus expect to find in the *Analects* something structurally similar to the Platonic idea of "recollection," and indeed we find throughout the text suggestions that self-cultivation involves merely the beautification of tendencies already present within the self. We have already mentioned 3.8, where it is said that "the rites come after," and where ritual training is portrayed metaphorically as the application of cosmetics to enhance an otherwise pleasing face. We have also discussed the importance for Confucius of first having the right "stuff" (*zhi* 質) before the process of cultural "adornment" (*wen* 文) can be successfully carried out. This sentiment is also sometimes expressed in terms of an organic metaphor. A certain Lin Fang asks about the "roots [*ben* 本] of ritual" in 3.4, and—after commending him for his excellent question—Confucius replies in a manner that suggests that *zhi* 質 is the "root" of *wen* 文: "When it comes to ritual, it is better to be simple than extravagant. When it comes to mourning, it is better to be overwhelmed with grief than overly composed."[75] The organic metaphor appears also in 1.2, where filiality and respect for one's older brother (*xiaodi* 孝弟) are described as the "roots of *ren*," and where Yuzi notes that "the gentleman applies himself to the roots; once the roots are planted [*li* 立], the Way will grow [*sheng* 生]."

Supplementing these "adornment" and "root" metaphors, we can find several passages in the text that suggest the existence of some kind of innate tendency toward the good. For instance, we read in 16.9 that some are "born knowing it," and although Confucius does not count himself among them (7.20), it is apparent that Yan Hui, at least, has some sort of intuitive grasp of the Way. In 2.9, Confucius describes how Yan Hui listens somewhat passively all day to his teachings in a manner that suggests he is somewhat stupid. When Confucius then secretly observes Yan Hui's private behavior, though, he finds that it manifests perfectly the Confucian Way. "That Yan Hui is not at all stupid," Confucius concludes. The implication is that Yan Hui did not ask questions because he already had some grasp—at least at an intuitive level—of what was being taught to him. This interpretation is strengthened by 5.9:

> The Master said to Zigong, "How would you compare yourself with Yan Hui?"
>
> Zigong answered, "How dare I even think of comparing myself with Hui? When Hui learns one thing, it allows him to immediately grasp ten. When I learn one thing, I am able to grasp two."
>
> The Master said, "No, you are not the equal of Hui. Nor am I. Neither of us is the equal of Hui."

Although in these passages Yan Hui is portrayed as requiring some instruction, he seems to have been something of a moral genius naturally inclined toward the Way. If nothing else, he possessed a kind of passion for learning that apparently cannot be taught, and which is unfortunately rare among Confucius's contemporaries. In 6.3, Confucius is asked by a ruler which of his disciples loves learning, and he replies somewhat wistfully:

> There was one named Yan Hui who loved learning. He never misdirected his anger, and never repeated a mistake twice. Unfortunately he was fated to live a short life. Since he passed away, I have heard of no one who really loves learning.

That a moral elite among humans possess some sort of natural inclination toward the Way is suggested in the observation in 17.3 that "the most intelligent . . . do not change [*yi* 移; lit. move]," and in 19.22 we even find the suggestion that such innate orientation toward the good is a universal quality: "The Way of Wen and Wu has not fallen to the ground, but is in people [*zairen* 在人]. . . . There is no one who does not have the Way of Wen and Wu in them." Although this late passage may reflect the beginnings of a Mencian-like internalist sect of Confucianism, we can see that it is not without precedents in the earlier strata of the text.

Of course, these internalist-leaning passages raise problems. If all that is necessary to possess *ren* is to love it, then why did Yan Hui, who is clearly even more naturally gifted than Confucius, have to push himself so strenuously and experience the sort of frustration we see him express in 9.11? Also, how are we to deal with the vast majority of people who, like Confucius, are not born "knowing it," but have to push themselves to learn it? In addition to the internal problems raised by these metaphors, there is also the problem of explaining how to reconcile them with the transformation-craft-effort metaphors that dominate the text. If Yan Hui possesses such wonderful "stuff," for instance, it is hard to see why he is told by Confucius in 12.1 that *ren* consists of "overcoming/defeating [*ke* 克] the self and returning to the rites," or why he needs to be so strictly warned:

> Do not look unless it is in accordance with the rites; do not listen unless it is in accordance with the rites; do not speak unless it is in accordance with the rites; do not move unless it is in accordance with the rites.

Let us turn now to this alternate set of metaphors, which serve to correct some of the problematic entailments of the adornment-organic metaphors, but that in turn raise problems of their own.

The Craft and Effort Metaphors

The occasional celebrations of innate endowment that we saw earlier are overshadowed in the *Analects* by passages that stress the difficulty of self-cultivation. There are, for instance, several passages that explicitly deny that virtue is the result of innate ability. In 14.33, we read that "a racehorse is praised for its Virtue, not for its strength [*li* 力]." The message here is that success as a racehorse is due to Virtue acquired through training, not through any inborn advantage of strength. A similar point is made in 3.16, where Confucius notes that, as set down in antiquity, "the point in archery is not to pierce the hide [of the target], because strength (*li* 力) varies from person to person." That is, the ancients designed the practice of archery to recognize and celebrate acquired skill (proper aim), not some merely inborn quality such as physical strength.[76] The fact that it is effort and perseverance—not inborn talent—that counts in self-cultivation is also indicated in Confucius's comment that he "has never seen a person whose strength was insufficient" (4.6). The problem is merely that people do not *try* hard enough.

We also saw in our discussion of the Confucian soteriological path the schemas of SELF-CULTIVATION AS CRAFT and SELF-CULTIVATION AS LONG JOURNEY, both of which entail the need for great effort and long-term commitment. Self-cultivation is compared to painstakingly building a mountain or leveling ground (9.19), or cutting, polishing and carving a hard, rough piece of jade (1.15), the implication being that one's innate emotions are *not* virtuous until they are restrained (*yue* 約) and regulated (*jie* 節) by traditional forms. Indeed, as his spiritual autobiography in 2.4 indicates, even Confucius himself apparently did not attain the state of truly loving *ren*—in the sense of being able to fully embody it in a wu-wei fashion—until after fifty-five years of intensive self-cultivation. Hence Confucius's description of himself in 7.34: "How could I dare to lay claim to either sageliness or *ren*? What can be said about me is no more than this: I work at it [*weizhi* 為之] without growing tired and encourage others without growing weary."

The response of one of Confucius's disciples, Gong Xihua, to this comment of the Master's indicates, however, one of the internal tensions in the craft-effort model. Commenting on Confucius's tireless devotion to the Way, he notes, "This is precisely what we disciples are unable to learn." This is a very revealing observation. In order to keep oneself moving forward along on the "long journey" of self-cultivation it is necessary that one genuinely desire to reach the destination. How, though, does one *teach* such desire to a person who does not already possess it? This is no doubt the source of much of Confucius's frustration with his current age, expressed most succinctly in 15.13: "I should just give up. I have yet to meet a person who loves ren as much as he loves the pleasures of the flesh." A similar sense of exasperation shows through in 9.24:

> The Master said, "When a man is rebuked with exemplary words after having made a mistake, he cannot help but agree with them. However, what is important is that he change [*gai* 改] himself in order to *accord* with them. When a man is praised with words of respect, he cannot help but be pleased with them. However, what is important is that he actually *live up* to them. A person who finds respectful words pleasing but does not live up to them, or agrees with others' reproaches and yet does not change—there is nothing I can do with one such as this."

Nominal assent to the Confucian Way is thus insufficient—if wu-wei perfection is to be attained, the student must *love* the Way, not merely understand it. How, though, do you teach someone love? As Confucius remarks somewhat impatiently in 15.16, "There is simply nothing I can do with a person who is not himself constantly asking, 'What should I do? What should I do?'" The problem, of course, is that it is hard to see how the teacher could instill this sort of passion or love in a student to whom it simply does *not* occur to ask, "What should I do?" In short, if unself-conscious, wu-wei perfection is the soteriological goal, the student cannot learn from the teacher unless he or she is passionately committed to learning, and this would seem to entail already possessing a genuine love for the Confucian Way. Here we have Confucius's version of the Meno problem—the paradox of wu-wei.

As we saw in 5.10, someone like Zai Yu, who presumably "gives assent" to the Confucian project but nonetheless lies sleeping in bed all day, is dismissed by Confucius as a piece of "rotten wood" that cannot be "carved." Here—although it is the SELF-CULTIVATION AS CRAFT metaphor that is being invoked—we find ourselves falling back again into emphasizing the need for quality "stuff." As I have argued above, it is in response to precisely this problem that we find the adornment-root metaphors mixed into the text. Similarly, the craft metaphors are invoked as a counterbalance to the adornment metaphors, entailing as they do the openness of the Confucian Way to everyone and the need for education, traditional forms, and effort. Therefore, both the adornment and craft metaphors serve crucial functions in compensating for the shortcomings of the other, but the two sets of metaphors are themselves not compatible.

One way of responding to this tension would be to try to unambiguously come down in favor of one set of metaphors or the other—that is, stating unequivocally whether it is inborn stuff or acquired adornment that is the determining factor in moral self-cultivation. We will see that both Mencius and Xunzi attempt to do precisely this. Of course, neither of these thinkers necessarily saw themselves as attempting to solve Confucius's "paradox of wu-wei"; they saw their mission merely as defending the Confucian vision against the attacks of increasingly articulate rival schools of thought.[77] Nonetheless, this task of making Confucianism plausible in the increasingly sophisticated world of Chinese thought inevitably involved addressing at least implicitly the paradox of wu-wei, because—as we shall see below—this theoretical Achilles's heel was a favorite point of attack for both Laozi and Zhuangzi. Both of these Daoist thinkers felt that the profound tension involved in training someone in traditional, artificial forms in order to allow them to act "naturally" was a fatal flaw in Confucian thought and could only lead to spiritual hypocrisy.

Chapter 3

自然
So-of-Itself: Wu-wei in the *Laozi*

The *Laozi* 老子 (also known as the *Daodejing* 道德經 or *Classic of the Way and Virtue*)[1] presents a religious vision that parallels in many ways that of Confucius. Laozi[2] is moved to write because he sees the world around him mired in corruption, far from the true Way, and proposes a soteriological method by which the individual and then the rest of humanity can be brought back into harmony with the universe. He also identifies particular barriers to achieving this state of harmony and specific methods for overcoming these barriers. Given these similarities, what is most striking is his singling out of Confucianism itself—or the sort of knowledge acquisition and acculturation advocated by Confucians—as *the* main factor contributing to the fallen state of human beings. Although no historical figures or schools are mentioned by name in the text, Laozi was clearly familiar with terminology and institutions that we would now identify as Confucian. Moreover, the metaphorical targeting of the type of soteriological path we have seen in the *Analects* is striking. Whereas the *Analects* urges us to cultivate (*xiu* 修; lit. adorn) the self by submitting to the culture (*wen* 文; lit. patterns, designs) of the Zhou, Laozi demands that we exhibit the "unadorned" (*su* 素).[3] Against the metaphor in *Analects* 1.15 of carving the self like a piece of jade ("as if cut, as if polished / as if carved, as if ground"), Laozi famously advocates becoming like "uncarved wood" (*pu* 樸). And while the Confucian soteriological process is portrayed as a sort of grueling, life-long journey, Laozi warns us to put a halt to this misguided trip—to turn back (*fan* 返) and return home (*gui* 歸) to our primordial Mother, to our origins or roots (*ben* 本).

Laozi is the pre-Qin thinker who is most often associated with the ideal of wu-wei, and as a term of art wu-wei certainly plays a greater role in the *Laozi* than in any other of the texts we will be considering. In this text, wu-wei becomes something of a polemical barb aimed at the Confucians: "not-doing" is held up as an ideal in order to pointedly contrast with the incessant and harmful "doing" or "regarding"[4] of those acting with the false assurance conveyed by conventional knowledge. It is thus in the *Laozi* that the ideal of wu-wei comes closest to being adequately rendered literally as "non-doing" rather than metaphorically as "effortless action." Even for Laozi, however, this wu-wei is still not to be understood as a state of genuine passivity, but rather represents an ideal state of harmony with the cosmos that brings with it personal efficacy and ultimately universal salvation. In addition, as we shall see, even in the *Laozi* wu-wei is ultimately understood figuratively and has its own metaphorical structure. As we might expect, the usual metaphors for lack of exertion and unself-consciousness abound, such as "going along with the flow" (*shun* 順) or "following" (*cong* 從). In addition, we see in the *Laozi* the debut of a new metaphorical system that comes to be associated with wu-wei throughout the "Daoistic" corpus: that of being empty or "tenuous" (*xu* 虛). For Laozi, such a state is accomplished by being without (*wu* 無) all of the usual possessions of the conventional world: fame, desire, knowledge, activity. After the Subject has successfully emptied the Self in this manner, the Essential Self is free to emerge and guide the Subject into a way of being that is "so-of-itself" (*ziran* 自然) or entirely natural. Such natural action shares the usual primary hallmarks of wu-wei action (lack of exertion and unself-consciousness), and thus Laozian wu-wei—despite its metaphorical innovations—maintains its essential continuity with the ideal of "effortless action" formulated by the other pre-Qin thinkers that we will be considering.

Fallenness

Laozi's work is replete with criticism for his contemporaries. His vision of the fallenness of his age is perhaps expressed most vividly in chapter 53:

> If I truly had knowledge, I would, when traveling along the great Way, know to fear nothing except being led astray.
>
> Although the great Way is smooth and flat, the common people still love the bumpy, crooked paths [*jing* 徑].
>
> The court is corrupt,
>
> The fields are overgrown,
>
> The granaries are exhausted.
>
> Yet some wear clothes with fancy designs and colors,
>
> Hang sharp swords from their belts,
>
> Stuff their bellies with food and drink,
>
> And possess more wealth than they need.
>
> This is what is called "bragging about being a robber."
>
> Far is this from the Way!

Here, as in the *Analects*, we find the motif of a corrupt ruling class leading the common people astray. Whereas for Confucius the great sin of the "Three Families" of Lu was their usurpation of ritual practices beyond their station, in the *Laozi* it is their unrestrained greed that comes under attack. The author of the "Explicating the *Laozi*" (*jielao* 解老) chapter of the *Hanfeizi*[5] explains what it means for those in power to "take the lead in robbery":

Whenever one embellishes one's knowledge [*zhi* 智] and thereby brings harm to the state, one's own clan will necessarily be enriched. This is what the text means by being "possessed of too much wealth." When there are people like this in the state, then the ignorant masses cannot but artfully imitate their behavior, and it is imitation of this behavior which gives rise to petty thievery. Looking at it this way, when great criminals arise petty thieves will follow; when the great criminals sing, the petty thieves will chime in. (Gao Ming: 84–85)

It is commonly noted that Laozi considers excessive desires (*yu* 欲) to be one of the primary causes of fallenness and disorder. Chapter 46—where it is implied that desire is responsible for the fact that the world is without the Way—is often cited in this regard:

> When the Way prevails in the world, fleet-footed horses are used to haul manure;
>
> When the Way does not prevail in the world, war-horses are raised outside the city walls.
>
> There is no crime greater than giving assent to desire;[6]
>
> There is no disaster greater than not knowing contentment;
>
> There is no calamity more serious than desiring gain [*yude* 欲得].
> Hence, in knowing the contentment of contentment, one will be enduringly content [*hengzu* 恆足].

What is less commonly noted, however, is that in Laozi's view desire is merely a symptom of a deeper malaise: knowledge, or the "regarding" (*wei* 為) that springs from knowledge. "Regarding" in the sense that is criticized by Laozi refers to making normative, not merely definitional, distinctions—to hold something in (high) regard. Such regarding causes a person to value one thing over another, and therefore provides ulterior motives for action.[7] The role of regarding in engendering social chaos is placed beside that of greed/excessive desires in the beginning of chapter 75:

> The people are hungry because too much food is taken in taxes.
>
> This is why people are hungry.
>
> The hundred clans cannot be governed because those in authority have that which they hold in regard [*youyiwei* 有以為].
>
> This is why the hundred clans cannot be governed.

The greed of the social elite is here blamed for the common people's hunger, and the regarding of those in authority is cited as the cause of their unruliness. That these two ills—excessive desire and regarding—are essentially linked is made quite clear in the description of the Way found in chapter 34:

> The Way is vast, reaching to the left as well as right.

It is successful and accomplishes its tasks and yet has no name.

The myriad things return to it and yet it does not regard itself [*wei* 為] as their master.

For this reason, it is enduringly free of desire,

and thus can be named "the small."

Yet because it does not regard itself as master even though the myriad creatures return to it,

It can also be named "the great."

Thus, the reason the sage is able to be great is that he does not regard himself [*wei* 為] to be great.

This is why he is able to be great.

Here the fact that the Way does not regard itself to be the master of the myriad things is cited as a causal factor in its ability to be without desire, as well as the secret to its greatness. Modeling himself on the Way, the sage can become great only because he does not deem himself great. The same sentiment is expressed at the beginning of chapter 2, where it is said that "When the whole world knows to regard the beautiful as beautiful, this is ugly; when the whole world knows to regard the good as good, this is bad." Jiang Xichang links this passage to the observation in chapter 34 that the Way is nameless (*wuming* 無名), describing the origination of names in terms of a falling away from an original state that was instigated by human regarding:

> In the past age of namelessness, there were originally no names at all. For this reason there was nothing called "beautiful" or "good," and so also nothing called "ugly" or "bad." Once human beings appeared, though, there arose names, and with names came opposition. Since there were now names for "beautiful" and "good," there were also names for "ugly" and "bad." As human civilization progressed, these interrelated connections became more and more complex, and opposing names became more and more numerous. Since this time the world has been thrown into confusion and turmoil, and human beings have not known a moment of silence or peace. (Gao Ming: 229)[8]

It is thus with the arising of names (the reification of individual acts of "regarding" into categories and labels) and the creation of knowledge (which is formulated in terms of names) that the fall from original namelessness and purity began, and this is also when desire and contention began to rear their ugly heads. As D. C. Lau has noted, the problem of desire can in this way be traced back to the more basic problem of knowledge or self-consciousness: "Desire is in a sense secondary to the knowledge upon which it is dependent. It is through knowledge of what is desirable that desire is excited. It is also through knowledge that new objects of desire are devised" (Lau 1963: 35). When one comes to know that something is beautiful or good, a desire for that something is created. Human

beings seem to have a unique ability to multiply these artificial desires indefi-
nitely, creating an ever-expanding web of wants that must then be filled. Such
self-consciousness not only produces a host of novel desires but also simultaneously alienates people from their true nature. Chapter 38 (which is actually the
opening chapter of the Mawangdui texts) describes the fall from the "highest Virtue" (original "power" in its pristine form) down through the various levels of
decline that represent gradually increasing degrees of self-awareness and conscious activity—a process that culminates in the ultimate hypocrisy of Confucianism:

> The highest Virtue is not virtuous, and so it possesses Virtue.
> The lowest Virtue never lets go of Virtue, and so is without Virtue.
> The person of highest Virtue is without action (wu-wei) and holds noth-
>   ing in regard [*wuwei er wuyiwei* 無為而無以為];
> The person of highest benevolence [*ren* 仁][9] acts, but also holds nothing
>   in regard [*weizhi er wuyiwei* 為之而無以為];
> The person of highest righteousness [*yi* 義] acts and also holds certain
>   things in regard [*weizhi er youyiwei* 為之而有以為];
> The person of highest ritual propriety [*li* 禮] acts and, when the people
>   do not respond, rolls up his sleeves and forces them to respond.
> Hence when the Way was lost there arose Virtue;
> When Virtue was lost there arose benevolence;
> When benevolence was lost there arose righteousness;
> When righteousness was lost there arose the [Confucian] rites.
> The rites are the wearing thin of dutifulness and trustworthiness
> And the beginning of disorder.

We are presented here with a very detailed picture of progressive decline. In
the primordial state of harmony with the Way, people possessed and exercised the
power given to them by Heaven without "having regard" for this power—that is,
without consciously valuing it. In this manner, they lived out their lives in harmony with others and themselves. They were wu-wei without even having a
name for it; it was simply how they lived. This was the period of true wu-wei and
the "highest" Virtue. Once this harmony was disturbed, the subsequent loss of
Virtue caused people begin to become conscious of Virtue for the first time, and
once Virtue became an object of conscious attention it was no longer the highest
Virtue. "When the Way was lost there arose Virtue" thus refers to the appearance
of the "lowest Virtue"—the Virtue "which never lets go of Virtue and so is without Virtue." A still further state of decline is represented by the appearance of the
Confucian virtues. Benevolence is the most innocuous of the bunch: one who
possesses this virtue "acts"—that is, is conscious of behaving in a "benevolent"
fashion—but does not therefore make the mistake of having any special regard
for themselves or their actions. Presumably Laozi is referring here to the truly
virtuous. They participate in public life and perform virtuous acts, but do so out
of spontaneous inclination rather than any forced sense of duty, and do not dwell
upon the goodness of their own acts. This contrasts quite sharply with those who
possess "righteousness" (*yi* 義). These sanctimonious individuals consciously

guide their behavior according to the dictates of what is "right," and this heightened self-consciousness causes them to put a definite value upon themselves and
their actions: they "know to regard the good as good," and this sort of self-esteem
is—as Laozi has noted in chapter 2—in fact "bad." Further depraved still are
those who know nothing but rigid adherence to the rites: to the sanctimonious-
ness of the righteous they add a petty urge to see their sense of what is right
imposed upon everyone around them. This imposition of artificial social forms
upon human affairs forces people to become hypocritical—encouraging them to
substitute empty forms of respect for genuine reverence and flowery protestations
of love for true affection. For Laozi, this triumph of image over substance is like
the rosy glow of a tuberculosis patient—the misleading outward symptom of a
deeply entrenched sickness:

> Thus when the Great Way falls into disuse
> We then[10] have "benevolence" and "righteousness" [*renyi*仁義];
> When "knowledge" and "wisdom" emerge
> The great hypocrisy [*dawei* 大偽] then begins;
> When family relations are not harmonious
> We then have talk of "filiality" and "parental affection";
> When the state is in darkness and chaos
> There then appear "upright ministers." (chapter 18)

The problem with Confucianism is that it encourages *wei* 為 in both senses:
engaging in action and in evaluative "regarding." Some scholars[11] have argued
that Laozi does not intend to criticize the Confucian rites themselves, but merely
concern with the external *form* of the rites rather than the virtuous dispositions
that should inform them. As we have seen in chapter 2, however, this is actually
the Confucian position itself: Confucius reserves his greatest scorn for the "village worthies" who carefully observe the forms of morality but possess none of
its inner spirit. Laozi's criticism clearly goes deeper than this, lashing out even at
the crown jewel of Confucian self-cultivation—the virtue of *ren* itself. "Heaven
and Earth are not benevolent [*ren*]; they treat the myriad creatures as straw dogs,"
we read in chapter 5. Similarly, "the sage is not benevolent; he treats the people
as straw dogs." Straw dogs were used by the ancient Chinese as offerings in rituals, during which time they were treated with the greatest respect and handled
with elaborate ceremony; once the ritual was over, however, they were simply
tossed aside and trampled underfoot. As the author of the "Summary of Customs
and Proverbs" (*qisushun* 齊俗訓) chapter of the *Huainanzi* remarks after describing this practice, "So who then really values them?" His point is that the straw
dogs are accorded artificial reverence during the ceremony because they serve a
symbolic purpose, but after the ceremony everyone goes back to treating them as
they ordinarily would: as just worthless pieces of straw. Laozi's position is that
Heaven and Earth are not benevolent—that is, they do not act out of self-conscious kindness—and that they treat the myriad creatures the way that straw dogs
are treated after the ceremony: as simply what they are. Gao Ming explains:

"Heaven and Earth are not benevolent" means that Heaven and Earth do not impose themselves upon the myriad creatures, but let them grow in their own way. "The sage is not benevolent" means that the sage does not impose himself upon the hundred clans, but rather lets them all flourish in their own way. . . . Laozi's metaphor of the "straw dogs" thus refers to treating things naturally. (Gao Ming: 144)

The problem with Confucianism is that it encourages people to treat straw dogs as if they were something other than what they are, thereby fostering artificiality and leading people away from simplicity and honesty. Hence, we read in chapter 65, "The people are difficult to govern because of their knowledge [*zhi* 智]." As Jia Dongcheng explains, "The people 'knowing too much'[12] refers to knowledge brought about by the Confucian advocacy of morality [*renyi* 仁義], the rites and music," which causes people to lose their "loyal, kind, simple, and genuine Heavenly nature" and become hypocritical and contentious (Jia Dongcheng 1989: 89).

The only way to truly uproot this hypocrisy and do away with contention is to eliminate the insidious external influences that caused them to arise in the first place. Were a true ruler to come and sweep away the trappings of Confucian artifice, the people would be able to return to their true natures.

> Cut off sageliness, discard wisdom,
> And the people will benefit a hundredfold;
> Cut off benevolence, discard righteousness,
> And the people will return to filiality and parental affection;
> Cut off cleverness, discard profit,
> And there will be no thieves or bandits.
> These three teachings[13] are mere cultural adornment [*wen* 文], and are insufficient;
> The people must therefore be made to have somewhere they belong.
> Exhibit the unadorned [*su* 素] and embrace[14] the uncarved wood [*pu* 樸],
> Reduce selfishness and make few the desires.
> Cut off learning and there will be no worries. (chapter 19)

A truly sage ruler—one who has heard the Way—can reverse the damage done by learning and Confucian hypocrisy. By gradually discarding the adornments of culture (*wen*) it is possible for such a person to reach a state of both non-doing (wu-wei) and non-regarding (*wuyiwei* 無以為), and to thereby regain the power of the "highest Virtue" that flows from such a state of being. Backed by the suasive influence of such powerful Virtue, this ruler could then lead the world as a whole back to simplicity in a "non-meddling" (*wushi* 無事) fashion:

> One who engages in study adds to himself day by day;
> One who has heard the Way takes away from himself day by day.
> He takes away and takes away more, in order to reduce himself to a state of no-doing (wu-wei),
> And when he is free of doing, he is also free of regarding (*wuyiwei*).

> One who is able to win the world is enduringly free of meddling [*wushi* 無事];
>
> Once one begins to meddle, one will not be equal to the task of winning the world. (chapter 48)

The "non-meddling" of one possessing the highest Virtue is no doubt meant to contrast with the most deluded of the figures mentioned in chapter 38: the person of highest ritual propriety, who rolls up his sleeves and forces the people to bend to his will.

It is clear, then, that were the ruler[15] able to purge himself of the corruption of the present age—Confucian hypocrisy, rampant desires, the stultifying effects of knowledge—and thereby regain his original Virtue, the world would then right itself. How, though, is this individual to realize such a perfected spiritual state? Laozi has a very definite answer to this question: by grasping the principle by which the Way functions (the law of reversal), the ruler can master it and so bring about both personal and universal salvation.

The Way, Nothingness (*wu* 無), and the Principle of Reversion

As was the case with Confucius, the qualities of Laozi's perfectly realized individual—the person of the highest Virtue—are modeled upon the Way itself. As we read in chapter 21:

> The behavior of one with great Virtue
> Follows [*cong* 從] the Way and only the Way.
> As a thing, the Way[16]
> Is vague, is obscure.
> Obscure and vague!
> Yet within it there is an image [*xiang* 象]!
> Vague and obscure!
> Yet within it there is a thing [*wu* 物]!
> Mysterious and dark!
> Yet within it is an essence [*qing* 情]!
> This essence is quite real [*zhen* 真],
> And within it is something which can be relied upon.

In chapter 42, the Way is described as giving birth to the myriad things, and similarly revealing by its mode of operation "something which can be relied upon"—that is, a precept for action:

> The Way gives birth to one;
> One gives birth to two;
> Two gives birth to three;
> And three gives birth to the myriad things.[17]

> The myriad things carry on their backs the *yin* 陰 and embrace in their
> arms the *yang* 陽, thereby harmonizing these two conflicting types of
> *qi.*
> There is nothing that people detest more than being "orphaned," "wid-
> owed," and "destitute,"
> Yet kings and lords use these terms to name themselves.[18]
> A thing is sometimes added to by being diminished
> Diminished by being added to.
> That which the ancients taught, I also teach to others:
> "The strong and violent will not die a natural death.'"
> I shall take this as my precept [*xue fu* 學父; lit. study-father].

Here the lesson to be learned from observing the Way is spelled out more explicitly: a thing can be added to by being diminished and diminished by being added
to. This is so because of the nature of the phenomenal world, which has its origin
in "Nothing" (*wu*). The puzzle of what it might mean to "add" to something by
diminishing it will be discussed in more detail later, but first it is necessary for us
to understand the relationship between "Nothing" and "Something" (*you* 有).

The progression from the Way to the One and then expanding outward in the
generation of the myriad things can be said to describe the production of "Something" out of "Nothing." The identification of the Way with Nothing is made clear
in chapter 40, where Nothing takes the place of the Way in being identified as the
source of the phenomenal world: "the myriad things in the world are born from
Something, and Something is born from Nothing." Many scholars have as well
noted the relationship between the Way and the "nameless" (*wuming* 無名),[19]
which is described (in chapter 1) as possessing cosmogonic powers:

> The Way that can be spoken of is not the enduring Way;
> The name which can be named is not the enduring name.
> The nameless is the beginning [*shi* 始] of the myriad things;
> The named is the mother [*mu* 母] of the myriad things.
> Hence, enduringly without desires [*wuyu* 無欲], I am able to gaze upon
>   its secrets,
> While also enduringly possessed of desires [*youyu* 有欲], I am able to
>   gaze upon its manifestations.[20]
> The two emerge together;
> Are given different names, but refer to the same thing:
> Mystery [*xuan* 玄] upon mystery—
> The door to a multitude of secrets.

The "nameless" and the state of being "without desires" correspond to Nothing,
while the "named" and being "possessed of desires" refer to Something. This correspondence allows us to more clearly understand the relationship between Nothing and Something. Although it has been argued by some scholars that Nothing
and Something (often rendered "Non-Being" and "Being") refer to two separate
ontological realms,[21] it is clear from the passages cited earlier that the two are
part of a single process of metaphoric procreation. "These two [Nothing and

Something, or the "Beginning" and the "Mother"] are given different names but refer to the same thing." As Wang Bi explains in his commentary,

> "These two" refer to the "beginning" and the "mother." "Emerging together" refers to the fact that they both emerge from out of mystery [*xuan* 玄]. Its head is referred to as the "beginning" and its tail is referred to as the "mother." The mystery is the dark and silent Nothingness from which the beginning and the mother emerge. (Gao Ming: 228)

Although Something and Nothing emerge together, it is Something that—to invoke Wang Bi's metaphor—forms the "tail" of Nothing, and in this sense the character of the positive terms in the world ("Something," "the named") is determined by the negative terms ("Nothing," "the nameless"). Feng Yulan has something like this in mind in saying of the Way, "Non-Being [i.e., Nothing] refers to its essence; being [i.e., Something] to its function."[22] The metaphors of beginning, birth, and "the mother" allow the reader to draw upon his or her conventional knowledge of procreation in order to understand the relationship of Something to Nothing. In literal procreation, the character of the parents determines the character of the offspring, and so a potential metaphorical entailment here is that by realizing the secret of Nothing one will possess the key to understanding and thereby mastering the phenomenal world. This entailment is explicitly spelled out in chapter 52: "Obtaining the Mother / You will understand the son / By understanding the son / You will return to holding fast to the Mother."

One might still wonder, though, how "Nothing" can give birth to "Something," or how something can be added to through being diminished. It is important here to realize that Laozi is speaking on two levels: the true and the conventional. In conventional terms, the Way is Nothing. It has no name, it has no form, it is tasteless and soundless. Yet in fact it is precisely this Nothing that gives rise to the riot of forms and colors and tastes that make up the world of Something, and all of these "somethings" in the end wear out and die and so return to the nothingness from which they originally emerged. The Nothing represented by the Way is "enduring" (*heng* 恆), whereas all of the sound and fury of the phenomenal realm is transient. In this sense, then, what is conventionally viewed as Nothing is in fact more real and enduring than all of the ephemeral "somethings" that people value and pursue. We can thus understand the phrase, "a thing is sometimes added to by being diminished and diminished by being added to," by using scare quotes to differentiate the conventional from the true: "a thing is sometimes added to by being 'diminished' and diminished by being 'added to.'" A true lord regards himself as "orphaned" or "widowed," yet of course he is in fact the most sought after and happy person in the world. In this way, what would conventionally be perceived as a diminishment in reality reflects an enhancement.

The arising of Something from Nothing, along with the eventual return of Something to Nothing, is seen by Laozi as something like a law of nature, and is given the technical name of "reversion," or "going back" (*fan* 反):

> Reversion is the movement of the Way;
> Weakness is the method of the Way.

The myriad things are born from Something,
And Something is born from Nothing. (chapter 40)

Here the Nothing is understood metaphorically as a place to which all the things that make up the phenomenal world eventually return, presumably through some sort of natural force such as gravity. Our experience of the physical world makes us familiar with the manner in which things in a high position are inexorably dragged down, and this serves as the basic schema that Laozi draws upon for his metaphors of the valley and water that will be discussed in more detail later. In any case, this "reversion" of the high to the low allows us to understand Laozi's treatment of value terms. Throughout the text we are presented with dyads of metaphorically "lower" and "higher" terms: soft/hard; weak/strong; empty/full. As Benjamin Schwartz notes, the "lower" (by conventional standards) term inevitably enjoys a higher true status in Laozi's scheme than the ostensibly "higher" term; water, as he puts it, is "in a profounder sense stronger than stone" (Schwartz 1986: 203). Such is the Way the world works: that which is conventionally "high"(e.g., strong) inevitably reverts to the low (weakness), and thus true strength thus lies in holding to "weakness."

One is able to endure by holding fast to the "roots" (to "Nothing" and the negative qualities associated with it) and not getting dragged "up" into the realm of doing and regarding. This law of reversion is also understood in terms of a balance metaphor in chapter 9, where we are told of the "tilting vessel"—said to have been in the temple of Zhou (or Lu)—which stands upright when empty but overturns when full:[23]

Grasping it and filling it to the rim[24]
Is not as good as stopping in time;
Sharpen the blade
And the edge cannot be preserved for long;
When gold and jade fill the room,
There is no way to guard it.
When wealth and honor lead to arrogance
Calamity naturally follows.
To accomplish one's task and then retire
Is the Way of Heaven.

The "Way of Heaven" is to "stop in time"—that is, to hold back from reaching the extreme. That which reaches the extreme will inevitably tip over and be ruined, and to avoid suffering such a reversion one should hold fast to the "beginning"—that is, the conventionally "lower" term of any dyad. The Way itself is thus described in terms of "lower" qualities that actually encompass their opposites ("empty yet full"), and the best advice is to emulate the Way and hold fast to the conventionally lower element of the dyad. Once one is able to accomplish this, both sides of the dyad will be obtained.

Laozi can provide no explanation for why the universe works as it does, but he cautions his readers that they ignore his words only at their own peril. The principle of reversion extends everywhere, and nothing in the universe is beyond its reach:

> To be courageous in being bold will lead to death;
> To be courageous in being timid will allow one to live.
> Of these two, one leads to benefit, the other to harm.
> Who knows the reason why Heaven hates what it hates?
> The Way of Heaven
> Excels in overcoming though it does not contend;
> In responding though it does not speak;
> In spontaneously attracting though it does not summon;
> In planning for the future though it is always relaxed.
> The Net of Heaven covers all.
> Although its mesh is wide, nothing ever slips through. (chapter 73)

This principle of reversion may seem fairly straightforward, but it is unfortunately not easily grasped or put into practice by the average person. This is the subject of Laozi's lament in chapter 78,

> The soft overcomes the hard,
> and the weak overcomes the strong.
> There is no one in the world who does not know this,
> And yet none are able to put it into practice. . . .
> Straightforward teachings seem paradoxical [*zhengyanruofan* 正言若反].

People immersed in society are resistant to accepting the simple truth that Laozi teaches. The Way of Heaven is therefore misunderstood or mocked even by the scholars (*shi* 士), let alone the common run of people:

> When the superior scholar hears of the Way,
> He is able to diligently put it into practice;[25]
> When the average scholar hears of the Way,
> He dwells upon it from time to time, but often forgets;
> When the inferior scholar hears of the Way,
> It causes him to break out in laughter.
> If he did not laugh at it,
> It would not be worthy of being the Way. (chapter 41)

The inability of people to comprehend the Way has not always presented a religious problem. During the Golden Age of antiquity everyone, even the common people, embodied the Way in their daily lives. In this pristine state of nature the common people did not possess any conscious understanding of the principle of reversion, nor will they need it once they are led back again to their natural state. Cognitive understanding of the Way is thus not a necessary precondition for behaviorally embodying the Way—when, that is, one lives under the salutary influence of a sage ruler. Cognitive understanding of the truth Laozi teaches *is* necessary, however, for the spiritual vanguard of our darkened age who are to bring the world back into a state of harmony with the Way, and the ability to grasp the Way in this manner seems to be limited to an elite. The truth that Laozi teaches is therefore an esoteric truth, available to the select few capable of grasping it. Hence, we have the birth of an image that becomes a common motif in later Chinese religious thought and literature: the sage clad in rags who nonetheless harbors on his person a priceless piece of jade:

> My teaching is very easy to understand and very easy to put into practice,
> And yet among people there are none who are able to understand it,
> None who are able to put it into practice.
> My teachings have an ancestor and my activities have a master;
> It is only because of ignorance that I am not understood.
> Because those who understand me are few,
> Those who model themselves upon me are honored.
> Therefore the sage dresses in sack-cloth while harboring in his breast a
>   piece of jade. (chapter 70)

Laozian Wu-Wei: The Behavioral and Cognitive Aspects

As I have noted earlier, although wu-wei comes closer to being portrayed in literal, negative terms (as "no-doing" or "no-action") in the *Laozi* than in any other text, it nonetheless retains its metaphoric sense of nonforced or effortless action—a positive, achieved state of harmony with the Way and with Heaven. Donald Munro likens the Daoist project of self-cultivation to the model-emulation practiced by Confucians, with the difference that "in this case the model is not necessarily a teacher, ancestor, or sage ruler. Instead, a person takes Dao (or [Virtue], which is the Dao in the individual) as the model, and reproduces its qualities in his conduct."[26] The task of the aspiring sage, then, is to come to embody the qualities of the Way or of Heaven in her own person, and it is a convenient and quite common practice to refer to these qualities in a general fashion by the term wu-wei. If we are to be more precise, however, we should see "no-doing" (wu-wei in the more literal sense) as a particular quality of the Way along with "no-regarding" (*wuyiwei* 無以為).[27] These two qualities in turn might best be seen as simply two aspects—the first behavioral, the second cognitive[28]—of a single spiritual state, which we might refer to as wu-wei in the broader, metaphoric sense. If the sage-ruler can achieve this perfected state by both behaviorally and cognitively emulating the Way, then success will follow as surely as water flows to the sea.

The value of wu-wei in the narrower, behavioral sense is extolled in chapter 63:

> Do that which consists of no doing [*weiwuwei* 為無為];
> Act in a way that is not acting [*shiwushi* 事無事];

Taste that which has no taste [*weiwuwei* 味無味].
Make large the small and many the few;
Repay injury with kindness [*de*].

The appearance here of the phrase, "repay injury with kindness" [*baoyuanyide* 報
怨以德],[29] is quite interesting, as this saying (which probably did not originate
with the author of the *Laozi*) is explicitly singled out for criticism in *Analects*
14.34:

Someone asked, "What do you think of the saying, 'Repay injury with
kindness [*de*]'?"

The Master replied, "With what, then, would one repay kindness? Repay
injury with uprightness, and kindness with kindness."

Confucius's project is, as we have seen, to bring about order through proper discrimination. Each type of behavior has a response proper to it: injury should be
met with sternness, whereas kindness is to be rewarded with kindness. Failure to
discriminate in this way is an invitation to chaos; as Huang Kan notes in his commentary to 14.34, "The reason that one does not repay injury with kindness is
that, were one to do so, then everyone in the world would begin behaving in an
injurious fashion, expecting to be rewarded with kindness. This is the Way of
inviting injury" (Cheng Shude: 1017). For Confucius, being impartial or just
(*gong* 公) means to discriminate properly, giving to each its due. For Laozi, on
the other hand, being impartial means to treat things as one. The Way does not
discriminate between injury or kindness and choose its response accordingly, but
nourishes equally all of the myriad things. It thus gives things life without
demanding "justice" in the Confucian sense—that is, demanding to be honored
and showered with ritual gratitude:[30]

The Way gives [the myriad things] life, raises them;
Causes them to grow, nourishes them;
Perfects and matures them;
Cultivates and protects them.
Giving birth to them and yet laying no claim;
Acting, but not dwelling upon the action;
Leading without being domineering—
This is called mysterious Virtue [*xuande* 玄德]. (chapter 51)

So rather than discriminating—imposing human distinctions upon the world—
one should emulate the Way and stick to the "lower" path: that is, to the element
of dyadic distinctions (such as kindness in the dyad "sternness/kindness") that is
closest to the Way. Thus we read in chapter 79 that the sage "takes the left-hand
tally, but exacts no payment from the people." The left-hand tally is the half of a
contract held by the creditor, and "uprightness" in the Confucian sense would
demand that this contract be fulfilled—that the debt incurred by the creditor be
paid. The Laozian sage, however, is undemanding in the same manner that the
Way is undemanding, understood in terms of the social metaphor of the mother:

he gives to the people and yet asks for nothing in return, holding fast to kindness and discarding the sort of sternness that would demand a quid pro quo.

Of course, it is precisely because the Way demands no gratitude or honor for having given things life that the gratitude and reverence of the entire world flows back to it:

> Among the myriad creatures
> There are none who do not revere the Way and honor Virtue.
> Yet the Way is reverenced and Virtue honored
> Not because they have been invested with any titles [*jue* 爵],
> But because [such reactions] continue to arise naturally [*ziran*]. (chapter 51)

We are presumably also to understand this spontaneous reverence in terms of the WAY AS MOTHER metaphor, in terms of which the Way-Mother gives life to and nurtures her children and so (ideally, at least!) enjoys their spontaneous love and gratitude. If the sage is able to follow the Way in emulating the mother, he can enjoy similar success. Thus,

> demanding nothing in return for his kindness, the sage in fact eventually obtains everything:
> The sage does not accumulate things.
> Yet the more he gives to others, the more he has himself;
> Having given to others, he is richer still. (chapter 81)

This method of sticking to the conventionally lower, more encompassing term—and thereby attaining in reality the higher term—is referred to by Laozi in chapter 22 as "holding to oneness" (*zhiyi* 執一):

> The crooked will be whole;
> The bent will be straight;
> The empty will be full;
> The exhausted will be renewed;
> The few will win out;
> The many will be thrown into confusion.
> Therefore the sage holds to oneness
> And in this way serves as the shepherd of the world.
> He has no regard for himself, and so is illustrious;
> He does not show himself, and so is bright;
> He does not brag, and so is given merit;
> He does not boast, and so his name endures.
> It is only because he does not contend that no one in the world is able to contend with him.
> When the ancients said, "The crooked will be whole," these were not idle words. Truly they return us to wholeness [*quan guizhi* 全歸之].

"Holding to oneness" refers to the behavioral aspect of Laozi's ideal: practicing wu-wei in the literal sense of "no-doing" (not showing oneself, not bragging, not boasting). This behavioral aspect is formulated in negative terms—holding to the "lower" of the dyadic terms and following the Way of Heaven in the sense of stopping before the extreme is reached—but this negative element should be viewed somewhat ironically, since it is precisely through "no-doing" that everything is done. "Wu-wei" is "no-doing" only from the perspective of the vulgar, because in fact it is the Way in which Heaven acts.

The cognitive element of Laozi's ideal—corresponding to "no-regarding" (*wuyiwei*)—is also often portrayed in negative terms, such as in those passages where the sage is described as a "fool":

> The multitude are loud and boisterous
> As if feasting at the *tailao* 太老 offering
> Or climbing terraces in the Spring.[31]
> I am instead tranquil and make no display,
> Like an infant that has not yet learned to smile,
> Drifting as though with no home to return to.
> The multitude all have more than they need.
> I alone am in want.
> I have the mind of a fool—how blank [*dundun* 沌沌]!
> The common people are bright,
> I alone am dull.
> The common people are clever,
> I alone am muddled.
> Vast! Like the ocean.
> Endless! As if never stopping.
> The multitude all have a purpose [*youyi* 有以].
> I alone am ignorant and uncouth.
> My desires alone are different from those of others
> Because I value being fed by the Mother. (chapter 20)

Of course, the nonregarding Laozian sage only appears "dull" or "muddled" from a conventional perspective. In truth, he harbors beneath his ragged sackcloth the valuable gem of true insight into the Way, which Laozi refers to as "illumination" (*ming* 明). In the few places where Laozi drops his ironic stance and discusses this Heavenly understanding directly, it is formulated in quite positive terms:

> If you desire that something contract,
> You must necessarily expand it;
> If you desire that something be weakened,
> You must necessarily strengthen it;
> If you desire that a thing be destroyed,
> You must necessarily raise it up;
> If you wish to take something away,
> You must necessarily give it.
> This is called subtle illumination [*weiming* 微明] (chapter 36).

"Subtle illumination" refers here to the understanding of one who has grasped the principle of reversion and learned to use it to her own advantage.[32] It is called "subtle" (*wei* 微) because it concerns an understanding of the Way, which is (as I noted earlier) mysterious and difficult to see. "The Way is shadowy and indistinct," we read in chapter 21, "yet within it there is an image." This "image" is the image of reversion or return, and once it is grasped one will be like Heaven itself: "Grasp [*zhi* 執] this great image, and the world will come to you" (chapter 35).

How *does* one, though, go about grasping this "image"? That is, what is the precise nature of Laozi's soteriological path? The answer to this question involves establishing a priority between the behavioral and cognitive aspects of Laozian wu-wei—a task that has provoked considerable disagreement among scholars.

Henri Maspero is perhaps the most prominent spokesman of the position that such "philosophical" Daoist thinkers as Laozi and Zhuangzi were merely the more educated and literate spokesmen of a larger movement focused on the attainment of immortality and magical powers, whose activities centered around a variety of physical practices such as breathing techniques, alchemy, and sexual gymnastics.[33] The behavioral aspect of wu-wei would clearly have priority under such an interpretation, and wu-wei would then be seen as a sort of psycho-physiological state—similar to trance or hypnosis—induced by means of such physical techniques. As J. J. L. Duyvendak would have it,

> Lasting vitality and long life are therefore the purpose and result of wu-wei. A special technique is developed to that end. Breathing exercises in which one tries to make the *qi* "air, breath, life force" circulate as intensively as possible through the entire body so that one breathes with his "heels" (*Zhuangzi* VI). A sexual hygiene in which one tries in the union of Yin and Yang to retain the life-force by remaining inactive. The search for medicinal herbs promoting vitality, such as the Ginseng (*Aralia quinquefolia*) and alchemy for preparing the pill of immortality. Daoist saints, devotees of such practices, attain the gift of levitation; they float freely on the wind and their dematerialized bodies, no longer requiring food, become imperishable. (Duyvendak 1947: 91)

Such an interpretation of the *Laozi* certainly has an ancient pedigree, extending back to one of the earliest commentators on the text, a certain Heshang Gong 河上公 (Lord above the River).[34] The Heshang Gong commentary portrays the *Laozi* as an extended metaphorical poem concerning the personal cultivation of the self, and takes much of the poetic and mystical language in the text to refer to specific physical practices. For instance, the commentary on the line from chapter 10, "The Heavenly gates open and shut," reads: "In cultivating the self, the 'Heavenly gate' refers to the nasal passages. 'Opening' this gate refers to inhaling, while 'closing' the gate refers to exhaling" (Gao Ming: 268).

This particular chapter as a whole is perhaps the passage most often cited by those would see the *Laozi* as a manual for physical practice:

> Carrying on your back your troubled earth soul [*yingpo* 營魄],
> Can you embrace the One [*baoyi* 抱一] and not let it go?
> Concentrating your *qi* until it is supple,
> Can you be like an infant?

Polishing and cleaning your mysterious mirror,
Can you leave it without a blemish?
Caring for the people and ordering the state,
Can you not employ knowledge?
Opening and closing the gates of Heaven,
Can you play the role of the female?
With your illumined clarity [*mingbai* 明白] reaching to the four quarters,
Can you not employ knowledge?

Heshang Gong argues that the "One" refers to the "cloud soul" (*hun* 魂)—the counterpart to the "earth soul" (*po* 魄)—and that this passage describes the harmonizing of these two elements of the self through a strict breathing regimen.[35] Many modern commentators thus cite chapter 10 as proof of the fact that Laozi was interested in such practices.

On a closer reading, however, one might just as reasonably conclude that the main concern of this chapter is that one "not employ knowledge" (*wuyizhi* 毋以知).[36] The knowledge that is to be eschewed is, of course, "knowledge" in the conventional sense: the sort of knowledge that would lead one to regard one thing as being better than another, or make one value one's own actions to the point that one regards oneself as worthy of authority or gratitude. This sense is reinforced if we include in our citation the final portion of chapter 10, which is usually passed over without comment by those more interested in seeing this chapter as a short manual on breathing practices:

It gives them life and yet lays no claim to them;
Leads them and yet is not domineering.
This is called mysterious Virtue [*xuande* 玄德].

"It," of course, refers to Heaven or the Way, which gives life to and nurtures the myriad things and yet does not "know" that it is to be honored or valued for such service. It is because the Way is not afflicted by this sort of conventional knowledge that it can act in a wu-wei fashion and possess the sort of universal power that it does—referred to here as "mysterious Virtue." It would thus seem that the key to Laozi's soteriological scheme is a sort of higher knowledge that transcends conventional knowledge. Its specific content is an understanding of the law of reversion, while its effect is to allow one to refrain from harmful "regarding" and thereby hold to the "One" (the lower term of any dyad pair, which in fact contains both elements) and act in the world in a wu-wei fashion. Lisa Raphals refers to this understanding as a kind of "metaknowledge," and portrays it as the basis for all of the other desiderata advocated in the text:

The *Laozi* uses no one term to denote metaknowledge. It is associated with *dao*, discernment [*ming* 明], and non-being [*wu* 無]. It has no Confucian or Mohist equivalent. On the linguistic level, metaknowledge is associated with the nameless [*wuming* 無名]. On the moral level, it is associated with the absence of desire [*wuyu* 無欲] and a virtue that is hidden and mysterious [*xuande* 玄德]. Finally, on the level of praxis, it is described as nonpurposive action [*wuwei* 無為], which operates by reversal and indirection. (Raphals 1995: 79)

Many other scholars of the text agree that it is the cognitive aspect of wu-wei that is the basis for the behavioral aspect.[37] In chapter 47, we find "knowledge" (*zhi* 知) being used unironically in the sense of Raphal's "metaknowledge," where it is clearly associated with illumination (*ming* 明) and is linked with wu-wei in the specifically behavioral sense:

Do not go out the door,
And in this way know the whole world;
Do not look out of the window,
And in this way know the Way of Heaven.
The farther out you go,
The less you know.
This is why the sage knows without going abroad [*xing* 行],
Achieves clarity [*ming* 明] without having to look,
And is successful without trying.

This is not to say that it is impossible that some sort of physical practices play a role in the Laozian soteriological process; as Donald Munro has noted, it is quite likely that Laozian self-cultivation involved both intellectual and physical training.[38] These physical practices might have included everything from reciting the text aloud to breathing or meditation. The point is merely that there is little indication in the text of the *Laozi* itself that such practices constituted any kind of organized or systematic regimen; on the contrary, practice-related imagery seems to be used primarily in an abstract and metaphorical sense. The main focus of the text itself is to have an effect—through the ideas it promulgates and the images it employs—upon the reader's mind. Its main purpose is to produce in the reader the right sort of *understanding*: an understanding of the law of reversion and a corresponding reluctance to make conventional value judgements. To put this another way, the primary focus of Laozi's project is cognitive and affective rather than behavioral.

Naturalness (*ziran* 自然) or the "So-of-Itself"

Once one has acquired "knowledge of the constant" (*zhichang* 知常)—that is, an understanding of the law of reversal—and thereby achieved illumination, one is able to reach a state that is characterized in chapter 16 with several sets of metaphors:

I attain the limit of tenuousness [*xu* 虛],
And hold firmly to stillness [*jing* 靜],
So that as the myriad things all rise up,
I am able to observe their return [*guanqifu* 觀其復].

As for things, though they sprout wildly and multiply,
Each will finally come home to its root [*fugui yu qigen* 復歸於其根].
Coming home to the root is called stillness,
And this is what is known as returning to fate [*fuming* 復命].
Returning to fate is constancy.
Knowing constancy is illumination;
Not knowing constancy is reckless ignorance [*wang* 妄];
Behaving in a reckless, ignorant manner leads to misfortune.
Knowing the constant leads to tolerance;
Tolerance leads to public-mindedness [*gong* 公];
Public-mindedness leads to kingliness;
Kingliness to Heaven;
Heaven to the Way;
And the Way to endurance [*jiu* 久].
[Achieve this, and] to the end of your life you will not meet with disas-
 ter.

The primary metaphors and expressions can be roughly categorized into three
sets—1) "tenuousness"/"stillness"; 2) "observing the return"/"coming home to
the root"/"returning to fate"; and 3) constancy/endurance—that are clearly associated with one another by the author(s). By maintaining a state of stillness and
tenuousness, the sage is able to resist the move toward frantic activity that characterizes most things in the world. This activity is all ultimately for nought, since
however far from their origin things travel they are inexorably drawn back to their
original stillness. Having never left this spot, the sage is able to observe both the
manner in which things arise and the way they come back to their origin. By thus
emulating the Way—that is, remaining still and constant—the sage not only
acquires a special form of knowledge (in turn, metaphorically understood as
"illumination") but partakes of the Way's "endurance" and lives out a long life.

The link with the cosmic order is made quite clear in chapter 68, where an
ability to hold fast to the lower term of any dyad is referred to as "matching up
with Heaven" (*peitian* 配天), and in chapter 25, where we encounter a principle
that encompasses many of the qualities we saw in chapter 16 and that serves as a
model for everything in the world, apparently being greater even than the Way:

There is a thing confusedly formed,
That was born before Heaven and Earth.
Silent! Void [*liao* 寥]!
It stands alone and does not change,
And yet can be taken to be the mother of the world.
I do not yet know its name,
And so I style it "the Way."
If forced to name it more specifically, I would call it "the great";
Being great, we can further call it "the passing away" [*shi* 逝],
Passing away, we can further call it "the far traveling" [*yuan* 遠],
Traveling far, we can further call it "returning" [*fan* 返].
The Way is great

Heaven is great
Earth is great
And the king also is great. . . .
The people model themselves on Earth,
Earth on Heaven,
Heaven on the Way,
And the Way on naturalness [*ziran*]. (chapter 25)

As I noted in chapter 1, the metaphor of *ziran* 自然 is based upon a combination of the ESSENTIAL SELF and SELF AS CONTAINER schemas. Meaning literally "so-of-itself," *ziran* refers to the way a thing is when its actions spring from its own internal Essence. Metaphorically, the image is that *ziran* actions emerge "naturally" out of the container of the Self—an example of the apparently cross-cultural NATURAL CAUSATION IS MOTION OUT metaphor. Scholars of the text have observed that there are multiple senses of what it means for something to be *ziran* in Laozi's thought. Zhang Qin 1995, for instance, notes two senses: "originally so"—the primordial state of a thing—as well as "uncoerced" or "uncaused," a state of affairs that has come about without any value-guided ("regarding") action or outside force (i.e., "effortless" behavior). To these two senses, Liu Xiaogan 1999 adds a third: "internal" and "enduring" in the sense of a state of affairs that has come about through development tendencies internal to the thing itself. Arguably, the second and third of these senses of *ziran* (uncoerced/uncaused and internal/enduring) represent direct entailments of the basic image schema of thing emerging naturally from the inside of a container (the NATURAL CAUSATION IS MOTION OUT schema), while the first (originally so) is an entailment that is attached to the concept by associating it with other metaphors such as that of the "infant") or the "uncarved wood," as will be discussed later.

Understanding *ziran* in this manner, it is thus Liu Xiaogan's third sense—the entailment of internalness—that is most direct and primary: the myriad things are containers that have within them some behavior-determining essence that naturally "comes out." This essence can be overridden by "outside" pressures, in which case behavior is forced or artificial. On the other hand, when this outside pressure is removed and the Essential Self is freed to emerge and determine a being's actual behavior, this behavior can then be said to be *ziran*—that is, "so-of-itself," uncoerced, or effortless. The NATURAL CAUSATION IS MOTION OUT schema is in turn likely based upon our experience with the birth of animals or germination of plants, which seem to emerge "effortlessly" (at least for the observer!) and spontaneously from within the container of the mother or seed. This conceptual connection allows us to link *ziran* to the metaphors of birth, motherhood, and the "root" mentioned earlier with regard to the qualities of the Way and Nothingness. The sense of "internal cause" and its connection to effortlessness is reinforced by our experience of the physical world of nature. Water, for instance, "internally" tends to flow downhill and eventually to the ocean. By exerting "outside" force upon it, however, it can be made to stop and gather behind a dam, or even to reverse its course and flow uphill. An entailment of this experience motivates Liu Xiaogan's association of "enduring" with "internal": it takes no energy to let a thing follow its natural course, and therefore such behavior is sustainable; on the other hand, the fact that active and constant exertion of external force is required to oppose a thing's essential tendencies dooms such action to eventual failure. Dams are eventually breached; pumps eventually fail. Similarly, *ziran* behavior is "uncoerced": no one has to force water to flow to the sea. In this way, the metaphor of *ziran* and its various entailments are an excellent illustration of how conceptual structures acquired in interacting with the physical world are directly mapped onto more abstract domains.

The "internal cause" and effortlessness entailments of the *ziran* metaphor are thus quite directly motivated by the basic schema. Other "senses" of the term, however, require a bit more of a conceptual stretch. For instance, it takes a little work to see how "originally so" belongs to the *ziran* complex, and why it might be cited by Zhang Qin and Liu Xiaogan as an aspect of *ziran*. Making this connection requires the invocation of other metaphor structures, and it is precisely through such metaphorical linkages that the author(s) of the *Laozi* both reinforce the direct entailments of the *ziran* metaphor and introduce a variety of associated entailments. We have seen an example of such metaphor mixing in my analysis of chapter 16 above, and this practice is in fact the rule rather than the exception in the *Laozi*. For instance, two of the more powerful metaphors for "naturalness" in the sense of an original, unspoiled state are the "infant" (*ying'er* 嬰兒) and the "uncarved wood" (*pu* 樸), both of which are portrayed in chapter 28 as representing the state of things before the fall:

> Know the male, but keep to the female,
> And be a ravine [*xi* 溪] to the world.
> Being a ravine to the world,
> The enduring Virtue will not leave you;
> When the enduring Virtue does not leave you,
> You will return again to being an infant [*fugui ying'er* 復歸嬰兒].
> Know glory, but keep to disgrace,
> And be a valley [*gu* 谷] to the world.
> Being a valley to the world,
> The enduring Virtue will be sufficient;
> Once the enduring Virtue is sufficient,
> You will return again to the uncarved wood.
> Know the bright, but keep to the dark,
> And be a model [*shi* 式] to the world.
> Being a model to the world,
> The enduring Virtue will not err [*te* 忒];
> When the enduring Virtue does not err
> You will return again to the limitless [*wuji* 無極].

Keeping to the lower half of the value dyad is here understood metaphorically as being a "ravine" or "valley" to the world. By taking the lower position in this way, one is able to rely upon the natural force of gravity to ensure that one will retain a sufficient quantity of the "enduring Virtue" (here understood as water), and can also be confident that this Virtue will not go away. Water, as we know, does not naturally flow uphill.

This achievement of a valley-like state is also understood as a "return" to being like an infant or uncarved block of wood—both metaphors for human beings' original, unspoiled nature.[39] Why do these connections seem logical (or "natural") to both the author(s) and the reader? Their force derives from the fact that their metaphorical linkage is not random, but is rather motivated by our physical experience of the environment. For instance, the image of the valley is a common one in text. The metaphorical identification we see in chapter 28 of a "lower" qualitative state (female, disgrace, darkness) with a literally low feature of the physical landscape allows us to apply conceptual structures derived from observations of the physical environment to the metaphorical spiritual world: just as water that has fallen as rain and been deposited in the highlands naturally flows back into the valleys, so everything in the world eventually returns to the sage who emulates the Way and takes the lower position.[40] In chapter 32 we read that the Way's relationship to the world is "like the rivers and oceans are to the valley streams"—that is, the great source from which the water arises and to which it inexorably and naturally returns. Similarly, in chapter 66 the rivers and oceans are portrayed as the "king" of the hundred valley streams, because they are "good at taking the lower position," and the sage is instructed to metaphorically emulate this stance by placing himself "below" the people. Thus, the abstract action of valuing and "holding to" the traditionally lower values is linked to the whole *ziran* complex (with its entailments of endurance and lack of coercion) through the physical metaphor of the valley or ocean. In this way the many claims made in the text about how the myriad things spontaneously "return" (*fu* 復 or *gui* 歸) to the Way (or the sage who is emulating the Way) seem quite reasonable to both the author(s) and the reader, since their common experience of the physical landscape allows the valley and ocean metaphors to motivate the "return," "naturalness" (in the sense of internal cause), and "originally so" metaphors.

This sense of "originally so" is also suggested by the chapter 16 metaphors of "coming home to the root" and "returning to fate," as well as the fact that the Way is described in chapter 25 as being "born before Heaven and Earth." This impression of primordiality is reinforced by the description of decline in chapter 38 or of the low-tech, agrarian utopia whose establishment is urged upon the sage-ruler in chapter 80:

> Reduce the size of the state and decrease its population.
> See to it that labor-saving devices are not employed,
> See to it that the people view death as a weighty matter and do not[41]
> move to distant places,
> See to it that,
> already possessing carts and boats, the people do not ride in them,
> already possessing armor and weapons, they do not deploy them.
> See to it that the people return to using the knotted rope,
> That they will
> Find sweetness in their food

Beauty in their clothes,
Joy [*le* 樂] in their habits,
And contentment [*an* 安] in their homes;
See to it that,
though neighboring states are within sight of one another,
and the sounds of chickens and dogs can be heard across the border,
the people will grow old and die without ever traveling abroad.

The "knotted rope" refers to a primitive method of calculation and record keeping supposedly employed prior to the development of literacy. Whereas Confucius located his lost Golden Age at the high point of the glorious culture of the Zhou, Laozi locates his in a preliterate age.[42] In the original state of society, people were not afflicted by knowledge or the value judgments and artificial desires that knowledge brings with it. They found "joy in their habits and contentment in their homes." Mori Mikisaburo argues that this primordial state of harmony represents the "original nature" of human beings, which has been lost, but can be realized again—and spread through the transformative influence of Virtue—by one who is able to eliminate knowledge and desire (Mori 1967: 12). Therefore, although he never explicitly discusses the issue of human nature with reference to the technical term *xing* 性, Laozi's conception of naturalness presents a fairly clear picture of the "nature" of human beings.

Another common metaphorical connection in the text is between "stillness" (*jing* 靜) and *ziran* results:

The Way is enduringly nameless.
If the lords and kings were able to hold fast to it,
The myriad things would be naturally transformed [*zihua* 自化].
If, in transforming, desire should arise among them,
I would suppress [*zhen* 鎮] it with the nameless uncarved wood.
Then they would have no desire.
If I attain stillness through not desiring,
The world would be naturally settled [*ziding* 自定].[43] (37)

Here the "enduringly nameless" Way is described as a primal force capable of transforming the myriad things in a *ziran* manner. The sage, through eliminating desire and thereby attaining stillness, makes himself like the Way and acquires its power. A similar connection between wu-wei, stillness, and spontaneous tranformative power is made in chapter 57:

Therefore the teaching of the sage is this:
I am without doing (wu-wei), and the people are naturally transformed;
I am fond of stillness, and the people are naturally rectified;
I am without action [*wushi* 無事] and the people naturally prosper;
I desire not to desire, and the people naturally become like the uncarved wood.

A common physical instantiation of stillness is water, and this connection is evoked explicitly in chapter 8: "The highest good resembles water / Water excels

at benefitting the myriad things while remaining still." This linkage between stillness and water allows all the various "powers" of water to be metaphorically
transferred to stillness. For instance, the text explains that water does not change
its "nature," and this is why, when it begins to flow, it is able to wear down mountains:

> In all the world there is nothing softer or weaker than water,
> And yet nothing is better than it for attacking the hard and rigid.
> This is because water does not allow anything to change [*yi* 易] it.

The metaphorical implication is clear: become still and enduring like water, and
then when you do take motion you will be able to overcome all obstacles. Hence
the claim in chapter 45 that "stillness wins out over action" and that clarity (*qing*
清) and stillness (both common attributes of water) can be used to "settle" (*ding*
定) the world. When stillness is described as "settling" the world, the connection
is made between still water and stationary objects, which creates a bridge
between the water metaphors and the many metaphors in the text involving physical stillness or inactivity. We then have a link between water and "no-doing"
(wu-wei) or "no-action" (*wushi*), knowing without stirring from home (chapter
47, discussed earlier), teaching without having to speak (chapters 2, 23, 43, 56,
73), and similar images in the text. The softness and suppleness of water further
allows it to be associated with the metaphor of the infant (who is soft and supple—chapter. 10), which in turns connects it with the idea of "originally so."

Thus, the inexorable and natural manner in which water flows back to the sea
and conquers all obstacles in its path is one of the primary physical models
according to which we are to understand the "so-of-itself," originally so, uncoerced, effortless fashion in which the Laozian sage's power operates. Water, however, is not the only physical metaphor relied upon. Another important image is
that of physical emptiness:

> Thirty spokes are joined to a common hub,
> But the usefulness of the cart
> Is to be found in the nothingness [*wu*] [between the spokes].[44]
> Clay is molded into vessels,
> But the usefulness of the clay vessel
> Is to be found in the nothingness [within].
> Doors and windows are carved out,
> But the usefulness of the room
> Is to be found in the nothingness [of these openings]. (chapter 11)

Consider also chapter 5 ("Is the space between Heaven and Earth not like a bellows? / Tenuous [*xu*] yet never exhausted / The more it works the more comes
out"), which echoes the chapter before it: "The Way is an empty vessel / And yet
as much as it is used, it can never be filled up" (chapter 4). The message here is
that the sage is to become empty and the powers accruing to emptiness will then
logically follow. In order to map physical emptiness metaphorically onto the Self,
the CONTAINER SELF metaphor must be invoked: the Self is a container that is to
be emptied of, to name a few examples, "doing" (*wei*), "regarding" (*yiwei*),

"actions" (*shi*), the heart/mind (*xin*), schemes and knowledge, desires, and even the "self" or body (*shen* 身) itself. Passages such as chapter 57 (cited earlier)— where the sage who has been emptied of doing, acting, and desires is described as transforming the people in a manner as effortless as the endless production of wind from a bellows—connect emptiness to naturalness, while passages such as chapter 13 explain the link between emptiness and endurance: "The reason behind my suffering trouble is that I have a self/body [*shen*] / Were I able to be without a body, what trouble would I have?" Once the emptying of the self is completed, then, the "source of trouble" will have been removed and the sage will prove impervious to external forces. This idea is expressed quite vividly in chapter 50:

> I have heard that those who are good at nurturing life
> Do not flee from the rhinoceros or tiger when traveling in the mountains
> And do not equip themselves with armor or weapons when serving in
> the army.
> [This is because] the rhinoceros can find no place to plunge in its horn;
> The tiger can find no place to grab with its claws;
> And weapons can find no place to bite with their blades.
> Why is this?
> It is because [those good at nurturing life] have no "execution ground"
> [*sidi* 死 地][45] within them.

By metaphorically emptying its Self, then, the Subject renders itself enduring and impervious to the outside world: since the Self has been rendered a void, there is no "execution ground" —that is, no place where the Subject may be attacked or harmed.

Another important system of metaphors related to naturalness centers on the image of the "root" (*gen* 根, *ben* 本) or "stem" (*di* 柢). In chapter 6, in the space of only a few lines, the root is linked with the valley, female, container, "thread," and endurance metaphors:

> The spirit of the valley does not die;
> This is called the mysterious female.
> The gate of the mysterious female
> Is called the root of Heaven and Earth.
> Like a fine, unbroken thread it seems to exist!
> Draw upon it and it will never be exhausted.

The mysterious female is here equated with the valley, and the female/valley spirit is described as "internal": dwelling within the self and accessible only by a "gate" (*men* 門). Passing through this gate is equivalent to possessing the root of Heaven and Earth—the power of the female spirit presumably producing life in the same way the root produces and anchors the full-grown plant. Both the female and the root are thus the origin of things (i.e., "originally so"), and both are described as enduring eternally—like an endless thread that never runs out. The sense of endurance is also powerfully evoked through the vegetative metaphor in chapter 59:

Pile high your Virtue and there will be nothing you cannot overcome;

Once there is nothing you cannot overcome, no one will know your limit.

Once there is no one who knows your limit, you will thereby be able to possess the state.

Once you possess the Mother of the state, you will thereby be able to endure a long time [*changjiu* 長久]

This is called having deep roots and firm stems [*shen'gen gudi* 深根固柢]—

The Way of living a long life and seeing many days.

As we have already seen, the natural or physical realms are not the only domains upon which the *Laozi* draws for metaphors related to naturalness. The metaphor of the Mother—who (considered earlier in my discussion of reversion) produces life, nourishes her offspring unselfishly, and in turn enjoys the spontaneous love of her offspring—invites the reader to draw upon her rich stock of associations arising from the social realm and apply these qualities to the sage (see chapter 52). Another important example of a social metaphor is to found in chapter 26, where—through a revealing mixing of metaphors—the "root" is equated with the "ruler": "The heavy is the root of the light / The still is the ruler of the active." Here we see a SELF AS SOCIETY metaphor, drawn from our experience of interpersonal relationships, and allowing us to map our vast knowledge about evaluative qualities of specific social relationship onto our inner lives. Chapter 26 invites us to use the evaluative social relationship ruler-ruled in order to cognize the relationship between different abstract aspects or qualities of the Self—in this case, stillness and activity.

The evaluative logic of the social metaphor is then reinforced by mixing it with the vegetative metaphor: just as the root controls the development of the plant, the ruler is the master of things, he who properly commands and controls. This same social metaphor is drawn upon in chapter 32, where we are told that "nothing in the world dares to treat the uncarved wood as a minister [*chen* 臣]"— that is, everything recognizes that the uncarved wood is the ruler, not the minister. Another structurally similar social metaphor employed in the text is that of the "ancestor" (*zong* 宗). In the literal social world, the ancestor is the one who— through past actions and hereditary endowment—has given rise to and largely determined the qualities of the present generation. Like the ruler, he enjoys (again, at least ideally) spontaneous reverence and obedience. In chapter 70, the ancestor metaphor is combined with the ruler metaphor to describe the pedigree and consistency of the *Laozi*'s message ("My teachings have an ancestor / My actions have a ruler"),[46] and in chapter 4 the Way itself is described as "Deep and vast! Like the ancestor of the myriad things."

We have yet to exhaustively discuss the metaphors found in the *Laozi* relating to naturalness. There are, for instance, the additional metaphors of the One (chapters 14, 56), standing for origination and primordial lack of distinctions; the shepherd (chapter 22); the "limitless" (*wuji* 無極); the "foundation" (*ji* 基); and the "Genuine" (*zhen* 真). We might also have examined more closely the metaphoric conceptualization of Virtue, which is sometimes portrayed as a substance that—unlike other aspects of the self—is positive and to be "piled high" (chapter 59) or possessed "thickly" (chapter 55), and at other times portrayed as a physical place that can be "returned home to" (chapter 60) or even as a companion that accompanies things as they return to their origins (chapter 65).[47] It suffices for our purposes to note that, in the *Laozi*, the specific expression "wu-wei" is situated at the center of the complex network of mutually motivating conceptual metaphor systems. Following the lead of scholars such as Zhang Qin and Liu Xiaogan, we might conclude by classifying these metaphor schemas under various headings to summarize the various senses of Laozian wu-wei or naturalness:

Lack of Exertion

The sage is still, like water, and yet "spontaneously" causes—simply through the power of his Virtue—various transformations in the world around him. One is here reminded of the sage-king Shun as described in *Analects* 15.5, or the Pole Star in 2.1. Like the stillness metaphor, the metaphor of "following" (*cong*) invokes a sense of effortlessness, and is found in the *Laozi* as well: "The behavior of the person of great Virtue follows the Way and nothing but the Way" (chapter 21). This strongly recalls the description of Confucius "following his heart's desire" in *Analects* 2.4 and never transgressing the bounds, and will surface again in *Mencius* 7:B:33. We also see in *Laozi* 30 the debut of a metaphor that will reappear with great frequency in the *Zhuangzi*: that of "dwelling" (*ju* 居) in "what cannot be stopped" (*budeyi* 不得已). All of these metaphors—accompanied by references to "softness" and "weakness"—point in various ways to the primary hallmarks of wu-wei: a lack of exertion on the part of the Subject.

Emptiness/Nothing (wu)

This aspect of Laozian wu-wei is related to the other hallmark of wu-wei— "unself-consciousness"—that is so often conveyed through the metaphor of object-loss: forgetting, losing the self, and so on. In the *Laozi*, however, unself-consciousness is conceived metaphorically by means of the CONTAINER SELF structure: the Self is a container, and it is only when it is emptied of everything extraneous that spiritual perfection is attained. These extraneous elements, as we have seen, include the heart/mind, desires, actions, the self/body (*shen*), "doing" (*wei*), and "regarding" (*yiwei*). Laozi's soteriological path is thus conceived of as a metaphorical "emptying" of the container of the self, so famously described in chapter 48:

> One who engages in study adds [*yi* 益] to himself day by day;
> One who has heard the Way takes away [*sun* 損] from himself day by day.
> He takes away and takes away more, in order to bring himself to a state of no-doing (wu-wei),
> And when he is free of doing, he is also free of regarding [*wuyiwei*].

It is worth noting that wu-wei is here understood in a unique metaphoric sense. More commonly, as discussed in the introduction, wu-wei is understood in terms of the OBJECT SELF schema, in which sense it refers to the lack of exertion of the Subject upon the Self. In the passage quoted here, it is understood instead in terms of the CONTAINER SELF schema, and refers to the absence of a substance ("doing") in the container of the Self. "Wu-wei" in this sense is therefore more directly linked to the notion of emptiness than that of effortlessness.

Despite this unique twist on the "unself-conscious" aspect of wu-wei and the metaphorical structure of the term itself, however, the first and second senses of naturalness are similar to what we have seen in the pre-Confucian and early Confucian material, and correspond to the two primary hallmarks of wu-wei. What is quite new in the *Laozi* is the introduction of the metaphor systems described later to the wu-wei complex.

Originally So

Wu-wei and the naturalness it releases work because they are "originally so." That is, if we recall the discussion above of the principle of reversion, that which comes first (the conventionally "lower" member of dyad pairs) is the source and ruler of what comes after (the conventionally "higher"). Metaphysically, then, the power of wu-wei and naturalness is based upon the logical and ontological priority of Nothing over Something. The specific metaphorical expressions of this primordiality are quite various:

1. travel: returning [*fu*], returning home [*gui*], reverting [*fan*];
2. unworked, unspoiled: the unadorned [*su*], the uncarved wood [*pu*];
3. vegetative: the root [*gen, ben*], the stem [*di*];
4. construction: the foundation [*ji*];
5. social: the Mother [*mu*], the ancestor [*zong*];

Of course, all of these "originally so" metaphors are directed against the Confucian portrayal of self-cultivation as the adornment or reformation of a raw material or the undertaking of a life-long journey. We were fine as we originally were, Laozi is saying, and it is only in departing from our primordial purity that we go astray. As we read in chapter 47 (cited earlier), "The farther out you go / the less you know."

Internal Essence

Within the Self there is an essence that determines the proper behavior of the Subject, and this essence spontaneously emerges once space within the Self has been cleared. "Emptiness" or "not-(having)" (*wu*) are thus viable metaphors for Laozi's perfected state only because the "container" of the Self, once emptied, spontaneously wells up with an internal force that has hitherto been suppressed.[48] Although the container language of "inner/outer" (*neiwai* 內外) that later becomes very popular is almost completely absent from the *Laozi*, this structure is clearly implied by the metaphor of *ziran*,[49] and later commentators thus freely make use of such terminology in explicating the text. The "Jielao" commentary on chapter 38, for instance, employs the inner-outer model to explain why it is that true Virtue cannot strive to be virtuous:

> Virtue is internal [*nei*]; "attaining" [*de* 得] is external [*wai*]. "The highest Virtue is not Virtue" refers to the spirit not spilling over to the outside. When the Virtue does not spill over to the outside,[50] then the self [*shen*] will be kept whole, and the self being whole is what is meant by Virtue. Virtue thus refers to "attaining" [*de* 得] one's self. In all cases Virtue is *accumulated through wu-wei*, perfected through being without desires, settled through being without thoughts, and solidified through being without use. (emphasis added)

While this earliest commentary on the text may employ terminology not found in the original, the basic metaphoric conceptualization is the same: Virtue properly resides in the self in its "natural" (in all of the senses I have discussed) state, and purification can be attained only through the elimination of unnatural external corruptions.

We thus find in the *Laozi* the beginnings of a metaphor that will become very prominent in later Daoist praxis: closing off the doors to the Self in order to keep insidious influence out and to keep Virtue in.

> Plug up the crevices [in the self (*shen*)],
> Close its gates,
> And you can complete your life without the self being exhausted.
> Open up the crevices,
> Meddle in affairs,
> And for the rest of your life you will be beyond saving. (chapter 52, cf. chapter 56)

As we will see in the *Zhuangzi* as well, there runs throughout the *Laozi* a metaphoric contrast between what is internal and proper to the self (the Way, Virtue) and what is external and harmful to the self. A basic characteristic shared by the soteriological paths advocated in these two texts is the desire to eliminate the latter so that the original, "natural" self might be recovered, as well as a belief that the self-conscious striving of the Confucians—oriented as it is toward such external attainments as fame and learning—is fundamentally antithetical to this project.

Enduring

Being the original and essential state of things, as well as the goal to which they are internally impelled, the state of naturalness or wu-wei is long-lasting and stable. We saw this theme in chapter 80, where people in their primitive village utopia are portrayed as being content and joyful, and have also seen it linked to the vegetative metaphor of being "deeply rooted." This aspect of the natural Way is the reason it and its principles are referred to as "the enduring" (*heng*) or "constant" (*chang*), and in human terms it is what endows the sage with longevity.

As we shall see, these innovative aspects of Laozian wu-wei—especially that of internal essence—will become an inextricable part of the wu-wei family of metaphors. As a result, the self-cultivation internalism they entail cannot be ignored by any of the thinkers that follow. Some embrace it enthusiastically (the authors of the "Inner Training" and the *Zhuangzi*), some attempt to co-opt it (Mencius), and some dramatically reject it (Xunzi), but the internalist/externalist-division it engenders becomes a central point of tension in subsequent East Asian religious thought.

"Contemplative" versus "Purposive" Daoism and the Paradox of Wu-wei

I have mentioned in passing the benefits accruing to one who has attained wu-wei. There are, of course, immense personal benefits: long life, increased vitality, and freedom from harm (See chapters 15, 44, 50 and 55). It is clear that the author of the *Laozi* was very much concerned with personal survival, and the ability to preserve one's person and move through a dangerous world with ease are certainly prominent among the benefits he promises to those who follow his Way. As we have noted, however, Laozi—like Confucius—saw the attainment of personal salvation as merely a catalyst for universal salvation. His soteriological project is thus much broader in scope than the mere seeking after personal longevity. As Li Shenglong notes, although the goal of universal salvation is less explicit in the *Laozi* than in the *Analects*, it is nonetheless an important element of Laozi's thought:

> Laozi repeatedly emphasizes his demand that the sage save other people as well as the myriad things, and that he should take possession of the world through wu-wei. The observation, "My teaching is easy to understand and easy to put into practice," is in fact an earnest remonstration prompted by altruistic intentions, strongly tinged by a sense of urgency. (Li Shenglong 1987b: 21)[51]

In chapter 54, we find a description (very reminiscent of *Analects* 2.21, 14.42 and the opening lines of the "Great Learning") of the manner in which "firmly established" personal perfection expands out in concentric circles from the individual to the family and state and, eventually, to the world as a whole:

> That which is well established cannot be pulled up;
> That which is held tightly cannot be snatched away;
> By means of sons and grandsons, the sacrificial offerings will never be
>   cut off.
> Cultivate it in your self [*shen*], and its Virtue will be genuine.
> Cultivate it in the family, and its Virtue will be more than enough;
> Cultivate it in the village, and its Virtue will last.

Cultivate it in the state, and its Virtue will be abundant;
Cultivate it in the world, and its Virtue will be universal [*bo* 博].

"It," of course, refers to the Way. By cultivating it in one's own self and thereby attaining a state of wu-wei and accumulating genuine Virtue, the aspiring ruler will have firmly established the roots of universal salvation. Once these roots are firm, the tree cannot but grow to eventually encompass the entire world. Of course, the manner in which the Laozian sage's Virtue exerts its influence on the world is quite different from that of the Confucian sage. Unlike the awesome pole star or the powerful wind bending the grass from above, Laozi's sage serves as a "model for the world" by remaining unseen and placing himself below the myriad things. By thus taking the "lower" position and transforming the world through the subtle influence of his Virtue, the Laozian sage-ruler leads the world back to naturalness. By not taking any action or engaging in meddling himself, he is able to cultivate the powerful and mysterious Virtue that gradually washes the people of the world clean of unnatural behavior and desires. By not personally engaging in "regarding" or the accumulation of conventional knowledge, the sage-ruler brings it about that the people will also be free of knowledge and desire and disinclined to act:

Do not honor the worthy, and this will keep the people from contention;
Do not value goods that are difficult to acquire, and this will keep the people from becoming thieves;
Do not display that which is desirable, and this will keep the people from unrest.
Therefore, the sage governs the people like this:
He empties [*xu*] their minds but fills their bellies,
Weakens their ambitions [*zhi* 志] but strengthens their bones.
He enduringly keeps them free of knowledge and desire,
And ensures that those with knowledge never dare to act.
Take no action, that is all,
And there will be nowhere that is not governed. (chapter 3).[52]

By returning to naturalness himself through the practice of wu-wei, the sage is able to bring the rest of the world back to naturalness along with him. This is what is meant by saying that the sage is able to "assist the myriad things in [returning to] naturalness" although he "does not dare to act" (chapter 64). "Returning to naturalness" represents a return to the state of "great flowing along with" (*dashun* 大順) that once prevailed in the world (chapter 65), and this idyllic state of affairs—which will come about again if a ruler in Laozi's own time could only grasp the Way—is described quite beautifully in chapter 32:

The Way is enduringly nameless. . . .
If the lords and kings were able to hold fast to it,
The myriad things would submit of their own accord [*zibin* 自賓],
Heaven and Earth would come together
And cause a sweet dew to fall,

Which—though no one orders it—would naturally spread itself equita-
bly among all the people.

In chapter 43 an anonymous sage extols the "benefits" (*yi* 益) of wu-wei, and
this issue of wu-wei "paying off" in the end—giving to others so that one in the
end will have everything one needs, for instance—brings up a tension that is central to the *Laozi* and closely related to the paradox of wu-wei. One approach to
this tension is represented by Herrlee Creel who, in his famous essay "What is
Taoism?"[53] introduced the distinction between "contemplative" and "purposive"
Daoism into English-language sinology. Each of these two types of Daoism is
described by Creel as possessing its own version of wu-wei: contemplative wu-
wei represents "an attitude of genuine non-action, motivated by a lack of desire to
participate in the struggle of human affairs" (Creel 1970: 74), whereas purposive
wu-wei represents merely a clever technique for gaining control over human
affairs. As I have noted in chapter 1, this idea of wu-wei as a mere instrumental
technique is quite clearly embodied in the writings of such Legalist thinkers as
Hanfeizi or Shen Buhai, but Creel is of the opinion that this brand of wu-wei
characterizes the *Laozi* as well.[54] The *Laozi*, he feels, "is less concerned with the
vision of the *dao* as the great whole, and more with the *dao* as a technique of control" (Creel 1970: 6). Along with such scholars as Feng Yulan, Arthur Waley, J. J.
L. Duyvendak, Kanaya Osamu, and Michael LaFargue,[55] Creel sees the *Laozi* as
a practical manual advocating a technique for surviving a chaotic world, obtaining long life, and ruling effectively. The Laozian sage, as Duyvendak would have
it,

> keeps to the weak and lowly, and refrains from any conscious effort, any
> striving after a set purpose. In a sense therefore he may be said to have a
> purpose. His wu-wei is practiced and conscious design; he chooses this
> attitude in the conviction that only by so doing the "natural" develop-
> ment of things will favor him. (Duyvendak 1954: 10–11)

The Laozian sage seems harmless, Duyvendak notes, but in fact is as "amoral"
and "cynical" as any Legalist statesman. A less stark but similar point is made by
Kanaya Osamu, who—like Creel—distinguishes between the more contemplative and "religious" Zhuangzi and the more cynical and this-worldly minded
Laozi. Reviewing the chapters that explain the law of reversion, Kanaya observes
that the Laozian sage is merely making use of this law to get what he wants. In
this way, Laozi's sage is not really that different after all from ordinary people: he
shares their mundane values and their desire to get ahead, but is merely more
clever and successful in realizing these ends. Kanaya feels that unlike Zhuangzi—who possesses genuinely religious ideals—Laozi has not in the final analysis really transcended "secular" values (Kanaya 1964: 5–6). In a similar vein,
some scholars (particularly in mainland China) feel that Laozi's vision is atheistic
and "materialistic" in the sense of modern scientific theory. Noting Laozi's
emphasis upon the importance of the principle of reversion, Yang Darong claims
that Laozian wu-wei "involves merely acting in accordance with objective laws"
(Yang 1994: 54), while Liu Xuezhi believes that Laozian naturalness has the

"materialist significance of following the independent laws inhering in the myriad things" (Liu 1986: 72).

I have cited many passages from the *Laozi* that certainly lend themselves to these sorts of instrumentalist interpretations. Perhaps the most potentially sinister passage is the discussion of "making the people ignorant" in chapter 65, and the split between purposive and nonpurposive interpretations is often revealed by where an interpreter comes down on this particular passage. As Roger Ames notes, the doctrine of "making the people ignorant" could be taken in two ways: 1) an authoritarian technique for stultifying the people, where only the ruler possesses the Way; or 2) a means for leading the people to their own fulfillment, where the ruler helps the people to find the Way as well. Ames observes that, although neither interpretation is entirely ruled out by the text ("The ambiguity of the *Laozi*," he writes, "is such that it can quite comfortably accommodate both interpretations"), the second "has the positive feature of establishing consistency between the metaphysics and the political philosophy of the text" (Ames 1994: 8). That is, the sage-ruler is to model his actions upon the Way itself, and in passages such as chapters 10 and 51 we find the Way described as attaining its own ends only through nourishing and contributing to the flourishing of the myriad things. Commenting upon chapter 3 ("emptying their minds and strengthening their bones," etc.), Ames argues against a Legalistic interpretation:

> In the context of Daoist philosophy, to interpret "emptying the people's minds," "weakening their sense of purpose," and "ensuring that the people are without knowledge" as a stupefying policy of political oppression is to ignore the whole thrust of Daoist thought as the emulation of the natural Dao. . . . The principal idea presented in Chapter 3 is that the sage-ruler, by adhering to a policy of wu-wei, creates a situation in which the people are free to express their own untrammeled potentiality and to develop naturally and fully without suffering the contaminations of externally imposed "purposes." (Ames 1994: 42–43)

Other scholars are in accord with Ames on this point. Liu Xiaogan observes that the policy of "making the people ignorant" refers not to the clever taking advantage of the foolish, but rather to "honesty, simplicity and straightforwardness" (Liu 1999). With regard to passages such as chapter 7 ("Is it not because he is without thoughts of himself that he is able to accomplish his own private ends?") and chapter 66 ("Therefore, if the sage desires to be above the people / he must in his teachings put himself below them"), D. C. Lau notes that the doctrine of putting oneself below so that one may be above takes on a sinister connotation

> only so long as we have the preconceived notion that the *Laozi* advocates the use of "scheming methods." But if we approach [such passages] with an open mind, we begin to see that there need not be anything sinister in what is said, which is no more than this. Even if a ruler were to aim at realizing his own ends he can only hope to succeed by pursuing the ends of the people. If he values his own person he can only serve its best interests by treating it as extraneous to himself. What

is said here about the realization of the ruler's private ends is reminiscent of what is sometimes said about the pursuit of happiness. A man can achieve his own happiness only by pursuing the happiness of others, because it is only by forgetting his own happiness that he can become happy. This has never been looked upon as a sinister theory. No more need be the theory in the *Laozi.* (Lau 1963: 39–40)

We can thus conclude that, while it is clear that there are instrumentalist elements in the *Laozi* that made it attractive to later Legalist thinkers,[56] it would be mistaken to view the text as a systematic blueprint for effective political control.[57] A crucial element that any instrumentalist interpretation of the *Laozi* overlooks is that the text possesses an essentially religious[58] element. This is Liu Xiaogan's point in observing that the various strands of instrumentalist interpretations of the *Laozi* manage to highlight certain aspects of the text, but in the end fail to capture its central theme:

While it is certainly not a gross distortion to view the *Laozi* as a manual for politics, military strategy or *qigong* 氣功 , such explanations of the text fail to penetrate the surface and get to the deeper, more substantial and unified principle that informs the philosophy of Laozi. A reverence for "naturalness" is the most distinguishing characteristic of the Daoist scheme of values, and is what most clearly separates it from Confucian theory, which extols hard work and striving. (Liu 1999: 211–12)

Jia Dongcheng has something similar in mind when, after noting the practical benefits of wu-wei—achieving a long and vigorous life, succeeding in military actions, bringing the world into harmony—he adds:

Although all of these benefits would seem to be related to the political technique of "doing nothing and leaving nothing undone," it is my opinion that their more important function is to display a level of quiet kindness and tolerance and the spiritual state of the "one who is a skilled soldier" or the "sage." This demonstrates the degree to which Laozi is exploring a deeper spiritual and psychological level than those interested in the merely mundane and concrete problems of government or military strategy. (Jia 1989: 91)

We can thus dismiss any crudely instrumentalist interpretation of the text, for it is clear that the Laozian sage no longer shares ordinary human desires or values. The fact does remain, however, that the sage still possesses *some* values: she values, for instance, being without ordinary human values, or being "fed by the Mother." This sort of regarding is set off by Laozi from the values of the multitude, for—unlike vulgar values—the Way and the "Mother" are things which genuinely *are* to be valued. There is a parallel here with the Daoist "metaknowledge" discussed earlier that leads the sage to eschew conventional sorts of "knowledge." Valuing being "fed by the Mother," then, can be seen as a kind of metavalue, because it exists on an entirely different plane than ordinary human values. Nonetheless, there is still something of a paradox involved in valuing being without values, and it is not entirely clear whether or not calling this a "metavalue" really allows us to escape the dilemma cleanly. This brings us right to the center of the paradox of wu-wei as it manifests itself in the *Laozi*.

Most readers come away from the *Laozi* with the sense that its teachings are somewhat paradoxical, and the desire to unravel this paradox may be part of the enduring appeal of the text. To begin with, though, it is necessary to dispose of the all-too-common notion that the paradox in Laozi's thought is to be located in the principle of reversion. At first glance, it seems paradoxical that Laozi advocates holding to weakness so that one might be strong, since it would seem that this strength, once obtained, would eventually cycle back into weakness. As we have seen above, however, reversion is not a cycle in which strength becomes weakness and vice versa, but rather a law of return in which the "Something" (the conventionally strong, hard, etc.) reverts back to the "Nothing" (weakness, softness, etc.). As D. C. Lau notes,

> To turn back [*fan* 反] is to "return to one's roots," and one's roots are of course the submissive and the weak. All that is said is that a thing, once it has reached the limits of its development, will return to its root, i.e. decline. This is inevitable. Nothing is said about the development being equally inevitable once one has returned to one's roots. (Lau 1963: 27)

Holding to weakness is thus the key to true, enduring strength. Similarly, the apparent paradox in preferring to be weak so that one might be strong is resolved when one understands that the "weakness" that is preferred is "weak" only in the conventional sense. Laozi's words are only paradoxical if one fails to see the distinction between ironic and nonironic uses of such words as "weakness" and "knowledge." The principle of reversion is a "straightforward teaching which seems paradoxical," but this paradox lies only on the surface.

The deeper paradoxes are those that—as we shall see—appear to plague any internalist position. To begin with, there is the "theodicy" problem:[59] if we are "naturally" in harmony with the Way (in all of the senses of "natural" noted earlier), how did the world ever fall away from such perfection, and why is so much effort required to bring us back? Chapter 37 in particular begs this question:

> The Way is enduringly nameless.
> If the lords and kings were able to guard [*shou* 守] it,
> The myriad things would transform of their own accord [*zihua* 自化].
> If, in transforming, desire should arise among them,
> I would suppress [*zhen* 鎮] it with the nameless uncarved wood.
> Then they would have no desire.

If desire is not natural, though, why does it continue to arise? And is not "suppressing it" an example of the worst sort of unnatural force? To phrase this question another way, if our essential selves are really already in harmony with the Way—and will lead us to accord with it "of-ourselves"—how did they ever get covered up? The Laozian sage boasts, "The multitude all have a purpose [*youyi* 有以] / I alone am ignorant and uncouth/ My desires alone are different from those of others / Because I value being fed by the Mother" (chapter 20). If the sage really is so different from other people, though, in what way can his Way be said to be "natural" for us all? Perhaps the opposite is true: that it is natural for us to *have* a purpose, to *be* clever and to ignore "the Mother." The implicit admonition to love the primordial Mother in this passage seems like an example of the worst sort of forced filiality condemned in chapters 18 and 19.

Related to the theodicy problem is the more conceptual problem of how it is possible to try not to try. Laozi urges us behaviorally to "do wu-wei" (*weiwuwei*) and cognitively to "grasp oneness" (*zhiyi* 執一) or "grasp the image" (*zhixiang* 執象) of the Way, while at the same time he of course systematically condemns doing and grasping.[60] He urges us personally to reduce our desires and politically to reduce the size of the state, while at the same time warning us that human nature is a piece of uncarved wood that should not be touched, and that the state is a "sacred vessel" that should not be handled:

> I see that those who wish to take the world and do something to it
>   [*weizhi* 為之]
> Will not be successful.
> The world is a sacred vessel—not a thing that can be worked upon [*wei* 為].
> Work on it and you will ruin it;
> Try to grasp it and you will lose it. (29)

Perhaps a more sympathetic reading of Herrlee Creel's distinction between "contemplative" and "purposive" Daoism is to see it as a kind of response to these deep tensions in the internalist position. Creel writes of the two "types" of Daoism that they

> are not merely different. Logically and essentially they are incompatible. For the calm and poise and inner power that comes from a complete detachment from human affairs are necessarily lost the moment one seeks to intervene in human affairs. . . . The Daoist works are ingenious in informing us that these activities are not in fact meddling with things, but only designed to return the people to their natural state, but this does not really alter the case. (Creel 1970: 45)

If one were genuinely without regarding or normal human desires, Creel believes, one would be unable to act in the world, whereas an ability to act in the world and achieve certain ends reveals the presence of hidden desires and values. Although we have rejected his specific categorizations, we should observe that Creel has managed to put his finger on the crux of this aspect of paradox of wu-wei in the *Laozi*, and would have no truck with the sort of "ingenuity" that would try to resolve it.

Many such ingenious attempts have been made, of course. David Loy has devoted some effort to resolving the problem of how one might "wei-wu-wei"—a problem he describes as the most basic paradox of Daoism. He believes the answer to be a kind of "nondual action," where "there is no bifurcation between subject and object: no awareness of an agent that is believed to *do* the action as being distinct from an objective action that is *done*" (Loy 1985: 73). This seems merely to be a displacement of the paradox, however, for the question remains of how one can consciously (that is, with awareness) try to become unaware of something. Other scholars have approached the problem by distinguishing between two or more different levels of wu-wei. Zhang Qin, for instance, distinguishes between a "higher" sort of wu-wei, which characterizes the Way or Heaven and is entirely free from conscious purposes or purposive action, and a "lower" sort of wu-wei, which merely involves eliminating unnatural actions and does not necessarily rule out consciously and actively seeking to follow the inherent nature of the myriad things (Zhang 1995). One problem with this theory, though, is that Heaven is apparently *not* wu-wei in either the sense of non-doing or being without purposes. Heaven *does* quite a bit—it is, in fact, the generator and nurturer (along with the Earth) of all of the myriad things and the entire phenomenal world. At the same time, it would seem to have certain purposes of its own: for instance, to press down the high and raise up the low, or take from that which has excess and give to that which is deficient. If even Heaven is not "wu-wei" in Zhang Qin's "higher" sense, then it would seem that such an attempt to distinguish different levels of wu-wei is not a viable solution to the paradox.

Another notable attempt is that of A. C. Graham. In response to the question, "Does the sage *prefer* being without desires to having desires?" Graham tries to finesse the issue by answering the question in the negative: "No, for that would imply analysis and calculation of means to end. The sage, perfectly illuminated about his situation, gravitates towards his survival with the spontaneity of a natural process" (Graham 1989: 230). This answer is part of Graham's larger project of providing an account of Daoist spontaneity in terms of pure "awareness of the situation."[61] This is not the place for a full discussion of the merits of Graham's project, which in any case was formulated more with Zhuangzi than Laozi in mind. We can only note that the text of the *Laozi*, at least, would seem to contradict Graham here. As we have noted above, the Laozian sage clearly engages in regarding of a certain sort—knowing to "value being fed by the Mother"—and his actions are guided by a kind of metaknowledge. Although the sage does take natural processes as metaphorical models to be emulated, this is not to say that the sage himself *becomes* a natural process, whatever that might even mean. In addition, Graham is also assuming an impersonalized conception of "natural process," whereas "nature" (as embodied in Heaven or the Way) in Laozi's scheme has purposes of its own, and thus continues to possess a certain anthropomorphic character.

That there is a paradox involved here did not escape the notice of the authors of the *Laozi* themselves, and it might be helpful to look at their treatment of it. It is precisely this paradox that is being played with in the famous lines that open the Mawangdui versions of the text (chapter 38 of the Wang Bi edition), "The highest Virtue is not virtuous, and so it possesses Virtue," and let us recall as well the opening chapter of the received Wang Bi version (chapter 38 in the Mawangdui texts):

> The Way that can be spoken of is not the enduring Way;
> The name which can be named is not the enduring name.

The nameless is the beginning of the myriad things;
The named is the mother of the myriad things.
Hence, enduringly without desires [*wuyu* 無欲], I am able to gaze upon
its secrets,
While also enduringly possessed of desires [*youyu* 有欲], I am able to
gaze upon its manifestations.[62]
The two emerge together;
Are given different names, but refer to the same thing:
Mystery [*xuan* 玄] upon mystery—
The door to a multitude of secrets.

As I have noted above in my discussion of this passage, it is by being without desires that one can participate in the realm of "Nothing" (the realm of Heaven and the Way) and thereby acquire the secret to success in the realm of "Something" (the phenomenal, human realm). That this requires simultaneously being without desires and being possessed of desires is what the author seems to mean by saying that "the two emerge together / Are given different names, but refer to the same thing." That there is a paradox involved in this demand is what is meant by saying that this teaching involves a "mystery upon mystery" (*xuan zhi you xuan* 玄之又玄). As Alan Fox has noted in his discussion of the term *xuan*,

> In our modern culture, we have trivialized the word "mystery" by asso-
> ciating it with detective novels and television shows, where we know
> that this "mystery" will be solved by the end of the story. But tradition-
> ally, however, a mystery was not something that *had not yet* been solved,
> but which *never could be* solved. It is in this sense that, for instance, the
> Christian trinity is described as a mystery—the three persons of God
> which are nevertheless understood to constitute a single God. The infini-
> tude, the unfathomable variety of possibility is itself a mystery, the fact
> that things could be other than what they are, even their own opposite.
> (Fox 1995: 11–12)

Laozian wu-wei, properly understood, can thus be seen as an attempt to com-bine and therefore transcend Creel's two categories of "contemplative" and "pur-posive." The text actually gives expression to a subtle religious sensibility that is built around the deepest level of the paradox of wu-wei: the mystery of trying not to try, desiring not to desire. Free of desires, the Laozian sage participates in the realm of Nothing and gazes upon the secret of the law of reversion; possessed of desires, she applies this principle in the world, thereby both attaining her own ends and helping the myriad things to return to naturalness. Creel is perfectly cor-rect in arguing that the two states—being free of desires and possessed of desires—are logically contradictory, but it is precisely an ability to transcend this contradiction that Laozi requires of his reader. Hence the series of questions we saw in chapter 10:

Carrying on your back your troubled earth soul,
Can you embrace the One and not let it go?
Concentrating your *qi* until it is supple,

Can you be like an infant?
Polishing and cleaning your mysterious mirror,
Can you leave it without a blemish?
Caring for the people and ordering the state,
Can you not employ knowledge?
Opening and closing the gates of Heaven,
Can you play the role of the female?
With your illumined clarity [*mingbai* 明白] reaching to the four quarters,
Can you not employ knowledge?

Participating in the mystery of straddling both desire and nondesire—caring for the people and yet not employing knowledge, having one's illumination penetrate to the four quarters and yet remaining ignorant, benefitting the myriad things and yet not dwelling upon it—is what allows one to arrive at Laozian's ideal spiritual state and attain the cosmic power of "mysterious virtue."

What is particularly interesting in the passage just cited is the suggestion of physical practices. Although we questioned earlier the claims of those such as Maspero or Roth that the *Laozi* as a whole should be understood as a manual for meditative or other physical techniques, the argument that the authors of at least part of the text were familiar with such techniques or even themselves practitioners is not implausible. Chapter 10 in particular—with its mentions of "concentrating the *qi*" and "cleaning the mysterious mirror"—reveals an awareness of meditative and/or breathing techniques that we later[63] find described in a much more elaborate form in such texts as the "Inner Training" (*neiye* 內業) and "Techniques of the Mind" (*xinshu* 心術) chapters of the *Guanzi*, or in the recently discovered medical texts from Mawangdui.[64] These cryptic references to meditative practices point in the direction of an interesting new strategy of circumventing at least one aspect of the paradox of wu-wei by means of the body. That is to say, although it leaves the theodicy problem unresolved, one way of dealing with the cognitive paradox of "trying not to try" is turn away from the cognitive and toward the behavioral: for instance, toward a regimen of meditative or breathing practices designed to bring about psycho-physiological changes in the self. Faced by the problem of how to desire not to desire, then, one solution might be a purely physical set of exercises that, for instance, alter the *qi* in such a way that desire is eventually nipped in the bud at the physiological level.

One might argue that a rather vague version of this is something like what Confucius actually had in mind, in the sense that ritual practice, music, and study—though consciously pursued in the early stages of education—eventually bring about changes in one's "native substance" (*zhi* 質) and psycho-physiological disposition. The sort of practices hinted at in chapter 10 of the *Laozi*, however, represent an entirely new level of sophistication concerning the psycho-physiological makeup of the self, accompanied by similarly advanced and specific technologies for altering this makeup. It is important that we first examine these new techniques before moving on to our treatment of *Mencius*, for we will find in the *Mencius* a reformulated internalism that not only attempts to defuse some of the conceptual tensions inherent in Laozian wu-wei, but that also responds to—either by incorporating or rejecting—some of the new techniques for altering the self that had arisen to challenge Confucianism since the time of the *Analects*.

Chapter 4

方術

New Technologies of the Self:

Wu-wei in the "Inner Training" and the

Mohist Rejection of Wu-wei

In this chapter I will briefly review two developments in Warring States thought that will have an impact on the rest of my discussion. The nature of these developments is hinted at in *Mencius* 3:B:9, where we are treated to a short account of the heresies that have forced Mencius to resort to disputation:

> The teachings of Yang Zhu and Mo Di [Mozi] fill the world—if you look at contemporary teachings, the ones that don't incline toward Yang incline toward Mo. Mr. Yang advocates egoism [*weiwo* 為我], which amounts to being without a ruler; Mo advocates impartial caring [*jian'ai* 兼愛], which amounts to being without a father. To be without a father or without a ruler is to live like a beast.

We find a similar description in 7:A:26:

> Yang Zhu adopts the stance of egoism. If he could benefit the world merely by pulling out a single hair he would not do it.[1] Mozi teaches impartial caring. If by shaving his skull or standing on his head he could benefit the world, he would do it.

The purpose of this chapter is to briefly fill out and balance this rather polemical account of Yang Zhu and Mohism, as well as to mention some other contemporary strands of thought that seem to have been factors in the development of Mencius's thought.[2] We will see that these new conceptions of the self and "new technologies" for dealing with it will have a powerful effect on Warring States discourse concerning wu-wei.

Yang Zhu and the "Discovery of the Body"

Very little is known of the life and thought of Yang Zhu, who is thought to have flourished between 370 and 319 B.C., based upon accounts of his audience with King Hui of Liang.[3] Unlike Mozi, no direct records of his teachings survive, and his doctrines must therefore be reconstructed on the basis of secondhand accounts. The most often cited and helpful of these is a passage in chapter 13 of the *Huainanzi*, which attributes three basic beliefs to Yang Zhu: keeping one's nature (*xing* 性) intact, protecting one's genuineness (*zhen* 真), and not letting the body be tied by external things. Certain chapters of the *Lüshi Chunqiu* have been associated with Yangism, and in 1962 Kuan Feng identified three chapters of the *Zhuangzi* (28, 29, and 31, to which A. C. Graham has added chapter 30) as Yangist works.[4] This later Yangist literature makes it possible for us to assess the import of the three beliefs mentioned in the *Huainanzi*. As Graham has observed, Yangism, like Mohism, is concerned with benefit (*li* 利), but this benefit is assessed in radically individualist terms:

> [Yangism] starts from the same calculations of benefit and harm as does Mohism, but its question is not, "How shall we benefit the world?" but "What is truly beneficial to man?", more specifically, "What is truly beneficial to myself?" Is it wealth and power, as the vulgar suppose? Or the life and health of the body and the satisfaction of the senses? The Mohists cared only for the useful, the Yangists ask, "Useful for what?" (Graham 1989: 56)

Based upon Graham's reconstruction, the "nature" that Yang Zhu sought to preserve refers to the capacity given by Heaven for one to live out one's years; "genuineness" refers to the spontaneous tendencies of one who is not yet corrupted by culture; and "not letting the body get tied by things" refers to valuing one's own life over the attainment of an official position. Such an egoistic doctrine represents quite a radical departure from the public-mindedness of Confucius or Mozi, and many scholars have argued that Yangism in fact represents a radical new conception of the self that emerged during the chaos of the Warring States period: the conception of the self as a biological individual independent of all social roles. John Emerson even goes so far as to attribute to Yang Zhu the "discovery of the body" in early China (Emerson 1996).

This rather overstates the case,[5] but points in the right direction. In Graham's view, Yang Zhu is the first Chinese thinker to thematize the subject of *xing* 性 (human nature),[6] and together with some other early thinkers such as Song Xing and the anonymous author of the "Inner Training" (*neiye* 內業) chapter of the *Guanzi*, Yang Zhu thus helped to shift Chinese religious and philosophical discourse away from an almost exclusive concern with social roles and the public good and toward the consideration of the private, biological individual. Song Xing is described as calling for a turn away from public standards of conduct championed by the Confucians and Mohists and urging the individual to concern himself with the "conduct of the heart/mind" (*xinzhixing* 心之行), while "Inner

Training" is considered by some scholars to be the earliest text in China that links self-cultivation to the development of such physiological factors as the *qi*. Next, I will briefly consider the "Inner Training"—probably the earliest extant example of this new genre of writing—in order to describe the outlines of this new model of the self that had such an influence on subsequent Warring States thought.

The New Model of the Self in the "Inner Training"

As scholars such as Harold Roth and Donald Harper have argued, the "Inner Training" and the metaphors it employs have to be understood in the context of the developing Warring States literature on medical theory, macrobiotic hygiene, and various occult practices—much of which is preserved only in relatively recently discovered archaeological texts—that were much more popular than the received textual tradition would indicate. Harper makes the point that this type of "natural philosophy" and occult practice was quite widespread in the third to second centuries B.C., and observes that

> were one to reconstruct the worldview of the Warring States elite based solely on the evidence of the tombs excavated to date, ideas related to natural philosophy and occult thought would occupy a prominent place—more prominent than would result from a reconstruction based on the received record, particularly were that record to be narrowed down to the writings attributed to the masters of philosophy. (Harper 1999: 820)

The earliest of the medical texts we possess is an inscription on a dodecagonal block of jade entitled "Circulating the *Qi*" (*xingqi* 行氣), thought to be from the late Warring States period (late fourth to early third century B.C.).[7] There are also the Mawangdui medical texts recently translated by Harper that, in his opinion, "are no earlier than the third century B.C.," with the Mawangdui manuscripts themselves being copied not long after the original editions were written (1998: 21). The actual origins of these practices and theories may be much older. Harper has noted the connection between physicians and shamans (1998: 43), and P. J. Thiel, A. C. Graham, Kristopher Schipper, and Jordan Paper have also associated natural philosophy and occult practices with venerable Chinese shamanistic practice communities.[8]

However venerable their origin, however, it is only in texts such as "Inner Training" and perhaps portions of the *Laozi* that we see evidence of such practices filtering up into the realm of philosophical debate. While acknowledging the clear relationship between these systems of natural and occult philosophy and "mystical" cultivation texts such as the "Inner Training"—sharing as they do a common set of vocabulary and metaphors (Harper 1995) and a concern with an overlapping set of practices, including circulating the *qi* and assuming proper physical postures—Roth still wants to distinguish between mere physical hygiene

and the "apophatic practice" of inner cultivation (Roth 1999: 168–172). He spec-
ulates that the adoption of naturalistic and occult terminology and practices was
the result of shamanistic and other technical practitioners (*fangshu* 方術) mixing
with philosophers at various pre-Qin "think-tanks" such as the Jixia Academy in
Qi (345–280 B.C.), the court of Lü Buwei in Qin (250–239) and the court of Liu
An at Huainan (150–122) (Roth 1999: 168). Among these technical practitioners
were healers and physicians of various sorts, whose technical terminology
enjoyed wide use in the developing field of medicine, whence it began to penetrate the lay lexicon and consciousness.[9] Whatever the specific pathway for the
entry of this new model of the self into common literary parlance, it is clear
that—beginning with the *Mencius*—it became the default model in terms of
which self-cultivation was discussed. We will thus find Mencius, Zhuangzi, and
Xunzi relying upon it in formulating their conceptions of wu-wei.[10]

In the opinion of Harold Roth, who has spent the past several decades studying early self-cultivationist texts, the earliest extant writing in this genre is the
"Inner Training" (*neiye* 內業) chapter of the *Guanzi*, a collection of writings that
originated circa 300 B.C. in the state of Qi, and which was added to until as late
as 26 B.C. Although the "Inner Training" is often discussed together with three
other texts from the *Guanzi*—the "Techniques of the Heart/Mind (parts 1 and 2)"
and "Purification of the Heart/Mind"—Roth believes the "Inner Training" to be
unrelated to and earlier than these other self-cultivation texts (Roth 1999: 18). In
the interest of brevity I will use the text of the "Inner Training"[11] as the focus of
my discussion.

Focus on the Body

Although sharing with the *Laozi* such soteriological goals as stillness or harmony
(*he* 和), the soteriological strategy of the "Inner Training" is much more explicitly physiological. Throughout the text there are concrete references to the physical body (*xing* 形) or parts of the body: the four limbs (*sizhi* 四肢), sense organs
(*ermu* 耳目), skin (*pifu* 皮膚), muscles and bones (*jingu* 筋骨).The ingestion of
food is portrayed as directly effecting the *qi* and the blood (91), and thus as something with physio-spiritual implications. Accompanying this increased focus on
the physical body is a slight shift in the manner in which the SELF AS CONTAINER
metaphor is conceptualized. As we have seen, this metaphor appears in the *Analects*, but there the categories of "inner" and "outer" are often used in a broad
sense that extends beyond the body to include certain actions and social relationships viewed as somehow proper to the self. In the *Laozi* there are vague suggestions of the physical body as the container, but this version of the metaphor is not
explicitly invoked with the terminology of "inner" and "outer." As its title would
suggest, the "Inner Training" makes systematic and explicit use of the SELF AS
CONTAINER metaphor, and here it is clear that the container involved is conceived
of as the physical body. For instance, in chapter 18 we read that:

> Once you have made the heart/mind whole within you [*zaizhong* 在中],
> It cannot be obscured or concealed.

It will be known in your actions and countenance,
And will reveal itself in the hue of your skin [*fusi* 膚色].

Here the heart/mind seems to be understood partially as an object located within the container of the body, and therefore not directly visible. The fact that it can be made "whole," however, indicates that is at least partially understood metaphorically as a kind of substance not coterminous with the physical organ—a substance that can somehow spread from the inside to the outside surface of the container-body. Once this substance is made whole, then, its state of being is revealed indirectly through one's actions and appearance, even affecting the "hue of one's skin." We will see that this metaphor of one's heart/mind or inner virtue as a substance that can spread from the inside of one's body to appear in the skin or in the pupils will become a common theme in post–"Inner Training" writings.

In chapter 21 we read, "Let a balanced and aligned [breathing] fill your chest / And it will swirl and blend in your heart/mind" (87). We see in this couplet a more physiological conception of the *xin* than we have seen previously: the *xin* is a concrete organ like the chest (*xiong* 胸) and can be affected by the mechanical motion of the chest. This is one aspect of a more general shift in the conception of the *xin* that we can discern in the "Inner Training" from a rather vague locus of will, emotions, and thought (as in the *Analects* and *Laozi*) to a concrete organ within the body serving as the locus of thought (*yi* 意) and intentions (*zhi* 志)— the "heart/mind" rather than the "heart." In chapter 5 we see the *xin* portrayed metaphorically as a container within which the Way can come and dwell (*chu* 處) or come to rest (*zhi* 止), and here we also see a connection established between a "cultivated heart/mind" (*xiuxin* 修心) and the "stilling of thoughts" (*jingyi* 靜意). It is also in the "Inner Training" that we first see the heart/mind singled out as the metaphorical "ruler" of the other parts of the self, and thus as the locus of self-cultivation:[12]

How does one release it?
[The secret] lies in putting the heart/mind at ease [*xinan* 心安].
If my heart/mind is ordered [*zhi* 治], my senses will be ordered.
If my heart/mind is at ease, my senses will be at ease.
The one who orders is the heart/mind;
The one who puts at ease is the heart/mind.
By means of the heart/mind one stores the heart/mind;
Within the heart/mind there is another heart/mind.
This heart/mind within the heart/mind represents thought [*yi*] before it
  becomes words.
Once there are thoughts, there is the physical body;
Once there is the physical body, there are words;
Once there are words, they are implemented;
Once they are implemented, there is order. (73)[13]

Another interesting development to note is that the description in chapter 21 of the breath or *qi* as "swirling and blending" (*lunxia* 淪洽), which marks the appearance in the elite textual tradition of the *QI* AS WATER metaphor. The locus classicus for the *QI AS WATER* metaphor can perhaps be identified as an essay in the *Guanzi* on the subject of water, which reads in part: "Water is the blood and *qi* of the earth, like the stuff that penetrates and flows [*tongliu* 通流] through the muscles and vessels of the body." In this essay water is characterized as "quintessential" (*jing* 精) and is described as possessing so many powers—"the standard for the myriad things . . . the basis for obtaining and losing . . . there is no place it does not fill, no place it does not dwell"—that the author is moved to declare: "This is why it is said that water is spiritual [*shen* 神]" (*Guanzi* Book 39; Rickett 1998: 100–101). Whatever its specific origins, this metaphorical conception of *qi* as water and the association of the *qi* with the quintessential and the spiritual is a theme found throughout the "Inner Training." *Qi* is described as "infusing" (*chong* 充) and "filling" (*ying* 盈) the heart/mind (59), and is connected to the quintessential and the spirit in various ways. While the connection between the *qi* and the quintessential is most direct—in chapter 8 the quintessential is simply defined as the "quintessential *qi*" (61)—the *qi*-spirit connection, though less direct, is no less clear. In chapter 19, for example, we are told that one should "concentrate one's *qi* like a spirit," and that the power of the ghosts and spirits represents the "culmination of the quintessential *qi*" (83). This conceptual link between *qi*, the quintessential, and the spirit allows the metaphorical qualities of *qi* to be transferred to these other terms, and hence the quintessential, for instance, can be described as "flowing" (*liu* 流) (47). Chapter 15, which describes sagehood as involving the accumulation of the "quintessential *qi*," extends the *QI AS WATER* metaphor to obtain several powerful new expressions:

> When the quintessential is preserved and allowed to grow of its own
>   accord [*zisheng* 自生],
> On the outside a sense of ease [*an* 安] will flourish.
> Stored inside, it can serve as a spring or source [*quanyuan* 泉原],
> Floodlike [*haoran* 浩然], harmonized and balanced,
> Serving as the deep pool [*yuan* 淵] of *qi*.
> If this deep pool does not dry up
> The four limbs will be firm;
> If this spring is not exhausted
> [The *qi*] can well up [*da* 達] through the nine apertures.
> Only then can one exhaust Heaven and Earth,
> And cover all within the Four Seas (75).

As we shall see, the parallels in language between this passage and Mencius's account of self-cultivation are too exact to be attributed to chance.[14] Although this new focus on the *qi* and its coordination with *jing* and *shen* is likely derived from the rising disciplines of medical theory and natural/occult philosophy, after the "Inner Training" it becomes a standard part of Warring States metaphysics.

Wu-wei and the Paradox of Wu-wei in "Inner Training"

We see almost all of the standard metaphors for wu-wei in the short text of the "Inner Training." The most common metaphors are from the "at ease" family—

an 安 (at ease) and *jing* 靜 (stillness) appear multiple times. We see many appearances of the "so-of-itself" metaphor from the *Laozi*—with many processes described as occurring in a "spontaneous" (lit. *zi* 自, "from-the-inside") fashion—and an instance of the "timeliness" (*shi* 時) concept familiar from the *Analects* combined with the following (*cong* 從) metaphor in a phrase that prefigures the conception of wu-wei found in the *Zhuangzi*: "[The sage] changes along with the times [*shi*] and yet is not altered / Follows [*cong*] the shifting of things and yet is not moved" (59). Unself-consciousness metaphors are less common, but not entirely absent, as we see in this description of the "solitary joy" that comes from following the "Inner Training" soteriological path:

> Enlarge the heart/mind and then let it go [*fang* 放],
> Relax your *qi* and let it expand,
> Put your body at ease [*an*] and be unmoving . . .
> [Then you will be:]
> Relaxed and restful [*kuanshu* 寬舒], and yet acutely sensitive [*ren* 仁];[15]
> Taking solitary joy [*dule* 獨樂] in the self.
> This is called the "revolving *qi*" [*yunqi* 運氣],
> [The state of] thoughts and behavior being like Heaven. (93)

Like the author(s) of the *Laozi*, the author(s) of the "Inner Training" are also aware at some level of the paradox of wu-wei. They are careful to note, for instance, that wu-wei cannot be forced. Describing the numinous *qi* that allows one wu-wei freedom and power, they warn:

> This *qi*
> cannot be stopped-detained [*zhi* 止] through exertion of effort [*li* 力],
> And yet can be put at ease [*an*] by means of Virtue;
> It cannot be summoned by speech,
> But can nonetheless be welcomed by one's awareness [*yi* 意]. (49)

The process of "welcoming it with the awareness," in turn, seems to be a rather sticky business, since is not something that can be consciously pursued:

> You think about it [*sizhi* 思之], think about it
> Then think about it some more.
> Think about it and yet never penetrate it.
> [In contrast], the ghosts and spirits are able to penetrate it
> Not because they have exerted effort [*li* 力],
> But because they represent the culmination of the quintessential *qi*.
> Simply align your four limbs
> And the blood and *qi* will be stilled.
> Unify your awareness and concentrate your heart/mind
> And then your ears and eyes will not overflow,
> And even that which is far-away will seem close. (83)

The key to attaining wu-wei, then, seems to be simply realizing that you already have it. The "ghosts and spirits" do not *try* to be spiritually powerful, they simply *are* powerful. How, though, does one realize this innate spiritual power? This passage seems to suggest that simply taking up a particular *physical* posture is enough: "Simply align your four limbs / And the blood and *qi* will be stilled." Note, however, that this is immediately followed by the injunction: "Unify your awareness and concentrate your heart/mind / And then your ears and eyes will not overflow." It thus appears that a combination of physical and mental discipline is required. We see a similar combination in the passage that follows this one. After advising the readers not to "make plans" (*tu* 圖), lest their vitality desert them, it is said:

> With regard to eating, it is best not to eat one's fill;
> With regard to thinking, it is best not to go too far.
> Equalize these things through regulation and fitting [*shi* 適]
> And then it [the quintessential *qi*] will naturally ["of-itself"] arrive [*zizhi* 自至]. (85; cf. 67)

The "Inner Training" soteriological path thus seems, like that of the *Laozi*, to have both behavioral and cognitive components. On the one hand, it is necessary to "clean out" the "lodging place" of the spirit through physical hygiene and posture, while, on the other, one must also "still one's heart/mind" and stop *worrying* about attaining the quintessential *qi* or spiritual power:

> There is a spirit that naturally resides in the self.
> One moment it goes, the next it returns,
> And no one is able to grasp it with thought [*si*].
> If you lose it, you will inevitably be disordered;
> If you get it, you will inevitably be ordered.
> Diligently clean out its lodging place [*she* 舍],
> And the quintessential will come of its own accord [*zilai* 自來].
> Still your efforts to reflect or think about it;
> And quiet your desire to contemplate or control it.
> Be reverent, awestruck, and diligent,
> And the quintessential will be naturally settled [*ziding* 自定].
> Get it and do not cast it aside:
> Then your ears and eyes will not overflow,
> And your heart/mind will have no other plans.
> Align your heart/mind within,
> And the myriad things will be properly dealt with. (71)

The behavioral side seems quite straightforward: it is necessary merely to align the body and regulate the intake of food. The problem, as we might expect by this point, is how one goes about the cognitive project of "aligning the heart/mind within." While claiming that we are "naturally" infused with the wonderful *qi*, the author(s) of the "Inner Training" are nonetheless aware that most of us are not in touch with this innate perfection. In chapter 3, an explanation of sorts is offered for this phenomenon:

> In general, the form of the heart/mind
> Is that it is naturally infused, naturally full [of *qi*],

It naturally gives birth to it, naturally perfects it.
The reason for losing [this state of perfection]
Is necessarily because of sorrow and joy, happiness and anger, and
desire for profit.
If you are able to reject [*qu* 去] sorrow and joy, happiness and anger, and
desire for profit,
The heart/mind will then return to equanimity.
This essential state of the heart/mind
Finds ease to be beneficial, and is thereby at peace [*ning* 寧].
Do not disturb it, do not disrupt it,
And harmony [*he* 和] will naturally be perfected. (51)

If it is the natural state of the heart/mind to be at ease, though, where do "sorrow and joy, happiness and anger" come from? More to the point, once afflicted by these pernicious emotions, how do we get rid of them? The answer suggested in the passage seems to be: "just do it." That is, just "reject" them. On the other hand, we cannot try *too* hard to reject them, since this would involve "planning" (*tu*) and thinking (*si*).

Do not pull, do not push
And fortune will return of its own accord [*zigui* 自歸]
And the Way will naturally come [*zilai* 自來] . . .
If you are still, you will get it,
If you are active, you will lose it. (95)

The paradox as manifested in this short text presents itself in the classic form faced by any internalist: if we already at some level possess perfection within, why do we not realize it already? These internalists urge us not to try too hard not to try, but if we do not try, how will we ever get there? Despite the suggestion of a new technique for circumventing the paradox of wu-wei by means of the body, the authors of the "Inner Training" still see a need for physical austerities to be accompanied by a kind of cognitive transformation, and thus do not escape the grasp of the paradox as we saw it in the *Laozi*: the problem of how one could try not to try. Nonetheless, they do manage to introduce to Warring States thought a new "technology of the self," perhaps derived from medical and other "natural" philosophies, but from this point on available to the philosophers as well: the idea of *qi*, the quintessential, and the spirit as active forces within the physical body that can be accessed and activated through physical and cognitive means. This suggestion that physiological forces within the self can be harnessed and allowed to do much of the work of wu-wei is a powerful one and will be adopted in different ways by all of the thinkers we have yet to consider.

The Mohist Rejection of Wu-wei

As he did not value wu-wei as a spiritual ideal, Mozi (5th c. B.C.) and his school will not detain us for long. There is one aspect of his thought, however, that is relevant to my discussion: his rather extreme rationalism and voluntarism, which in effect constitute a rejection of wu-wei. Mozi was perhaps the first person in the history of Chinese thought to concern himself with the formal aspects of argumentation and the logical evaluation of arguments, and his later followers became formidable logicians and theorists of language. We should note here that the Mohist concern with logic and formal argumentation—a "new technology" for altering the self—introduced a plethora of new technical terms into Warring States discourse. For instance, A. C. Graham notes that the terms *bian* 辯 (disputation), *shifei* 是非 (it is, it is not) and *qing* 情 (essence) appear as terms of art in the later Mohist *Canons*, and argues that the sense of these terms as they are used in the *Mencius*, *Zhuangzi*, and *Xunzi* cannot be understood except in the context of the Mohist conceptions of logic. In the *Canons*, Graham explains, "Discrimination [*bian*] proper is concerned, not with describing what is temporarily so of transitory objects, but with deciding whether something 'is this' or 'is not' [*shifei*], is ox or non-ox, and its judgements follow by strict necessity from the definition of names [*ming* 名]" (Graham 1978: 37). As for *qing*, "The *qing* of X is all that is conveyed in its definition, everything in it without which it would not be a genuine X, conceived as something behind its *xing* 形 ('shape') and *mao* 貌 ('looks')" (179).

Mozi's reason for devoting such attention to techniques of argumentation was his belief that a person could and would take up a belief once it had been adequately proven to them to be valid.[16] For instance, Mozi believed that the sorry state of his contemporaries was caused by partiality—that is, the sort of nepotism and cronyism he saw as encouraged by Confucian doctrines. He believed, though, that any reasonable person who objectively considered his doctrine of impartial caring (*jian'ai* 兼愛) would realize that adopting it would maximize benefits for all, and that this theoretical conviction alone would be enough to allow this person to put the principle into action. Self-cultivation thus has no place in Mozi's thought, since the adoption of right beliefs and practices is not a matter of transforming or developing dispositions within the self, but merely a matter of being logically convinced by an argument.

We can illustrate this phenomenon by considering the Mohist use of the metaphor of "extension" (*tui* 推 ; lit. pushing). Understood metaphorically, Mohist extension involves "pushing" one's understanding from its present location to a logically related "space." As it is defined in the Later Mohist *Canons*: "Extension involves using the sameness [*tong* 同] between what someone does not accept and what he does accept to propose the former" (Graham 1978: 482). Although this definition comes from the later *Canons*, extension in this sense is a technique employed by Mozi himself. For instance, his argument against offensive warfare made in chapter 17 is based upon extension in this sense:

If someone kills one person, we call this immoral [*buyi* 不義], and the perpetrator will necessarily pay for the crime with his own life. If we go along with [*wang* 往] this argument a bit further,[17] killing ten people should be ten times as immoral, and should be paid for with ten lives, while killing one hundred people should be one hundred times as immoral, and should be paid for with one hundred lives. At this point [*dangci* 當此], all of the gentlemen in the world know enough to condemn such behavior, and to call it immoral. And yet when we arrive at [*zhi* 至][18] the even greater act of immorality involved in attacking another state, they do not know enough to condemn it, and on the contrary praise it and call it moral. (Watson 1963: 51/ Wu Yujiang 1993: 198)

Misguided "gentlemen" know enough to condemn the murder of one, ten, or even one hundred people, but continue to praise offensive warfare (which kills hundreds upon hundreds of people) because they simply have failed to extend their reasoning far enough along the chain of analogies.

Mozi's belief seems to be that people, having now had pointed out to them the analogical connection between what they condemn in case #1 (murder) and yet praise in case #2 (mass murder in warfare), should be instantly able to "push" their condemnation of the first case to the second.

The process of extension as understood by Mozi requires very little expenditure of energy and can be accomplished instantaneously. There is thus no room in the Mohist picture for self-cultivation: people err as a result of improper beliefs (their understanding being in the "wrong place"), and the remedy is to move their understanding into a proper place through rational argumentation. As Nivison notes, "There is, for [Mozi] . . . no problem of inner psychic restructuring or nurturing needed to make a person morally perfect. In effect, he assumes this: a person is a kind of rational calculator" (1997: 96). Although this rather extreme rationalism and voluntarism was later moderated by the neo-Mohists discussed in chapter 5, the Mohist position nonetheless continued to preserve as one of its distinguishing characteristics this sort of self-cultivation externalist view of morality (*yi* 義), focus on rational persuasion, and lack of concern for the cultivation of dispositions—and hence for wu-wei. As we shall see, although Mencius at times understands "extension" in this logical, cognitive sense, he more commonly gives it a physiological, gradualist twist that allows the incorporation of self-cultivation technology derived from the "Inner Training."

Chapter 5

養端
Cultivating the Sprouts:
Wu-wei in the *Mencius*

Separated from Confucius by several generations, Mencius (fourth century B.C.) saw himself as being charged with carrying on and defending the Confucian religious vision in a new and largely hostile intellectual milieu. In the book that bears his name,[1] we find him responding to a wide range of questioners and opponents, from neo-Mohists to primitivist (Daoist) anarchists to cynical rulers interested only in the acquisition of power, wealth, and territory. Mencius has a response to all of these critics of Confucianism, defending the value of traditional Zhou culture, as well as the viability of Confucian wu-wei.

We find in the *Mencius* metaphors for wu-wei already familiar to us from the *Analects*—being "at ease" (*an*) or taking joy (*le*) in the Way—but these are overshadowed by new sets of metaphors developed in response to the challenges of the day. Perhaps most famous are Mencius's famous agricultural metaphors: being in touch with the root (*ben* 本)[2] of morality or cultivating (*yang* 養) the sprouts (*duan* 端) of virtue. In this way he associates Confucian morality with the "natural" (*ziran*) model of wu-wei championed by the *Laozi*. In addition,though, he links this family of metaphors with a separate, equally evocative water-based family: finding the "source" (*yuan* 原) of morality in order to access the "flood-like" (*haoran* 浩然) *qi*, allowing moral behavior to follow as inevitably and irresistibly as a spring breaking through the ground (*da* 達) or water bursting through a dike. The primal power of water also serves as the principal model for Mencius's conception of a force within the self that "cannot be stopped"—a metaphor for effortlessness seen only once in the *Laozi*, but one that becomes extremely important in the *Zhuangzi*. Finally, the water family of metaphors allows Mencius to link his project with the new physiological concern with *qi*, thereby giving him access to a range of liquid metaphors for wu-wei—such as "flowing" (*liu* 流) or "going along with the flow" (*shun* 順)—and providing him with a new conceptual schema for understanding the power of Virtue.

Contrasting Mencius's metaphorical conceptualization of wu-wei with that of the *Laozi* is also quite revealing. In place of Laozi's inert block of "uncarved wood," Mencius's primary metaphor is the dynamic "sprout," which has a natural direction and motive force of its own. In this way Mencius can portray the achievement of Confucian culture (*wen* 文)—rejected outright by the Laozian primitivists as unnatural—as the proper and unforced culmination of human nature. In other words, we can get the cultural "grain" without having to "tug on the sprouts," to borrow a metaphor from *Mencius* 2:A:2. The natural world is not static but has its own direction, and it is therefore no more "unnatural" for us to practice the Confucian rites than it is for wheat plants to produce a crop—in fact, it is precisely the Laozian/primitivist call for "return" that is truly unnatural. As I will discuss further, this agricultural metaphor also allows Mencius to deal with a tension that troubles a reader of the *Laozi*: why does one need to *try* to be "natural"? Nature for Mencius is not what the modern Chinese call *da ziran* 大自然 "the natural world" (i.e., untrammeled by human beings), but *domesticated* nature. Domesticated plants and channeled irrigation water thus represent for Mencius the perfect marriage of human effort with natural tendencies, and thereby serve as the ideal metaphors for the "cultivation" of wu-wei moral tendencies.

Barriers to Self-Cultivation

Many of the barriers to self-cultivation perceived by Mencius are similar to those noted by Confucius. Like Confucius, Mencius saw an obsession with material goods as a hindrance to morality (see 7:A:27 and 7:B:35), although enjoyment of these goods in their proper measure is not at all incompatible with the moral life. Mencius also shares Confucius's concern that excessive desire for social goods (a good name, honor) can similarly lead one astray; indeed, these sorts of goods are perhaps even more of a danger than material goods, since the corruption involved is more subtle and difficult to detect. Mencius, like Confucius, therefore reserves his most vicious criticism not for the profligate or glutton, but for the hypocritical "village worthy" (*xiangyuan* 鄉愿), who accommodates himself to the fallen ways of his contemporaries while still claiming to follow the Way of the ancients and of Heaven. By serving as a counterfeit model of virtue for the common people, the village worthy is in effect a "false prophet," not only blocking the development of true virtue in himself but also leading others astray. In a dialogue with his disciple Wan Zhang in 7:B:37, Mencius explains in great detail why it was that Confucius labeled the village worthy the "thief of Virtue" (*dezhizei* 德之賊):

> If everyone in a village praises a man as being worthy, and nowhere can you find someone who does not consider him worthy, what did Confucius mean by calling such a person a "thief of Virtue"?
>
> Those who try to censure him can find no basis; those who try to criticize him can find no faults. He follows along with all the vulgar trends and harmonizes with the sordid age. Dwelling in this way he seems dutiful and trustworthy; acting in this way, he seems honest and pure. The multitude are all pleased with him—he is pleased with himself as well—

and yet you cannot enter with him into the Way of Yao and Shun. This is why he is called the "thief of Virtue."

Confucius said, "I despise that which seems to be but in fact is not. I despise weeds [*you* 莠], for fear they will be mistaken for domesticated sprouts [*miao* 苗]. I despise glibness, for fear it will be mistaken for rightness. I despise cleverness of speech, for fear it will be mistaken for trustworthiness. I despise the tunes of Zheng, for fear they will be mistaken for true music. I despise the color purple, for fear it will be mistaken for pure vermillion. I despise the village worthy, for fear that he will be mistaken for one who truly possesses Virtue."

The gentleman simply returns to the standard [*jing* 經], that is all. Once the standard is properly arranged then the common people will be inspired; and once the common people are inspired, then we will see no more of deviant aberrations [*xiete* 邪慝].

The reference here to "deviant aberrations" brings us to the consideration of one barrier to proper self-cultivation that Confucius did not face, but which was perhaps the primary concern of Mencius: the deleterious effects of "deviant doctrines" (*xieshuo* 邪説). As we shall see, Mencius rejects the new idea (developed by the Mohists and logicians) that doctrines alone can be an effective motivator of proper behavior in human beings, but he was nonetheless aware of their potential to confuse people and lead them astray. It is for purely defensive reasons, then, that he was forced to gain "understanding of doctrines" (2:A:2) and to master the art of disputation (*bian* 辯). As an orthodox devotee of Confucian wu-wei, Mencius shares Confucius's aversion to speech and justifies his participation as a response to the exigencies of the age: "How could anyone think that I am fond of disputation! I simply cannot avoid it [*budeyi* 不得已]."[3] Defending Confucius's vision in the intellectual milieu of fourth century B.C. China, Mencius found himself confronting a wide variety of competing doctrines, many of which were explicitly critical of Confucianism. Whereas Confucius's mission was to preserve the culture of the Zhou for later generations, Mencius saw his task as defending this Way against the new heresies of Yang Zhu and Mozi:

> In an age of decline, with the Way hard to see, deviant theories and violent behavior arose. There were cases of ministers killing their rulers and sons killing their fathers. Confucius was alarmed and therefore composed the *Spring and Autumn Annals*. . . . No sage kings have arisen since then; the feudal lords have been able to give free rein to their wayward impulses, scholars without official position express their opinions without restraint, and the teachings of Yang Zhu and Mo Di fill the world. . . .

> If the Ways of Yang and Mo are not extinguished and the Way of Confucius not proclaimed, these heresies will deceive the common people and block the path of morality. . . . I am therefore alarmed. I wish to protect the Way of the Former Kings, put an end to Yang and Mo, do away

with other insidious teachings, and assure that advocates of deviant theories will not be able to arise again. (3:B:9)

These deviant teachings are of course not the only challenge Mencius faced. As we have seen, the rise of theories concerning the biological self and subsequent focus on the individual called for a reformulation of Confucius's vision in a way that would respond to the new state of the art in self-cultivation technology, which in turn required addressing the specific functions of the heart/mind (*xin*) and the *qi*. While the relative dating of the *Mencius* and texts such as the "Inner Training" is probably impossible to establish beyond doubt—and the question as to whether or not Yang Zhu was the first to thematize the issue of human nature is difficult to settle—it is nonetheless quite clear that Mencius was writing in an environment where the link between self-cultivation and physiological forces within the self was taken for granted, and where the subject of biological human nature could no longer be avoided. As Benjamin Schwartz notes, by the time of Mencius "Confucians might generally accept a common code of morality . . . but one could no longer avoid the question of the ontological source of this morality" (Schwartz 1985: 262). Confucius had postulated in a relatively vague fashion a cosmological source for the culture he sought to preserve, and even (as we have seen in chapter 2) provided hints that this culture might be grounded in human biology. It took Mencius, however, to fit such terse comments as Confucius's claim that "I have yet to meet the man who is as fond of Virtue as he is of sex" (*Analects* 9.18) into a systematic argument for a continuum between a fondness for Virtue and a fondness for sex and other basic human desires, and to present the ideal of Confucian moral perfection—symbolized by Confucius at age seventy, following the prompting of his heart and yet never transgressing the dictates of morality—as the perfect marriage of human biological dispositions and cultural mores. Not incidentally, demonstrating the link between Zhou cultural ideals and human biology also served to refute the Laozian/primitivist charge that Confucianism is unnatural and, as we shall see, helped to defuse the paradox of wu-wei as it existed in the *Analects*.

It is thus in response to a daunting constellation of challenges that Mencius developed his great innovations—the theory that human nature is good, the valorization of the unique role of the heart/mind, and the conception of the "flood-like *qi*"—and these innovations will be the main subject of this chapter. At the same time, it must also be understood throughout our treatment of Mencius that his thought remains essentially "Confucian," and the views examined in chapter 2 concerning the fallen state of humanity, the role of the gentleman in leading the world back into a state of harmony with the Way, the importance of the rites and the classics in self-cultivation, and the efficacy of Virtue will thus form the network of background assumptions against which we must assess the nature and scope of Mencius's own innovations.

Human Nature Is Good

Anyone even casually familiar with early Chinese thought is aware of the motto for which Mencius is most famous: "human nature is good" (*xingshan* 性善). Determining what exactly Mencius means by this claim requires us to look fairly closely at both of its elements. To begin with, the term *xing* 性 originally arose from the character *sheng* 生, and of course the two characters preserve a strong graphic relationship. *Sheng* refers to "life," an endowment from Heaven, and connotes of activity and productivity. *Xing* maintains this dynamic connotation, as well as the sense of being something granted by Heaven. In the opinion of A. C. Graham, *xing* comes to be distinguished from *sheng* to a certain extent by taking over the dynamic and developmental connotations of "life": "In the ordinary parlance of the fourth century B.C., the *xing* of an animate thing, in so far as it was distinguished from *sheng*, meant the course in which life completes its development if sufficiently nourished and not obstructed or injured from *outside*" (Graham 1967; emphasis added). The *xing* of a given thing thus refers to its natural course of development in many of the senses of "natural" (*ziran*) discussed in relationship to the *Laozi*: "originally so" in the sense of being present from birth; "uncoerced" or "effortless" in the sense of unfolding spontaneously; and "internal" in the sense of following a course of development independent from outside forces. We are thus justified in translating it as human "nature."

As Donald Munro has noted, *xing* has also a further specialized sense of the characteristic behavior of a thing—its *ergon* (Munro 1969: 66). The fact that *xing* can be used to refer to the characteristic behavior of a species is important for understanding certain exchanges in the *Mencius*, for many of the debates on this topic hinge upon a distinction between (a) *xing* in the more specific sense of those natural, developmental traits that are proper to human beings (and uniquely related to the project of morality) and (b) *xing* in a broader general sense of the entire collection of human propensities, including the amoral ones shared with animals. This is the point of 7:B:24, where Mencius grants that *xing* can be used in sense (b) to refer to the lesser desires for food and drink, but that since the pursuit of the objects of these desires is not the concern of the gentleman (who consigns them to "fate"), the gentleman holds to the proper sense (a) of *xing* (the moral tendencies):

> The disposition of the mouth toward flavors, the eye toward colors, the ear toward sounds, the nose toward scents, and the four limbs toward rest is human nature [*xing*]. Yet because there is fate [*ming* 命] involved,[4] the gentleman does not refer to them as human nature. The way benevolence pertains to the relationship between fathers and sons, dutifulness to the relationship between rulers and ministers, ritual propriety to the relation between guests and hosts, wisdom to worthiness, and sageliness to the Way of Heaven are all [somewhat dependent upon] fate. Yet because there is human nature involved, the gentleman does not refer to them as fate.[5]

We will see that, for Mencius, the Confucian virtues are portrayed, not as artificial qualities created through training in arbitrary forms, but rather as the natural fruition of inborn tendencies. Nevertheless, it is also important to keep in mind that one's "nature" is not to be confused with simply the set of traits and dispositions with which one is born, for there is a separate term that refers to one's endowment at birth, *gu* 故.[6] In saying that *xing* is *shan* 善, then, Mencius is not claiming that we are *born* fully good, but merely that we are *born for* goodness (Ivanhoe 1990a: 34). That is, our natural tendency—if we remain undamaged and are allowed to develop unhindered in a nurturing environment—is to become good.

This is the theme of 6:A:6, where Mencius is confronted with the views of the neo-Mohist[7] Gaozi 告子:

> Gongduzi said, "Gaozi says, 'There is neither good nor bad in human nature,' while others say, 'Human nature can be made good or it can be made bad, which is why the common people were fond of goodness when King Wen and King Wu arose, whereas the common people were fond of violence when King You and King Li arose.' There are also some who say, 'Some people are good by nature, and others are bad by nature...' Now you say that human nature is good. Does this mean that all the others are wrong?"

> Mencius replied, "As far as his essence [*qing* 情] is concerned, a man is capable of becoming good [*keyiweishan* 可以為善]. This is why I call it good. As for his becoming bad, that is not the fault of his innate stuff [*cai* 才]."

Many commentators have been puzzled by the fact that, having been questioned about *xing*, Mencius replies with a statement about *qing* 情. I think one of the more plausible explanations offered is offered by Kwong-loi Shun:

> Probably Mencius shifted from speaking of *xing* to speaking of *qing* in 6:A:6 to emphasize that although *xing* may be subject to the different influences that Gongduzi describes in putting his question to Mencius, all human beings have *something in common that is directed toward goodness and reveals what they are really like*, even if only some develop it. (Shun 1997: 216; emphasis added)[8]

This seems correct but—in light of the different senses of *xing* discussed earlier—there is perhaps another way of putting it. If we note that the lines that I have highlighted in the passage essentially describe sense (a) of *xing*, we can perhaps understand Mencius's retreat to the term *qing* as a response to the fact that Gongduzi in his initial question is clearly using *xing* in the looser, probably more common sense (b)—that is, what the people are given to doing in a particular environment where their less savory propensities might be brought to the fore. Mencius does not wish to dispute the fact that in a bad environment people will tend to be ruled by their "lesser" impulses (indeed, this is an observation that he himself makes on several occasions), nor that these impulses are foreign to human nature. By changing terms on Gongduzi, Mencius is essentially saying: you are using the term *xing* too loosely, so let me clarify what *I* mean when I say that "*xing* is good" by switching to some less ambiguous terminology.

The terms he then adopts— "essence" (*qing*) and "innate stuff" (*cai*; lit. timber)—are powerful new metaphorical tools. We have noted several times the dependence of the ESSENTIAL SELF metaphor on the SELF AS CONTAINER metaphor, with the essential self of a person being associated with the Subject and other aspects of the Self being relegated to the outside. By locating the goodness of human beings in their essence, Mencius is thus indirectly invoking the "so-of-itself"/"naturalness" (*ziran*) metaphor as well: goodness is what human beings do when they are acting "naturally" in all of the senses of that term noted in our discussion of Laozi. I will focus more on the second of these metaphors, though, because it belongs to what is probably the most prominent and vivid metaphor family in the text: that of agriculture. This metaphor system is crucial to understanding Mencius's claim about human nature because it does much of the cognitive work for both him and his audience, allowing them to draw upon conceptual structures grounded in a concrete domain with which they are quite familiar (agriculture and the behavior of plants) and apply them to the unfamiliar and abstract realm of moral self-cultivation.

As many scholars have noted, Mencius's claim about human nature does not refer merely to an empty "capacity" for good, but rather to an active tendency toward good[9] modeled upon the observable tendency of seedlings to grow into certain specific types of plants. As A. C. Graham puts it, human beings are "capable of being good" in the same way that they are capable of living to a ripe old age: under normal conditions, and assuming no untoward accidents or disease, human beings will live out their full life span. If someone dies at age twenty, this is not the fault of her "innate stuff" but rather is attributable to her growth having been injured (Graham 1967: 34–35). The agricultural metaphor is explicitly linked to moral development in the famous parable of "Ox Mountain" in 6:A:8, which incidentally also makes it clear that the link between innate stuff (*cai* 才 ; A. **dz'âi*) and timber/lumber (*cai* 材; A. **dz'âi*) is not accidental:

> The trees on Ox Mountain were once quite fine. But because the mountain is located on the outskirts of a great walled state, its trees are constantly subjected to the blows of the woodsmen's axes—how could it possibly retain its fineness? Because of the respite they get in the day and in the night, and the moistening from the rain and the dew, there is no lack of shoots and new leaves [*mengnie* 萌蘖] sprouting up from their stumps, but then the cattle and sheep are brought to graze upon them. That is why the mountain looks so bare. Seeing only its bareness, people assume that it never had any timber [*cai* 材]. But how could you say that this condition represents the nature [*xing*] of the mountain?
>
> As for what is originally present in [*cunhu* 存乎 ; lit. stored in] human beings, how can we deny that it includes the heart/mind of morality [*renyizhixin* 仁義之心]? As for a person's letting go of his pure heart/mind [*liangxin* 良心], it is like the woodsmen's axes and the trees: if day

after day they are chopped, how could they possibly retain their fineness? With the respite this person gets in the day and in the night, and the effect of the morning *qi* on him, his likes and dislikes again begin to resemble those of other people. But then in the course of his daily activities this *qi* is agitated and stirred up, and this agitation and dissipation are repeated day after day, to the point that the evening *qi* is no longer sufficient to replenish it. Once this has occurred, the person is reduced to a state not far removed from that of the beasts. Seeing his beastliness, people assume that he never had any innate stuff [*cai* 才]. But how can you say that this condition represents the essence of human beings [*renzhiqing* 人之情]?

Therefore, there is nothing that will not grow if given the proper cultivation [*yang* 養]; similarly, there is nothing that will not wither away if deprived of it.

While this passage might appear to be a "wild nature" rather than agricultural metaphor—especially to a modern Westerner accustomed to viewing suburban forests as parks—I believe that it is more appropriate to see Ox Mountain as a source of timber than as a kind of nature preserve, and therefore to understand the trees growing upon it as a managed resource requiring human intervention. That is to say, the entailment intended is not that *we* should stop cutting trees or grazing our livestock on Ox Mountain (i.e., that we should leave our moral nature alone), but rather that we need to stop neglecting Ox Mountain by allowing *others* to abuse it. That is, we (as metaphoric rulers) cannot allow the pressure of Ox Mountain's environment—the demands of woodsmen and grazers who are inevitable components of a semi-urban area—to cause it harm through lack of regulation. In other words, we need to take steps to actively *protect* from harm our own moral nature and the moral nature of others.[10]

The Ox Mountain parable thus vividly weaves together the "essence"/ "endowment" metaphors in the context of an agricultural framework: the essence of human beings is like a fragile seedling or sprout naturally destined to grow into morality if given the proper cultivation, nourishment, and protection from environmental harm. One of the most basic entailments of this MORAL HEART/MIND AS SPROUT metaphor is that the failure of a seedling to grow into a full-grown plant can only be the result of interference with its essential telos. The story also nicely links the agricultural metaphor system to contemporary medical theories and the literal[11] nourishment of the *qi* within human beings—a link that is crucial for Mencius's project of self-cultivation and that is reinforced throughout the text in the form of mixed agricultural-water metaphors.[12]

The Ox Mountain parable also gives some content to the term "good" (*shan* 善): to be good in Mencius's view is to be moral in the Confucian sense. The formulation we find in 6:A:8—*renyi* 仁義 (lit. benevolence and rightness; translated as morality)—is one of the shorthand terms for this morality,[13] but a more detailed description is given in 6:A:6. If we recall where I left off in my discussion of this passage, Mencius was explaining that observable bad behavior in people is not to be blamed upon their innate endowment. He goes on to claim that this is because by nature human beings are endowed with the four cardinal Confucian Virtues in the form of the four "hearts" (*xin* 心):[14]

> The heart of compassion is something possessed by all people, as are the heart of shame, the heart of deference, and the heart of right and wrong [*shifei* 是非]. The heart of compassion pertains to[15] benevolence [*ren*], the heart of shame to rightness [*yi*], the heart of deference to observance of the rites, and the heart of right and wrong to wisdom.

In English we tend to distinguish between cognitive and affective capacities or tendencies in human beings, generally referring to the former in terms of the "mind" or "thoughts" and the latter in terms of the "heart" and "feelings." The difficulty in rendering *xin* properly is that the actual organ or "orb"[16] to which it refers—the "heart/mind," as we have been rendering it since it the "Inner Training"—has in the Chinese view both cognitive and affective capacities and tendencies, and in addition serves as a kind of "container" for settled dispositions to act in a certain way, thereby including what we might refer to as the "will." On top of this difficulty is added the fact that Mencius uses *xin* to refer not only to the organ itself (which is the seat of conscious agency) but also—as in 6:A:6—to various specific cognitive/affective tendencies (and the feelings to which they give rise) that spring from and are essentially related to the heart. In Mencius's view, many feelings possess an extremely limited cognitive content: as I will discuss later, emotions aroused through the senses (hunger, lust, etc.) are not capable of much more than the simple recognition of their object, and are then bound to respond to this object in a mechanical stimulus-response fashion. There is a special class of feelings and feeling-capacities, however, that is associated with the heart/mind and that contains a fairly complex cognitive aspect. Such feelings relate to their objects in such a way that they reveal "a perceived import of the object, a significance seen in it" (Yearley 1990: 96). They have an influence on what features of a situation appear as salient to us, and also provide an affective motivation for action.[17] For instance, Kwong-loi Shun notes of the heart of right and wrong that it involves "more than just knowing what is proper or improper . . . [but also] approving of what is proper and disapproving of what is improper."[18] Mencius refers to these special feelings and feeling capacities as "hearts" (*xin*) in order to mark them off from the lesser emotions, as well as to note their special relationship to the organ/orb.

It is this "heart of morality," then, that represents the essence "stored up" inside human beings. An entailment of this INNER ESSENCE metaphor is that the *xin*, in representing our essence, also should be recognized as the most important part of us. In claiming that human nature is "good," then, Mencius is not merely referring to the presence within human beings of the heart/mind and its special feeling capacities but is claiming for it a status that takes priority over lesser parts of ourselves, as well as the feelings and desires that go along with these lesser parts. As P. J. Ivanhoe puts it, Mencius not only describes a certain content for human nature but provides it with a *structure* as well, with the *xin* at the top (Ivanhoe 1990: 31–32). This supreme position for the *xin* is already implicit once it is established as our metaphoric essence, and Mencius relies upon this implicit status in urging people to pay more attention to the heart/mind:

> Among the parts of the body, some are noble and some base, some great and some small. Never harm the greater parts for the sake of the lesser; never harm the noble parts for the sake of the base. Those who cultivate the lesser parts are petty (lit. "small") people, whereas those who cultivate the greater parts are great people. (6:A:14)

That the heart/mind is the "great" or "noble" part is made quite clear in 6:A:11, where Mencius laments the fact that people have no trouble keeping track of their material possessions, but forget what is truly valuable when it comes to caring for the self:

> Benevolence is the heart of human beings; rightness is their road. To discard this road and not follow it—to let this heart escape and not know to go after it—this is a tragedy indeed! If a person has a chicken or dog that has escaped, they know enough to go after it, but the opposite is the case when it is the [moral] heart that has escaped. The Way of study and learning is none other than this: to go after this escaped heart, that is all.

In this passage, Mencius does not first have to prove to us that the heart/mind is to be valued over mere livestock, for this is an unspoken entailment of the HEART/MIND AS ESSENTIAL SELF metaphor. His task as moral psychologist is— after helping people to realize what it is that they really should value by identifying the *xin* with the human essence—to get them to see how their current behavior makes no sense in light of this deeper value. This point is brought home in the conclusion to 6:A:14 through the invocation of both agricultural and medical analogies:

> Now consider a head gardener who ignored the *wu* 梧 and *jia* 檟 trees in order to cultivate the sour grass.[19] We would certainly consider this a sign of a despicable gardener. Or consider a physician who focused so much upon treating [*yang*; lit. cultivating] one of your fingers that he inadvertently caused you to lose your shoulder or back.[20] We would certainly consider this the sign of a quack. [In the same way], a person who cares only about eating and drinking is despised by others because he allows the great to be harmed by the cultivation of the small.[21]

This is Mencius at his rhetorical best, gently guiding us in applying evaluative judgments drawn from concrete domains (what makes a good gardener or physician) to the more abstract realm of moral self-cultivation. The moral heart/mind is the essence of what it means to be human, and therefore what makes us great. To ignore it in order to pursue the pleasures of the flesh is simply to be a despicable and incompetent human being.

We have noted that the presence of the four hearts does not by itself guarantee the presence of the four cardinal virtues: human beings are not born virtuous, but merely with an inborn propensity to *become* virtuous. Understanding the nature of the relationship between the hearts and the full-blown virtues to which they pertain is thus perhaps the key to understanding what it means to say that human nature is "good" and—not incidentally—the Mencian conception of wu-wei. In 6:A:6 the relationship between each of these hearts and their related virtue is not made explicit, but fortunately the relationship is clarified in 2:A:6, where the agricultural metaphor is invoked again in the claim that the four hearts are embodied in our endowment in the form of four "sprouts" (*duan* 端) of virtue:

> The heart of compassion is the sprout of benevolence; the heart of shame is the sprout of rightness; the heart of deference is the sprout of ritual propriety; and the heart of right and wrong is the sprout of wisdom. People have these four sprouts in the same way as they have four limbs. Possessing these four sprouts, one who declares himself incapable is a robber [*zei* 賊] of himself.

We will return to this "robbing" metaphor below. For now, let us explore one of the entailments of this "sprout" metaphor that opens up for Mencius a whole host of strategies for demonstrating to dubious rulers or rivals in debate the fact that they are born for goodness: since our hearts exist in the form of sprouts, they are a "constantly *visible* and *active*, not *hidden* or *latent*, part of the self" (Ivanhoe 1993a: 27), and their presence and influence should thus be manifested in human behavior in various ways.

An example of this strategy is Mencius's wonderful exchange with King Xuan of Qi in 1:A:7. Mencius has been lecturing the king about being a "true King," and the king asks Mencius if he thinks him capable (*keyi*) of becoming such a true King. Mencius answers that he is, indeed, capable of doing so. "How do you know I can?" the king counters, a bit dubious. In other exchanges in the *Mencius*, he has noted his fondness for (amoral) courage, money, and women, and apparently thinks himself completely lacking in the resources Mencius claims he possesses. Mencius responds to his doubts with an anecdote:

> "I heard the following from Hu He:
>
> The king was sitting in his elevated throne when someone led an ox through the courtyard below him. The king noticed it and asked, 'Where is the ox being led?' The response was: 'It is going to be used to conse-crate a bell'[22] The king replied, 'Spare it. I cannot bear [*buren* 不忍] its look of abject terror, like an innocent person going to the execution ground.' 'In that case,' the servant asked, "should the bell consecration ceremony be abandoned?' 'That is out of the question! Substitute a lamb in its place.'
>
> I wonder, is there any truth in this report?"
>
> The king replied, "There is."
>
> "The heart [that motivated you then] is sufficient to enable you to become a true King. The common people all thought that you begrudged the additional expense of the ox, but I know for certain that it was because you could not bear to see its suffering."

"That is so," said the king. "The common people may talk, but even though Qi is a small state, how could I begrudge the expense of a single ox? It was simply because I could not bear its look of abject terror, like an innocent man going to the execution ground, that I substituted a lamb in its place."

"You should not think it strange that the people thought you miserly. You substituted a small animal for a large one—how were they to know the reason? If you commiserated with a creature going innocently to the execution ground, what difference does it make whether it was the ox or the lamb?"

The king laughed, saying "What was I thinking?[23] It is not that I begrudged the expense, but considering that I did substitute a lamb for an ox, it is not unreasonable that the people should have considered me miserly."

"There is no harm in this. It is, in fact, the technique of benevolence [*renzhishu* 仁之術].[24] You saw the ox; you never saw the lamb. The attitude of the gentleman toward beasts is this: having seen them alive, he cannot bear to see them die; having heard their cries, he cannot bear to eat their flesh. That is why the gentleman keeps his distance from the kitchen."[25]

The king said, "In the *Book of Odes* we read,
> The other person has a heart,
> But it is I who can gauge it.

This describes you. Even though the action was mine, when I looked into myself for a motivation I could not find my own heart. Your telling of it went straight to my heart and greatly moved me."

Mencius is here performing a sort of moral psychoanalysis. Through a process of questioning he causes the king to come to an understanding of his own true motivation, which hitherto had been opaque—not only to others but even to the king himself. Mencius demonstrates to the king that this motivation was in fact the heart of compassion, which the king mistakenly thought he did not possess.

In the famous "child and the well" passage (2:A:6), Mencius attempts to support the broader claim that *all* people—not merely King Xuan of Qi—possess this "heart unable to bear the sufferings of others" (*burenrenzhixin* 不忍人之心):

My reason for saying that all people possess the heart unable to bear the suffering of others is this. Anyone suddenly confronted with the sight of a child about the fall into a well would experience a heart of alarm and compassion. This reaction would not arise because this person wanted to get into the good graces of the child's parents, nor because of a desire to be praised by their fellow villagers or friends, nor because they were loath to get a bad reputation [for not having helped]. From this it can be seen that a person lacking the heart of compassion is inhuman, a person lacking the heart of shame is inhuman, a person lacking the heart of deference is inhuman, and a person lacking the heart of right and wrong is inhuman.

As in 1:A:7, Mencius is here challenging the listener/reader to discover something essential about her own motivations by considering a spontaneous or unguarded reaction. The element of spontaneity is key in both cases: King Xuan's sparing of the ox was so uncalculated that he himself did not understand why he acted as he did, while the response to the child crawling toward the well strikes one suddenly. It is this instant, spontaneous quality of the reaction that marks it as something *ziran*—"so-of-itself" in the sense of being uncoerced and unforced.

The universality of the 2:A:6 claim is bolstered in passages such as 6:A:10, where Mencius refers to examples of human behavior to show that the desire for rightness (*yi*) over even biological life itself is not something limited to him or other "moral people," but rather something which—at some basic level—is shared by even vagrants and beggars:

> Fish is something that I desire; bear's paw is also something that I desire. If it is not possible for me to get both of them, I would give up the fish and take the bear's paw. Preserving my own life is something that I desire; rightness is also something that I desire. If it is not possible for me to get both of them, I would give up life and take rightness. Preserving my life is certainly something that I desire, but there is something that I desire more than life, which means that I will not simply pursue life at any cost. Death is something that I hate, but there is something that I hate even more than death, which means that there are certain troubles from which I will not flee. . . . Desiring some things more than life and hating some things more than death is not a heart possessed only by the worthies, but is rather possessed by all people. The worthies simply do not lose it.

Similar examples of how this inherent repugnance to what is not right (*yi*) or ritually proper (*li*) are offered in the examples of the gamekeeper to the Duke of Qi, who refused at the risk of death to answer a ritually improper summons (3:B:1, 5:B:7), or the charioteer Wang Liang, who was ashamed to drive for a dishonest hunter despite the promise of great gain (3:B:1). All of these individuals present us with something analogous to our own unpremeditated, wu-wei reactions: the behavior of uncultivated, uneducated people—representatives of simple innate endowment (*cai*). Presumably, none of these lowly people have ever studied the rites or read the classics, and therefore their spontaneous displays of righteous behavior serves as strong prima facie proof that the feeling of morality is as innate and universal as the possession of four limbs.[26]

In his exchange with King Xuan, Mencius seems to have won the first round, as it were: he has convinced the king that he possesses innate moral tendencies. Unfortunately, the possession of such an innate moral tendency alone is not sufficient to guarantee actual moral *conduct*. Witness King Xuan himself. In an unguarded moment he spares an ox, but we are to understand that he spends the majority of his time oppressing and burdening his people. How does one close the gap between moral potentiality and actuality? That is, how can King Xuan transform his momentary, spontaneous outburst of compassion for an animal into a full-blown disposition to treat his people compassionately in a wu-wei fashion? The answer to these questions is the subject of my next section: Mencius's theory of self-cultivation.

Mencian Extension

Let us move to the second stage of Mencius's discussion with King Xuan of Qi in 1:A:7. The king has granted that Mencius has seen into his heart in divining his true motivation for sparing the ox, but still fails to see how this fleeting instance of compassion for an animal has anything to do with being a true king. "What did you mean," he asks, "by saying that this heart is the means by which I could accord with the way of a true King?" Mencius answers with an analogy:

> "If someone said to you, 'I have enough strength to lift a hundred *jun* 鈞[27] but not enough to lift a single feather; I have vision acute enough to observe the tip of a fine hair, but not to see a cartload of firewood,' would you find this reasonable?"

> "No."

> "Now, your kindness [*en* 恩] is sufficient to reach [*ji* 及] the beasts, and yet your achievements [in government] fail to reach the common people. Are you any different from this hypothetical person? That a single feather is not lifted is because strength is not applied to it; that a cartload of firewood is not seen is because vision is not directed toward it; that the common people are not cared for is because kindness is not bestowed upon them. Therefore, your failure to become a true King is due to a refusal to act [*buwei* 不為], not an inability to act (*buneng* 不能)." . . .

> "Treat the aged of your own family in a manner that respects their seniority, and then cause this treatment to reach [*ji*] the aged of other families. Treat the young ones in your family in a manner appropriate to their youth, and then cause this treatment to reach the young of other families. Once you are able to do this, you will have the world in the palm of your hand. . . . All that is required is to pick up this heart here and apply it to what is over there. Thus one who is able to extend [*tui* 推] his kindness will find it sufficient to care for everything within the Four Seas, whereas one who cannot extend his kindness will find himself unable to care for his own wife and children. That in which the ancients greatly surpassed others was none other than this: they were good at extending what they did, that is all. Now, why is it that your

kindness is sufficient to reach the beasts and yet your achievements fail to reach the common people?"

Mencius upbraids the king for claiming to be incapable of becoming a true king when this is clearly not the case. The understanding behind Mencius's frustration is that it is easier for human beings to care for other human beings (especially their own family) than to take pity upon animals, and yet the king has shown himself equal to this comparatively difficult task.[28] Therefore, his failure to apply this feeling he had toward the ox to his own family and then to his people is simply due to a refusal to act, rather than an inability to act.[29] What the king needs to learn to do is to "pick up this very heart here" (the heart that caused him to spare the ox) "and apply it to what is over there" (to his everyday dealings with the people), a process that Mencius terms "extension" (*tui* 推).[30]

In discussing extension, Mencius is shifting to an EVENT-LOCATION metaphor: one's current affective state or state of character is a "place," a normative affective state is a desired destination, and the process of cultivation itself is a kind of movement. The literal meaning of *tui* is "to push," so extension in this formulation involves the Subject metaphorically pushing the Self—instantiated in the form of the "hearts" or feelings—from one place to another.[31] As we have noted, the "hearts" contain cognitive as well as affective aspects, so the implication is that "pushing" them in the proper direction will necessarily involve a kind of cognitive/affective therapy. The details of this therapeutic method are worth considering. As P. J. Ivanhoe observes, in 1:A:7 Mencius is concerned not only with establishing that the king possesses a certain kind of moral sense but also with helping the king to realize: 1) what this sense feels like; 2) what some of its general characteristics are (including how it differs from other types of motivations; and 3) how to go about looking for, focusing on, and appreciating this moral sense.[32] Mencius accomplishes the first task by getting the king to recall the incident of the ox—to imaginatively reconstruct what he perceived and felt in the moment, consciously focusing upon this heart with a clarity that is possible only in retrospect. Mencius's presentation of alternate explanations for the king's behavior accomplishes the second task by leading the king to imaginatively consider other "hearts" (such as miserliness or greed), to distinguish them from the "heart incapable of bearing the suffering of others," and to confirm that it was indeed the latter heart that motivated his action. Mencius has the same task in mind in 2:A:6, where he invites the reader to imaginatively consider their reaction to the child crawling toward the well, and to acknowledge that this heart is something to be distinguished from other, selfish motivations (such as a desire to get into the good graces of the parents, etc.). The third task involves providing a way for the king to focus upon and further develop this heart, and this Mencius accomplishes by suggesting ways in which the king can go about immediately extending this heart: "Treat the aged of your own family in a manner befitting their venerable age and extend this treatment to the aged of other families; treat your own young in a manner befitting their tender age and extend this to the young of other families, and you can roll the world on your palm."

It is extremely important to note that this describes a process of gradual therapy or *cultivation*. Some commentators have emphasized the cognitive aspect of Mencius's argument with the king, suggesting that by demonstrating the analogy between showing kindness to the ox and showing kindness to the people, Mencius has given the king an abstract, rational *reason* for moral action that the king cannot ignore without being rationally inconsistent.[33] We see a similar argument from analogy in 6:A:10, where Mencius laments the fact that people are unable to extend their aversion to what is not ritually correct or right in small matters to what is not proper in large matters. Recall his observation that even a vagrant or beggar would ignore food proffered in an insulting or demeaning fashion, even if his life depended upon it.

> Yet when it comes to ten thousand bushels of grain one accepts it without debating whether or not it is ritually correct or right to do so. What good are ten thousand bushels of grain to me? Do I accept them for the sake of a beautiful dwelling, the services of wives and concubines, or for the gratitude my needy acquaintances will shower upon me? What just before I would not accept when it was a matter of life and death I now accept for the sake of a beautiful dwelling; what I would not accept when it was a matter of life or death I now accept for the services of wives and concubines; what I would not accept when it was a matter of life or death I now accept for the sake of the gratitude my needy acquaintances will shower upon me. Is there really no way of putting a stop to this? This is what is referred to as losing one's original/root heart [*benxin* 本心].

The conceptual dissonance between these two cases is designed to illustrate a common situation where extension from something easy (the visceral reaction against accepting food offered in an insulting manner) to something more difficult (turning down riches offered improperly) has not been made, and a similar cognitive element is clearly present in 1:A:7. Mencius is there asking the king to sense an analogical resonance—the presence of a category (*lei* 類) relationship—between his kindness for the ox and the potential kindness toward his family and the common people, and to reflect upon the fact that he has not been able to extend the one to the other. Nonetheless, this cognitive element would seem to be only part of the process of extension. It serves to refocus the attention of one who is confused about or ignorant of his own potential, but this cognitive realization is only meant to point the king in the right direction—to set him upon the road of Confucian self-cultivation.

To express this more precisely in terms of the EXTENSION metaphor structure, what is being "pushed" is the emotional Self (the *qi*) rather than just the mental consciousness. As we shall see, although one's intention (*zhi* 志) might be quite "mobile" (able to instantly make analogical inferences), true virtue requires that the *qi* be brought along as well. Conceived of metaphorically as a liquid substance that needs to gradually accumulate or a plant that takes time to grow, the *qi* can be led in a certain direction by the intention, but cannot be forced to move *too* fast. So, even though the king may logically see Mencius's point—that is, although he may be able to "push" his understanding of his spontaneous kindness from point A (the ox) to point B (his family and the common people)—consciousness or intention is easier to push than other, equally crucial instantiations of the Self. In other words, cognitive understanding or logic cannot by itself bring about true, wu-wei virtue.

It is in response to this problem that Mencius proposes a moral regimen by means of which the king might learn to further develop and appreciate this moral heart of his, beginning with what should be easiest (extending it to his immediate family members) and eventually leading to what is hard (extending it to the people, and so bringing the entire world into submission under the power of his moral suasion). Mencius is thus not trying to analytically *prove* something to the king so much as he is trying to focus the king's attention in the proper direction and set him on the road to personal perfection. In 6:A:7, Mencius compares our innate moral hearts to our preferences for fine food, elegant music and beautiful women:

> Were the nature [*xing*] of the relationship of the palate to flavors to vary from person to person in the same way that dogs and horses differ from me in kind, then how could it come about that all the palates in the world follow that of Yi Ya[34] in their relationship to flavor? The fact that in matters of flavor the whole world looks to Yi Ya is because all the palates in the world are alike. It is the same with the ear as well. When it comes to sounds, the whole world looks to Shi Kuang,[35] which is because all the ears in the world are alike. It is the same with the eyes as well. When it comes to Zidu,[36] everyone in the world knows to appreciate his beauty, and whoever does not is simply blind. Hence it is said, all palates have the same preferences when it comes to flavors; all ears hear the same thing when it comes to sounds; and all eyes are similarly entranced when presented with beauty. When it comes to hearts, then, how could they alone lack this kind of common agreement? Upon what do all hearts agree? That which we refer to as good order [*li* 理] and rightness. The sage is simply the first person to discover that with which my heart agrees. Thus reason and rightness please my heart in the same way that fine meat pleases my palate.

On this analogy, which sets up the metaphor MORAL SENSE AS TASTE, the sage is something like a moral connoisseur, who helps us to develop our moral sensibilities in the same way a great chef can help us to develop our sensibility for food. I can perhaps get you to allow that, since you derive pleasure from eating instant frozen dinners, acquiring a taste for more fresh, carefully prepared, and subtly flavored dishes is the natural extension of this pleasure. This cognitive assent does not, however, suddenly *create* such taste in you. At most, it may cause you to feel a bit dissatisfied with—or even embarrassed or ashamed about—your present state of culinary crudeness, thereby encouraging you to embark upon the process of cultivating such a taste. This is all that Mencius hopes to do; indeed, it is all that he thinks a teacher is *capable* of doing. The admonitions and teachings of the sages therefore do not in themselves provide us with proper dispositions or reasons to act morally, but rather serve to stimulate us in extending our own inborn tendencies.

One Source, One Root

Although we have rejected the voluntarist interpretation of Mencian extension—the idea that cognitive extension could immediately bring about extension of one's motivations—this sort of voluntarism was not completely unheard of in Mencius's age. Indeed (as I noted in chapter 4), this is precisely the manner in which extension was understood by the later Mohist dialecticians, from whom Mencius appropriated the term. By the time of Mencius, however, it is apparent that the Mohist school (or at least certain thinkers within the Mohist school) had moderated this scheme somewhat, substituting for it a "two-root" picture of moral development. We get a somewhat sketchy portrait of their position in 3:A:5, where Mencius indirectly debates with the neo-Mohist Yi Zhi through an interlocutor. Mencius criticizes Yi Zhi for giving his parents a lavish burial, which seems to violate the Mohist imperative of frugality. Yi Zhi's response is as follows:

> "When the Confucians say, 'The ancients [cared for the people] as if they were caring for an infant,' what is the point of this teaching [*yan* 言]? I think it means that there should be no gradations in caring, although in applying it one must begin with one's parents."

> Xuzi reported this to Mencius.

> Mencius said, "Does Yi Zhi genuinely think that a person loves his brother's son no more than his neighbor's infant? . . . When Heaven gives birth to things, it causes them to have a single root [*yi ben* 一 本]; Yi Zhi is mistaken because he believes them to have two roots [*erben* 二 本]."

There are several things one could note about this response, but for the moment I am most interested in the comment about the two roots, which seems a bit cryptic at first glance. David Nivison has argued that it should be understood as follows:

> I have a basic affection-capacity which reveals itself in a basic way—in this case as parental and familial affection. Having this capacity, I am then able to apply it to others, in accordance with my *beliefs* about how it should be focused—i.e., in accordance with the doctrines to which I adhere or my moral reasons for these doctrines. Morality on this view depends on two things, which are independent of each other: what I *think* I should do, and could state in *words* and reason about; and my capacity to feel certain emotions, which I can steer and shape so as to be *moved* to do what my principles tell me I should. (Nivison 1997: 102; cf. Nivison 1997: 134)

On this interpretation, Yi Zhi believes that morality has "two roots": a basic feeling capacity with one direction (i.e, toward one's parents), and a completely separate belief—derived from a teaching or doctrine (*yan*)—about the direction this affection *should* take (i.e., equally toward all people).[37] Extension in this sense thus involves taking the inborn feelings of affection, which supply a source of motivation, and then modifying and reshaping these inborn feelings according to the dictates of an externally acquired belief. This represents an advance of sorts over the more extreme rationalism of Mozi in that one is harnessing the emotions to aid one in realizing one's ideals, but it is still anathema to Mencius because it involves fundamentally altering our innate endowment. As he says in 6:A:6, "Benevolence, rightness, ritual propriety and wisdom are not welded onto [*shuo* 鑠] me from the outside; they are something I possess from the beginning." That this is the substance of Mencius's objection to Yi Zhi becomes very clear when we read on to the conclusion of 3:A:5:

> Mencius said, "Presumably in previous ages there were once cultures where the people did not bury their parents—when their parents died, they just picked up the bodies and tossed them into drainage ditches. Subsequently, though, when they passed by the ditches and noticed the foxes feeding on and the flies swarming over the corpses, sweat would break out on their foreheads and they would turn away, unable to bear the sight. This reaction was not an outward show put on for other people—it was a case of that which was in their hearts spontaneously welling up [*da* 達][38] and manifesting itself in their countenance. Presumably they were eventually moved to return home for shovels and baskets in order to bury the remains. If this primitive burial really was the right thing to do, then the burying of parents by filial sons and benevolent men must similarly have its justification."

> Xuzi reported this to Yi Zhi, who was taken aback for a moment before replying, "I have taken his point."

The point, of course, is that rightness and ritual propriety are not something one acquires by means of an external doctrine (they are not "welded on from the outside"), but are rather something that wells up in a spontaneous fashion from our own essential heart-mind. Rightness and ritual propriety—along with the other cardinal Confucian Virtues—are thus properly understood to have one root, not two. Understanding the "one root–two root" debate in this way is very helpful because it allows us to link it to the debate between Gaozi and Mencius concerning human nature and the issue of whether rightness is internal or external, as well as to the discussion of self-cultivation in 2:A:2. Essentially at stake in this debate is the viability of Mencian wu-wei as opposed to Mohist *wei* 為.

In 6:A:1 through 6:A:6, Mencius engages in debate (sometimes through a proxy) with a certain Gaozi on the topics of the character of human nature and whether rightness is internal or external. I have already discussed 6:A:6, so let us focus on some of the other sections of this chapter, trying to understand them in terms of the "one root–two root" scheme.

6:A:1

Gaozi said, "Human nature is like the *qi* 杞 willow. Rightness is like cups and bowls. To make morality [*renyi* 仁義] out of human nature is like making cups and bowls out of the willow tree."

Mencius replied, "Can you follow [*shun* 順; lit. flow with] the nature of the willow in making your cups and bowls? Or is it in fact the case that you will have to mutilate [*qiang'zei* 戕賊] the willow before you can make it into cups and bowls? If you have to mutilate the willow to make it into cups and bowls, must you then also mutilate people to make them moral? Misleading the people of the world into bringing disaster upon morality—surely this describes the effects of your teaching [*yan*]!"

6:A:2

Gaozi said, "Human nature is like a whirlpool. Cut a channel to the east and it will flow east; cut a channel to the west and it will flow west. The lack of a tendency toward good or bad in human nature is just like water's lack of a preference for east or west.

Mencius replied, "Water certainly does not have a preference for either east or west, but does it fail to distinguish between up and down? The goodness of human nature is like the downhill movement of water—there is no person who is not good, just as there is no water that does not flow downward.

"Now, as for water, if you strike it with your hand and cause it to splash up, you can make it go above your forehead; if you apply force and pump it, you can make it go uphill. Is this really the nature of water, though? No, it is merely the result of environmental influences [*shizeran* 勢則然]. That a person can be made bad shows that his nature can also be altered like this.

The water analogy in 6:A:2 takes on added significance if we recall the QI AS WATER metaphor that had by this time become part of common parlance.[39] In Gaozi's view, the human *qi* is neutral, possessing no inherent tendency of its own. This at first glance seems difficult to reconcile with 6:A:4, where Gaozi seems to be attributing an inborn sense of "benevolence" (*ren* 仁) to human beings:

Gaozi said, "The drive to eat and have sex is nature. Benevolence is internal, not external; rightness in external, not internal."

"Why do you say," Mencius asked, "that benevolence is internal and rightness external?" . . .

"My younger brother I love, whereas the younger brother of a man from Qin I do not love. This is because the deciding factor[40] in this case is me, and this is why I call it internal. I treat an elder from Chu as an elder, and I also treat an elder of my own family as elder. This is because

the deciding factor in this case is their elderliness, and this is why I call
it external."

The two passages do cohere, however, if we understand that in 6:A:2 the topic of
the discussion is not just any inborn tendencies, but inborn tendencies toward
"good" or "bad." More specifically, then, Gaozi's argument is that human nature
has no *morally relevant* internal preferences of its own. It is clear that the desires
for food and sex are morally neutral, but the presence within human beings of a
tendency toward "benevolence" would still seem to present a problem for Gaozi's
claim. It is in this respect that seeing Gaozi as a neo-Mohist becomes important
for understanding the debate.[41] Recall that Yi Zhi in 3:A:5 also allowed that
affection for one's parents is natural, and that this affection is something that is
drawn upon in the moral life. However, for a neo-Mohist like Yi Zhi this affection
is not *in itself* moral—it is no different from the sort of affection felt by animals
for others of their own kind, and if allowed to develop unchecked would lead to
precisely the sort of partiality and strife that Mozi so deplored. This affection
only becomes specifically moral when it is molded and redirected in accordance
with an external doctrine: in the Mohists's case, the doctrine that human beings
should practice "impartial caring" (*jian'ai* 兼愛). In Yi Zhi's "two-root" conception of morality, one's natural affections are a raw material to be molded into a
form determined by an external teaching (*yan*). If we understand Gaozi to be a
compatriot of Yi Zhi, the import of the debate in 6:A:1–4 suddenly becomes
much more clear. 6:A:1 presents a craft metaphor for the "two-root" model of
morality, with human inborn tendencies serving as the raw material to be carved
and cut; 6:A:2 (and 6:A:3, not cited) describe the lack of any sort of inherent
moral direction in human nature, implicitly making the point that this direction
must be supplied externally; and 6:A:4 completes the attack on the Mencian conception of human nature by reducing "benevolence" to simple animal affection
and noting that any sort of moral order (*yi*) must come from without.

Mencius takes many tacks in responding to Gaozi. In 6:A:2 he subverts
Gaozi's own metaphor, noting that water—looked at in a different way—*does*
indeed have an inherent direction; in 6:A:3 and 6:A:4, he shows his familiarity
with later Mohist theories of reference and naming by engaging Gaozi at the level
of his use of terminology. Much has been written concerning the technical features of this debate,[42] a detailed consideration of which reveals much about early
Chinese theories of language. In order to avoid sidetracking this discussion, however, I would like to focus on what I feel to be Mencius's main objection to the
"rightness-is-external" or "two-root" conception of morality: the fact that Mohist
ethics go against the natural tendencies of human nature.

This point is made in 6:A:1 through combining the agricultural and water
metaphors with another of Mencius's favorite metaphors: that of "robbing" or
"injuring" (*zei* 賊) human nature. The metaphoric structure set up in 6:A:1 is
clear: human beings have a certain endowment (their moral nature) that tends to
"flow" in a certain fixed direction, just as a willow tree tends to grow in a certain
way. A person attempting to work this innate endowment "against the flow"
(*bushun* 不順) will only damage it, in the same way that carving a willow tree to

make utensils will result in injury to the tree, and injuring people in such a way would result in disaster. Mencius is here basically arguing a position we have seen in the *Laozi*: human beings have within them certain "so-of-themselves" (*ziran*) tendencies like the teleologies observed in the natural world, and a morality working against these natural tendencies is doomed to failure. In 6:A:2, Mencius even evokes a very Laozian metaphor—human beings move toward goodness with the same spontaneous force as water flowing downhill (ESSENTIAL SELF AS DOWNWARD-FLOWING WATER)—but spells out an important entailment of this metaphor that was left implicit in the *Laozi*: water can be forced to do "unnatural" things like splashing above the forehead or flowing uphill, but only through the application of violent force. As would be clear to anyone living in a society where the manipulation of water for irrigation and flood control played an important role, the generation of such force is resource-intensive and ultimately unsustainable. Hence Mencius's valorization of the legendary sage-king Yu 禹, whose engineering feats were successful precisely because they worked *with* nature rather than against it:

> Bogui said, "In regulating the flow of water [*zhishui* 治水], I would say that I surpass even Yu."

> Mencius replied, "You are quite mistaken. In regulating water, Yu took advantage of its natural course [*dao* 道]. Hence he used the four seas to serve as his drainage ditch. You, on the other hand, use neighboring states as your drainage ditch. When one [in this fashion] forces water to flow against its nature [*ni* 逆], the result is what is referred to as "flood waters." "Flood waters" represent a "deluge," and this is something that a benevolent person hates. No, sir, you are very mistaken." (6:B:11)

Water naturally flows to the sea; in regulating it, Yu simply helped it to its natural "home" along a course that also proved beneficial to human beings. The harm caused by Yu's counterparts in Mencius's age—who try to control water by applying unnatural force, with disastrous results for their neighbors—is analogous to the injury caused by the neo-Mohists and their "two-root" strategy, which fails to "flow along with" (*shun*) human nature. In 4:B:26, the "going with the flow" strategy exemplified by Yu is explicitly linked by Mencius with the ideal of effortlessness and—in a very Laozian fashion—contrasted with the sort of harm caused by the "clever" or falsely wise (*zhizhe* 智者):

> What is so detestable about the clever is the way they try to force their way through things [*zuo* 鑿; lit. bore through wood]. If these clever people would just emulate the manner in which Yu guided the waters, there would be nothing detestable about their cleverness. In moving the waters, Yu guided them in a way that required no effort [*wusuoshi* 無所事]. If the clever could also guide things in a way that requires no effort, then their wisdom would be great indeed. Despite the height of the heavens and the distance of the stars, one who is able to seek out their former patterns [*gu* 故] can predict celestial events a thousand years in the future without leaving his seat.

The patterns of Heaven are constant, and going along with them allows one almost supernatural power with only the slightest exertion of effort. If the rulers of Mencius's age could only employ this sort of wisdom, they would be able to embody this power in their ruling of the people:

> The subjects of a hegemon [*ba* 霸] are happy, while the subjects of a true king are expansive and content like the heavens. The king can execute them without stirring up resentment, and can benefit them without receiving credit for it. The common people move daily toward goodness without being aware of who is bringing it about. This is because everything the gentleman passes by is transformed; everywhere he dwells is infused with spiritual power [*shen* 神], and above and below he joins together with the flow [*liu* 流] of Heaven and Earth. (7:A:13)

The Physiological Aspects of Mencian Wu-Wei: The "Flood-like *Qi*"

We can thus find all of the metaphorical elements of Laozian "naturalness"—lack of effort, unself-conscious efficacy, primordiality, internal motivation, and constancy—present in the *Mencius*. What is new about Mencius's use of these metaphors is not just that they are being marshalled in a defense of Confucian culture but also the manner in which they are linked to the new technologies of the self that were emerging in fourth century B.C. China. This linkage allows Mencius to circumvent the paradox of wu-wei as it is manifested in the *Analects* by providing him with a plausible model of how Confucian self-cultivation—which seems on the face of it to be a strenuous, unnatural undertaking—in fact represents the effortless expansion of physiological forces within the self. One of the most striking metaphors for this process is that of ESSENTIAL SELF AS HYDRAULIC FORCE, which allows him to portray the development of Confucian morality as being as natural and inexorable as the gushing forth of water from a spring or the power of a river flowing to the sea.

Perhaps the best entrée into this hydraulic metaphor system is *Mencius* 2:A:2. The passage begins with a disciple asking Mencius whether or not the prospect of being given a high official position and thus being able to put the Way into action would cause any "stirring" (*dong* 動) in his heart/mind. Mencius replies that since the age of forty he has possessed a "heart/mind that does not stir" (*budongxin* 不動心), which in itself is not a terribly difficult achievement, since (he says) Gaozi achieved such a heart/mind even before he did. A discussion of various types of courage follows. Eventually—and more to the point of my discussion—the disciple asks,

> "I wonder if I could get to hear something about the master's heart/mind that does not stir as compared to that of Gaozi?"

"Gaozi says, 'If you fail to get [*de* 得] it from doctrine [*yan*], do not look for it in your heart/mind; if you fail to get it from your heart/mind, do not look for it in your *qi*.' It is acceptable to say that one should not look for it in the *qi* after failing to get it from the heart/mind, but it is not acceptable to say that one should not look for it in the heart/mind when one fails to get it from doctrine. As for the intention [*zhi* 志], it is the commander [*shuai* 帥] of the *qi*, whereas the *qi* is that which fills [*chong* 充] the body. The intention is of utmost importance, whereas the *qi* is secondary. Hence it is said, 'Grasp firmly to your intention and do not do violence to your *qi*.'

"You just said that the intention is of utmost importance, while the *qi* is secondary. What, then, is the point of going on to say, 'Grasp firmly to your intention and do not do violence to your *qi*?'"

"When the intention is unified it moves [*dong*] the *qi*, and yet when the *qi* is unified it can also move the intention. For instance, stumbling and hurrying impact the *qi*, and yet this in turn moves the heart/mind."

"May I ask about the master's strong points?"

"I understand doctrines, and I am good at cultivating my flood-like *qi* [*haoranzhiqi* 浩然之氣]."

"May I ask what the 'flood-like *qi*' is?"

"It is difficult to explain in words. As a form of *qi*, it is the most expansive and unyielding. If it is cultivated with uprightness [*zhi* 直] and not harmed, it will fill the space between Heaven and Earth. It is the form of *qi* that complements rightness and accompanies the Way. Without these it will starve. It is something produced only by an accumulation [*ji* 集] of rightness; it is not something that can be acquired through a sporadic attempt at [*xi* 襲; lit. ambush of] rightness. The minute one's actions fail to please one's heart/mind, it will starve. This is why I said that Gaozi never understood rightness: because he looked upon it as something external.

This is a very rich passage and provides a great deal of material for discussion. One of the first questions that must be answered is the identity of the "it" that one "gets" from doctrine, the heart/mind or the *qi*. There has been some interpretative controversy on this issue, but it is almost certain that "it" refers to one's conception of rightness (*yi*), which in turn is the key to moral self-cultivation.[43] The fact that Gaozi gets "it" from doctrine confirms our picture of what it means to have an external view of rightness and a "two-root" picture of morality. Mencius has criticized such a view in passages I have cited before, and he rejects it here again, but now he provides us with a psycho-physiological explanation for why an external view of morality will not work. Let us review his argument.

To begin with, Mencius introduces the term *zhi* 志. *Zhi* has often been translated as "will," but "intention" might be better, as many commentators have noted that it does not refer to a distinct faculty, but rather to "the heart/mind [*xin*] when it is regarded as having a specific orientation."[44] The intention is described as existing in an interesting state of interdependence with the *qi*. On the one hand, a social metaphor is invoked in the description of the intention as the "commander" (*shuai*) of the common foot soldier *qi*. The entailment is clear: it is the job of the commander to give guidance to his troops, who, left to their own devices, would simply mill about in confusion. Indeed, Mencius in several passages notes the dangers of letting the *qi* run uncontrolled, in which case it will fixate upon external things.[45] It is necessary, then, for the mind to guide and restrain the *qi*, and this accords with Mencius's approval of the maxim, "if one does not get it in the mind, do not look for it in the *qi*." On the other hand, an entailment of the INTENTION AS COMMANDER metaphor is that the intention/mind is also somewhat dependent upon the *qi*, because a general cannot fight a battle without his troops. This INTENTION AS COMMANDER METAPHOR also possesses entailments that explain why Mencian extension, in contrast to Mohist extension, is not instantaneous: although the demonstration of analogical resonance may convince the commander (intention) that it is proper to move from point A to point B, he still needs to marshall his troops (*qi*) and gradually get them moving in the direction that he orders. This metaphorical entailment of dependence is reinforced by the concrete and physiological observation that "stumbling and hurrying impact the *qi*, yet this in turn moves the heart/mind"—with both terms meant in the very literal senses of the "breath" (*qi*) and the physical organ (*xin*)[46]—but this literal dependence of the heart/mind upon the *qi* in turn serves as a medical metaphor for a more profound, metaphysical dependence. There exists a certain form of *qi*—the "flood-like" *qi*—that, when properly "cultivated," expands to fill the world and to "complement rightness and accompany the Way," and the manner in which this flood-like *qi* supports rightness and the Way is analogous to the manner in which *qi* in the more literal sense infuses the self with motive force—that is, conceptualized as a kind of hydraulic force, it provides the psychological and physical *motivation* to undertake acts that are right or in accordance with the Way.

This hydraulic image is not ad hoc. Throughout 2:A:2 Mencius is relying upon the QI AS WATER metaphor derived from contemporary medical theories: *qi* "fills" (*chong*) or fills the body, where it can be "accumulated" until it becomes *haoran* 浩然 —like a surging expanse of floodwater—at which point it can support righteous action. This metaphor of the vital essence serving as a kind of vast hydraulic power source providing the motive force (if not the actual direction) for moral behavior is invoked again in 4:B:14, where we see it combined with both the interior essential self and lack of exertion metaphors:

> The gentleman is able to deeply immerse [*shenzao* 深造] himself in the Way because he desires to get it himself [*zidezhi* 自得之]. Getting it himself, he is able to dwell [*ju* 居] in it with ease [*an* 安]; dwelling in it with ease, he can draw upon it [*zi* 資] deeply; drawing upon it deeply, he finds its source [*yuan* 原] everywhere he turns.[47] Thus the gentleman desires to get it himself.

Although 4:B:14 does not specifically mention the *qi*, the use of water imagery supplies the conceptual link, and the image of an innate resource upon which one can "draw deeply" ties in nicely with the concept of the flood-like *qi*.[48] One can only attain a wu-wei degree of ease and perfection when the source lies within oneself—that is, when the action is approved of by the heart/mind and supported by the flood-like *qi*.

The entailments of the metaphors strongly support Mencius's argument that self-cultivation cannot be rushed in the Mohist fashion—that rightness cannot be "ambushed." In order to acquire a reservoir a dam must be built (i.e., some effort must be made), but springs and rivers flow at a constant rate, and thus a vast accumulation of water can only be achieved gradually over time. Switching to the social metaphor, although the role of the heart/mind is to guide the *qi* in the direction of rightness like a commander marshalling his troops, it cannot push the *qi* too far or the "troops" might revolt. In order to make the relationship between the intention and *qi*—that is to say, between effort and non-effort—entirely clear, Mencius switches back to his trusty SELF AS DOMESTICATED PLANT metaphor at the end of 2:A:2.

> "You must put some work [*shi* 事] into it, but you must not force [*zheng* 正] it. Do not forget about the heart/mind entirely, but do not try to help it to grow either. Do not be like the man from Song. In Song there was a man who—worried because his sprouts of grain [*miao* 苗] were not growing—decided to pull on them. Without any idea of what he had done he returned home and announced to his family, 'I am terribly worn out today—I've been out helping the sprouts to grow!' His sons rushed out to the fields to take a look and saw that all the sprouts had shriveled and died.
>
> Rare are those in the world who can refrain from trying to help their sprouts to grow. Then there are those who think that there is nothing they can do to help and therefore abandon all effort entirely. They are the people who fail to weed their sprouts. Those who try to help along the growth are the 'sprout-pullers.' Not only do their efforts fail to help, they actually do positive harm."

In abstract self-cultivation, as in the literal cultivation of the fields, effort is required, but one should not *try* too hard not to try. Like the man of Song's grain sprouts, *qi* and the heart-sprouts it supports grow at their own natural pace, and any attempt on the part of the intention to force them to grow faster will be futile. This is why the support of the *qi* needed to perform right acts must be gradually accumulated or cultivated, beginning with easy acts (for instance, being kind to one's own parents), and gradually advancing to more difficult acts (being generous to one's people).

The farmer of Song parable makes it quite clear now why Mencius did not expect King Xuan of Qi to immediately begin acting like a true king on the basis of a fleeting moment of pity for a frightened animal. This would be to force benevolence, and it is better to have genuine indifference than forced benevolence. Invoking the SELF AS DOMESTICATED PLANT metaphor again, Mencius notes:

> The five domesticated grains are the finest of all edible plants, but if they are grown in such a fashion that they do not ripen, you would have been better off sticking with their wild cousins.[49] When it comes to benevolence as well, the important thing is making sure that it ripens, that is all. (6:A:19)

In 7:A:44, Mencius notes that "one who advances sharply falls back rapidly as well," and in 7:A:24 he switches to the water metaphor in comparing the process of self-cultivation to the manner in which flowing water moves toward the sea, in that "it does not proceed until it has filled all of the hollows in its path." Water and agricultural metaphors are found together again in 4:B:18:

> Xuzi said, "Several times Confucius praised water, saying, 'Water! Oh, water! (*Analects* 9.17)' What was it he saw in water?"

> Mencius replied, "Water from an ample spring [*yuanquan* 原泉] flows day and night without ceasing, proceeding on its way only after filling all of the hollows in its path, and then eventually draining into the Four Seas. All things that have a root [*ben* 本] are so, and what Confucius saw in water is simply this and nothing more. If a thing lacks a root, it is like rain water that accumulates after a late summer storm. Although all the gutters and ditches may be filled, you can just stand for a moment and watch it all dry up."[50]

Water and agricultural metaphors are used interchangeably here, the image of water flowing from an ample spring being conceptually blended with the image of a plant growing up from its roots. Because of the commonly accepted QI AS WATER metaphor, the juxtaposition of the two families of metaphors here reinforces the dual flowing/growing model of *qi* development we saw in 2:A:2.

In 4:B:18, then, Mencius is able to transform Confucius's famously cryptic expression of admiration for water into an endorsement of Mencius's own "one-root" morality and new metaphorical models for self-cultivation. Extension must be gradual because the ESSENTIAL SELF is like a rooted seedling growing at its own pace or water from a source flowing step-by-step to the sea or accumulating behind a dam. Any attempt to rush this process through the imposition of external force is to try to have "two roots"—just as ridiculous an image as that of the poor farmer of Song pulling on his sprouts to make them grow. The extreme voluntarism of the Mohists is thus doomed to failure.

Mencian Wu-wei: ESSENTIAL SELF
AS IRREPRESSIBLE FORCE

The SELF AS DOMESTICATED PLANT and SELF AS HYDRAULIC FORCE metaphors not only provide the entailments for refuting Mohist-style morality but can also be seen as representing attempts by Mencius to circumvent the paradox of wu-wei. On the one hand, some effort is required: in the agricultural metaphor, one has to weed and water (the Subject needs to "cultivate" the Self), whereas in the hydraulic metaphor, one needs to build a dam for the reservoir (the Subject needs to "feed" the Self with "uprightness"). On the other hand, one cannot force the matter: the Subject cannot "pull on" the Self to make it grow faster, nor can it make the Self flow or accumulate any faster than it is naturally inclined to. Finally, despite the need to "put some work into it," the whole process can still be understood as "effortless" because the Subject is still allowing the natural tendencies of Self to do most of the *real* work.

We have seen that one cannot "get it" from doctrine, and that a two-root conception of morality is doomed to failure. Since rightness is internal, what one hears from external doctrine is only to be followed if it can also be "found" in the heart/mind, and it is found in the heart/mind only if the heart/mind approves of it and also has the support of the floodlike *qi*. From the agent's perspective, the primary indication that one possesses the support of the *qi* is a feeling of satisfaction or joy (*yue* 悦 or *le* 樂) that accompanies all truly virtuous action. If one can take joy in a "right" act, this reveals that one has the support of both the heart/mind and the *qi*. Similarly, forcing such an act in the absence of joy will only do damage to the *qi*. This is what Mencius means when he says of the floodlike *qi*, "The minute one's actions fail to please one's heart/mind, it will starve." The importance of taking genuine satisfaction in the Way is emphasized in 6:B:13, where Mencius hears that a certain Yuezhengzi is going to be appointed to a high office and is so overjoyed that he is unable to sleep. Apparently puzzled at Mencius's reaction, Gongsun Chou questions him concerning this man's character:

"Does Yuezhengzi possess great strength of character?"

"No."

"Is he knowledgeable and thoughtful?"

"No."

"Is he widely learned?"

"No."

"Then why were you so happy that you could not sleep?"

"He is the type of person who is fond of goodness [*haoshan* 好善]."

"Is that enough?"

"To be fond of goodness is more than enough to master the entire world, let alone the state of Lu! If one is truly fond of goodness, then everyone within the Four Seas will come—thinking nothing of the distance of a thousand *li*—in order to bring to his notice what is good."

Because virtuous acts must be done with genuine pleasure if they are to be anything more than empty hypocrisy, a "fondness" for the good is valued more than strength of character, intellectual ability, or broad learning, because all of these depend for their full realization upon the ability to take joy in the good. Such affective feedback is necessary not only to avoid hypocrisy but also to sustain one during the long process of self-cultivation. As P. J. Ivanhoe notes, "The joy of a given act marks it as right, and it is this feeling that makes self-cultivation a practical possibility. At least this latter point is true for all ethics of self-cultivation. Self-cultivation must in some clear and direct way produce satisfaction, for this is what leads us to strive for future improvement."[51] The performance of genuinely virtuous acts—acts done with a sense of joy, approved of by the heart/mind, and supported by the *qi*—allows one to gradually "cultivate" the four sprouts, supporting them at every step with an ever-accumulating "flood-like" *qi*. Joy is what makes possible the long process of cognitive/affective extension from what is easy (the serving of one's parents and obedience to one's older brothers) to what is difficult (adorning and regulating these basic feelings until they are transformed into the full Confucian Virtues), and Mencius—playing upon the commonly used pun between "music" (*yue* 樂) and "joy" (*le* 樂)—likens the unconscious ease of one who has completed this process to the pleasure of one who has surrendered to the irresistible rhythm of a song:

> The substance [*shi* 實] of benevolence is the serving of one's parents; the substance of rightness is being an obedient younger brother; the substance of wisdom is to understand these two and not let them go; the substance of ritual propriety is the regulation and adornment of them; the substance of music is the joy one takes in them. Once such joy is born, it cannot be stopped [*wukeyi* 惡可已]. Once it cannot be stopped, then one begins unconsciously to dance it with one's feet and wave one's arms in time with it. (4:A:27)

This metaphor of a force that "cannot be stopped" is found throughout the *Mencius*, although it is given various expressions.[52] Of course, we saw this metaphor in the *Laozi* expressed as "what you cannot get to stop" (*budeyi* 不得已), and this is the idiomatic form in which it will appear in the *Zhuangzi*. Despite its various expressions, the conceptual structure is the same: the ESSENTIAL SELF AS IRREPRESSIBLE FORCE, with an entailment of effortlessness because the Subject is simply carried along for the ride by the Self.

The SELF AS IRREPRESSIBLE FORCE metaphor can perhaps be singled out as the most general expression of Mencian wu-wei, encompassing many of the more specific expressions we have already examined. For instance, I noted in my discussion of Mencian extension that the general structure of the EXTENSION metaphor is the Self moving from point A to point B, with no specification as to the manner in which this movement is effected. The metaphors from 1:A:7 previously discussed—physically "pushing" (*tui*) or "causing to reach" (*ji*)—both entail a sort of forced movement, and are therefore employed by Mencius on occasions where he is goading his audience (like the reluctant king) into action. In this sense, extension represents part of the "voluntarist residue" in the *Mencius* that I will turn to in my discussion of the paradox of wu-wei. More commonly, however, the structure of EXTENSION is conveyed by means of water metaphors in order to emphasize its naturalness and efficacy:

> People all have that which they cannot bear. To allow this to spread [*da* 達] to what they can bear is benevolence. People all have that which they will not do. To allow this to spread to what they are willing to do is rightness. If a person is able to fill out [*chong* 充] [with *qi*] his innate heart opposed to harming others, then there will be a surplus of benevolence. If a person is able to fill his innate heart opposed to boring holes and climbing over walls, then there will be a surplus of rightness. If a person can fill the substance of his unwillingness to be addressed familiarly,[53] then there will be no place he can go where he will not exhibit rightness. (7:B:31)

Although primarily a spatial term (as suggested by the "walk"/"travel" radical) meaning to "pass through" or "penetrate" to a certain point, *da* is used in 2:A:6 to describe the spontaneous welling up of a spring—"in all cases, if you who possess the fours sprouts within you simply know enough to expand [*kuo* 擴] them all and fill [*chong*] them, it will be like a fire beginning to burn or a spring beginning to well up [*da*] through the ground"— and its consistent association in the *Mencius* is with this spontaneous "welling up" or "spreading out" process.[54] In both 7:B:31 and 2:A:6 *da* is used in conjunction with *chong*, which—as we know from 2:A:2—is the fluid-like manner in which *qi* fills the body. Together, these two metaphors make use of the basic EXTENSION structure in a manner quite different from *tui* or *ji*: rather than the Subject "pushing" the Self from point A to point B, the Self naturally "reaches" point B in the way a spring breaks through the ground, or "fills" the space between points A and B in the way that downward-flowing water effortlessly fills all the hollows in its path.

This "effortless" sense of EXTENSION is cleverly tied back together with the physiological in 3:A:5 (cited earlier), where that which was in the hearts of the sons who had failed to bury their parents "spontaneously welled up [*da*] and manifested itself in their countenance." A similar idea is expressed in passages such as 7:A:21,[55] where the Confucian virtues—rooted (*gen* 根) in the heart/ mind—are described as being so perfectly developed in the gentleman that, "manifesting themselves in his countenance as a vigorous flush [*zuiran* 晬然],[56] they appear in his face, filling up [*ang* 盎] his back and spreading [*shi* 施] through his four limbs, thus physically revealing their presence without the need for words [*yan*].[57] As one would imagine, this grounding of Virtue in the liquid *qi* and its physiological manifestations can serve a useful diagnostic function:

For discovering what is stored up [*cun* 存] within a person, there is nothing better than the pupils of his eyes, for they cannot conceal his badness. When that which is within his breast is correct, a person's pupils are clear and bright; when it is not correct, they are cloudy and murky. Listen to his words, observe the pupils of his eyes—where can a person possibly hide? (4:A:15)

A wonderful example of someone who has—against the warnings of 2:A:2—attempted to "ambush" rightness and is then given away by his wu-wei, physiological reactions is found in 7:B:11: "A man who is after fame might be able to give away a state of a thousand chariots, but if this is not the type of person he really is,[58] in giving away a basket of food or a bowl of soup [his reluctance] will be visible in his face." Therefore, someone eager to acquire a reputation for generousness might be capable on occasion of making grand public gestures, but the emptiness of such gestures will be revealed in the details of his everyday life. Giving away a bit of coarse food is easy; giving away a state of a thousand chariots is difficult. Attempting to skip over the easy tasks and go right to difficult ones—motivated by a desire for fame or a wish to accord with some doctrine one has heard—is what is meant by trying to "ambush" rightness. Since such a person has not yet accumulated the floodlike *qi* required to for true Virtue, the result is a complete failure at all levels of moral agency: his lack of character will constantly be revealed in small but significant actions, and eventually he will prove equally incapable of maintaining his grand public deceit. To recall a metaphor from 4:B:18, because his apparent goodness "lacks a root," you can stand and "watch it dry up" like an unseasonal rainfall.

We have seen, then, that the SELF AS IRREPRESSIBLE FORCE metaphor serves as a basic expression of Mencian wu-wei. In 4:A:7, the force is an irresistible musical beat; in the SELF AS DOMESTICATED PLANT metaphor it is the germinal force of the sprouts; and in the SELF AS HYDRAULIC FORCE metaphor it is the inexorable force of water flowing downhill or a spring breaking through the ground. The cognitive equivalence of these various metaphoric expressions is revealed by their frequent mixing; to the many examples we have already seen, we might add for good measure the observation in 1:A:6 that after a torrential spring rain formerly dry sprouts "spring up [*xing* 興] out of the ground with the force of pouring water [*boran* 浡然] . . . who could stop them?" Perhaps the most powerful evocation of the irresistible nature of true morality is the account of the legendary Shun's attainment of sagehood in 7:A:16, where the ESSENTIAL SELF is described as spontaneously, effortlessly, and inexorably flowing forth from the depths of his own heart/mind at the slightest instigation:

When Shun lived in the depths of the mountains, he dwelled among the trees and stones, and roamed together with the deer and wild pigs. At that time, there was very little to distinguish him from the other uncouth hillbillies. But as soon as he heard his first good word and witnessed his first good deed, it was like opening a breach in the dyke of the Yangzi or the Yellow River—nothing could restrain the torrential force.[59]

Like Confucius at age seventy, then, Mencius's perfected moral person spontaneously moves within the bounds of morality. Describing the legendary Yao and Shun, for instance, Mencius says: "in their movements and countenance, everything accorded perfectly [*zhong* 中] with the rites" (7:B:33). For Mencius, though, the Confucian Way is not something learned from tradition, but rather represents "the ultimate fullness / flourishing (*sheng* 盛)[60] of Virtue" (7:B:33)—that is, the fullest expression of an inborn nature conceptualized as a latent force that, once sufficiently accumulated, is ready to pour out into the world like a surge of water released from a dyke. Mencian wu-wei thus involves the perfect embodied harmony of external teachings, the heart/mind, and the *qi*, representing both the fulfillment of human nature and the reverent realization upon earth of Heaven's will. The themes of effortlessness, flexibility, and the spontaneous movements of everyday life are of course not new to Confucianism, but by grounding them in state-of-the-art models of human physiology Mencius gave the traditional Confucian ideal of wu-wei morality a powerful new conceptual metaphorical expression.

The Paradox of Wu-wei

This new conceptualization of wu-wei brings with it, as we might expect by now, its own new tensions. Recalling the conception of wu-wei as it appeared in the *Analects*, we will remember that the end state idealized by Confucius is arguably identical to the ideal advocated in the *Mencius*: so fully embodying the Confucian virtues in one's dispositions that moral action follows spontaneous and naturally. The difficulty in the *Analects* arose because achieving this perfected state involved intensive training in cultural forms in order to fundamentally transform the inborn nature—which is in itself unformed—into the perfected moral nature. One is then left with a problem of motivation, because the transformation cannot occur unless the student genuinely *desires* to be moral and loves morality for its own sake—rather than as a means to some other end—and yet it would seem that such love for the good is the very thing that is to be instilled over the course of the training itself. As David Nivison has noticed, Mencius's theory that human nature inherently tends toward the good provides him with a solution to at least this particular form of the paradox of wu-wei: "Mencius's solution is that we all have genuine moral motivation. The teacher's job is to perform a sort of moral psychoanalysis, get one to catch oneself in a moral-making response . . . so that one notices one's real 'heart'" (Nivison 1997: 40).

The paradox as Confucius faced it thus dissolves.[61] Deep down, we are always already possessed of a love for the good, and merely need someone to help us recognize it. In his discussion in 1:A:7 with King Xuan of Qi, then, Mencius's main purpose is to help the king to see that in his heart of hearts he already possesses the sprout of benevolence: if he would only become aware of this sprout, clear away the weeds that have been choking it, and provide it with some sunlight and water, it will naturally expand to realize its full potential and allow the tyrant to become a true king. As Nivison notes, "Mencius's theory arguably does the same job as Plato's recollection" (1997: 237)—that is, we can learn to be good because we already contain the good within ourselves, at least in potential form.[62] Mencius's agricultural and water metaphors, along with his grounding of Confucian self-cultivation in the physiological make-up of the self—free him up for an end-run around the paradox in a manner similar to the "Inner Training": simply engage in certain practices such as the rites or studying of the classics—understood as metaphorical watering, weeding, or opening up a dike—and the natural force of the growing sprouts or surging water will take care of the rest. As I have mentioned, Mencius's agricultural model also allows him to get around certain aspects of the paradox as it existed in the *Laozi*, in the sense that it explains how something that is natural can also require effort: "nature" is not some inert chunk of uncarved wood, but rather delicate and dynamic sprouts that need nurturing and care, but that possess their own primordial and innate telos.

Unfortunately, the paradox of wu-wei seems to be something like the hydra of Greek mythology—chop off one head, and two spring up in its place. This is quite literally what occurs in Mencius's solution to Confucius's paradox: having solved the problem of moral motivation, Mencius is now presented with at least two new tensions, both of which revolve around incompatible metaphor systems.

Wild versus Domesticated Nature Tension: The "Voluntarist" Problem

David Nivison has noted what he refers to as a "voluntaristic residue" in the thought of Mencius and observes that "perhaps all self-cultivation philosophers must have it, believing as they do that in some sense one can seek to become what one sees that one is not, at least at the level of effective moral agency" (Nivison 1997: 132). We can find this residue of voluntarism throughout the *Mencius*, particularly in those passages where Mencius attributes moral failure to a simple failure of effort:

> Cao Jiao asked, "Is it really the case that all people are capable of becoming a Yao or Shun?"
>
> "Yes, that is so," Mencius replied.
>
> "I heard that King Wen was ten *chi* tall and Tang was nine *chi* tall. Now, I am nine *chi*, four *cun* tall, and yet all I can do is sit around and eat millet all day long. What can I do about this?"
>
> "What is the difficulty? All you have to do is try at it [*weizhi* 為之]. . . . Is the trouble with people that they do not have the strength? No, it is that they do not try, that is all. One who walks slowly behind his elders is called a proper younger brother, whereas the opposite of true of one who walks quickly and overtakes his elders. Now, is walking slowly really something people are not capable of? No, it is just that they do not

try. The Way of Yao and Shun consists of nothing more than being a filial son and proper younger brother . . .

"The Way is like a wide road. How is it hard to find? The trouble with
people is simply that they do not seek [*qiu* 求] it out." (6:B:2)

The problem faced by this strapping, healthy young man who nonetheless cannot
find it in himself to do anything other than sit around and eat millet is unfortunately not uncommon. Like Confucius, Mencius often describes this kind of
moral failure in a general sense as a failure to "seek" (*qiu* 求) the Way.[63] He goes
a step further than Confucius, though, in tracing this general moral failure to a
failure to utilize a specific human capacity: the heart/mind's ability to "think" or
"concentrate" (*si* 思).[64]

Benevolence, dutifulness, ritual propriety and wisdom are not welded on
to me from the outside; they are in me originally. It is only that I do not
concentrate (*si* 思) on them. That is why it is said, "Seek and you will
get it; let go and you will lose it." (6:A:6)

The heart/mind is naturally the greatest and most important part of ourselves,
and its unique capacity—the ability to think—is thus the most crucial of human
capacities. Whereas the lesser organs (the eyes, ears, nose) are passively led to
their objects in an almost mechanical fashion, the mind is able to choose its
objects and to focus where it will. The difference between Cao Jiao, who merely
sits around eating millet, and the sage-king Yao is that Yao chose to use his heart/
mind to focus upon his innate endowment, whereas Cao Jiao continues to muddle
along under the sway of the lesser organs:

Gongduzi asked, "We are all equally human, and yet some become great
men, others become petty men. Why is this?"

Mencius said, "Those who follow [*cong* 從] the greater part of their
bodies become great men, those who follow the lesser parts of their
body become petty men."

"If we are all equally human, though, why do some follow the greater
part, others the lesser part?"

"The ears and the eyes cannot think [*si*], and are therefore obscured by
things. When one thing [an external object] impinges upon another thing
[the sense organs], it can do nothing more than simply attract [*yin* 引] it.
The organ of the heart/mind, on the other hand, is able to think. Only
after having thought about something does it obtain it; without thinking
it will not get it. This is what Heaven has given me, and if you first take
your stand on that which is great within you, those things that are petty
cannot wrest you from your spot. As for becoming a great person, this is
all there is to it. (6:A:15)

Ordinary people, then, have allowed their true nature to "stray" (as Mencius puts
it in 6:A:11) by allowing their lesser, animal parts (the passive organs) free reign

and by failing to focus upon that great thing that distinguishes them from the animals: the heart/mind. All that a person needs to do, though, is to exercise his
heart/mind's capacity to think or concentrate, and his good "sprouts" will be able
to flourish. This is why Mencius upbraids King Xuan of Qi with the accusation
that his "failure to become a true King is due to a refusal to act [*buwei* 不為], not
an inability to act [*buneng* 不能]." All people possess the true heart of goodness,
but most allow it to get away from them. The decision to go after one's original
heart in turn seems to involve a simple act of will.

So, despite his belief that human nature is "good," Mencius seems to be
aware of the problems involved in translating this potential into reality. Our moral
potentialities are somewhat different from our biological potentialities, in that the
former need to be actively developed, whereas the latter do not.[65] Mencius
thereby attempts to get around the paradox as it faced Laozi by combining effort
and effortlessness in an interesting way. Laozi urges us to be natural, but when
presented with the question of why we have to try to be natural, cannot supply a
satisfactory answer. Mencius also urges us to be natural, and when presented with
the question of why we have to try, he answers: because by "natural" I do not
mean the manner in which *weeds* grow, but the manner in which crops grow.
Hence the comment put in Confucius's mouth in 7:B:37: "I despise the weeds for
fear they will be mistaken for domesticated sprouts." Similarly, in the context of
the water metaphor family, the achievements of Yu are in *taming* wild rivers for
the purposes of irrigation and flood control. The SELF AS DOMESTICATED PLANT
and SELF AS CHANNELED WATER metaphors thus neatly combine inner telos with
the need for some external effort and guidance on the part of the Subject, and
thereby serve as a model for a special kind of effort perfectly harmonized with
nature.

This, unfortunately, does not bring Mencius entirely out of the woods. One
could imagine a Laozian retort (and indeed this is essentially the Zhuangzian
response) to the effect that it is not crops but rather the very weeds that Confucius
and Mencius so disdain that are in fact the natural state of plants, or that it is not
channeled irrigation ditches but rather the wild river that is the natural state of
water. Put physiologically, the Daoists would argue that *qi* that has been guided
and shaped by the heart/mind is no longer pristine but has been exhausted
through alteration, in the same way that domesticated grains lose their hardiness
or channeled irrigation water has its energy dissipated. Granted, the Daoists
might say, the sense organs cannot "think" and are merely "attracted" by things
(6:A:15), but what is wrong with being spontaneously attracted to something? Is
this not the innate tendency of the *qi*? Is this not what it means for a response to
be "natural" and truly effortless? Once thinking or focusing has been introduced
to the process, what you have is no longer true spontaneity. From the Daoist perspective, the sort of "weeding" that Mencius proposes is just as violent and unnatural as the Mohist carving of metaphorical cups and bowls out of the willow tree
of human nature.

Indeed, we do not even have to turn to the Daoist critique to feel this tension,
for it exists within the *Mencius* itself in the form of a rather schizophrenic metaphoric conceptualization of nature. On the one hand, we have a valorization of

domesticated nature—sprouts of grain growing in their rows, irrigated water safely confined by dikes flowing into the sea—combined with a disdain for wild nature. In 3:A:4, in a conversation with a follower of the primitivist Xu Xing,[66] Mencius paints a bleak picture of the original state of nature:

> In the time of Yao the world had not yet been tamed. Great flood waters surged randomly across the countryside, inundating the entire world. Grasses and trees flourished and formed tangled thickets, among which the birds and beasts bred and multiplied. The five domesticated grains were not raised. The birds and beasts encroached upon human beings, and the tracks and traces these wild creatures criss-crossed throughout the Middle Kingdom. Yao alone was alarmed by this state of affairs, and raised up Shun in order to bring order [*zhi* 治] to the world. Shun appointed Yi to master fire, after which Yi put the flame to the mountains and marshes and burned them, causing the birds and beasts to flee and hide. Then Yu helped the nine rivers to flow, controlling the Ji and Ta rivers by channeling them into the ocean, then dredging the Ru and Han and building up dykes along the Huai and Si in order to channel them into the Yangzi. Only after all these tasks were accomplished could the people of the Middle Kingdom get enough to eat.[67]

The rivers thus did not *originally* flow into the oceans, but rather flowed randomly back and forth (*hengliu* 橫流) across the land; they had to be guided to the ocean by the efforts of Yu. People do not naturally live well off the land, but only find comfort after wild nature is eradicated and agriculture and the division of labor are introduced. The term "wild beast" (*qinshou* 禽獸) is almost always used in the *Mencius* as a byword for the undesirable and subhuman, and at the end of 3:A:4 it is explicitly argued against the primitivists[68] that to try to reverse the development of human history would in fact be the most "unnatural" thing in the world: "I have heard of people emerging from the dark valleys to move into the tall trees," Mencius admonishes the follower of Xu Xing, "but I have never heard of people coming down from their tall trees to descend back into the dark valleys." Similarly, in 7:A:16, Shun's original bucolic way of life—dwelling among the trees and stones and roaming around idly with the wild animals—is dismissed as the way of a crude hillbilly, and we are to understand that it is something he gave up once the "torrential flood" of Confucian virtue burst forth in him.

This 7:A:16 passage, though, gets right to the heart of the tension between wild and domesticated nature metaphors that we are discussing. As we have seen, Shun's virtue is there approvingly described as bursting forth like a "breach in a dike" whose primal power "cannot be restrained," yet elsewhere in the text the wild force of an untamed flood is portrayed as the worst kind of disaster, and the job of the gentleman as being precisely to *tame* such outbursts. Similarly, the manner in which the people "return home" to virtue is positively described as like wild animals running off into the fields in 4:A:9, whereas in 6:A:11 we are warned to go after our "strayed" heart/mind in the same way we chase after escaped domestic animals. If we are to admire the spontaneous energy of wild animals running free into the fields, one might well ask, why are we also asked to restrain the wanderings of our heart/mind? There is a real tension here that arises out of genuinely incompatible entailments. Although it does not really fit well with his dominant domesticated nature metaphors, Mencius's occasional valorization of wild nature perhaps reflects a sense that the agricultural or flood control metaphors are a bit *too* tame, and so fail to capture certain important aspects of natural phenomena. Despite the beauty and refined flavor of the domesticated grains, they *do* need to be coddled in order to produce, and there is thus something appealing about the sheer vigorousness and spontaneous consistency of their "wild cousins." In any case, this tension between domesticated or wild nature as appropriate models for wu-wei behavior will be Zhuangzi's main point of attack. In contrast to Mencius, Zhuangzi celebrates of the wild diversity of creation and valorizes the "weeds" of humanity—the cripples, the criminals, the ugly—who have been driven out of the carefully tended Confucian fields.

Tension between Self-Cultivation Internalist and Externalist Metaphors   The second new tension arises from Mencius's strong internalism and concerns the individual's relationship to tradition. We have noted that the teachings of the sages might be viewed as something like a "moral cookbook." As Nivison puts it:

> We all have natural tastes, that are more or less alike because we are all human. We tend to agree upon what is beautiful to see, beautiful to hear, and delicious to eat. Similarly, our hearts tend to like the same things, viz., *li* 理 and *yi* 義, "what is orderly and right." Tradition gives us standards about this—in the language of Mencius's world-view, the civilization-creating sage-kings have left us their teachings. But this simply means that the sages got there first. Just as a famous cook of past times might have written a cookbook to which we prudently turn for good recipes—since this cook, with his or her excellent taste, has anticipated what we are all going to find we like—so also the teachings of the sages can be thought of as a moral cookbook. (Nivison 1997: 41)

Another metaphor for the role of traditional forms is provided by P. J. Ivanhoe. The rites and the teachings found in the classics serve as a "trellis" upon which the four moral sprouts can grow.

> They guide and support their development until the sprouts are able to stand on their own. But these supports do not alter or inhibit natural growth. A healthy, vital specimen which grows undamaged will follow the course and assume the shape described by these supports. (Ivanhoe 1990: 94)

The trellis is no doubt useful in anchoring the plant and helping it to grow, and it is also true (as anyone who has grown tomatoes or beans has observed) that a plant can grow to a greater height and be more productive with the help of such a trellis. Nonetheless, the trellis is not essential, and even without such support the plant will eventually come to assume something like its ideal shape and form. We see an excellent illustration of this principle in the story recounted in 3:A:5, where a group of dutiful sons spontaneously create a crude funeral ritual in response to the distress they feel upon seeing their parents' bodies rotting by the side of the road. There is no doubt that they would have been better off if there had already been a funeral rite at their disposal: they could have avoided this distress which "brought sweat to their brows" altogether, and the rite that they improvised on the spot clearly suffers in comparison to the elegant and subtle rites of burial and mourning developed by the early sage-kings. Still, by listening to the dictates of their own heart/minds, they were able to independently create a new "recipe," and one presumes that over time this crude rite they devised would become increasingly polished and elegant.

A related issue is the degree of independence vis-a-vis traditional forms displayed by the Mencian gentleman. This is, of course, not an entirely new theme: flexibility, sensitivity to context, and a certain degree of autonomy in putting ritual into practice are all valued by Confucius. Indeed, it is through the efforts of Mencius that Confucius came to be known as the "timely sage"—that is, the sage whose efforts were always perfectly in harmony with the demands of the situation.[69] We have also noted that the *Analects* holds open the possibility that actual modification of the rites themselves is even permissible, if in the judgment of the gentleman this modification does no harm to the spirit of the rite.[70] Mencius went beyond Confucius in this respect in repeatedly emphasizing that it is both the duty and the right of the gentleman to temporarily suspend or even actively violate the dictates of ritual or morality when the situation dictates it.[71] This position is most succinctly and forcibly stated in 4:B:6, where Mencius observes that "A ritual that is contrary to the spirit of the rites, a duty that goes against the spirit of rightness—these are things a great person will have nothing to do with."[72] It is clear that this increased autonomy vis-a-vis traditional norms allowed to the gentleman in Mencius's scheme grows out of his strongly internalist conception of "rightness." As Ivanhoe has noted, the development from Confucius to Mencius marks a shift in the locus of authority for moral decisions from the rites to the heart/mind (Ivanhoe 1990: 92)—from traditional norms to the moral intuitions of the individual. This degree of independence from tradition reveals itself not only in a flexibility in applying or suspending the rites but also in Mencius's hermeneutical stance toward the Confucian classics. The text of the *Odes*, for instance, should not always be taken literally; the point is to use one's intuition to understand the *meaning* of the *Odes*.[73] In one case, Mencius even goes so far as to reject portions of the *Book of History* because they do not accord with his own moral intuitions.[74]

To be sure, certain metaphysical assumptions prevent Mencian internalism from degenerating into extreme antinomianism or relativism. It is easy for someone living in the post-foundationalist West to imagine that this strong internalist aspect to Mencius's thought might lead to a sort of moral relativism, with each individual being charged with acting in accordance with the idiosyncratic dictates of her own heart/mind. It is therefore important to briefly note the metaphysical assumptions behind Mencius's project—more specifically, the belief that human nature and the system of morality that grows from it possess a universality endowed by Heaven.[75] As I have already observed in my discussion of human nature, Mencius claims that all human beings share the four sprouts of virtue, and makes use of various types of arguments to demonstrate the universal existence of these sprouts. This argument for a shared human nature allows him to follow Confucius in claiming a similar sort of universality for the specifics of the Confucian Way:

> Shun was an Eastern barbarian: he was born in Zhu Feng, moved to Fu Xia, and died in Ming Tiao. King Wen was a Western barbarian: he was born in Qi Zhou and died in Bi Ying. The places where they lived were over a thousand *li* apart, and the ages in which they lived were over a thousand years removed. Yet when their intentions [*zhi*] were realized in the Middle Kingdom, it was like the matching up of two halves of a jade contract. The measures of the former sage and of the latter sage were completely identical. (4:B:1)

Their measures were identical, of course, because they were derived from a shared heart/mind. It is this same heart/mind that allows Mencius to meet the intention [*zhi*] of the anonymous sage authors of the *Odes* with his own understanding, and which also allows him to diagnose corruptions in the heart/minds of his contemporaries by examining the faults in the doctrines they espouse (2:A:2). In addition to the factual claim about human nature—that it has certain characteristics and is shared by all people in the same way that all people share a taste for meat or physical beauty—Mencius adds a normative edge in claiming this nature (and particularly the "higher" or moral aspect of it) derives from Heaven (*tian* 天).[76] In this way, Mencius combines his strong motivational internalism with a profound religious faith. Because the heart/mind is so intimately related to Heaven, by fully developing it the sage is not only according with his own innermost self, but is also in a very important sense serving Heaven: "One who fully explores his heart/mind will understand his own nature, and one who understands his own nature will thereby understand Heaven," we read in 7:A:1. "Preserving [*cun*] one's heart/mind and cultivating one's nature are the means by which one serves Heaven."[77]

Despite these metaphysical safeguards against wild relativism or individualism, however, the sort of independence vis-a-vis tradition that the individual possesses in Mencius's scheme continues to raise the implication that traditional Confucian forms represent nothing more than optional aids in the task of self-cultivation—an implication that most Confucians would find quite disturbing. Mencius himself seems troubled by the implications of his internalism, and this causes him to continue emphasizing the necessity of traditional forms and the historical sages who invented them. In 3:A:4, defending the division of labor that allows the sages to worry about the larger affairs of the people against the primitivist teachings of Xu Xing, Mencius describes the gradual accumulation of culture built upon the historic efforts of the sage kings. In a passage that might have come from the hand of Xunzi himself, he describes how the Confucian virtues must be instilled in the common people through strict education and discipline:

> Hou Ji taught the common people how to farm and cultivate land, and how to plant the five kinds of domesticated grains. Once these five

grains ripened, the people were well nourished. There is a tendency in people, though: once they have full bellies and warm clothes on their backs, they become lazy and fail to seek of instruction, degenerating into a state not much different from the birds and beasts. The sage king was concerned about this, and so appointed Xie as the Minister of Education, whose duty it was to instruct the people concerning proper human relations [*renlun* 人倫]: love between father and son, rightness between ruler and minister, distinction between husband and wife, precedence of the old over the young, and trust between friends.[78]

Traditional norms are necessary not only for the common people but even for the aspiring gentleman. In another very Xunzian passage, Mencius invokes what will become one of Xunzi's favorite metaphors in explaining that it is impossible to succeed by relying solely upon one's own natural abilities and efforts and ignoring cultural standards:

> Even the keen eyesight of Li Lou or the technical skill of Gongshuzi would not allow you to draw squares or circles without the help of a carpenter's square or a compass [*guiju* 規矩]. Even the sharp hearing of Shi Kuang would not allow you to properly regulate the five notes without the help of pitchpipes [*liulu* 六律]. Even the Way of Yao and Shun would not allow you equitably to govern the world without the help of benevolent government institutions [*renzheng* 仁政]. Now, there are some who have benevolent hearts and good reputations, yet fail to benefit the people or set an example for posterity. This is because they do not practice the Way of the Former Kings. This is why it is said,
>
> Goodness alone is not enough to govern properly,
> While laws alone cannot apply themselves.
> The *Book of Odes* says,
> Do not go astray, do not forget [former ways];
> Follow and be guided by the ancient rules.
> There has never been a case of someone who observed the laws of the
>   Former Kings going astray. (4:A:1)[79]

Contrast this emphasis on the importance of the carpenter's square and compass with, for instance, the observation in 7:B:5 that "The carpenter or wheelwright can pass on his square or compass [*guiju*] to others, but cannot thereby make them skillful." Several commentators have noted the revealing parallelism between 7:B:5 and the story of Wheelwright Pian in the *Zhuangzi*, both of which have as their point the idea that knowledge cannot be transmitted externally but must, as Zhu Xi puts it, be "intuited with the mind" (*xinwu* 心悟).[80] Similarly, it is difficult to see why we need to consult the laws of the Former Kings considering the famous claim in 7:A:4 that "the myriad things are all possessed in their entirety [*bei* 備] within me." As in the case of his appeals to voluntarism, then, the occasional externalist fragments in the *Mencius* are difficult to reconcile with the main thrust of his moral vision.

Analogous to the observation that motivates Mencius's voluntarism—the fact that the process of developing the four moral sprouts is somehow different from simply growing four limbs—the introduction of scattered, somewhat anomalous externalist elements in the text might be seen as a response to a realization that external institutions and doctrines play some sort of non-optional role in the moral life. The problem is that Mencius's model of human nature and his program of self-cultivation cannot easily handle such non-inclinationally based elements. I believe that Lee Yearley puts his finger on the heart of this problem in observing that the so-called preservative virtues, such as courage, do not play a central role in the *Mencius.*[81] One of the possible explanations for this that Yearley considers is the fact that Mencius's developmental model of self-cultivation causes him to focus upon inclinational virtues:

> This leads him to think inclinational virtues, like benevolence, are the paradigmatic virtues. Moreover, it also leads him to picture perfected virtuous action as spontaneous, free of real conflict, and simply pleasurable. Ordinary courage, however, is a preservative virtue; moreover, reflexivity, some form of conflict, and a complicated relationship to pleasure define it. (Yearley 1990: 145)

I would phrase this a bit more strongly and propose that inclinational virtues are the *only* sort of virtue that Mencius recognizes; they are not only his "paradigmatic virtues" but also his sole paradigm *for* virtue. For instance, courage serves as Yearley's paradigm for the preservational virtues. In his discussion of Aquinas, he notes how eventually, through the Gift of Courage, "the direct action of deity produces a state where a preservational virtue becomes an inclinational virtue." At this point, courage "ceases to exhibit any of its distinctive marks"—that is, consciousness of conflict among competing goods, reflexivity, need for overcoming momentary psychological state—and becomes something of an altogether different quality.[82] In contrast, it would seem that Mencian courage is portrayed as a purely inclinational virtue from the very start, involving as it does the steady accumulation of rightness (*yi*) and gradual expansion of *qi* until one reaches the ultimate stalwartness represented by the "the heart/mind that does not stir" (*budongxin* 不動心), rooted in the irresistible power of the floodlike *qi*. There would seem to be no room in this picture of courage for doubt, regret, or the slightest moment of confusion. The kind of supreme confidence that, for Aquinas, represents an extraordinary gift from the Holy Spirit seems in Mencius's vision of self-cultivation to permeate every step of the way. The Mencian sage is from the very beginning supremely *unvexed*, and yet it seems that a certain degree of vexation—of painfully overcoming temptation, or striking a perhaps less than fully satisfying balance between mutually incompatible goods—is an essential component of a morally lived life.

The extreme internalist and inclinational elements of Mencius's position go against the intuition that living a moral life involves some kind of commitment to external norms, as well as the potential for tension between these external norms and inner inclination. A purely inclinational account seems incoherent when dealing with such moral phenomena as, for instance, the institution of marriage. Inclination certainly plays an important role in marriage, and in the model of marriage now common in the modern West it is accorded perhaps the central role.[83] As this model would have it, marriage is entered into in an essentially inclinational manner, as the result of romantic love or physical passion, and ideally a combination of the two. However, even in this inclination-dominated model, it is recognized that the commitment to the external institution may—at least in exceptional situations—require at times the exercise of preservational virtues, which in turn involve suppressing or going against one's momentary inclinations. The need to counterbalance momentary inclination with something more firm and lasting seems the very raison d'être of the institution itself; indeed, the social institution of marriage is arguably meaningless if the commitment involved is conceived of solely in inclinational terms. Marriage is a conscious, "preservational" commitment. Ideally, this conscious commitment remains fully in harmony with one's inclinations, but in exceptional situations it might involve a degree of reflexivity, some form of conflict between competing inclinations, and—as Yearley quite nicely puts it—"a complicated relationship to pleasure."

Mencius was not blind to the problem of relying solely upon inclination, and recognized that our inclinations often lead us in the wrong direction. He was clearly aware at some level that the moral life often involves difficult choices, tensions, and decisions—that unlike plants naturally growing toward the light or water flowing downhill, people sometimes need to fight *against* the pull of natural inclinations in order to be moral. Since his primary metaphors for self-cultivation and virtue acquisition all involve going along with the natural tendencies of things, they cannot easily accommodate this insight, and Mencius is therefore forced to occasionally supplement them with the sort of externalist metaphors noted earlier, or with a related set of metaphors having to do with the application of strong external force by the Subject upon the Self. We had a taste of this in the metaphoric formulation of extension found in 1:A:7, which involves the Subject physically "pushing" the Self from one place to another. The conceptual scheme of external force is found in other passages—such as 7:A:4, where we are advised to "force" (*qiang* 強) sympathetic understanding, or 3:A:3, where a king is urged to "apply strength" (*li* 力) in his practice[84]—and these external force metaphors do not sit well with the dominant metaphors of ease or effortlessness. This tension is perhaps made most clear in 6:B:15:

> Heaven, when it is about to lay a heavy responsibility upon a person, must first embitter [*ku* 苦] his heart/mind and intention, belabor [*lao* 勞] his muscles and bones, starve his body, exhaust his personal resources, and frustrate or throw into confusion all that he does. Heaven does this in order stir up his heart/mind [*dongxin* 動心] and cause him to take responsibility for his nature [*renxing* 忍性] and make good his areas of inability. It is always the case that a person is able to change [*gai* 改] only after making mistakes, and is only able to innovate [*zuo* 作] after experiencing trouble [*kun* 困] in his heart/mind and conflict in his deliberations [*hengyulu* 衡於慮] . . . Thus we know that people flourish when

placed in trouble and adversity and die when coddled by ease [*an* 安] and joy [*le* 樂].

Here we see Mencius incongruously portraying the "stirred heart/mind" as a *desideratum*, approving of "change," "trouble," and deliberation, and dismissing with disdain the very sort of "ease" and "joy" that is valorized elsewhere in the text.[85]

This tension arguably represents merely an alternate expression of the domesticated versus wild nature tension—both being permutations of the basic paradox of wu-wei we have been tracking—and it similarly stands out as a point of weakness in Mencius's position. Just as the tension between domesticated and wild nature became a target of Zhuangzi's subsequent criticism of Mencian-like positions, this tension between inner prompting and external restraint becomes the central focus of Xunzi's very explicit criticism of Mencius, motivating him to come down strongly on the side of external standards and to develop his own family of metaphors for self-cultivation drawn from the domains of technology and craftwork. It is hoped that the process of tracing the metaphoric innovation involved in the Zhuangzian and Xunzian reformulations of the ideal of wu-wei over the next two chapters will help to convey the inexhaustively productive power of the paradox of wu-wei in all of its various permutations.

Chapter 6

虛

The Tenuous Self:
Wu-wei in the *Zhuangzi*

The Zhuangzian[1] ideal of wu-wei resembles in certain respects that of Mencius, in that it represents a state in which one's actions are perfectly harmonized with one's "natural," spontaneous inclinations. But whereas Mencius understands the "natural" in terms of human hierarchies and inherited cultural forms, Zhuangzian naturalness requires a transcendence of the human—particularly of the categories and valuations associated with that faculty so treasured by Mencius, the human heart/mind (*xin* 心). Like Laozi, Zhuangzi uses wu-wei in a polemical fashion: as a tool to uncover the hidden tensions and difficulties in the thought of his predecessors. While Confucius and Mencius remain fairly silent on the subject of the paradox of wu-wei, Zhuangzi seems to take delight in it. Wu Kuang-ming has commented upon the manner in which Zhuangzi—by calling for such blatantly paradoxical feats as "losing oneself" or fasting away the "essence" (*qing* 情) of what makes us human—seeks to bring out into the open the tension that lies at the heart of earlier theories of self-cultivation and use it as a tool to further human self-understanding:

> [Seeing that this tension exists as well in Confucian thinkers], we are thus aware that this is not a new absurdity invented by Zhuangzi. He merely used a few novel expressions ("wu-wei," "I have lost myself" [吾喪我]) to frankly bring into the open the type of difficulty that arises when the human condition encounters language. The Confucian sages did not mention this problem. Zhuangzi not only brings it into view for us, but also actively makes use of this type of difficulty—plays with this sort of problem—in order to shock us into awareness or understanding. (Wu Kuang-ming 1989: 317)

Although all of the thinkers we are examining share wu-wei as a spiritual goal, this ideal—understood by Zhuangzi as a transformation or transcendence of everyday conscious human activity—plays a more dominant role in the thought of Zhuangzi than in any other major pre-Qin thinker. It is also in the *Zhuangzi* that we find the most complex and potentially confusing network of metaphoric conceptualizations of the wu-wei state in early Chinese sources. We of course find the usual metaphors for lack of exertion—following (*cong* 從 or *yin* 因) and

175

flowing with (*shun* 順)—supplemented with some new concepts and conceptual metaphors, such as "responsiveness" (*ying* 應) or "playing/wandering" (*you* 遊). We also encounter again the SELF AS OBJECT POSSESSION formulation of unself-consciousness, where the Self can be "forgotten" (*wang* 忘) or "lost" (*sang* 喪) by the Subject. Probably under the influence of "Inner Training"–type physiological theory, though, metaphorical "forgetting" of the self is closely linked to the schema of SELF AS CONTAINER, where unself-consciousness is understood as the making "tenuous" (*xu* 虛) of the "inside" of the Self. As we will see below, this metaphorical emptying of the Self then alternately (depending upon which metaphor systems is subsequently invoked) releases the ESSENTIAL SELF—that is, previously suppressed powers within the Self—or clears a space for the "entry" into the Self of the normative order, portrayed as a physical substance or human guest. Flipping this metaphor around, the normative order is at other times cognized by means of the NORMATIVE ORDER AS LOCATION schema, where the Subject can enjoy lack of exertion through "lodging" (*yu* 寓), "fitting" (*shi* 適), or "properly dwelling" (*yi* 宜) in it. As we have come to expect, although these metaphor schemas are at times literally incompatible, they are skillfully woven together by Zhuangzi into a conceptually coherent soteriological strategy.

Fallenness

In the story of the unfortunate seabird who is feted by the Marquis of Lu, Zhuangzi poignantly contrasts the foolishness of contemporary people with the wisdom of the ancients. This bird alights in the suburbs of Lu and is treated to feasts and music as if it were a visiting dignitary:

> But the bird only looked dazed and forlorn, unwilling to eat a single bit of meat or drink a single cup of wine, and after three days it died. The marquis was trying to nourish [*yang* 養] a bird with what would nourish *him* rather than with what would nourish a bird. Someone who knows how to nourish a bird with what nourishes a bird would let it nest in the deep forest, wander [*you* 遊] among the sandbars and bogs, float on the rivers and lakes, eat mudfish and minnows, fly in formation with the rest of the flock and then come to a rest, and live comfortably and contentedly. . . . Things necessarily differ from one another because they have different likes and dislikes. This is why the former sages did not demand that things display the same abilities or engage in the same types of activities. Names stopping when they have identified objects,[2] rightness established upon what is suitable [*yisheyushi* 義設於適]—this is what is referred to as "comprehending principle and thereby holding onto good fortune." (W194–95/G621)

The former sages knew how things differed and never tried to force them into uniformity, letting each thing live and flourish in its own natural and spontaneous way. They used "names" (language) to pick out things in their world and left it at that—they did not let language overstep its bounds and become reified into rigid concepts and categories. Therefore in determining what was right (*yi* 義), they relied not upon linguistic preconceptions or traditional conventions (for instance, that it is "right" to welcome a visiting dignitary with banquets and music) but looked rather to what "fit" (*yi* 宜) the situation. Following the venerable association of *yi* 義 with *yi* 宜 ,[3] Lu Deming explains: "The 'right' is the 'fitting': it is established in accordance with what fits, merely following the nature [of the situation or thing], and not imposing one's own model upon the other" (G623).[4] In short, the ancients understood the "suitable" (*shi* 適): how to accord with things in their naming and valuing. Zhuangzi describes this in chapter 2 as the highest form of knowledge, and chronicles as well the various stages in its gradual decline:

> The knowledge of the ancients really got somewhere. How far did it get? There were those who believed that there had never even been things in the worlds—they reached the highest, most exhaustive form of knowledge. Nothing can be added to it. Below them were those who believed that things existed but that there had never been boundaries [*feng* 封] between them. Farther down still were those who believed that there were boundaries but that there had never been 'right' or 'wrong' [*shifei* 是非]. The glorification of 'right' and 'wrong' is what caused the Way to be harmed, and that which caused the Way to be harmed also caused love to become complete. (W41/G74)

The progress of the fall is quite clearly delineated: first people starting noticing that things existed; then they began distinguishing among them (setting boundaries); finally they reified these distinctions and attached value judgments to them. It is at this point that the Way became "harmed" and "love became complete"—that is, the natural spontaneous caring of people for one another (a manifestation of the Dao) became disrupted, "love" became a conscious issue, and people began making a show of "benevolence" (*ren* 仁).[5] The process of decline is also described in chapter 2 as originating with the "deemed 'it is' [*weishi* 為 是]":[6]

> The Way has never had boundaries [*feng* 封], and teachings/words [*yan*] have never had constancy [*chang* 常]. But with the "deemed 'it is'" we begin to have demarcations [*zhen* 畛]. (W43/G83)

Boundaries become piled upon boundaries, progressing from distinguishing left and right to making theories (*lun* 論), discriminating among things (*bian* 辯), competing (*jing* 競) and finally becoming embroiled in contention [*zheng* 爭). This passage concludes with a very Laozian call to stop this advance of knowledge and return to the inexhaustible resources of the natural—here, as throughout the *Zhuangzi*, identified with Heaven or the Heavenly (*tian* 天):

> Knowledge that stops at what it does not know is the best. Who can know the wordless discriminations,[7] the Way that is not spoken? The

ability to know this is referred to as the Storehouse of Heaven [*tianfu* 天府].⁸ Pour into it and it will never become full, ladle it out and it will never run dry, and yet no one knows where it comes from. (W44–45/ G83)

People today, Zhuangzi laments, have become cut off from this source, this "Storehouse of Heaven." The primary symptom of this fall is the rise of "discrimination"⁹ (*bian* 辯) and the consequent emergence of ideas of *shi* 是 and *fei* 非 . As we saw in chapter 5, these terms literally mean "it is" and "it is not." The fact that a judgment that something does or does not fit a given name usually carries with it a normative element—this thing *is* good, this person *is* a king—also gives *shifei* a normative force that is reflected in our rendering as "right" and "wrong."¹⁰ Zhuangzi clearly does not condemn wholesale the practice of discrimination; as we saw in the quotation above, the former sages themselves picked out objects by means of names. However—and this is crucial—they *stopped* at this stage where names are merely used to pick out objects and "what is right is established upon what is suitable." This is the "great discrimination" (the discrimination that does not speak), that leads to "great knowledge" (*dazhi* 大知). By saying that the great discrimination "does not speak," Zhuangzi seems to mean that one discriminating in this way lacks any kind of foundational justification for why she is calling a given thing "X" in a certain situation.

The problem is that people of Zhuangzi's age claimed an absolute, foundational basis for their discriminations, and thus could not but cling to them and "parade them before others"—an activity that involves a great deal of speaking indeed. The judgments of "right" and "wrong" that result from such overly conscious discrimination—a collection of which constitutes an *yi* 義, a systematized code of "what is right"—are reified into rigid distinctions, which lose the flexibility to accord with what is "fitting" (*yi* 宜). The result is "petty knowledge" (*xiaozhi* 小知) and all of its attendant suffering:

> Great knowledge is broad and expansive; petty knowledge is cramped and divisive. Great words/teachings are quiet and clear; petty words are loud and garrulous. When asleep, people's *hun*-spirits interact [*jiao* 交]; when awake, their bodies open up wide [*kai* 開], and everything they touch becomes an entanglement. Day after day they use their heart/ minds [*xin*] to stir up trouble. Some become boastful, some unfathomable, some secretive. They are consumed with anxiety over petty matters, but remain arrogantly oblivious to the things truly worth fearing. Their words shoot out of their mouths like crossbow bolts, which is why they are called the "arbiters of right and wrong." They cling to their positions as though they had sworn an oath, which is why they are said to "hold onto victory" [*sheng* 勝].¹¹ Their decline is like fall fading to winter—this describes the way they dwindle day by day. They drown in what they do—you cannot make them turn back. They become suffocated, as though sealed up in an envelope—this describes the senility of their old age. And as their heart/minds approach death, nothing can cause them to turn back toward the light [*yang* 陽]. (W37/G51)

The conceptual rigidity of little understanding cuts people off from both the "Storehouse of Heaven" and the world itself. Since they no longer possess the flexibility to respond to the world in a fitting manner, people come into conflict with things and wear out both their bodies and their heart/minds:

> Once people receive their mature [*cheng* 成][12] bodies, they cannot forget them as they wait for the end. Clashing with things, grinding against things, they charge ahead to the end like a galloping horse, and nothing can stop them. Is it not pathetic? They struggle to the end of their lives without ever seeing results, laboriously wearing themselves out without ever knowing the way home [*gui* 歸]. Can you help but pity them? People say, well at least I'm still alive!, but what good is that? Their bodily forms change and then their heart/minds follow—can you deny the sorrow of this? (W38/G56)

In a later passage, Zhuangzi describes the thing that has been lost by these "pathetic" masses as the "Heavenly impulse" or "Heavenly Mechanism" (*tianji* 天機) that guided the ancients:

> The True Person of ancient times slept without dreaming and awoke without worries; he simply ate what was put before him, and his breathing was deep and profound. The True Man breathes with his heels; the multitudes breathe with their throats. Oppressed and bent, they cough up their words as though they were retching. Those with deep passions and desires [*qiyu* 耆欲] are shallow when it comes to their Heavenly mechanism [*tianji* 天機]. (W78/G228)

As with Laozi, then, the natural or the "Heavenly" is also the primordial: the original state enjoyed by the perfected people of some past Golden Age. Again, in a parallel with Laozi, the fall from this state is associated with the rise of desires. These include unnatural or excessive bodily passions (*qi* 耆), but both Laozi and Zhuangzi reserve most of their scorn for what we might call the "social desires": the pursuit of fame (*ming* 名) and the wrangling over questions of "right" and "wrong" that passes for knowledge (*zhi* 知) among their contemporaries. In chapter 5, Confucius is described as one "punished by Heaven" because "his pursuits are motivated by the foolish illusion of fame and reputation, and he does not know that the Perfect Man views these as handcuffs and fetters upon the self" (W72/G204). Just as the pursuit of excessive physical passions harms the body, the pursuit of fame and knowledge agitates or stirs up (*dang* 蕩) one's Virtue (W55/G135). As in the "Inner Training" and the *Mencius*, Virtue is conceptualized metaphorically as a liquid and (as we will see later) associated with the *qi*, but rather than being gradually accumulated through righteous acts, it is portrayed as something of which we have a full stock at birth and which is in fact *depleted* by the very sorts of activities encouraged by Mencius.[13]

Why is it that people fail to note the "dissipation" of their Virtue—that is, to see the futility of such pursuits? Because, Zhuangzi implies, they are distracted and blinded by pride—by a false sense of their own importance and abilities. The little quail who makes fun of the great Peng Bird (W31/G14), the "village worthy" who glows because he has attained a name in his little community (W31/ G14), and even Liezi who can ride on the wind (W32/G17) or the great Lord of the River swollen with the floodwaters (W175/G568) are so full of their own self-importance that they are unable to perceive the Way. This is why the "Nameless Man" in chapter 7 advises Tian Gen that he must "allow no room for selfishness [*si* 私]" if he wishes to be able to "flow along with the natural current of things"[14] (W94/G294), and this is what Zhuangzi means by saying that "The Way is hidden by petty achievements" (W39/G63). The scope of "petty achievements" includes not only personal fame or gain but the supposedly more noble pursuit of the Confucian virtues:

> Yi Erzi went to see Xu You. Xu You said, "How has Yao been helping you?"
>
> Yi Erzi said, "Yao said to me, 'You must personally submit to the discipline of benevolence and righteousness and learn to speak clearly about right and wrong [*shifei*].'"
>
> "Then what are you doing coming to see *me*?" replied Xu You. "Yao has already tattooed you with benevolence and righteousness and cut off your nose with right and wrong.[15] Now how are you going to be able to freely wander along the distant, carefree, transforming path?" (W89/ G278–79)

The conventions and values inherited from the past are nothing but sedimented collections of *shifei* discriminations, and therefore only serve to blind one to the Way. Conceptualizing this metaphorically as a form of mutilation—tattooing or amputation—brings to heart/mind the Mencian metaphor of "injuring" (*zei* 賊) one's natural endowment, although again the metaphor is subverted: here it is the very practice of Confucian culture, not its rejection, that does the damage.

It is not just traditional Confucian morality that presents a danger but more fundamentally the language in which it is formulated, preserved, and passed down. Language is the repository of conventional distinctions, and thus should be approached with caution. Zhuangzi does not deny a positive role to language ("Words are not just blowing wind," he observes. "Words have something to say"—W39/G63); indeed, he himself was a master of Chinese style, and takes obvious delight in both playing with words and using them as a medium to convey his insights. Language is necessary if people are to live together and flourish. There is, however, the ever-present danger of becoming trapped by words: allowing the *shifei* distinctions they represent to get inside and harms one's Virtue, rather than simply using them and then letting them go. Indeed, the tendency to fall under the sway of *shifei* distinctions seems to Zhuangzi to be a deeply rooted human disposition: he refers to it as the characteristic "essence" (*qing* 情)[16] of human beings (that which distinguishes human beings from other living beings), and describes it as something that the Daoist sage must learn to do without:

> [The sage] has the physical form [*xing* 形] of a human being but lacks the human essence.[17] Because he has the form of a human, he flocks

together with other people. Lacking the human essence, though, right and wrong [*shifei*] cannot get to his true self [*shen* 身].[18] Lowly! Small! In this way he belongs to the realm of the human. Elevated! Great! He alone perfects his Heavenly endowment.[19] (W75/G217)

True to form, the logician Huizi (Zhuangzi's friend and traditional "straight man") immediately questions the logic of this statement:

Huizi said to Zhuangzi, "Can a person really be without [the human] essence?"

Zhuangzi replied, "Yes."

Huizi: "But a human without the essence of a human—how can you call him a human?"

Zhuangzi said, "The Way gave him this appearance [*mao* 貌], Heaven gave him this physical form [*xing* 形]—how can you not call him a human?"

"Having already called him a human, how can he be without the essence [of a human]?"[20]

"What I am referring to as 'essence' is [making distinctions of] 'right' and 'wrong' [*shifei*]. So when I talk about 'lacking the essence,' what I am referring to is a person not allowing likes and dislikes [*haowu* 好惡] to get inside and harm his true self. He is constant in following [*yin* 因] the natural and doesn't try to help life along."

"If he doesn't try to help life along, how does he manage to hang onto his body [*shen*]?"[21]

"The Way gave him his appearance, Heaven gave him a physical form, and he never lets likes and dislikes get inside and harm his true self. Now, as for you—you put your spirit [*shen* 神] on the outside and exhaust your quintessential [*jing* 精] [*qi*]. [When out walking], you lean against a tree, huffing and puffing; [when lecturing], you slump over your podium and fall asleep. Heaven picked out this physical form for you and you use it to twitter pointlessly about petty logical distinctions!"[22] (W75–76/G220–22)

Zhuangzi's point here is that the "essence is not the essence." That is, the quality that is conventionally taken to be the essence of human beings (the ability to make *shifei* distinctions) is actually only a flaw that has a deleterious effect upon our *true* essence: our *shen* 神 (spirit) or *jing* 精 (quintessential).[23] When Zhuangzi says that the sage does not allow "likes and dislikes" (i.e., the emotions stirred up by *shifei* 是非 distinctions) to "get inside," and when he chides Huizi for putting his spirit on the outside, he is invoking the SELF AS CONTAINER metaphor and claiming that these vital powers (spirit and energy) are properly inside us from the beginning, and only later become alienated or harmed through the insidious effects of discrimination.

Despite his impatience with his friend Huizi and his frustration with the foibles of his society at large, Zhuangzi is nonetheless troubled by the suffering that people in his age have brought upon themselves. His writings are thus aimed at dispelling the "fallen" habits of heart/mind that have cut humanity off from the Dao—the ultimate source of life. He points to a state of salvation, which (as we shall see) is metaphorically conceptualized in various ways, but which is explicitly identified as "wu-wei" by a School of Zhuangzi writer in chapter 18:

> Now, as for what ordinary people do and what they find happiness in, I don't know whether such happiness is in the end really happiness or not. I look at what ordinary people find happiness in—what the masses all flock together to pursue, racing after it as though they couldn't stop— and I don't really know whether those who say they are happy are really happy or not. In the end is there really happiness or isn't there?
>
> I take wu-wei to be genuine happiness, even though it is something ordinary people think very bitter. Hence the saying, "Ultimate happiness is without happiness; ultimate acclaim is not acclaimed." What the world takes to be right and wrong can in the end never be settled [*ding* 定]. Nonetheless, wu-wei can be used to settle right and wrong. When it comes to attaining ultimate happiness and invigorating the self [*shen* 身], only wu-wei can get you close. (W191/G611–12)

Below we will discuss the barriers which Zhuangzi feels prevent human beings from achieving the state of wu-wei, as well as the techniques he proposes to overcome these barriers.

The Cognitive Aspect of Zhuangzian Wu-wei: Tenuousness and Clarity

How does one avoid alienating one's vital power, or at least regain powers that have already been lost? In other words, how does one resist the inborn human tendency toward fallenness? We have noted that language and the heart/mind, in which the linguistic capacity resides, are singled out by Zhuangzi as the root causes of fallenness, and it is therefore the heart/mind and its distinction-making tendency that are the primary targets of his soteriological strategy. One of the most detailed accounts of the cognitive aspect to Zhuangzian wu-wei is found at the beginning of chapter 4, in an exchange between Confucius (acting as a mouthpiece for Zhuangzi) and his favorite disciple, Yan Hui. Yan Hui comes to ask permission to travel to the state of Wei in order to remonstrate with its young and unprincipled ruler, whose selfish and foolish policies have caused much suffering among his people.[24] Confucius is very dubious about his chances of success—or of even coming back with his head still attached to his shoulders. The problem is that Yan Hui is being guided by teachings/words (*yan* 言) he has heard from the master ("Leave the state that is well ordered and go to the state in chaos!"), his confidence in his superior knowledge of right and wrong, and—Confucius rather sharply observes—his own desire to achieve fame as a "virtuous" man. Yan Hui suggests several different strategies, and they are all rejected by Confucius ("You are still making the heart/mind your teacher [*shi* 師]!" he complains). Finally Yan Hui gives up:

> Yan Hui said, "I have no other suggestions. May I ask about the proper technique [*fang* 方]?"
>
> Confucius responded, "You must fast! Let me tell you: do you think it is easy to act under the guidance of [the heart/mind]?[25] Those who do think so are not deemed fit [*yi* 宜] by Bright Heaven."
>
> Yan Hui said, "My family is poor, so I haven't drunk wine or eaten meat for several months. Can this be considered fasting?"
>
> "That is the kind of fasting one does before a sacrifice; it is not the fasting of the heart/mind [*xinzhai* 心齋]."
>
> "May I ask about the fasting of the heart/mind?"
>
> Confucius said, "Unify your intention [*zhi* 志]! It is better to listen with your heart/mind than to listen with your ears, but better still to listen with your *qi* than to listen with your heart/mind. Listening stops with the ears and the heart/mind stops with matching things up [*fu* 符],[26] but *qi* is tenuous [*xu* 虛] and waits upon things. Only the Way will gather in tenuousness [唯道集 [於] 虛].[27] Tenuousness is the fasting of the heart/mind."
>
> Yan Hui said, "Before I was able to put this into practice, I was full of thoughts of myself. But now that I am capable of putting it into practice, [I realize] that my self has never existed. Can this be called tenuousness?"
>
> The Master answered, "You've got it! I tell you now: you may go and wander in his cage without being moved by fame. If he is receptive, then sing; if not, keep silent. Be without gates and without schemes. Reside in oneness and lodge [*yu* 寓] in what cannot be stopped [*budeyi* 不得已]. Then you will be close to getting it." (W57–58/G146–48)

This is an extremely rich passage, and it will take us the next few sections to unpack it completely.

Let us begin with the three levels of "listening": with the ears, with the heart/mind, and with the *qi*. We cannot resist seeing this hierarchy in terms of the discussion in *Mencius* 2:A:2 described in chapter 4.[28] In commenting upon Gaozi's maxim that "what you fail to get from doctrines [*yan* 言], do not try to find it in your heart/mind; and what you fail to get in your heart/mind, do not try to find it in your *qi*," Mencius rejects the first injunction and agrees with the second. That is, getting "it" (morality, a sense of "rightness") in the heart/mind is primary, while getting it through doctrine or the *qi* is secondary. Mencius further speaks of how the "flood-like *qi*" is then cultivated to support the heart/mind, being born through "gathering righteousness" or "letting righteousness gather" (*jiyi* 集義). Whether Zhuangzi is reacting directly to this Mencian doctrine or merely independently to Gaozi-like maxims that were current at the time, it is clear that he is quite dramatically subverting the Mencian picture of self-cultivation. As David Nivison notes:

> In Mencius's cultivation *yi*, righteousness, "accumulates." In Zhuangzi, it is *dao*, the Daoist "Way," that "accumulates." In Mencius, our *qi* is "starved" [*nei* 餒] if this "accumulating" doesn't happen. Zhuangzi transvalues the image, making his cultivation itself a psychic "fast." (Nivison 1997: 129)

For Zhuangzi, what we get when we listen with our ears (doctrine) is not as valuable as what we get when we listen with our heart/mind (morality), and this thing we get through our heart/mind is still less valuable than what we get through listening with our *qi*. This is because the ears can get no deeper than the surface of words, and the heart/mind can get no deeper than coordinating things with words, whereas *qi*—being "tenuous"—is open to things-in-themselves, the patterned interrelationship of which constitutes the Dao. Zhuangzi feels we must "starve" the heart/mind that we have been given, purging it of the accumulated deposits of *shifei* distinctions that constitute language and conventional conceptions of righteousness, in order to create a clearing of tenuousness in which the Way will gather. Let us now turn to an exploration of the various metaphorical schemas involved in this "fasting of the heart/mind" passage, beginning in this section with the more cognitive aspects.

SELF AS OBJECT

Yan Hui equates the state of tenuousness with a loss of self ("my self has never existed"). This is also the theme of a story that opens chapter 2, where a certain Zi Qi of Southwall, after making "his body like dry wood and his heart/mind like dead ashes" through a sort of meditative technique, declares that "I have lost myself" (*wu sang wo* 吾喪我) (W36/G45). The question of what precisely it might mean for one to lose oneself has always troubled interpreters of the text, and has inspired much ingenuity among recent Western commentators.[29] Fortunately, though, the SUBJECT-SELF schema makes it clear what the metaphoric structure of this event is: the basic schema is the Self as an object that can be possessed or lost by the Subject. This is a structure also common to English and other Western languages, a common instantiation of which is the metaphor of SELF-CONTROL AS OBJECT POSSESSION.[30] In English, for instance, we speak of "losing ourselves" in an activity or "getting carried away." There are cases of this specific instantiation of the object-self metaphor in the *Zhuangzi*, and it in fact appears to be a conventional Warring States metaphor. For example, we read in chapter 7 of a second-rate shaman who is confronted with a true Daoist master that "before he had even fully come to a halt, he lost himself [*zishi* 自失] [i.e., 'lost his nerve'] and ran away" (W96/G304). Similarly, in chapter 6 a person who is seduced by fame and external concerns is described as having "lost himself" (*shiji* 失己) and "ruined his true self" (*wangshen* 亡身) (W78/G232).

Despite the importance for Zhuangzi of the Subject maintaining possession of the "true self" and not allowing any harm to come to it, however, he seems to feel that most of our ordinary instances of Self are harmful to the Subject, and therefore makes use of the SELF-CONTROL AS OBJECT POSSESSION metaphor primarily to transvalue it, giving us the new metaphor: SUBJECT ESCAPES CONTROL OF FALSE SELF BY ELIMINATING OBJECT POSSESSION. One of Zhuangzi's primary soteriological goals is thus purging the Subject of the Self (or, at least, the false instantiations of the self), and this is how we are to understand the perfected state attained by Zi Qi of Southwall and Yan Hui after he has learned from Confucius the secret of the fasting of the heart/mind. In a later but obviously related story in chapter 6, the process of Yan Hui's cultivation (or *de*cultivation) is treated in more detail and described as a process of "forgetting" (*wang* 忘). Twice Yan Hui appears to update Confucius on his progress ("I'm improving!" he excitedly reports each time): at the first stage, he has forgotten benevolence and rightness (*renyi* 仁義), and at the second he has forgotten the Confucian rites and music (*liyue* 禮樂). "That's not bad," Confucius says both times, "But you are still not there." The third time, though, his progress makes a greater impression upon Confucius:

> They met again on another day, and Yan Hui said, "I'm improving!"
>
> "What do you mean by that?"
>
> "I can sit and forget [*zuowang* 坐忘]!"
>
> Confucius looked surprised and said, "What do you mean, sit and forget?"
>
> Yan Hui replied, "I let my limbs and my body fall away, dismiss perception and intellect, separate myself from physical form and get rid of knowledge, and make myself identical with the Great Thoroughfare [*datong* 大通]. This is what I mean by sitting and forgetting."
>
> Confucius said, "Being identical with it, you must be free of likes; Having been transformed [*hua* 化], you must be free of constancy. So you really are a worthy man after all![31] I humbly request to become your follower." (W89–90/G282–85)

This act of forgetting the Self is here conceptualized as an active destruction of the object Self on the part of the Subject, or (through an invocation of the SELF AS CONTAINER metaphor) as the forced expulsion from the Self of those elements not proper to it: perception (*congming* 聰明), consciousness of the physical form, knowledge (*zhi* 知), likes and dislikes (*haowu* 好惡), and "constancy" (*chang* 常)—that is, clinging to rigid forms of behavior.[32] All of the things that can get "inside" and harm one's *qi* or spirit (*shen*) have been eliminated, and Hui is now free to harmonize himself with the "Great Thoroughfare" (i.e., the Dao).

A similar theme is found in the School of Zhuangzi story of Woodcarver Qing, who creates bellstands of such beauty that people think them the products of ghosts or spirits. He explains to the Marquis of Lu how he prepares for his work:

> When I am going to make a bellstand, I am always careful not to exhaust my *qi* in the process, so I fast in order to still [*jing* 靜] my heart/mind. After fasting for three days, I no longer dare to cherish thoughts of con-gratulations or praise, of titles or stipends. After fasting for five days, I no longer dare to cherish thoughts of blame or acclaim, of skill or clum-siness. After fasting for seven days, I am so still that I forget I have four limbs and a physical body. Once I've reached this point, there is no more ruler or court. My skill [*qiao* 巧] is focused and all outside distractions disappear. Only now will I enter the mountain forest and observe the Heavenly nature [*tianxing* 天性] of the trees. If I come across one of perfect shape and form, then I am able to see the completed bell stand in it and simply apply my hand to the task; if not, I let it go. In this way I am merely taking the Heavenly [within] and joining it [*he* 合] with the Heavenly [without]. This is probably why people suspect that the final product was made by spiritual beings [*shenzhe* 神者]." (W205–6/G658)

Here again we find the theme of fasting the heart/mind, with the resultant state being described as "stillness" (*jing*) rather than tenuousness. The import, how-ever, is clearly the same. Once the heart/mind has been stilled, everything "out-side" is forgotten—social rewards, social values, and even the existence of the physical body itself. The result is that Qing is able to be open to the Heavenly nature (*tianxing*) of the mountain trees and skillfully harmonize his inner state (the "Heaven" within) with the Way (the "Heaven" without).

ESSENTIAL SELF + SELF AS CONTAINER

In the case of both Yan Hui and Woodcarver Qing, the "forgetting" of everything extraneous to the true self—from social values to personal greed to the existence of the body itself—results in a state cf inner peace. The OBJECT LOSS metaphor is thus alternately conceived of in terms of the SELF AS CONTAINER metaphor, with the process of forgetting understood as an emptying of the Self of everything which has been produced by the "essence" of human beings: that is, all of the human distinctions that have accumulated and thereby blocked one's access to the Way. Once these barriers have been removed (that is, once the Self has been emptied), the Subject is able to reestablish contact with the normative order—the Way, Heaven, or the "Great Thoroughfare"—and thereby escape fallenness and move smoothly through the world. The importance of forgetting/expelling exter-nalities if one is to harmonize one's internal skill with the Way is emphasized throughout the School of Zhuangzi chapter (chapter 19, "Understanding Life") that contains the Woodcarver Qing story. For instance, Confucius explains at one point that one can be a skillful swimmer only when one has "forgotten the water" (i.e., has lost one's socially acquired fear of water), and brings up the example of archery:

> If you're betting for pottery tiles in an archery contest, you are skillful [*qiao* 巧]. Once you begin betting for belt buckles, you become worried about your aim. By the time you begin betting for solid gold, you're completely petrified. Your skill is the same in all three cases, but on account of your greed you emphasize what is on the outside. It is a general rule that those who emphasize what is outside become clumsy on the inside. (W201/G642)

Similarly, the almost supernaturally skilled swimmer who is able to negotiate the treacherous waters of Lu-liang falls explains that he does so by "following along [*cong* 從] with the way of the water and never allowing selfishness [*si* 私] to be involved" (W204–5/G657). As in the *Laozi*, this metaphoric emptying of the Self is often conveyed by means of the existential verbs *you* 有 (there is) and *wu* 無 (there is not). The post-fast Yan Hui notes that "my self has never existed" (*Hui weishi you* 回未始有 —literally, "there has not yet begun to be a Hui"), and we read in chapter 1 that "the perfected person is without (*wu*) a self, the spiritual person is without achievement, the sagely person is without fame" (W32/G17). The parallel correlation here of self (*ji* 己) with achievement (*gong* 功) and fame (*ming* 名) as equally negative possessions eschewed by the Daoist sage makes it quite clear that the instance of the Self that is to be eliminated from the Subject is the Self constituted by social reknown, social recognition, and similar extraneous concerns.

This SELF AS CONTAINER metaphor is consistently combined throughout the text with the ESSENTIAL SELF metaphor in a conceptual blend that we saw in the *Laozi*, the "Inner Training," and the *Mencius*,[33] giving us the following conceptual structure:

> Inside of $\longrightarrow$ Real Self (Fits Subject/Essence)
> Container

> Outside of $\longrightarrow$ False Self (Does Not Fit Subject/Essence)
> Container

For instance, in the fasting of the heart/mind passage in chapter 2, Confucius rejects one of Yan Hui's suggested schemes because the king he wishes to set straight will not really listen to his preachy advice. "Outwardly he will accord [*he* 合] with you," Confucius warns him, "but inside he will be unrepentant" (W56/G141). In other words, he will falsely ("on the surface," as we would say in English) agree with Yan Hui's advice, but he will not really take it to heart. As in English and the other Warring States texts we have examined, this coordination of "inner" with the Essential Self and "outer" with the False Self seems to be a universally accepted convention that would not need to be justified or explained to the reader.

Thus, it is precisely by eliminating the (false) self—forgetting it or making it empty—that one is able to realize the true self—Yan Hui's "oneness" or Woodcarver Qing's "Heaven within."[34] The true self is usually associated with the Heavenly, while the false self is associated with the human and everything related to the human "essence"—the heart/mind, right and wrong, fame, cultural standards and knowledge, and so on. We see this expressed in a line from the fasting of the heart/mind passage, where Yan Hui advances a scheme in which, as he explains to Confucius, "I will be inwardly straight [*zhi* 直] while outwardly compliant [*qu* 曲—lit. crooked]. . . . Inwardly straight, I will serve as the follower of Heaven; outwardly compliant, I will serve as the follower of humans" (W56–57/ G143). Here Zhuangzi manages in a few words to combine the SELF AS CONTAINER + ESSENTIAL SELF metaphor with a SOCIAL SELF metaphor (the Subject's relationship to Heaven or human beings is like a follower to his or her master) and the schemas of LIFE AS PATH + OUTSIDE FORCES AS OBSTACLES IN PATH, which yields the entailment:

Straight path   ⟶   True to (Inside) Essence (i.e., loyal follower of Heaven)

Crooked path   ⟶   Accommodating (Outside) Forces (i.e., apparent follower of human beings)

It might be helpful at this point to stop and summarize the various forces and instantiations of the Self and where they stand in Zhuangzi's SELF AS CONTAINER + ESSENTIAL SELF schema:

PROPERLY INTERNAL THINGS	PROPERLY EXTERNAL THINGS
(Related to Essential Self)	(Not Related to Essential Self)
Heaven (*tian* 天)	Human (*ren* 人)
qi	"full" heart/mind (*xin*)
spirit (*shen*)	knowledge (*zhi* 知) or scheming (*mou* 謀)
Virtue (*de*)	fame (*ming* 名) or achievements (*gong* 功)
True Self (*shen* 身)	cultural standards (e.g., *renyi* 仁義 "morality")
the numinous (*ling* 靈)	"likes and dislikes" (*hao'e* 好惡) life and death (*shengsi* 死生) the political world (*tianxia* 天下) the physical form or body (*xing* 形) sensory perception (*congming* 聰明)

The power of this metaphor schema is that it motivates a variety of entailments that have crucial soteriological significance and yet can be understood without need for justification or argument by anyone familiar with the use of containers.

> 1. Properly external things inside   ⟶   Subject in bad state
> container

This entailment motivates the perceived danger of allowing "likes and dislikes to internally harm the true self" (W75/G221), the undesirability of "hoarding up [*cang* 藏] benevolence and using it to make demands upon others" (W92/G287), and the admonition not to "serve as a storehouse [*fu* 府] for schemes" (W97/G307). It also provides the logic for the statement that:

> Death and life, preservation and destruction, failure and success, poverty and wealth . . . all these represent the vagaries of affairs and the movement of fate. Day and night they alternate before you . . . but they are not worth disturbing your harmony, they should not be allowed to enter into the Storehouse of the Numinous [*lingfu* 靈府]. (W73–74/G212)[35]

> 2. Properly internal things outside   ⟶   Subject in bad state
> container

This explains the perceived danger of "allowing Virtue to be agitated-spilled out [*dang* 蕩] by fame" (W55/G134) and the warning that "now you are putting your spirit on the outside" (W76/G222).

> 3. Properly external things outside   ⟶   Subject in good state
> container

This entailment fits the description of the sage progressively "putting on the outside" the world, things, and life, and finally reaching the point where he can "enter into [the realm of] no-death and no-life" (*ruyu busi busheng* 入於不死不生) (W82–83/G252).

> 4. Properly internal things inside   ⟶   Subject in good state
> container

One of the most interesting illustrations of this entailment is the metaphoric conception of Virtue, which—as in all the post-"Inner Training" texts we will be considering—is metaphorically conceived of as a liquid-like substance. In the *Zhuangzi*, this liquid substance is something with which the Self is originally filled through the action of Heaven, and it is important not to let it leak out. This explains the admonition, "internally preserve it and externally do not allow it to be agitated" (*neibaozhi er waibudang* 內保之而外不蕩) (W74/G214), and the fascinating description in chapter 7 of a sage who is portrayed as having a "mechanism" that "plugs up" the Self so that his virtue does not leak out: the "plugging up virtue mechanism" (*dude ji* 杜德幾) (W95/G299). Heaven fills the Self up with a full tank of Virtue at birth; if it does not leak out, we can get to use it all up ourselves, "preserve" our true self and live out our full life: "use up completely [*jin* 盡] all that you have received from Heaven" [W97/G307].[36]

Based upon the entailments 1–4, and drawing upon our common knowledge of the behavior of substances in containers, we obtain the further entailments:

> 5. Pervious barrier between inner   ⟶   Undesirable state
> and outer

This explains the problem of "entanglements" resulting from the fact that "when asleep, people's *hun*-spirits interact [*jiao* 交]; when awake, their bodies open up wide [*kai* 開]" (W37/G51).

> 6. Impervious barrier between inner   ⟶   Desirable state
> and outer

This entailment underlies the explanation that the sage Song Rongzi could reach a state where "the whole age could praise him and he would not be encouraged, and the whole world could condemn him and he would not be discouraged" because he had "firmly established the distinction between inner and outer, and clearly marked off the boundary between glory and disgrace"[37] (W31/G16). Similarly, after being shocked into an awareness of his own ignorance (and thus reaching the highest stage of understanding), the sage Liezi is described as returning to his home, not going out for three years, and finally entering a spiritual state in which all selfishness and socially derived distinctions have been expelled and an "air-tight" seal between inner and outer has been established:

> He replaced his wife in the kitchen, fed the pigs as though he were feeding people, and had no preferences regarding the kinds of things that he did. Carving and polishing[38] were replaced by a return [*fu* 復] to the uncarved wood [*pu* 朴]; like a clod he would let his body stand alone. In the face of entanglements he remained sealed [*feng* 封], and in this oneness he ended his life. (W97/G306)

Consider also the admonition to "make it so that day and night you are without cracks [*xi* 郤]" (W74/G212) or the description of the True Person of ancient times, who is said to have "preferred to close himself off [*bi* 閉]" (W79/G234).

Self as Location, Normative Order as Person

We have seen that, in one metaphoric conceptualization, the Self is portrayed by Zhuangzi as a container that must be emptied of extraneous elements and kept tightly sealed against the outside. In a permutation of this schema, Zhuangzi explains how this clearing of the container of the Self allows it to serve as receptacle for the accumulation of the normative order (metaphorically conceived of, like Virtue, as a liquid substance) or—equally—as a location where the normative order or its representatives can come to dwell. We can recall the fasting of the heart/mind passage, where we read that "only the Way accumulates [*ji* 集] in tenuousness" and that the tenuous *qi* "waits upon [*dai* 待] things." Here, the things-

in-themselves—the patterned relationship of which constitutes the Way—are portrayed as visitors who are formally received in the tenuous space of the Self. This
metaphor is reinforced in Confucius's final words to Yan Hui at the end of the
passage:

> You have heard of the knowledge that knows, but you have not yet heard
> of the knowledge that does not know. Gaze into that closed space
> [*quezhe* 闋者], that tenuous chamber where brightness is born [*xushi
> sheng bai* 虛室生白]! Good fortune and blessings rest in restfulness [*zhi*
> 止]. . . . Let your ears and eyes communicate with what is inside, and put
> your heart/mind and knowledge on the outside. Then even ghosts and
> spirits will come to dwell [*she* 舍], not to mention people! (W58/G150)

The "tenuous chamber" refers of course to the tenuous self: once the self is
cleared of extraneous elements—that is to say, once the distinction between inner
and outer (the Heavenly and the human) is understood and the border between the
true and false selves is thereby closed off—cognitive brightness or "clarity"
(*ming* 明) will be spontaneously born and the representatives of Heaven (good
fortune and blessings, the ghosts and spirits) will come to dwell. The Daoist sage
who has reached this state is no longer a prisoner of conventional valuations of
"right" and "wrong" or "good" and "bad," which are normally apprehended by
the senses and then "approved of" by the heart/mind in a predetermined fashion,
but is rather able to understand that these distinctions dissolve from the point of
view of Heaven.

The Behavioral Aspect of Zhuangzian
Wu-wei: Response and Fit

Having discussed the metaphor schemas more closely related to the cognitive
aspect of Zhuangzian wu-wei—the dominant metaphor for which is "brightness"
or "clarity"—we turn now to those associated with the more behavioral aspect. In
Zhuangzi's soteriological scheme, it appears that the cognitive project (the "fasting of the heart/mind") comes first. It is designed to empty the container of the
Self, thereby clearing the way for the Subject to come into contact with the normative order. As we shall see below, the manner in which this contact is conceptualized metaphorically varies quite a bit, but in all cases it allows the Subject to
move through the world in an effortless, unself-conscious and perfectly efficacious manner.

*Wu-wei as Object (Subject) Responding Automatically
to Another Object (World)*

Seeing the world with clarity does not entail entirely rejecting *shifei* distinctions,
but rather making them in a special kind of way. The sage—rendered tenuous and

thus receptive to the Way—no longer perceives the world in terms of *shifei* distinctions and through the veil of language as ordinary people do, but rather sees things "in the light of Heaven"—that is, as they really are in themselves (*ziran*).[39] Clarity frees the sage from the confines of a single human viewpoint, thereby providing him with unmediated access to reality.[40] The sort of cognitive understanding provided by this clarity is portrayed by Zhuangzi as giving rise to a sort of mechanical, automatic response on the part of the Subject to the world. For instance, in chapter 2 we read that:

> Following a "right" entails also following a "wrong"; following a "wrong" entails also following a "right." This is why the sage does not go this route, but rather illuminates things by means of Heaven. He still follows a "this" [*yinshi* 因是], but in such a fashion that his "this" is also a "that," his "that" is also a "this." His "that" is equally "right" and "wrong"; his "this" is equally "right" and "wrong." . . . When "this" and "that" have no opposite [*ou* 偶], this is called the pivot of the Way [*daoshu* 道樞]. Once the pivot is centered in its socket, it is able to respond [*ying* 應] inexhaustibly. . . . Thus it is said, nothing compares to using clarity. (W40/G66)

Here clarity is portrayed as causing an inevitable response in the subject in the same way a properly fitted pivot responds to force exerted upon it. Such perfect sensitivity and responsiveness both to things in the world and to other people is also conceptualized by Zhuangzi metaphorically in terms of the functioning of a mirror:

> Do not serve as an embodier of fame or a storehouse for schemes; do not be an undertaker of projects or a proprietor of knowledge. Fully embody that which cannot be exhausted and wander where there are no signs. Use to the fullest what you have received from Heaven but do not think that you have gotten anything special. Just be tenuous, that is all. The Perfected Person in using his heart/mind is like a mirror: he does not lead, nor does he welcome; he responds [*ying* 應] but does not store. This is why he is able to win over things and not be harmed. (W97/G307)

We see in this passage the mirror analogy being nicely linked to the SELF AS CONTAINER metaphor: a mirror works only because it is itself "empty," and merely responds spontaneously to what is put in front of it. Similarly, the heart/mind of the Perfected Person—once emptied through psychic fasting—is completely open and responsive to things. The mirror-response is thus the behavioral correlate to cognitive emptiness or clarity.

Wu-wei as Object (Subject) Following Another Object

Another common and related metaphor for perfected action in the *Zhuangzi* is that of "following" or "adapting" (*yin* 因). We saw this expression above in the description of the sage who has been able to get rid of the essence of human beings (making *shifei* distinctions) and can therefore "constantly follow the naturalness" (*chang yin ziran* 常因自然), and we will see it again below in the story of Butcher Ding, who is able to adapt to the fixed make-up of the ox (*yinqi guran* 因其固然) as he wields his blade. Situating this "adaptive" responsiveness more explicitly in the context of *shifei* distinctions—and thus linking it to the cognitive project—it is described by Zhuangzi as *yinshi* 因是 ("the adaptive 'it is'"), the practice of which allows one to move through the confused human world like a hot knife through butter:

> Thus you may deem [*weishi*] something to be a slender reed or a great pillar, a gruesome leper or beautiful Xishi,[41] but the Way penetrates [*tong* 通] through all—the strange as well as the fantastic—and makes them one. . . . Only the ultimate person [similarly] knows how to penetrate things and make them one. Such a person does not deem 'this is X' [*weishi*], but rather lodges [*yu* 寓] everything in the usual. The usual is the useful [*yong* 用]; the useful penetrates; that which penetrates gets it; and once you get it you're almost there. 'Adapt to 'it is' [*yinshi* 因是], and stop there. Stopping there, and not even being aware that one is doing so—this is what we call the Way. (W40–41/G70)

Here we have the effortless accordance of "following" linked nicely with the motif of unself-consciousness, and these two main hallmarks of wu-wei are jointly being praised as "the Way." The passage goes on to illustrate the usefulness of practicing adaptive 'it is' with the story of an animal trainer who is able to handle smoothly the arbitrary willfulness of a pack of monkeys—who incidentally serve as a metaphor for the mass of ordinary people who "belabor their spiritual clarity [*shenming* 神明] trying to make things one without realizing that they are the same":

> When the monkey trainer was giving out nuts, he said, "You will get three in the morning and four in the evening." All the monkeys were furious about this, so the trainer said, "Alright, then, I'll give you four in the morning and three in the evening." All the monkeys were thereupon delighted. Without anything being missed out either in name or substance,[42] their pleasure and anger were put to use. This, too, is *yinshi* 因是. This is why the sage uses right and wrong in such a way that he harmonizes with them and is able to rest on the Heavenly Potter's Wheel [*tianjun* 天鈞]. This is called walking two roads [*liangxing* 兩行]. (W41/G70)

A. C. Graham points out that *liang* 兩 has a technical Mohist sense meaning "both sides," and refers to alternatives between which those making discriminations must decide (Graham 1978: 192–93). By "walking two roads," the sage follows a *shi* 是 that—because it is held to provisionally and flexibly—ultimately encompasses both *shi* and *fei*, and this is what is meant when it is said that the sage's "that" is equally "right" and "wrong" and his "this" is equally "right" and "wrong." Such cognitive flexibility leads to behavioral wu-wei: the sage can effortlessly "rest" (*xiu* 休) on the "Heavenly Potter's Wheel" and be naturally smoothed out by this cosmic "tool" in the same way that wet clay is evened out by the literal tool.

Wu-wei as Object (Subject) Physically Fitting Another Object (World)

The monkey passage mentions "harmonizing" (*he* 和) with *shi* and *fei*, which brings us to another family of common metaphors for wu-wei responsiveness in the *Zhuangzi*, all having to do with a physical object (metaphorically representing the Subject) matching up or fitting with another physical object (the world or the Way).[43] Most concretely we have the metaphors of "joining" (*he* 合) or "fitting" (*shi* 適). We find this metaphor in the description of the post-fast Woodcarver Qing, who—having become "still" (*jing*) like a mirror by eliminating extraneous elements from the Self—has removed all barriers to the Heavenly within him "joining" with the Heavenly nature of the mountain trees. A similar example is the portrayal of Artisan Chui, who can draw freehand as perfectly as if he were using a compass or a carpenter's square[44] because

> his fingers followed [*yu* 與] things in their transformations [*hua* 化] and he allowed his heart/mind to linger. Thus his Numinous Tower [*lingtai* 靈臺] was unified and unobstructed. You forget your feet when the shoe fits [*shi* 適],[45] and forget your waist when the belt fits. [Similarly], you forget right and wrong when the heart/mind fits, and remain unwavering on the inside and unmoved by the outside when events come together in a fitting fashion. You begin with what is fitting and never experience what is not fitting when you experience the comfort [*shi* 適] of forgetting what is comfortable. (W206-7/G662)

Here the "fitting" of the Subject to reality is understood in terms of properly sized clothing fitting the body, and is also nicely linked to the cognitive project through both the OBJECT LOSS "forgetting" and the SELF AS CONTAINER + ESSENTIAL SELF metaphors.

At a more abstract level, taking the two entities to be sounds rather than physical substances gives us the metaphor of "harmonizing" (*he* 和), seen in account of the monkey trainer. We find this metaphor again—combined with a metaphor from the "going along" or "following" family— in the advice given to a young man who is going off to serve as the tutor to an unruly young crown prince: "In your outward appearance, it is best to stay close [*jiu* 就] to him, and in your heart/mind it is best to harmonize [*he* 和] with him" (W62/G165). At the most abstract level, this harmony with the world and the normative order is described as "fitting" (*yi* 宜). The original graph for this word was composed of the graph for "many" or "much" under a house roof and above the floor, which Karlgren characterizes as a "well furnished house" (Karlgren 1923: 83)—hence the sense of "proper," "fitting," or "right." Zhuangzi plays upon the relation between this word and *yi* 義 to reinforce his point that it is what is "fitting" to the situation at hand that is truly "right." The True Person of ancient times is described in chapter 7 as "being fitting in his relationship with things" (*yuwu youyi* 與物有宜) (W78/G231). Similarly, it is only when Yan Hui has fasted the heart/mind and given up any kind of rigid conception of morality that he is "considered fit [*yi* 宜] by Bright Heaven."

Wu-wei as Location

The behavioral flexibility displayed by the post-fast Yan Hui brings us back to the issue of *weishi* 為是 (the "deemed 'it is'"). To deem "it is" in a contrived fashion means to reify a *shi* 是 distinction into a fixed judgment, and use this as a guide for future action.[46] The Zhuangzian sage is not guided by the ordinary certainties provided by *weishi*, but rather "lights his way with the brightness of chaos and doubt. He does not *weishi*, but rather lodges all in the constant [*yong* 庸]. This is what is called using clarity" (W42/G75). In terms of this metaphor scheme, to *weishi* a position or judgment is to take out a thirty-year mortgage on it—that is, to settle down in it, grow attached to it. The sage practicing *yinshi* 因是 , on the other hand, takes up a position the way a traveler lodges in an inn: temporarily, and always ready to move on.[47] This mode of understanding gives the sage the sort of flexibility that we have seen evinced in acts of skill, and also allows the unique details of each new situation to be fully appreciated because they are not being screened out by a web of preconceived notions.[48] The metaphor of "lodging" (*yu* 寓) appears frequently throughout the *Zhuangzi*, and describes the proper way both to hold to a position and to be in the world. It serves as a bridge between the PERFECTED STATE AS LOCATION metaphor and the schemas I will discuss next.

Normative Order as Irresistible Force

What it means to "lodge everything in the constant" is clarified by Confucius's advice to Yan Hui after he has completed the fasting of the heart/mind: he tells him to have no predetermined plans or preconceived notions, but to "make oneness your house and lodge [*yu*] in what cannot be stopped [*budeyi* 不得已]" (W58/G148). Here "that which cannot be stopped" is understood metaphorically as a moving place in which the Subject can temporarily dwell and thereby be carried along in the proper manner. Throughout the *Zhuangzi* we see the theme of effortlessness cognized in terms of a normative order—either the Way or Heaven, or simply the disposition of things-in-themselves—that provides an irresistible force capable of carrying the Subject along with it.

This is an alternate way of cognizing both the Pivot of the Way and Heavenly Potter's Wheel metaphors discussed under responsiveness: the sage occupies the pivot or "rests" upon the potter's wheel, and it is these cosmic "tools" that then provide the motive force behind responsiveness. Zhuangzi also draws upon the more standard wu-wei metaphor of "flowing" (*shun* 順). For instance, the manner of one who trains ferocious tigers is presented as a metaphor for how to deal with other people and the world in general:

> [When feeding the tiger], he is timely [*shi* 時] with regard to its appetite
> and understanding of its ferocious nature. Tigers can be made to feel

affection for their keepers—even though they are an entirely different breed from us—if you flow along [*shun*] with them. Those who get killed are the ones who go against them [*ni* 逆].[49](W63/G167)

The metaphor of flowing is often associated in this way with "timeliness" [*shi* 時]. In chapter 3, we see timeliness combined with flowing, the container metaphor, and the venerable Confucian metaphor of "being at ease" (*an* 安) in a nice example of the normative order being conceptualized of as a moving place in which the sage can dwell and be carried away:

When it was fitting [*shi* 適] to come, your master was timely; when it was fitting to go, your master floated away [*shun* 順]. Be at ease in time-liness and dwell in the flow [*anshi er chushun* 安時而處順],[50] and then sorrow and joy will not be able to enter [*ru* 入]. (W52–53/G128)

In a wonderful metaphor in chapter 6, the Way is conceptualized as a great river that represents our original home, and returning to this river is associated with the motif of unself-consciousness:

When the springs run dry and the fish are left stranded together on the land, they keep each other damp with their slime and moisten each other with saliva, [and so stay alive]. It would be better, though, if they were simply able to forget each other in the rivers and lakes. Now, when it comes to praising Yao and condemning Jie, wouldn't it be better to for-get them both and transform along with your Way? (W80/G242)

As Yang Darong 1994: 52 has noted, the pitiful spitting of the stranded fish is Zhuangzi's metaphor for the self-conscious, petty kindness of the Confucians, which cannot compare with the unself-conscious joy of returning to our true home.

"Wandering" or "playing" (*you* 遊) is perhaps the most famous expression of Zhuangzian effortlessness and unself-consciousness. Its literal sense of physi-cally easy wandering metaphorically represents an effortless manner of moving through the world—a manner in which the Subject is not required to exert force upon the Self. Most commonly in the Inner Chapters, wandering is structured metaphorically in terms of the NORMATIVE ORDER AS IRRESISTIBLE FORCE schema that I have been discussing here. That is, the Subject is understood as being able to luxuriate in effortlessness because it has hitched a ride, as it were, on the normative order:

He can mount [*cheng* 乘] the rightness of Heaven and Earth and take the reins [*yu* 御] of the discriminations of the six forms of *qi*, and thereby wander in the inexhaustible. . . . (W32/G17)

Mounting the clouds and *qi*, taking the reins of the flying dragons, and wandering outside the Four Seas. (W33/G28)

Therefore the sage wanders in the inescapable tendencies of things [*wu zhi suo budedun* 物之所不得遯] and everything is preserved. (W81/G244)[51]

Of course, "Free and Easy Wandering" (*xiaoyao you* 逍遙遊) constitutes the title of the first chapter of the *Zhuangzi*, and this image of effortless movement is a common one in the text, often being linked with unself-consciousness: "Unself-consciously [*mangran* 芒然][52] they roam [*fanghuang* 彷徨] outside the dusty realm, drifting easily [*xiaoyao* 逍遙] in the service of wu-wei" (W87/G268). Such ease and unself-consciousness is possible only because the Subject has given up attempting to impose itself upon the Self or the world, and is thus able to relax and simply, as we might say as well, "go with the flow."

Essential Self as Irrepressible Force

Most of the behavioral metaphor systems examined so far portray effortlessness through the image of the Subject allowing the world or normative order to do the work, either through provoking automatic response, providing a fit, or serving as a kind of vehicle carrying the Subject along in the proper fashion. However, the final metaphor—that of "wandering" or "playing"—points in the direction of an alternate way of expressing the theme of effortlessness: the image of an instantiation of the Self, rather than the normative order, providing the motive force for action. For instance, the response of the "nameless man" in chapter 7 to someone seeking advice about how to order the world combines the flowing metaphor with the "joining" schema, the container schema, and the metaphor of wandering:

> Let your heart/mind wander in a state of lazy contentment, let your *qi* join [*he* 合] with silent stillness. Flow along with the naturalness [*ziran*] of things, make no room for selfishness, and then the world will be ordered. (W94/G294)

Here the concept of effortlessness is formulated in terms of the Subject relinquishing control of particular elements of the Self: the heart/mind is allowed to wander on its own recognizance, as it were, in the state of contentment,[53] and the *qi* is allowed to join up with some cosmic reservoir of "silent stillness" (*mo* 漠). Similarly, in the Butcher Ding story (to be discussed in detail later), the skillful exemplar is described as "letting his blade play [*youren* 遊刃]" in the spaces between the joints and tendons of the ox he is dismembering—that is, his blade is metaphorically conceptualized as an instantiation of the Self that can find its own way through the complex tangle facing him. In chapter 4 we see an interesting mixture of schemas: "Ride upon things in order to let your heart/mind wander; consign yourself to what cannot be stopped in order to cultivate the mean" (W61/G160). Here the "ride" provided by the movement of the normative order allows the Subject to give free reign to the heart/mind and cultivate a "heart/mind of harmony with the mean."[54]

It is important to note the existence and intermingling of both of these schemas—that is, both the normative order and an instantiation of the Self being conceptualized as providing the motive force behind wu-wei behavior—because Zhuangzi is often portrayed as advocating a kind of "no-self" doctrine.[55] It is particularly Zhuangzi's celebration of "tenuousness" (*xu*) or "losing" the Self that lends itself to this sort of interpretation.[56] This is an excellent illustration of a point made in my introduction that *all* of the various and sometimes literally incompatible metaphor schemas used to convey a given idea such as wu-wei must be considered together if we are to arrive at a full understanding of the concept. The SELF AS CONTAINER schema and its metaphor of tenuousness, taken by itself, *does* suggest a kind of no-self picture, as does the PERFECTED STATE AS OBJECT LOSS schema ("forgetting" or "losing" the Self). Once we understand the purpose of each metaphor schema, however, we are in a better position to understand how it fits together with and is supplemented by other schemas. The metaphors of tenuousness and forgetting are aimed at removing *cognitive* flaws in human beings: our tendencies to be "full" of ourselves or "stuck on" our values and ideals. As with Michael LaFargue's concept of "aphorisms" discussed in the introduction, these metaphor schemas have their own particular "targets," and their intent is often "exhausted in making their point against their target" (LaFargue 1998: 271). That is to say, despite their apparent amenability to a no-self interpretation of wu-wei, we find that they are contradicted when we turn our attention to the metaphor schemas related to the behavioral aspects of wu-wei. In these schemas, we find the supposedly "tenuous" Subject happily giving free reign to various instantiations of the supposedly "forgotten" Self. The co-occurrence of these apparently incompatible metaphor schemas could (as we have seen before) indicate a genuine tension in the concept they represent, but in this case the two schemas, though *literally* incompatible, do not seem *conceptually* contradictory, for each has its own purpose to serve in Zhuangzi's overall conception of the wu-wei state. Tenuousness is to be understood, not in terms of some complete annihilation of the Self, but rather as a kind of clearing or openness created by the Subject that either allows the normative order itself to enter the Self or—as in the cases we will explore below—releases normatively positive instantiations of the Self that had previously been repressed.

We saw in the *Mencius* how the ESSENTIAL SELF in the role of the sprouts or conceptualized as a raging flood of righteous *qi* served as one motivating component in Mencian wu-wei. Another way in which the importance of the ESSENTIAL SELF was expressed by Mencius was in the social metaphor of the heart/mind (in the form of the intention) as the "commander" (*shuai* 帥) of the *qi,* or (using an agricultural metaphor) as a valuable tree situated among noxious and worthless weeds. Zhuangzi is targeting both of these Mencian metaphors[57] when he sharply challenges the assumption that it is the heart/mind that is the proper "ruler" or most valuable instantiation of the Self:

> Pleasure and anger, despair and joy, concerns and regrets, vacillation and inflexibility, modesty and abandon, candor and posturing—they are all music produced by tenuousness [*xu*], like mushrooms emerging from dampness. Day and night alternate before us, and no one knows where they sprout from. . . . It seems that they are controlled by a True Master [*zhenzai* 真宰], and yet it is particularly difficult to find a trace of it. That it can cause my self [*ji* 己] to act is certain, but I cannot see its physical form [*xing* 形]. It has essence [*qing*] but is without physical form.

The hundred bones, the nine orifices, and the six organs are all put together and exist here [as my body], so which part should I feel closest to? Do you take joy in them all equally, or is there one you favor more? If not, are they all equally servants? But if they are all equally servants, wouldn't it be impossible for them to keep order among themselves? Maybe they take turns being lord and servant. Or do they have a True Lord [*zhenjun* 真君] among them? Whether or not I manage to seek out its essence or not, this would neither add to nor detract from its truth. (W37–38/G51–56)

It would seem, then, that there is indeed some sort of ruler, despite its absence of physical form and the corresponding difficulty of discovering its essence. Mencius is mistaken, though, in assuming that it is the heart/mind. Indeed, to take the heart/mind as the ruler is in fact one of the main causes of fallenness itself.[58] Zhuangzi's soteriological goal is, as we have seen, to escape the domination of the heart/mind and come under the sway of a different "ruler"—this "True Master" who "has essence and yet is without physical form."

Who or what, though, is this master? Despite Zhuangzi's coyness in the cited passage, he is elsewhere less reluctant to identify this normatively positive force within the Self. If we recall our previous discussion of fallenness we will remember the mention of something called the "Heavenly Mechanism" (*tianji*), which is "shallow" in the multitudes but presumably deep in the True Person. This term appears again in one of the School of Zhuangzi chapters in the description of a millipede who explains to a one-legged creature astounded by the skill required to manage ten thousand little legs, "I just put into motion my Heavenly Mechanism, but I don't know how it works" (W183/G593). Although it functions in a manner mysterious to the Subject, then, this Heavenly Mechanism clearly *works*, and represents an instantiation of the Self that enables effortless, unself-conscious behavior.

The metaphor of the Heavenly Mechanism appears only twice in the Inner Chapters, where this powerful, normatively positive instantiation of the Self is more commonly identified as the spirit (*shen* 神). The workings of the spirit is the theme of what is possibly the most famous story in the Inner Chapters, the account of Butcher Ding cutting up an ox:

Butcher Ding was cutting up an ox for Lord Wen-hui.[59] At every touch of his hand, every bending of his shoulder, every step of his feet, every thrust of his knee—swish! swoosh! He guided his blade along with whoosh, and all was in perfect tune—one moment as if he were joining [*he* 合] in the dance of the Mulberry Grove, another as if he were in a performance of the Jingshou symphony.[60]

Lord Wen Hui exclaimed, "Ah! How wonderful! Can technique [*ji* 技] really reach such heights?"

Butcher Ding put down his cleaver and replied, "What I care about is the Way, which goes beyond mere technique. When I first began cutting up oxen, all I could see was the ox itself.[61] After three years, I no longer saw the ox as a whole.[62] And now—now I meet it with my spirit [*yi shen yu* 以神遇] and don't look with my eyes. My sensory knowledge is restrained and my spiritual desires are allowed to move/act.[63] I follow [*yi* 依] the Heavenly pattern [*tianli* 天理], thrusting into the big hollows, guiding the knife through the big openings, and adapting my movements to the fixed nature of the ox [*yin qi gu ran* 因其固然]. In this way, I never touch the smallest ligament or tendon, much less a main joint. . . .

Lord Wen Hui exclaimed, "Wonderful! I have heard the words of Butcher Ding and from them learned how to cultivate life!"[64] (W50–51/ G117–24)

Many interesting observations can be made about this story.[65] To begin with, in the midst of his activity Butcher Ding's body parts are portrayed acting in a literally autonomous fashion. Metaphorically, of course, this is an expression of wu-wei: it is the various instantiations of the Self (the hand, shoulder, etc.) that are doing the work for the Subject (Ding). In the middle of the story, the Subject reasserts control, "taking hold of" or "using" (*yi* 以) one instantiation of the Self (his spirit) rather than another (his eyes) in order to interact with the world. Finally, the SELF AS MOTIVATING FORCE schema reappears when Ding explains that he "stills" or "restrains" (*zhi* 以) his sensory knowledge, thereby allowing his spiritual desires (*shenyu* 神欲) to be free to move or act.

Let us focus now on this positive instantiation of the Self, the "spirit," which seems to be the central theme of the Butcher Ding story. Our understanding of spirit can be enhanced when we see it as being both closely linked with the *qi* and as giving one unique access to Heaven or the Way. Both points allow us to establish a conceptual connection between the otherwise incompatible NORMATIVE ORDER AS IRREPRESSIBLE FORCE and ESSENTIAL SELF AS IRREPRESSIBLE FORCE metaphor schemas, so let us explore them in turn.

In the "human essence" passage from chapter 6, Huizi was criticized for putting his spirit and "quintessential" (*jing* 精) on the outside. The conjunction of the two terms suggests that they are linked. In this context, it is worth noting that the opening passage of the "Inner Training" describes the "quintessential" as the most purified form of *qi*, and claims that it constitutes the essence of the "spiritual" and descends from Heaven to give life to all beings:

In all things the quintessential
Is that which brings them life.
Below it produces the five grains,
Above becomes the constellations.
When flowing in the space between heaven and earth,
It is referred to as the ghosts and spirits [*shen* 神].
When it is stored within the breast
[The one who can do so] is called the sage.[66]

Although no such explicit link between *qi* and spirit is made in the Inner Chapters,[67] the criticism of Huizi shows that at least an implicit connection is present, especially if we see the sort of metaphysical picture described in the "Inner Training" as an assumed background to the *Zhuangzi* as well as the *Mencius.*[68] In Cook Ding's account, spirit is described as being able to be used to "encounter" things in a manner analogous to *qi*'s ability to "wait upon things" that is mentioned in the dialogue between Confucius and Yan Hui cited earlier. Indeed, it might be appropriate to view spirit as the dynamic aspect of *qi*—as the tenuous *qi* in motion within a human being and issuing forth to interact with things. The connection between the two becomes clearer when we see the spiritual progression that Cook Ding describes above in terms of the three levels of "listening" portrayed in the conversation between Confucius and Yan Hui.[69] As Pang Pu 1994 interprets it, Cook Ding's progression can be understood as follows:

(1) Sensory Perception (*guan* 官) (Looking with the eye): seeing nothing but the brute fact of the ox as an object confronting him as an object. This corresponds to "listening with the ear."

(2) Use of Knowledge (*zhi* 知) (No longer seeing the ox as a whole): discriminating now between the various parts of the ox and understanding their connections to each other. This is deeper than level (1), but still not good enough, and corresponds to "listening with the heart/mind" (which can go no further than making correspondences).

(3) Guided by Spirit ("Meeting it with the spirit"): being open by means of the tenuous *qi* to the "Heavenly pattern" of the ox, and following along with these patterns under the guidance of the *qi* in motion (the spiritual desires). This is the model not only for keeping one's knife sharp but also for preserving life itself, and corresponds to "listening with the *qi.*"

To further reinforce the analogy between Cook Ding's progress and the advice given to Yan Hui by Confucius, we might also note a passage from one of the Outer Chapters (chapter 11) that echoes Confucius's advice, only with "spirit" taking the place of *qi*:

Don't look and don't listen; embrace the spirit by means of stillness [*bao shen yi jing* 抱神以靜] and the physical form will correct itself. You must be still and pure [*qing* 清]; do not belabor your physical form and do not agitate your quintessential.[70] Only then you can live a long life. When the eye does not see, the ear does not hear, and the heart/mind does not know, then your spirit will protect the body, and the body will enjoy long life. (W119/G381)[71]

For Zhuangzi, as we have seen throughout this chapter, neither the senses nor the heart/mind are proper to the ESSENTIAL SELF. In order to have access from the inside to a positive guiding impulse, it is necessary to get in touch with an internal force such as the spirit, which is composed of and flows out of the refined *qi*.

What invests the "spiritual desires" or the "Heavenly Mechanism" with a normative quality not possessed by ordinary human desires is, of course, their connection to Heaven and the Way. It is this connection to the normative order that provides the conceptual link between the normative ORDER AS IRREPRESS-

IBLE FORCE and ESSENTIAL SELF AS IRREPRESSIBLE FORCE metaphor schemas. While the association of the "Heavenly Mechanism" or Woodcarver Qing's "Heaven within" with the normative order is self-evident, the link between the spirit and Heaven/the Way is best illustrated with a few examples. The many "skill stories" in the *Zhuangzi* provide a wealth of indirect links between the two. For Butcher Ding, for example, following the spiritual desires gives him access to the "Heavenly pattern" of the ox. Similarly, when Woodcarver Qing matches up the Heaven within with the Heaven without, people think that his work must be the products of "spiritual beings" (*shen* 神者). Many similar stories are to be found in chapter 19 ("Mastering Life"), the work of a "School of Zhuangzi" writer. In one, Confucius runs into a hunchbacked cicada catcher who seems to possess supernatural skill because he is able to focus on the cicada wings to the exclusion of all other considerations. Confucius explains to his disciples, "He does not allow his intention [*zhi* 志] to become divided and thereby becomes focused in his spirit" (W200/G641).[72] Artisan Chui, whose story I discussed above, is able to draw perfect circles and lines because his actions are under the unimpeded direction of his "Numinous Tower" (*lingtai* 靈臺), a metaphor for a heart/mind filled with the spirit,[73] and a preternaturally skilled ferryman is described as handling his boat "as if he were a spirit" (*ruo shen* 若神).

It is clear in these stories that spirit is associated with marvelous ability and perfect harmony with the way of the world. The "School of Zhuangzi" author of this chapter even goes on to make an explicit link between spirit and Heaven:

> [The Perfect Man] guards and keeps intact his Heavenly [nature]. His spirit has no cracks in it, so how can things enter into him? When a drunken person falls out of a cart, although the cart may be going very fast, he won't be killed. His bones and tendons are the same as other people, and yet he is not injured as they would be. This is because his spirit is intact [*qi shen quan* 其神全]. He was not aware that he was riding, and is equally unaware that he had fallen out. Life and death, alarm and terror cannot enter his breast, which is why he can come into contact with things without fear. If a person can keep himself intact [*de quan* 得全] like this by means of wine, how much more so can he stay intact by means of Heaven! The sage hides in Heaven, and therefore nothing is able to harm him. (W198–99/G634–36)

Here we have the unself-consciousness of wu-wei action portrayed metaphorically as a kind of intoxication, with spirit conceptualized as a substance that can be made "intact" by wine (at least temporarily!). This highlights spirit's link with human physiology and the *qi*, while the parallelism of the passage suggests that it represents the sage's Heavenly nature. It is interesting that in this passage spirit is (invoking the SELF AS CONTAINER metaphor) understood as a kind of indestructible core that protects and seals off the unself-conscious Subject from harmful external elements. A similar link (only here described as obtaining between spirit and the Way) is found in chapter 6, where we read that spirit is a substance invested in things by the Way: "It gave spirituality [*shen*] to the spirits and to the Lord on High" (W81/G247).

As is usually the case, however, it is in the Outer and Miscellaneous Chapters that we find the most explicit metaphysical accounts of the spirit-Heaven/Way connection. In chapter 11, the NORMATIVE ORDER AS IRREPRESSIBLE FORCE scheme is invoked in the claim that the sage "is moved by the spirit and follows along (*sui* 隨) with Heaven, obedient and content in wu-wei" (W116/G369). Switching to the ESSENTIAL SELF AS IRREPRESSIBLE FORCE metaphor, the chapter goes on to explain that "what is spiritual and cannot but be put into action (*bukebuwei* 不可不為), this is Heaven" (W124/G398). In chapter 12, spirit is associated with the quintessential (*jing* 精), and (in a passage that Graham identifies as being the product of a "School of Zhuangzi" writer) it is claimed that a "settled" (*ding* 定) spirit is necessary if one is to be "carried along" (*zai* 載) by the Way (W134/G433–34). In chapter 15, "content and wu-wei, moving at the impetus of Heaven"[74] is described as part of the way of cultivating the spirit (W169/G544), and it is said that the quintessential and the spirit (*jingshen* 精神) "reach [*da* 達] to the four directions, flowing [*liu* 流] everywhere—there is no place to which they do not extend"(W169/G544).[75] It is thus quite clear that spirit is conceived of by Zhuangzi as connecting the Subject with Heaven and with the workings of the Way, and that (along with *qi* and the quintessential) it serves as powerful instantiation of the Self that—when released from the external forces that normally repress it—will carry the subject along in a wu-wei fashion. The fact that this wu-wei activity arises from a Heavenly endowment possessed by the Subject is why it is at times described as "using to the fullest what you have received from Heaven" (W97/G307).

Finally, the existence of this metaphor scheme of an instantiation of the Self providing the motive force for proper action bears upon the issue of whether or not Zhuangzi has a conception of human nature, and—if so—what that conception might be.[76] Although Zhuangzi does not discuss explicitly the question of human nature in the same way that Mencius does, the existence within human beings of a locus of action—the spirit or Heavenly Mechanism—that is normally suppressed or warped by the activities of the human heart/mind, and that has "desires" of its own, should be seen as representing a kind of "nature." That these spiritual desires might encompass even such things as a parent's love for his child is suggested by the story of a metaphorically named Mr. Lin Hui 林回 (lit. Forest Returning), who—in fleeing from the state of Jia 假 (lit. Falseness)—throws away a valuable piece of jade and takes his infant son with him instead. When asked incredulously why he would discard such a convenient and valuable item in order to save a bothersome, relatively worthless infant, Lin Hui replies that "the jade and I were joined by profit, while the infant belongs to me through the action of Heaven" (W215/G685). The fact that the relationship between a parent and his child is associated with Heaven and portrayed as more essential and enduring than relationships of mere profit is very Mencian in flavor, and it would thus seem that at least some human affections are natural to human beings, and will spontaneously emerge once the grip of the heart/mind upon the self has been loosened through fasting and the true Heavenly nature is allowed to emerge.

Heavenly Freedom and Human Necessity

The issue of freedom and necessity in the Zhuangzi is another example of why it is necessary to understand the intended target range of the metaphor schemas employed in the text. Some of the passages involving "wandering" or "playing" seem to describe a kind of release from the phenomenal world, speaking as they do of "wandering outside the Four Seas" (W33/G28; W46/G96) or "going out beyond the Six Ultimates [*liuji* 六極] and wandering to 'Possessing Nothing At All' Village in order to dwell in its broad and untrammeled wilds" (W93/G293). Indeed, paeans to freedom often take a fantastic form in the *Zhuangzi*, where the sage is described as cavorting with the "Creator of Things" (*zaowuzhe* 造物者), drinking dew, and riding on dragons. These "freedom" passages are usually based upon the metaphor schema, HUMAN WORLD AS CONTAINER, with freedom conceived of as going outside the container. This scheme, considered in isolation, would suggest that wu-wei involves a complete transcendence of the world as we know it. As I will discuss later with regard to "no-self" interpretation of the text, however, this sort of freedom metaphor must be understood in the context of other related metaphor schemas (such as "fitting" with the world or being carried away by it). Understood this way, it becomes clear that the "container" that the sage escapes is the *human* world, rather than the larger world of nature and the Way.

Having fasted away or "forgotten" (*wang* 忘) her human essence, the Zhuangzian sage has reestablished a connection with the Heavenly essence that the ancients took for granted. The freedom that comes with this intoxicating forgetfulness can only be envied from afar by those such as Confucius, who remain trapped within the human realm and all of its conventions. In chapter 6, we read of Confucius's stubbornly obtuse disciple Zigong—upon being sent by Confucius to offer condolences to a group of Zhuangzian sages upon the death of one of their friends, and being scandalized by their lack of ceremony—rushing back to complain of it to Confucius:

> "Who *are* these men?" he asked. "They display not the slightest trace of decorum [*xiuxing* 修行] and pay no attention to[77] their physical bodies. In the presence of the corpse they break out in song, without even changing the expression of their faces. I cannot come up with a name to describe them. Who *are* they?"

> "Men like that," answered Confucius, "wander [*you* 游] beyond the human realm [*fang* 方], whereas I am the kind of person who wanders within it. Beyond and within can never meet, and yet I sent you to go and offer condolences. That was loutish of me. As we speak they are joining as men with the Creator of Things and wandering in the unified *qi* of Heaven and earth. They look upon life as a swelling tumor or a protruding wart, and upon death as the draining of a sore or the bursting of a boil. How could you expect people like this to think of life being put first or death being put last? They consign themselves to a common

body cobbled together from various creatures. They forget their internal organs and put away their senses, returning and reversing, ending and beginning, unaware of where they start or finish. Unself-consciously they roam beyond the dusty world, wandering free and easy in the service of wu-wei. How could you expect people like that to bustle about performing the rituals of this vulgar world in order to provide a show for the masses?" (W86–87/G267–69)

Having opened themselves to Heaven, these sage men can now "wander free and easy in the service of wu-wei." Being freed of the dominion of the heart/mind and the tyranny of the human is thus metaphorically conceptualized as a sort of escape from the mundane or vulgar world.

We see this theme of release being also understood as an escape of the Subject from domination by undesirable aspects of the Self—those external elements such as the heart/mind, fame, distinctions. The SUBJECT AS PRISONER OF SELF metaphor informs the contemptuous attitude toward Confucius taken by a Daoist sage in chapter 6, cited earlier: "his pursuits are motivated by the foolish illusion of fame and reputation, and he doesn't know that the Perfect Man views these as handcuffs and fetters upon the self" (W72/G204). Here the pursuits of the foolish illusions of fame and reputation represent the parts of the Self that falls for their temptation, and this aspect of the Self is conceptualized as a force that fetters the subject. A similar idea is expressed by the metaphor of "release" (*jie* 解), which is based upon the metaphor of WORLD AS IMPRISONING FORCE. Wu Kuang-ming believes that this metaphor motivates a play on words in the Butcher Ding story, because the word translated as "cutting" (*jie*) also means to "loosen" or "release" (as well as to "understand" or "explicate"). Wu points out (Wu Kuang-ming 1990: 322) that it appears in the otherwise somewhat mysterious words of certain Zhang Wuzi near the end of chapter 2:

One who dreams of enjoying wine may wake up crying, and one who dreams of crying may bounce up in the morning and go off to enjoy the hunt. When we are dreaming we do not know that we're dreaming. Sometimes we even try to analyze our dreams while we are in the middle of them, and only after waking realize that it was all a dream. So one day there will be a great awakening where we will realize that all of this is one big dream. And yet the foolish believe that they are awake—so clever and perceptive, they are sure of it. Is there really any distinction between a so-called "ruler" and so-called "common shepherd"? Confucius and you are both dreaming, and my telling you this is itself equally a dream. You may dismiss what I am saying as exceedingly strange, but when after a myriad generations we encounter a great sage who knows how to liberate [*jie* 解] us, my words will seem quite commonplace. (W47–48/ G104–5)

Here the theme of "loosening" or "undoing" is combined with the metaphor IGNORANCE AS DREAM, UNDERSTANDING AS BEING AWAKE, and clearly involves a radical alteration in the Subject's relationship to the ordinary world.

These metaphor schemas, when focused upon exclusively, have led some commentators to see Zhuangzi as advocating a philosophy of "absolute freedom" or "complete liberty"—that is, of complete transcendence of the limitations of the material realm.[78] Again, such an interpretation involves a failure to understand such metaphor schemas within their larger conceptual context, and thereby to understand the range of their intended "target." The "traveling outside," being "released," or "waking up" metaphors are targeted at normal human limitations; they do not preclude the existence of some form of greater, Heavenly limitations. If we recall the metaphor of the normative order as a physical object to which the Subject must "fit" or with which he must "join," as a moving force that carries the Subject along, or as an "inescapable tendency of things" (W81/G244) along with which the Subject may wander, it becomes clear that in following the promptings of the spirit the sage is not completely transcending the material realm, but is rather for the first time actually able to perceive and spontaneously accord with its dictates. This sort of spontaneity[79] is described very well by A. C. Graham:

> The man who reacts with pure spontaneity can do so only at one moment and in one way; by attending to the situation until it moves him, he discovers the move which is "inevitable" [*budeyi*, the one in which he 'has no alternatives'] like a physical reflex.[80] Unlike Moists and Yang-ists seeking grounds for the right choice, Zhuangzi's ideal is to have no choice at all, because reflecting the situation with perfect clarity you can respond in only one way (Graham 1989:190).

This captures very well not only the phenomenology of Zhuangzi's skillful exemplars such as Butcher Ding or Woodcarver Qing but also the feeling of inevitability that accompanies certain artistic achievements: when an artist is successful, it often seems to her that the lines she has drawn and the colors she has chosen could not be otherwise. This sort of activity is felt not so much as a creation of order out of nothing, but the *discovery* of something—of the proper way pigments on a canvas are to be combined to reflect a landscape, or the way a knife is to be wielded if an ox is to be butchered. As Alan Fox 1996:64 notes, "[Butcher] Ding does not decide where he *wants* to cut—he *finds* the space between the bones." The freedom that Zhuangzi advocates is a freedom to act *properly* in response to a given situation, and thus represents a subtle combination of freedom and constraint.

Indeed, it is not merely the physical world of things that imposes a constraint upon the sage's actions but the structure of human society as well. Many scholars have interpreted Zhuangzi as advocating a complete withdrawal from social life,[81] and passages from the Outer and Miscellaneous Chapters are often cited in support of such interpretations. However—although eremitism was a prominent path taken by later self-proclaimed followers of Zhuangzi—the position of Zhuangzi himself and his closest followers would seem to be significantly more nuanced. While there begins to be signs of "world-renouncing" tendencies in writings such as chapter 19 ("Mastering Life"),[82] it is clear that the Zhuangzi of the Inner Chapters perceived the essential futility of attempting to flee from the world in pursuit of some sort of personal hedonistic pleasure, or simply in an attempt to preserve one's physical body (as in the philosophy of Yang Zhu).[83]

Zhuangzi seems to have felt that human beings are always already members of a given society—that we are inescapably social animals—and therefore cannot avoid certain aspects of social life. We see this theme in the metaphor—often overlooked in the *Zhuangzi*—of "fate" as an "order" (*ming* 命) from Heaven in a story from chapter 4, which is, not incidentally, entitled, "In the Human World." In this story Confucius advises someone who is soon to be sent off on a mission of the importance of knowing the inevitability of both fate and social duty:

> In the world there are two great constraints [*dajie* 大戒]: one is fate [*ming*], the other is duty [*yi* 義]. That a son loves his parents is due to fate—you cannot dislodge [*jie* 解] this emotion from his heart. That a minster serves his lord is a matter of duty—there is no place he can go where he is not subject to his lord, nowhere in the entire space between Heaven and Earth to which he could escape. These two are called the great constraints. Therefore, to serve your parents and be at ease [*an* 安] with every aspect of this service represents the perfection of filial piety [*xiao* 孝]. To serve your lord and be at ease with every task required of you represents the flourishing of role-specific duty [*zhong* 忠]. To serve your heart/mind in such a fashion that sorrow and joy do not run circles around it, understanding that there are things that you can do nothing about [*bukenaihe* 不可奈何] and accepting it contentedly [*an*] as fate— this represents the perfection of Virtue.
>
> As a minister or a son, there will certainly be things that cannot be stopped [*budeyi* 不得已]. If you act in accordance with the essence of events and forget about yourself, then what time will you have left to love life and hate death? . . .
>
> Let your heart/mind wander by mounting upon [the tendencies of] things, and nourish what is inside by trusting yourself to what cannot be stopped[84]—this is best. . . . Nothing is as good as following orders (obeying fate) [*zhiming* 致命],[85] and therein lies its difficulty. (W60–61/ G155–60)

The mention in this passage of filial piety and other Confucian virtues has led some commentators to suggest that this passage is a later Confucian or Huang-Lao school interpolation.The difficulty in integrating this passage into Zhuangzi's larger vision only arises, however, if one is committed to seeing Zhuangzi as a resolutely anti-Confucian advocate of "absolute liberty" and "social irresponsibility."[86] Taking a larger view of his thought, however, we can see the connection between this and similar passages and the more obviously "Daoist" stories such as that of Butcher Ding or Woodcarver Qing. In this respect, Billeter's comment on the passage cited above is quite insightful:

> [The *Zhuangzi*] is often taken as an apology for carelessness [*l'insouci-ance*], abandonness, escape—in short, for "liberty." However, Zhuangzi

is from the beginning a philosopher of non-liberty. "Nothing is as good," he says, "as following orders (obeying fate),[87] and this is what makes it so difficult." There is no liberty for him outside of the recognition of necessity—or more precisely outside of the practical realization of necessity at the heart of our activity. The most striking examples offered to us are therefore not based upon any type of escape (necessarily illusory) that a person might expect from "liberty," but rather upon the necessary activities engaged in by the ferryman, the cook and the woodcarver—as well as by Zhuangzi himself in his philosophical project. (Billeter 1993: 558)

Submitting oneself completely and contentedly to the necessities of physical reality, of fate, and of one's place in the social realm can thus be seen as one of the central themes of the *Zhuangzi*. It would thus not be accurate to say that the Daoist sage is free to do anything whatsoever that he wants; rather, he is free to do what he *must*, and do so with joy and a sense of ease. He "lets his heart/mind wander free by following along with things"—that is, his freedom lies in according with the orders of Heaven. When this accordance is not coerced from the outside, but rather springs from normative forces within the Self, we can truly say that the perfection of Virtue has been attained.

Zhuangzi's ideal thus strikes an interesting balance between freedom from normal human constraints and submission to a higher sort of necessity. This corresponds to a kind of balance struck by the sage between the Heavenly and the human. In exhorting people to "use to the fullest all that you have received from Heaven" (W97/G307), while at the same time realizing that it is necessary to act in the physical and social realms, Zhuangzi is calling for a metaphorical "walking of the two paths" with regard to the Heavenly and the human. This theme is sometimes also conveyed by means of the social metaphors of companionship and competition, as when the True Person of ancient times is described as having attained a state where:

> What he liked was one and what he did not like was one. His being one was one and his not being one was one. In being one, he was serving as a follower of Heaven. In not being one, he was serving as a follower of humans. When the Heavenly and the human do not defeat one another, then we may be said to have a True Person. (W79–80/G235)

Zhuangzi is here asking us to draw upon our knowledge of social relations in order to understand the abstract relationship between the Heavenly and human. Most of us have experience negotiating situations where our social ties or personal loyalties extend to people who may not be amenable to one another, or who may in fact be in open conflict. Just as we have learned how to negotiate such complex situations of mixed loyalties, the sage is able to harmonize the apparent conflict between the Heavenly and the human, using each to inform the other. He is in touch with the Heavenly realm, and so understands that—from Heaven's perspective—things are one. However, acting in the world, as I noted earlier, requires some form of discrimination between *shi* and *fei* (or *ran* and *buran*)—

Woodcarver Qing, for instance, must decide whether to put his hand to the work
or withhold it—and so the sage must discriminate. When this discrimination is
informed by the Heavenly perspective it is "great discrimination": a temporary
"lodging" in a given *shi* or *fei*. This is described by Zhuangzi as the "flourishing
of knowledge":

> One who knows what Heaven does and also knows what humans do is
> the best. Knowing what Heaven does, his [actions] are born of Heaven.
> Knowing what humans do, he uses the awareness of that knowledge to
> cultivate an awareness of what he does not know, and so lives out his
> Heavenly lifespan without dying halfway along the road. This is the
> flourishing [*sheng* 盛] of knowledge. (W77/G224)

The Zhuangzian ideal thus somewhat resembles the vision of being "in the
world but not of it" presented in the New Testament (John 17).[88] An exemplar of
this mode of living is presented in the form of the swallow, "wisest of all the
birds," described in chapter 20:

> If its eyes do not find a suitable [*yi* 宜] place, it will not look twice. If it
> happens to drop the fruit it is carrying, it will simply abandon it and con-
> tinue on its way.[89] It is wary of people, and yet it lives hidden among
> them,[90] protected within the altars of grain and soil. (W218/G692)[91]

We should thus see that true transcendence of the fallen aspect of human nature
requires not the dogmatic rejection of the worldly, but rather a transformation of
the self in which one properly balances the human and the Heavenly. Such balance allows one to move through the human realm without stirring up trouble,
like an "empty boat" that can bump into another boat without eliciting anger or
even much notice. Zhuangzi comments on this image of the empty boat, "If a person is able to make himself tenuous and thereby wander through the world, then
who can do him harm?" (W212/G675). Perhaps one of the most extraordinary
exemplars of this ideal is Beigong She, the skillful tax collector.[92] He displays an
extraordinary facility in collecting the funds needed by a ruler to cast a set of ceremonial bells without encountering any resistance. Like Lord Wenhui after
observing the performance of Cook Ding, he is asked by his amazed Duke,
"What art [*shu* 術] is it that you possess?"

> Beigong She replied, "In the midst of unity, how could I dare to "pos-
> sess" anything? I have heard it said, 'Give up carving and polishing
> [*diaozhuo* 彫琢] and return to simplicity [*pu* 樸].'[93] Dull, I am without
> comprehension; free of concerns, I simply dawdle and drift. Moving
> along with the herd, unself-conscious, I see off that which goes and wel-
> come that which comes; I do not reject the latter, and do not try to stop
> the former. I follow [*cong* 從] people when they are feeling strong and
> violent, trail after [*sui* 隨] them when they are feeling weak and com-
> plaisant, adapting to [*yin* 因] each emotion as it naturally plays itself out.
> Thus I am able to collect taxes from morning to night without meeting
> with the slightest resistance." (W213/G677)

Similarly, after hearing some Daoist advice in chapter 20, Confucius gives up teaching and retires to a great swamp, living in rags and eating whatever he could gather himself. "He could walk among the animals without alarming their herds, walk among the birds without alarming their flocks," we read. "If even the birds and beasts did not resent him, how much less would men!" (W214/G683)

The Paradox of Wu-Wei in the *Zhuangzi*

This, then, is Zhuangzian wu-wei: emptying the container of the Self of all human elements so that it might be filled with the Heavenly, and then keeping this container sealed so that the newly freed Subject may follow along with the natural tendencies of things is a state of complete ease and unself-consciousness.

Of course, we should expect that this conception is not free of tensions. We can, I think, distinguish at least two different tensions in the Zhuangzian conception of wu-wei. The first centers on the relationship between the Heavenly and human. Zhuangzi urges the sage to be a "companion" to them both, and not to allow one to "defeat" the other. One might well ask, though, why the two are in conflict in the first place. Aspiring sages are urged to "use to the fullest" what they have received from Heaven, yet in order to effect a proper balance between the Heavenly and human it is necessary for the sage to fast away the human "essence" (*qing*). Is not our "essence," though, by definition what we have gotten from Heaven? Zhuangzi would of course reply that it is fact the spirit and *qi* that represent our ESSENTIAL SELF, and that the heart/mind, knowledge of right and wrong, physical passions, yearning for fame, and all of the other ills that trouble us are merely "externalities" that must be expelled from the container of the Self. If they are mere externalities, though, how did they ever get inside in the first place? That is, if Heaven did not put them there, who did? If it is Heaven's will that we expel them from the Self, why did Heaven not simply leave them outside us from the very beginning? To relate this to the paradox of wu-wei, why do we need to *try* so hard not to try?

We can rephrase this concern by considering the debate between Zhuangzi and Huizi where the propensity for making "right/wrong" (*shifei*) distinctions is portrayed by Zhuangzi as both the "essence" and the major flaw of human beings. If we recall this exchange, we cannot help but feel a bit of sympathy for Huizi's position. We might reformulate and somewhat bolster Huizi's objections and ask of Zhuangzi, if it is the essence of human beings to make distinctions of right and wrong, why should we try to eliminate this essence? Put another way, if human beings are by their very nature prone to evaluate the world in terms of right and wrong, is this not (as Mencius would argue) the most "natural" way for them to live? Turning the question around again, if evaluating the world in terms of right and wrong is indeed "unnatural," why are we born unnatural and why do we have to work so hard in order to *become* natural? Some readers might find themselves nodding in agreement with Huizi's exasperated rejoinder, "If he doesn't try to help life along, how does he manage to hang onto his body?" It would seem that we human beings are born problem-solvers who use reason and instrumental thinking in order to control and manipulate our environment, in order to further our own existence and the existence of our kind. Is this not our natural way of being in the world? One might also note that the Way is said by the author of chapter 22 to be everywhere, including in the urine and excrement (W240–41/ G750). If this is so, why can the Way not be found in the exercise of human beings' Heaven-endowed rationality as well? This tension between the Heavenly and human became, as we shall see in the next chapter, the target of Xunzi's criticism of Zhuangzi, and is the motivation for his disapproving comment that "Zhuangzi was obsessed by Heaven and did not understand the importance of the human."[94]

This first tension is related to a second, perhaps deeper one. We have seen the metaphor schemas NORMATIVE ORDER AS IRREPRESSIBLE FORCE or ESSENTIAL SELF AS IRREPRESSIBLE FORCE used to convey the behavioral aspect of Zhuangzian wu-wei. The problem with these metaphors, though, is that even a cursory examination of Zhuangzi contemporaries in the chaotic period of the Warring States would suggest that the normative order as a motivator of human behavior seems quite repressible indeed. If the river of the Way is simply waiting to take us away, why are more of us not already floating down it?

The answer, of course, is that we need to *do* something first before we are ready to flow with the Way—that is, we need to try not to try. We thus encounter again the problem we saw in both Laozi and Mencius—and which seems endemic to the internalist position—of why we have to try so hard not to try, or how it is even possible at all to try not to try. Is it not the case that deciding by means of the heart/mind to fast away the heart/mind is a contradictory undertaking? Does not the conscious desire for a state of desirelessness involve overcoming an insurmountable difficulty?

There have been modern scholarly attempts to reconcile this form of the paradox. One common tactic is to—much like Herrlee Creel in his approach to the *Laozi*—postulate two different "types" of wu-wei, one "active" (i.e., serving instrumental purposes) and one "nonactive" (i.e., "contemplative"). Mori Mikisaburo has noted that passages such as the Cook Ding story reveal the presence in the *Zhuangzi* of the first type of wu-wei ("activity naturalness"), which is the culmination of a great deal of effort, but feels that the second type of wu-wei ("nonactivity naturalness") is more prevalent and expresses better Zhuangzi's true spirit (Mori Mikisaburo 1967; cf. Mori 1972: 61). The first type of wu-wei would thus be something that can be acquired through training, whereas the second would not. As I noted in my discussion of the *Laozi*, the problem with this sort of approach is that it does little to genuinely resolve the tension, for it continues to be present in the "contemplative" or "non-activity" form of wu-wei. Another approach is to attack the tension head-on by postulating different levels of the self or different types of agency. Framing his discussion in the language of Husserl and Merleau-Ponty, Wu Kuang-ming has argued that the Zhuangzian sage attains wu-wei through a dialectic process of reduction. Through this process, the sage proceeds from living in a state of "trying" (under the domination of the "empirical self") through a "meta-effort" that eventually culminates in perfect effortlessness (the "self"):

> The self can be characterized as a being in the realm of effort, which is a *wei*. To go out of it is an "act" of *wu-wei*, a radical re-positioning of *wei* on a new plateau. It is a *wei*-ing of *wei*, a meta-effort to posit the self out of the *wei*-realm, where there is a conflict between doing and not-doing (Wu 1981: 148).

This is an interesting idea, as is Wu's similar attempt to explain how the Zhuangzian sage moves from "doing" to "non-doing" by postulating two levels of the self: the *wu* 吾 -self and the *wo* 我 -self. Unfortunately, such attempts to understand Zhuangzian wu-wei seem in the end not much more successful than the first approach, as they merely transfer the tension into a different set of philosophical terms.

There are suggestions in the *Zhuangzi* that we *do* in fact have to try not to try—that is, that wu-wei represents the culmination of a long period of training. In the story of Butcher Ding, for instance, Ding had to cut up oxen for many years and pass·through several levels of skill before he finally reached a state of spirit-guided wu-wei. We see Zhuangzi here playing the same game as Mencius, but from a different side: whereas Mencius feels the need to spice up his dominant metaphors of cultivation or effort with a few piquant pinches of "wild nature" abandon, Zhuangzi's celebration of "wild nature" is muted by an apparently recognized need for cultivation. The manner in which this tension plays itself out in terms of Zhuangzi's metaphors is also quite similar to the *Mencius*: we have a dominant set of metaphors representing sudden transformation or release—"forgetting," "losing," "wandering," "release/undoing" (*jie* 解),—uneasily coexisting with a small contingent of such "effort" metaphors as "cultivating" (*yang* 養) life or "getting rid of" (*qu* 去) knowledge.

A. C. Graham sees this as evidence that Zhuangzi felt that we need to train in order to develop and realize our true natures—that "we do not possess from birth that selfless mirror-like objectivity which ensures that every prompting is the 'impulse from Heaven'" (Graham 1981). In support of his position Graham cites a passage from the Outer Chapters, "it is by adorning-cultivating [*xiu* 修][95] our nature [*xing* 性] that we return to [*fan* 反] Virtue" (W132/G424). On the other hand, there are passages in the *Zhuangzi* that state unequivocally that wu-wei is *not* something one can consciously cultivate, as we see in an imaginary dialogue between Confucius and Laozi in chapter 21:

> Confucius said, "Your Virtue, Master, matches up [*pei* 配] with Heaven and Earth, and yet even you must rely upon the perfect teachings [of the Way] in order to adorn/cultivate [*xiu*] your heart/mind. Even among the gentlemen of ancient times, then, who could have avoided such effort?"

> "That is not so!" replied Lao Dan. "Water has a wu-wei relationship to clarity—clarity is simply the natural [*ziran*] expression of its innate endowment. The Perfected Person's relationship to Virtue is the same: he does not engage in cultivation [*xiu*], and yet things cannot get away

from him. It is as natural as the height of Heaven, the depth of the Earth, and the brightness of the sun and moon. What is there to be cultivated?" (W226/G716)

It is interesting that this most Confucian of metaphors—*xiu*—appears only twice in the Inner Chapters in the sense of "cultivate" or "adorn" (W55–56/G139 and W86/G267) and is in both cases associated with Confucianism and given a negative valuation, whereas a split develops in its usage among the later followers of Zhuangzi: some using it positively to express the kind of effort engaged in by Butcher Ding and others explicitly rejecting it as anathema to the "Daoist" project.

This seems to indicate the development within the *Zhuangzi* textual tradition of a split between what we might call "gradualist" and "sudden" camps. In fact, we do not even have to leave the Inner Chapters to see evidence of such a growing tension. Let us recall the two versions of the encounter between Yan Hui and Confucius recounted in chapters 4 (W57–58/G146–48) and 6 (W89–90/G282–85). In the first version, the two have a single meeting where a simple verbal description by Confucius of the "fasting of the heart/mind" apparently induces sudden enlightenment in Yan Hui, who is instantly freed of the burden of a self. In the second telling the process takes much longer, with Yan Hui actually leaving Confucius's presence after each progress report and apparently going off to engage in some kind of practice—we are not told what it is. He finally wins Confucius's approval when he returns to report that he is able to "sit and forget," a process that involves the "falling away" (*duo* 墮) of limbs and body, the active "dismissing" or "driving out" (*chu* 黜) of perception and intellect, "separation from" (*li* 離) physical form, and "getting rid of" or "expelling" (*qu* 去) knowledge. The structure of this second story, along with its more active metaphors and suggestion of some sort of sitting technique, makes it read like a more "gradualist" or practice-oriented version of the chapter 4 story.[96]

One final approach to the paradox as it manifests itself in the *Zhuangzi* that we should mention is suggested by scholars such as Mori Mikisaburo who emphasize the role of trust or "faith" (*shinrai* 信賴)[97] in Zhuangzi's thought. Along with Kanaya Osamu, Mori wishes to distance Zhuangzi from the "secular" implications of an instrumentalist reading of wu-wei and emphasize the "more religious" character of Zhuangzian wu-wei.[98] What he means by characterizing Zhuangzi's thought as "religious" is that it is essentially founded upon an unbounded faith in the natural Way. Both Mori and Kanaya would come down on the anti-practice side of the paradox of wu-wei, emphasizing as they do that the Zhuangzian sage has no technique or conscious goals he desires to attain, but merely commits himself to the Will of Heaven as the swimmer in chapter 19 throws himself into the raging water at the foot of Lü-liang falls, trusting that the natural flow of the river will bring him through intact (W204–5/G657). I believe that in emphasizing the role of faith in the *Zhuangzi*, Mori is on the right track in helping us to understand not only Zhuangzian wu-wei but also how the spiritual ideal of wu-wei functions in all of the Chinese thinkers we have considered so far. Focusing on passages such as the description of the Zhuangzian sage "being drunk on Heaven" or the discussions of "being at peace with it as fate" (*anzhiruoming* 安之若命), Mori observes:

> The vast, numinous impulse that manifests itself after human knowledge has been abandoned is nothing other than the "Way." Once the worldly perspective that inheres in subjective human actions has been surrendered, the natural, numinous force of providence is able to reveal itself. An absolute faith in natural providence is thus the basic foundation supporting Daoist philosophy. . . . Zhuangzi's position, which is of a much more religious character than that of Laozi, is to accept naturalness in the form of fate [*unmei* 運命]. Therefore, Zhuangzi's ideal of wu-wei/ naturalness carries the connotation of giving up all forms of knowledge and living in accordance with fate. (Mori 1967: 7)

Understanding the transition from "doing" to "non-doing" as a surrender in faith to the Way is a helpful way of understanding Zhuangzi's religious vision. Surrendering conscious control of the heart/mind is a desirable goal only if one is confident that the force that will then be allowed to manifest itself (the spirit) will guide one in the proper direction. Entering into the state of wu-wei for Zhuangzi thus involves surrendering the self to something greater than the self—surrendering the heart/mind to the spirit, or the merely human to the Heavenly—in the faith that this will lead one to the Way.

This understanding of wu-wei is also of significance for early Chinese thought in general because a similar release into faith would seem to be necessary for one to commit to the Confucian program of self-cultivation or to resolve to embody the principle of reversion in one's person in the Laozian sense. Although Confucianism and (arguably) Laozi's brand of Daoism are significantly more practice-oriented than the *Zhuangzi*, they both require a similar sort of submission to an ideal and a confidence in its viability if one is even to get started on the Way. I will argue later that one can find such an element of faith even in Xunzi's rather austere program of self-cultivation. Zhuangzi is unique among these early Chinese thinkers, though, in making the need for this type of surrender the virtually exclusive focus of his religious vision. The Confucians and Laozi ask their devotees to sign up for a fairly well-defined program of cultivation that, it is promised, will bear very specific personal, social, and political fruit. Zhuangzi offers the prospective devotee much less in this regard. The promise of a full and healthy life is at times proffered, but is in other places undermined by the argument that true freedom and happiness is only to be found in surrendering to the transformations of Heaven without any thought for what might become of the self. It is sometimes said that only the sage is fully successful in realizing his true potential and in developing to the full his inner power, but this augmentation or realization of the self is only to be achieved through sincere self-abnegation.It is in this sense, then, that we can say that Zhuangzi develops the ideal of wu-wei to its extreme, making it a goal in itself gather than a means to another spiritual end. The sage is to leave behind the human and become drunk upon Heaven, with no more thought for the future or for himself than the drunken man falling from the cart.

Unfortunately, even this model of wu-wei as a form of submission to faith does not seem to get us entirely out of the woods. In both Mori Mikisaburo 1967 and 1972, Mori quite perceptively notes parallels between Zhuangzi, Chan Buddhism, and devotional forms of Chinese Buddhism such as Pure Land. This last connection is less commonly made, but makes sense in terms of our present discussion. The reader is referred to Mori 1967 and 1972 for the details of his argument; for the moment, let us just mention that we see in the Pure Land school the emergence of a tension that looks suspiciously like the paradox of wu-wei. To briefly sketch this out in Japanese context, the central teaching of the Pure Land School (*Jodo Shu*) as formulated by Honen (1133–1212) is the superiority of "other power" (*tariki* 他力) over "self-power" (*jiriki* 自力): whereas previous (and "inferior") forms of Buddhism believed that one could become a Buddha through one's own efforts, the Pure Land School teaches that human beings are so weak and corrupted that it is only by submitting to the grace of Amida Buddha that salvation is possible. Hence Pure Land employs the simple technique of *nembutsu* 念佛 —"chanting to the Buddha"—as a means for anyone to express and experience their absolute submission to Amida's grace. There arose a disagreement in the school, however, concerning this practice of *nembutsu*: some believed that a single, sincere invocation was sufficient, while others believed that it required constant repetition and needed to be accompanied by good works. This tension came to a head with the founding by a disciple of Honen named Shinran (1173–1263) of what eventually became an autonomous sect, the *True* Pure Land School (*Jodo Shinshu*). Whereas Honen and his more conservative followers believed that *nembutsu* needed to be maintained as a practice and accompanied by monastic discipline (that is, that "faith" needed to be accompanied by "good works"), Shinran believed that any recourse to good works indicated a dangerous lack of faith in Amida's ability to erase all imperfections. All that is required for salvation is a single moment of *sincere* (here is the rub!) submission to Amida's grace, which will result in a "natural" realization of *samadhi*. We have here again, in another form, the paradox of wu-wei. For any Pure Land practitioner, in order for *nembutsu* to be sincere it must be without conscious intent (that is, free of selfish motives) and genuinely selfless. How, though, do we *try* to be "genuine" and "selfless"?

Honen and his more conservative followers essentially took a more gradual-ist-externalist approach to the problem (practice of good works, meditation), while Shinran rejected such techniques as leading inevitably to hypocrisy and advocated instead a sudden-internalist approach.[99] The tension, though, is the same one we have been tracing all along, and it would thus seem that interpreting wu-wei as a kind of submission to faith will thus not enable us to get out of the paradox of wu-wei. As I have suggested several times, the universality and tenacity of this debate indicates that we may be dealing with a genuine paradox that is not amenable to rational solution. Nonetheless, I will conclude in my final chapter with an examination of a final pre-Qin attempt to solve the paradox of wu-wei by clinging unabashedly to the externalist-gradualist horn of the dilemma.

Chapter 7

直枸木

Straightening the Warped Wood:

Wu-wei in the *Xunzi*

Considering his outspoken opposition to the naturalistic theories of his time—exemplified in his pointed glorification of "conscious activity" (*wei* 偽) against Daoist and Mencian brands of wu-wei—it might seem strange to think of Xunzi 荀子 (b. ca. 310 B.C.)[1] as nonetheless sharing wu-wei as a spiritual ideal. Yet he surely does, and in fact has a vision of wu-wei as the culmination of a long process of unflagging self-cultivation that probably reflects more accurately the original vision of Confucius than does Mencius's ideal, although most modern Chinese are accustomed to thinking of Mencius as the orthodox successor of the Master. Certainly there are many aspects of Xunzi's thought that might strike us as rather "un-Confucian": his detailed discussions of methods for strengthening or enriching the state;[2] his advocation of controlling the populace through the use of carefully promulgated laws and consistently applied punishments;[3] and his discussion of military strategy (KII:108–9). One way to view these features of the Xunzi's thought, however, is to see them as a response to the challenge of defending the Confucian vision not only against the opponents Mencius faced (the Mohists and Yangists) but against an entire range of relatively new and attractive ways of thought that were flourishing in his age.[4] The impressive success of the state of Qin—which was organized along Legalist principles—and the popularity of the new theories of military strategy and statecraft made it impossible for Xunzi to defend the Confucian Way except by showing its relevance to the concerns of his age. To this end, he adopted many ideas that can be traced to Mohism, Legalism, and even Zhuangzi and Laozi.[5] Yet to the end he remained staunchly Confucian, and perhaps one of his greatest achievements was his successful absorption of Legalist, Mohist, and Daoist ideas into a Confucian framework, which involved defending certain core Confucian beliefs such as the efficacy of Virtue, the relevance of the rites and classics, and the viability of the wu-wei ideal while adapting these ideas to the concerns and temperament of his age.[6]

Xunzi saw himself as defending the teachings of Confucius not only against non-Confucian opponents, but also against the heterodox "false Confucians" who had sprung up in the generations since the Master's death.[7] When we turn to his conceptualization of wu-wei, we do indeed find ourselves confronting a constellation of metaphors that hark back to the *Analects* and were conspicuous by their relative absence in the *Mencius*. In the *Xunzi*, as in the *Analects*, wu-wei is portrayed as the "destination" at the end of a long, arduous trip, or as the respite or "ease" (*an*) enjoyed after a lifetime of bitter training and submission to external forms of behavior and thought. Xunzi's metaphors are much more explicit in their externalism than anything seen in the *Analects*, however, with our inborn nature conceptualized as a recalcitrant raw material in need of violent reshaping so that it might be "transformed" (*hua* 化) into a shape dictated by external standards or measuring tools: the carpenter's square and ruler (*guiju* 規矩), the inked marking line (*shengmo* 繩墨), or the balance scale (*heng* 衡). Xunzi also (as we might expect) formulates a much more elaborate metaphorical conceptualization of the heart/mind than anything seen in the *Analects*, borrowing freely from his philosophical opponents and putting their metaphors to work in advancing his own agenda. The result is a sophisticated argument in favor of an externalist approach to wu-wei that—despite the Song Dynasty turn toward Mencius—largely determined the manner in which Confucianism was understood and institutionalized during the early imperial period.

Fallenness: The Essential Role of Tradition

Like all of the thinkers we have considered so far, Xunzi has the very strong sense of living in a corrupted age that has fallen completely away from the Way of the ancients. Like Confucius, he is mainly concerned with the loss or degradation of traditional ritual forms, which has caused the world to sink into anarchy:

> Those who have forded a river place markers [*biao* 表] to indicate the deep places; if these markers are not clearly maintained, later people trying to ford the river will drown. Those who governed the people have placed markers to indicate the Way; if these markers are not clearly maintained, the result will be social chaos. Ritual serves as these markers [*biao* 表]. To condemn ritual is to darken the age, and a benighted age is characterized by great chaos. Therefore if every aspect of the Way is made clear, the distinction between inner and outer [*neiwai* 內外] will be marked, constancy will be established with regard to what is hidden and manifest, and the deep places in which people drown will be avoided. (KIII:21/W318–19)

Both of the primary metaphor schemas invoked in this passage are familiar from the *Analects*: LIFE AS JOURNEY (with the "Way" [*dao* 道] as the proper "path" along which to take this journey) and MORALITY AS BOUNDED SPACE, which informs the metaphor of the "mean" (*zhong* 中)—literally, the "center." Here the Way is portrayed as a demarcated ford across a dangerous river, the boundaries of which are indicated by the rites. We find a similar portrayal of metaphoric bounded space in the "Discourse on Ritual" chapter:

> During important occasions, the gentleman can rise to the task of being lavish; on humble occasions, he understands completely how to be understated, and in his everyday dealings dwells in the mean [*chuzhong* 處中]. Even when running, hurrying or in haste, he does not depart from [*wai* 外] this mean. This is the gentleman's arena [*tanyu* 壇宇], his noble dwelling place [*gongting* 宮廷; lit., palace quarters]. (KIII:62/W358)

The gentleman "dwells" at the center of the bounded space of morality, does not go outside of it, and rests in it as comfortably as an emperor in his personal palace quarters.

This MORALITY AS BOUNDED SPACE schema appears throughout the text, where it is often associated with the "mean" or "center" and described as a place where the gentleman can dwell at ease.[8] Thus we read in chapter 13 that the gentleman "is at ease with regard to ritual, music and profit . . . which is why he can make a hundred suggestions without making a single mistake [*guo* 過—literally, going outside the bounds] (KII:203/W256–57).[9] The restraining qualities of ritual are often portrayed by Xunzi in terms of this bounded space metaphor. "The gentleman's words remain within the bounds [*tanyu* 壇宇 ; lit. "arena"] and his actions are guarded by boundaries [*fangbiao* 防表]," he writes. "This is why he allows his intention and sentiments to run [*cheng* 騁] only within the bounds of his arena and noble dwelling place" (KII:83/W146). We see a similar conceit in chapter 27, where knowledge of the Way is portrayed as a bowl or pan that constrains the movement of heterodox doctrines: "Rolling [*liu* 流] balls come to a rest [*zhi* 止] in a bowl or pan; wayward [*liu*] doctrines are put to rest [*zhi*] by one who knows" (KIII:234/W516).

An entailment of the MORALITY AS BOUNDED SPACE metaphor is that, in order to position oneself properly vis-à-vis the normative order, it is necessary to have a clear idea of where the boundaries lie. This accounts for Xunzi's concern with establishing firm distinctions and—especially in the face of the confusion being engendered by the host of heterodox doctrines "rolling" about in the world—properly ordering language. We can recall Confucius's concern in *Analects* 13.3 with "using names properly" (*zhengming* 正名) and his warning to the gentleman not be "arbitrary (*gou* 苟) where teaching/doctrine (*yan* 言) is concerned," lest "the common people not know where to put hand and foot." Confucius too was interested in the use of proper verbal distinctions in order to demarcate moral space. Xunzi reinforces the message of 13.3 by taking *zhengming* 正名 as a technical term ("rectifying names"), and devotes an entire chapter to the issue. Noting that, when the true king establishes names, "names are settled [*ding* 定] and things are distinguished [*bian* 辨], the [king's] Way can be carried out and his intention widely understood [*tong* 通], and in this way care taken to guide the common people and be single minded with respect to names," he bemoans the fact that names in his contemporary world have become confused even among the cultural elite:

> Now the sage kings are gone, the preservation of names is neglected, strange propositions have arisen, the relationship between names and things [*mingshi* 名實] has become confused, and the outline of right and

wrong has become unclear. Even the officials who preserve the laws and
the Confucians who recite and explicate the classic texts have become
confused. (KIII:128/W414)

In Xunzi's metaphoric conception of the function of language, names are
things (social or mental objects) that can be correctly or incorrectly matched up
with other things (physical objects in the world). Although there is no inherent
"rightness" to words because they are created by social convention, the distinctions in the world that they pick out are quite real, and therefore once names have
been established a kind of "appropriateness" or "fit" (*yi* 宜) is involved (KIII:130/
W419–20). Names are created, Xunzi says, by "following" (*sui* 隨) the "defining
characteristics" (*zheng* 徵) of things. He employs an interesting social metaphor
to explain the process of perception, playing upon the dual meaning of *guan* 官:
literally "official" and (by common metaphorical extension) "sense organ." The
defining characteristics of things are known to the heart/mind only after the
"Heavenly Officials/Sense Organs" have officially "registered" (*bo* 簿) them in
the appropriate "category" (*lei* 類) (KIII:130/ W417–18).[10] These natural categories are derived from differences (*yi* 異) between things, and throughout the *Xunzi*
we are advised of the importance of properly distinguishing (*bian* 辨), differenti-
ating (*bie* 別) and demarcating (*fen* 分) in order to assure that names are correct
and firm (*ding* 定), because otherwise the bounded space of morality will not be
clear and the proper path of life cannot be followed.[11] Once the Xunzian sage
firmly establishes right and wrong the common people can be free of doubts (*yi*
疑) and confusion (*huo* 惑 or *luan* 亂) (KIII:107/W401).

It is interesting to note that this concern with establishing and maintaining
traditional boundaries and distinctions plays a less prominent (though by no
means nonexistent) role in the *Mencius*. The reason for this relative absence is
reflected in Xunzi's remark that confusion regarding traditional names has led to
the "boundary between right and wrong" being obscured. If we will recall, for
Mencius the ultimate source for moral knowledge—including that of right and
wrong—is the individual's own heart/mind; against Gaozi, he maintains that if
one cannot "get it" in the heart/mind, there is no use looking for it in doctrine.
With such an internalist conception of morality, it is no wonder that Mencius was
primarily concerned with motivating individuals to look within and recognize
their own moral potential—any degradation of traditional cultural forms or doctrines would for him be merely a temporary symptom of a failure on the part of
individuals to identify and cultivate their inner sprouts of Virtue.[12] For Xunzi, on
the contrary, human beings are completely lacking in such innate resources, and
therefore cannot rely upon their own instincts or initiative in restoring the traditional "ford-markers" once they have been torn down.

This concern with traditional norms is expressed in Xunzi's metaphor of the
Way as an external standard or measuring tool. We see the Way, ritual, or the sage
characterized as a carpenter's square and ruler (*guiju* 規矩), a inked marking line
(*shengmo* 繩墨), or a scale (*heng* 衡 or *quanheng* 權衡) throughout the text.[13] It
is by means of such external standards that the sage king is able to put things in
their proper places:

Measures [*cheng* 程] serve as the standards [*zhun* 準] for things. The rites functions as the standard for regulation [*jie* 節]. Measures are used to establish techniques of calculation; the rites are used to settle human relations [*dinglun* 定倫]; Virtue is used as a basis for evaluating people for official positions [*wei* 位]; and ability is the basis for awarding government offices. (KII:208/W262–63)

Human Nature Is Bad (*e* 惡)

The tradition inherited from antiquity is thus an essential tool for the aspiring sage.[14] A breakdown in the transmission of traditional teachings and culture therefore represents an unmitigated disaster and *the* primary cause of fallenness, since the doctrines of the sages and the true Confucian teachers who help one to understand them are absolutely necessary if the individual is to become a moral person. Indeed, Xunzi often emphasizes the fact that the great achievements of gentleman or sages are not the result of any inherent difference in ability from an ordinary person, but rather stem from the fact that they are simply "good at relying upon [external] things" (*jiayuwu* 假於物):

> I once spent the entire day in thought, but it was not as useful as even a single moment of study.[15] I once stood on tiptoes and gazed about me, but what I saw could not compare with the broad vista obtained by climbing to a high place. If you climb to a high place and wave, your arm is no longer than it usually is, but your signal can be seen from farther away. If you shout downwind your voice is no louder than it normally is, but your message can be heard more clearly. One who relies upon a cart and horses does not make his feet any better, yet he can travel a thousand *li*; one who relies upon a boat and paddles does not thereby make himself a great swimmer, and yet he can cross rivers and even seas.
>
> The gentleman is not born different from other people. He is simply good at relying upon external things. (KI:136/W4)

What is special about human beings is our ability to use external tools to enhance our otherwise meager native talents. The aspiring sage finds his "tools" through studying the Way of the Former Kings, and this tool is essential if one is to learn to make the proper sort of distinctions, since relying upon one's own intuitions is an invitation to disaster:

> The Way has served as the proper scale [*zhengquan* 正權] from ancient times down to the present. Someone who abandons the Way and tries to internally make decisions on his own initiative [*neizize* 內自擇] clearly does not understand where good fortune and disaster lie. (KIII:137/ W430)

Xunzi at one point cites this dependence upon external standards as proof of his claim that human nature is bad—"if human nature was good, then we could get rid of the sage kings and dispense with the rites and morality" (KIII:156/ W441). That dispensing with these standards is not a viable option is, Xunzi believes, obvious to anyone who thinks clearly about it. Contemplate our basic desires and urges, he asks us, and then imagine the consequences were we to indulge them in a manner unrestrained by external limits:

> Now, human nature is such that we are born with a love of profit. Going along with [*shun* 順] this nature thus causes aggression and conflict to arise and courtesy and deference to be lost. Human beings are born with feelings of envy and hatred. Going along with such feelings causes violence and thievery to arise and loyalty and trustworthiness to be lost. Human beings are born with the desires of the ears and eyes, which cause them to be fond of attractive sounds and beautiful women. Going along with such desires causes licentious and chaotic behavior to arise and ritual and morality [*liyi* 禮義], refinement and pattern [*wenli* 文理] to be lost. This being the case, following [*cong*] human nature and going along with the human emotions [*qing* 情] will necessarily give birth to aggression and conflict, encourage the violation of class distinctions [*fen* 分], throw the ordered pattern [*li* 理] into chaos, and cause the world to return to [*gui* 歸] violence.

> Hence the need for people to transformed by teachers and laws [*shifa* 師 法] and guided by ritual and morality. Only after such a transformation do we see the birth of courtesy and deference, the encouragement of refinement and patterned order, and a return to order. Considering this, it is quite clear that human nature is bad, and that goodness is the result of conscious activity [*wei* 偽]. (KIII:151/W434)

Xunzi is here arguing for the existence at birth of irrepressible and harmful instantiations of the Self that will lead to Subject "back" (*gui*) into chaos and disorder if they are "followed" (*cong*) or allowed to carry the Subject along with the flow (*shun*). He employs many of the wu-wei metaphor schemas we have seen in Mencius or the Daoists, but reverses their valuations: "going with the flow" leads to disaster rather than salvation, and we can expect to "return home" to a state of brutish violence, not a peaceful agricultural utopia. Hence the valorization of *wei* 偽 (conscious activity) that seems directly targeted against the wu-wei ideal.

Many commentators have claimed that there is no genuine contradiction between Xunxi's motto "human nature is bad" and Mencius's proposal that "human nature is good," and that the two thinkers were merely emphasizing different aspects of the moral project[16] or working with different but complementary definitions of human nature (*xing* 性).[17] A. C. Graham even claims that "it is indeed far from easy to locate any issue of fact on which they disagree."[18] Perusing the passage alone, however, would seem to provide us with a wealth of such facts. For instance, recall that Mencius located the roots of benevolence and rightness in human beings' prereflective inclinations, noting most famously in 7:A:15:

> What a person is able to do without having studied is their "proper ability" [*liangneng* 良能]; what they are able to know without having deliberated [*lü* 慮] is their "proper knowledge" [*liangzhi* 良知]. Among toddlers there are none who do not know to love their parents, and when they grow older there are none who do not know to respect their elder brothers. Loving one's parents is benevolence; respecting one's elders is rightness. Simply allow these two feelings to extend to [*da* 達] the whole world—nothing else needs to be done.

Mencius is here making empirical claims about human inborn sentiments—that all people are born with sprouts of benevolence and rightness in the form of natural, spontaneous feelings of affection and respect—that are quite directly denied by Xunzi, and to the refutation of which he devotes an entire chapter (chapter 23, "Human Nature is Bad"). While Mencius feels that even in the state of nature a younger brother feels natural respect and affection for his older brother, Xunzi presents a rather different picture of the state of affairs that will result when brothers simply follow their spontaneous inclinations:

> Love of profit and greed constitute human beings' essence and nature [*qingxing* 情性]. Now, imagine some younger and older brothers who need to divide up valuables among themselves, and further imagine that they follow along with [*shun*] their essence and nature—that is, their love of profit and their greed. In such a situation the younger and older brothers would end up struggling among themselves and robbing each other. . . . Thus following along with one's essence and nature will lead to conflict even among brothers. (KIII:154/W438–39)

This claim is aimed directly at *Mencius* 7:A:15. Nourishing and "extending" the sprouts of one's inborn nature would, in Xunzi's view, lead to nothing but a forest of weeds: strife, disorder, and violence. Whereas for Mencius the beginnings of courtesy and deference are to be found in our innate feelings and reactions, Xunzi states quite firmly that these are qualities that only appear in one who has been transformed through the influence of a teacher, the model of the ancients, and carefully guided by ritual forms and the principles of morality. Empirically, Mencius would expect to find at least crude forms of benevolence and rightness being practiced among a group of children shipwrecked and grown up isolated upon a desert island, whereas Xunzi would expect a nightmarish scenario out of *Lord of the Flies*. Pace A. C. Graham, then, it would seem that there are important issues of fact upon which the two thinkers disagree.[19]

The differences between the two thinkers are perhaps seen most clearly, however, on level of conceptual metaphor rather than empirical claim. The contrast between the Xunzian and Mencian metaphors for the heart/mind and—especially—self-cultivation is quite stark and philosophically significant, and this metaphorical contrast will be the subject of the following two sections.

Conception of the Heart/Mind

We have seen that, since individuals lack the internal resources that would allow them to live a moral life, the quality of the tradition—the appropriateness of names and the positioning of the ritual markers—is for Xunzi a prime concern. We have also seen that even Mencius devoted some effort to combatting "heresies" such as Mohism and Yangism that threatened to lead the common people astray. For an externalist such as Xunzi, however, the danger presented by such heresies was much more systemically threatening, and the stamping out of false doctrines thus becomes in Xunzi a central task to be undertaken in a careful, orderly fashion. He devotes two entire chapters to this end: chapter 6 ("Denouncing Twelve Philosophers") and chapter 21 ("Removing Obscurations"). In this latter chapter, he borrows and develops the Zhuangzian metaphor (based upon the apparently universal metaphor schema KNOWING IS SEEING) that human fallenness stems from visual "obscurations" or "blocks" (*bi* 蔽) caused by "partiality"—by seeing from the perspective only one corner of the great Way:

> A flaw to which human beings are generally prone is having their vision obscured [*bi* 蔽] gazing upon the Great Patterned Order [*dali* 大理] from the cramped perspective of one tiny corner. If this flaw is corrected, they can return to the classical standard [*jing* 經], but if they remain undecided between two paths [*liangyi* 兩疑] confusion will result. The world does not have two Ways, and the sage is not of two heart/minds.

> Now, since the feudal lords all govern in different ways and the Hundred Schools explain things differently, it is necessarily so that some are right and some are wrong, that some will produce order and some disorder. Even when it comes to rulers of chaotic states and people from disorderly schools, their genuine intention [*chengxin* 誠心] is to find what is correct, and no doubt from their own point of view believe that this is what they have done. Through partiality, though, they have misunderstood the Way, and the result is that others are able to lead them astray by pandering to their tastes.

> Partial [*si*] to what they themselves have accumulated, they fear only hearing it be criticized. Because they lean so heavily upon their selfishness [*si*], when they are presented with a technique that differs from their own, they fear only hearing it be praised. In this fashion they run farther and farther away[20] from the one who can correct their flaws, and yet think they are correct for doing so. Is this not a case of being obscured in a cramped corner and missing the very thing you seek? If the heart/mind is not employed [*shi* 使] in the task, black and white could be in front of a person's eyes and yet he will not see them, thunder and drums can be sounding next to his ear and yet he will not hear them. How much harder would this be if his heart/mind was obscured![21](KIII:100/W386)

Xunzi agrees with Zhuangzi that the heart/mind itself can become obscured and blinded by partial doctrines, and that the great mass of human beings are deluded in this manner by doctrines that lead them astray and close them off to experiencing the true Way. Once mired in such a state, it is difficult for the heart/mind to free itself from obscuration. Xunzi's soteriological strategy, however, is not—like Zhuangzi—to propose curing this blindness by fasting away the heart/mind and doing away with its doctrines altogether, but rather to "employ the heart/mind" toward grasping the one true doctrine: the Confucian Way. Indeed, Zhuangzi's goal of "walking the two paths" (*liangxing* 兩行) and "lodging" temporarily in a given position is seen by Xunzi as part of the problem, causing people to depart from the "classical standard" (*jing*) and become mired in confusion. Xunzi is quite determined to combat internalist doctrines in any form, whether they look for guidance in the depths of the heart/mind or in the promptings of the spirit [*shen* 神]. The only viable source of true morality is to be had from the teachings and cultural forms possessed by the Ancient Kings and preserved by Confucius. The only hope for his contemporaries to lift themselves out of their morass of confusion and violence is to rebuild the "markers" of the Ancients that have been pulled down, but whose location is still recorded in the classics and the inherited wisdom of the Confucian teachers. Since our innate tendencies are of no help in this task, it is necessary for those who wish to return to the "universal Way" to use their heart/minds to reform their nature, and this process of slowly transforming the desires and eliminating obsession is referred to by Xunzi as "conscious activity" (*wei* 偽).

We have seen that, in Xunzi's opinion, brothers relying merely upon their native instincts and emotions would rob each other without a hint of remorse for the sake of material gain. Once these same brothers have been trained in ritual forms and the dictates of morality, however, Xunzi claims that they would be willing to yield to each other even the claim to their own country (KIII:154/ W439). This is the extraordinary power of the traditional forms devised by the sages, which is based upon the capacity that all human beings have to overcome their innate nature. These forms do not apply themselves, however. To become an effective component of the self they must be appropriated through the proper use of the heart/mind. Lee Yearley has noted what he describes as two radically different views of the heart/mind in Xunzi: in one, the heart/mind is the director of activity, while in the other it is more of a passive receptor.[22] Neither of these two metaphorical conceptions in itself is unique to Xunzi, and he most probably borrowed each of them from his philosophical opponents. Mencius, as we have seen, portrays the heart as the "ruler" or "commander" of the self, and Zhuangzi's "fasting of the heart/mind" (*xinzhai* 心齋) is designed to make the container of the heart/mind "tenuous" (*xu* 虛) so that it will have room to "receive" or "gather" the Way. What is unique to Xunzi is the manner in which he combines these two metaphors for the heart/mind with some of his own contrivance to form a powerful new ideal of a heart/mind both entirely in control of the self and yet thoroughly receptive to tradition. This dual aspect to the heart/mind is what allows Xunzi to reconcile his strong voluntarist bent with his equally strong conservatism.

Heart/Mind as Receptor

The more passive heart/mind as receptor metaphor is employed by Xunzi in his discussion of the "obscurations" with which the heart/mind can be afflicted and which obscure one's view of the Way. In his call to remove such obscurations by making the heart/mind tenuous, unified and still, he combines this HEART/MIND AS CONTAINER schema with the Zhuangzian HEART/MIND AS STILL WATER metaphor, as well as with the common Warring States metaphors of HEART/MIND AS LIGHT SOURCE and HEART/MIND AS MANIPULABLE SUBSTANCE:[23]

> What do human beings use to know the Way? I say that it is the heart/mind. What does the heart/mind make use of in order to know? I say it is tenuousness [*xu* 虛], unity [*yi* 壹] and stillness [*jing* 靜]. The heart/mind never stops storing [*cang* 臧], but it still possesses what is called tenuousness. The heart/mind never stops being divided [*liang* 兩], but it still possesses what is called unity. The heart/mind never stops moving [*dong* 動], but it still possesses what is called stillness.
>
> When people are born they begin to acquire a degree of awareness [*zhi* 知], and with awareness comes intention [*zhi* 志]. Intention is the result of storing.[24] However, there is still that which is called tenuousness: not allowing what has already been stored up [in the heart/mind] to harm what is about to be received [*shou* 受] is what we call tenuousness. As soon as we are born the heart/mind begins to accumulate awareness. With awareness comes differentiation. Differentiation implies the simultaneous awareness of two things, and the simultaneous awareness of different things leads to division [*liang*]. However, there is still that which is called unity: not allowing awareness of one thing to harm awareness of another thing is what we call unity. When the heart/mind is asleep it dreams; when it is unoccupied, it wanders off on its own; and when it is employed, it schemes. Therefore, the heart/mind never stops moving, but it still possesses that which is called stillness: not allowing dreams or fantasies to disorder one's awareness is what we call stillness.
>
> One who has yet to attain the Way but is seeking it should be told about tenuousness, unity, and stillness. Once these qualities are attained, the tenuousness of one who intends to receive the Way allows it to enter;[25] the unity of one who intends to serve the Way allows him to do so completely; and the stillness of one who wishes to contemplate the Way will allow him to be discerning [*cha* 察]. One who, understanding the Way, is discerning and able to put it into practice is an embodier of the Way. Tenuousness, unity, and stillness are what is referred to as the Great Clear Brightness [*daqingming* 大清明]. (KIII:104–5/W395–97)

As diverse as the metaphor schemas invoked here are, they combine to form a coherent mental image. The HEART/MIND AS CONTAINER schema and the tenuousness metaphor allow us to understand how the heart/mind can "accumulate" memories and knowledge while still maintaining "room" for more information to enter; borrowing an image from Zhuangzi, the tenuous heart/mind still contains enough space to allow the Way to "enter." Cognizing the heart/mind as a physical substance that can be "divided" allows us to understand mental distraction as the literal dividing of the heart/mind by an external object, and "concentration" or "focus" as resisting such division. As we saw earlier, In Xunzi's view it is important to realize that "the world does not have two Ways and the sage does not have a divided heart/mind [*liangxin* 兩心]" (KIII:100/W386). While sharing Zhuangzi's concern that the heart/mind can become obscured by partial doctrines or perspectives and borrowing his language to describe a perfectly unsullied and receptive state of heart/mind, the Way that appears to the Xunzian sage is not some undefined and ultimately ineffable responsiveness to things as they are, but is rather a clearly delineated value system that allows the sage to unambiguously *know* what is right and what is wrong and impose this knowledge upon the world:[26] Xunzi emphasizes the importance of unity by quoting the poetess of Ode 3 whose longing for her departed soldier interferes with her work:

> "I pick and pick the curly ear,[27]
> But it does not fill my shallow basket.
> I sigh for my beloved man,
> Who fills those ranks of the Zhou."

> A shallow basket is easy to fill, and curly ear is easy to obtain, yet she cannot manage to get it done because [her attention] is divided [*er* 貳] by [her man serving in] the ranks of the Zhou. Therefore I say: if the heart/mind branches off [*zhi* 枝] it will lack knowledge; if it is tilted [*qing* 傾] it will not be concentrated [*jing* 精], and if it is divided [*er* 貳] then doubts and confusion will arise. . . . Categories [*lei* 貳] cannot be divided; therefore the wise person selects one and unifies everything with it. (KIII:106/W398–99)

Tenuousness is related to unity is the sense that the Way serves for Xunzi as an external standard that must be "received" by the heart/mind if external things are to be properly distinguished so that the sage can make clear and focused decisions. Earlier on in chapter 21, Xunzi uses the metaphor of the suspended balance to describe the external, universal quality of the Way as an independent standard of judgment:

> [The sage] lays out side-by-side all of the myriad things and centers the suspended balance [*xuanheng* 懸衡] among them. In this way the multitude of different perceptions cannot obscure one another and so confuse their proper positions [*lun* 倫]. What serves as the balance? I say that it is the Way. This is why it is not permissible for the heart/mind not to know the Way. (KIII:103/W394)

The Xunzian sage, then, makes himself tenuous in order to be receptive to an external standard that will in turn allow him to weigh and assess things, determining their proper category and then treating them appropriately. Zhuangzi's soteriological project stopped at the point of making the heart/mind tenuous;

everything after that was left to the spirit and to Heaven. For Xunzi, on the other hand, this state of heart/mind is (as David Nivison has noted) "a means to clear thinking and correct judgment, not a religious goal, not an end in itself" (Nivison 1991: 136).

A suspended balance must of course be level (*zheng* 正) if it is to function properly, and we saw above how Xunzi warned against allowing the heart/mind to become "tilted" or off-balance (*qing* 傾). This metaphor of the heart/mind being "tilted" in turn links the metaphors of the unified heart/mind and suspended balance to the metaphors of stillness and clarity, because water in a level bowl is still and clear, and is stirred up (*dong*) only when the pan is tilted. This connection is made explicit later on in chapter 21, where the qualities of stillness and clarity are further linked to brightness (*ming* 明) and the metaphor of the mirror:

> The human heart/mind is like a bowl of water. If it is placed on a level [*zheng* 正] surface and not moved [*dong*], the impurities will settle to the bottom and the surface will be so clear and bright [*qingming* 清明] that you will be able to see individual whiskers and eyebrows and discern the pattern of wrinkles on your face. If the slightest breeze passes over the surface, though, the impurities will be stirred up [*dong*] from the bottom, ruining the clarity and brightness of the surface, so that you will be unable to get a correct impression of even the general shape of the face.

> The heart/mind is just like this. Thus, if you guide it with the ordered pattern, cultivate it with clarity, and do not allow any external things to tilt [*qing* 傾] it, then you can use it to establish right and wrong and to resolve errors and doubts. If even the smallest thing is allowed to pull on it so that its level [*zheng*] orientation to the outside is changed and the heart/mind is internally tilted, then it will be insufficient to differentiate even the crudest of patterns. (KIII:107/W401)[28]

Still water, which is "clear and bright," reflects images like a mirror, and the mirror metaphor is associated with the HEART/MIND AS LIGHT SOURCE scheme and "brightness" (*ming*) metaphor through a connection that is perhaps not too much of a leap for a native English speaker, but which was even more natural to a Warring States Chinese reader, for whom mirrors were thought to gather up and project—not merely reflect—light.[29] It is this natural brightness of a still and level bowl of water or clean mirror that is obscured (*bi* 蔽) by heresies and other wrong understandings. In a revealing contrast to the "drunk on Heaven" passage from the *Zhuangzi* discussed earlier, where alcohol renders a person's spirit "intact," Xunzi notes that the distorted perception of a drunken person is evidence that alcohol has "disordered" his spirit, and invokes the water/mirror metaphor to explain the link between inner stillness and proper understanding: "When water is moving [*dong*] and its reflections waver, people do not use it to establish beauty or ugliness" (KIII:109/W404).[30]

Heart/Mind as Ruler   On their own, the series of metaphors dealing with the image of the heart/mind as receptor possesses many entailments that make several important points for Xunzi: the heart/mind needs to be open to learning and receiving external standards, and it must be focused and still. By itself, however, the receptor schema gives an overly passive flavor to Xunzi's conception of the heart/mind, which is why Xunzi needs to complement it with metaphorical schemas that portray the heart/mind in a more active role. One of these schemas is that of the tool user. Once the heart/mind has received the "suspended balance" of the Way through tenuousness, it is necessary for it to actively wield this tool in the measuring of things. The metaphor of tool using serves an important function for Xunzi in conveying the need for application and effort in moral activity.

In chapter 23 it is said that human beings' moral potential (*neng* 能) is a tool (*ju* 具) that can be "used" (*yi* 以)—literally, "grasped with the hand"—but cannot be "employed" (*shi* 使)—that is, delegated a task in the way one would entrust a mission to a representation or envoy (*shi* 使) (KIII:159/W443). In other words, our potential is an inert object that needs to be actively handled rather than a kind of autonomous agent that can be entrusted with a task. Xunzi often conveys the need for initiative on the part of the Subject through the use of social metaphors. For instance, the metaphoric portrayal of heart/mind as a social superior is invoked to conceptualize the most important ability of the heart/mind: that of approval (*ke* 可). Having through tenuousness received the "classical standard" of the Way, the heart/mind then must take an active role in determining whether or not something accords with (i.e., is in the "category" of) the Way. This "approval" function of the heart/mind provides a link between the passive and active conceptualizations of the heart/mind. "Only after the heart/mind knows the Way can it approve (*ke* 可) of the Way," we read in chapter 21, "and only after it approves of the Way can it abide by the Way and thereby ban what is contrary to it" (KIII:104/W395). Here the heart/mind is portrayed as a human agent with the authority to grant or withhold official approval, and to issue bans (*jin* 禁) against things that do not receive this approval.

The kind of autonomous power wielded by the heart/mind is one of the features that distinguishes Xunzi's conception of the heart/mind from that of Mencius,[31] despite the fact that both employ the social metaphor of HEART/MIND AS RULER. Despite his picture of the heart/mind as the most valuable part of the self and the ruler of the other parts, the *xin* 心 for Mencius is intimately linked to the emotions and desires. Although the *xin* possesses the important capacity to concentrate or focus (*si* 思), the exercise of this capacity leads it inevitably (in a "seek and you will get it, abandon it and you will lose it" fashion) to the moral desires that constitute the "four sprouts." Although there is (as we have noted) a voluntaristic element to the Mencian heart/mind in the sense that it is free to *choose* to concentrate or not, this seems to be the extent of the heart/mind's capacity for innovation: the act of concentration does not lead to cognitive innovation, but merely serves to "switch on" and nurture the set of moral desires. Consider, for instance, *Mencius* 6:A:15. The organs of hearing and sight are described as being drawn automatically toward their objects, whereas the heart/mind is different in that it can concentrate: "It will get it only if it does concentrate; otherwise, it will not get it. This is what Heaven has given me." Although the heart/mind can choose to concentrate or not, once it does concentrate it is immediately drawn to its proper object—it "gets" what Heaven has designed it to get (i.e., the four sprouts). The role of the heart/mind in Mencius's scheme, then, is essentially to act as activator and nourisher of the innate feelings—it is, to invoke the social metaphor, a fairly *laissez faire* ruler, confining itself to simply "employing" (*shi* 使) or guiding the native faculties.

One way to view this relative weakness of the Mencian "ruler" is to see it as stemming from the lack of strong distinction (or "rank," if you will) between morality and desire in the *Mencius*. Like Zhuangzi, Mencius sees desire—a special kind of desire, but desire nonetheless—as the prime and proper motivator of moral agency. Xunzi is therefore quite radical in arguing that a person's actions are properly determined not by desire but by fiat—that is, by what one approves (*ke*):

> Desires do not await being satisfiable, but rather what is sought follows what is approved of [*suoke* 所可]. That desires do not wait upon being satisfiable is what is received from Heaven. That what is sought follows upon what is approved of is what is received from the heart/mind. . . . [32]

> Of the things people desire, the most important is life; of the things people hate, the worst is death. Nonetheless, there are some people who abandon life and follow death. It is not that they do not desire life and rather desire death; it is that [in a given situation] they do not approve of life but rather approve of death. Thus, when desires become excessive and yet one's actions do follow through upon them, it is because the heart/mind stops [*zhi* 止] them. . . . In cases where the desires are not strong enough and one's actions must be made to exceed one's desires, this is possible because the heart/mind causes [*shi* 使] the actions to be so. . . . Thus, the difference between order and disorder lies in what the heart/mind approves of and not with the desires that belong to our essence. (KIII:135/W427–28)

Bryan Van Norden (1992: 174) has noted the similarity of the phrasing at the beginning of this passage to that of *Mencius* 6:A:10. We will recall that in 6:A:10 Mencius appeals to the observation that people will choose death rather than living in violation of morality (*yi* 義) to prove the existence of higher, moral desires: the desires of the heart/mind. In the Mencian picture of moral agency, choosing to starve to death rather than accept a bowl of rice given with abuse is to allow one's desire for ritual propriety and rightness to trump one's animal desire for life-giving sustenance at any cost. Xunzi thinks that focusing solely upon moral "desire" indicates a fundamentally flawed understanding of the moral life. Like desire and other instantiations of the Self, Xunzi at times conceives of the heart/ mind metaphorically as an object, but more commonly portrays it in terms of the HEART/MIND AS RULER schema in order to indicate that it is fundamentally different from and superior to the other instantiations of the Self:

> The heart/mind is the ruler of the physical form and the master of the spiritual brightness [*shenming* 神明]. It issues commands but does not receive commands. Of its own volition [*zi* 自], it forbids, causes to be,

renounces, selects, allows to proceed or stops. Thus, the mouth can be compelled and made to be silent or to speak, and the physical form can be compelled and made to crouch down or stretch out. The heart/mind, however, cannot be compelled and made to change its ideas. If it deems something right, it will accept it; if it deems something wrong, then it will reject it. Therefore, it is said that the capacity of the heart/mind [*xin-rong* 心容] is such that of necessity it perceives what it will, of its own volition—its choices [*ze* 擇] cannot be constrained, its objects are broadly diverse, and its perfected concentration [*jingzhizhi* 精之至] cannot be divided.[33] (KIII:105/W397–98)

The heart/mind is thus an entity of an entirely different order than other parts of the body, and its power of fiat as ruler is thus completely distinguishable from desire. The heart/mind is the commander of these desires, allowing their satisfaction only when the object of desire has been approved of. It can select among desires, initiate or stop the activities of other parts of the body, and enforce its decisions upon both the body and the "spiritual brightness" or "intelligence." It is thus a radically more powerful and voluntaristic organ in Xunzi's scheme than in the thought of Mencius.

At the same time, the proper standard that determines whether or not something should be approved of lies outside of the heart/mind, in the Way as it is revealed in the models passed down from the sages and the example of one's teachers.[34] This is how the two families of Xunzi's metaphors for the heart/mind fit together: the HEART/MIND AS CONTAINER schema is required in order to make room for the "balance" of the Way upon which all things are to be evaluated, while the HEART/MIND AS RULER schema is needed to impose these evaluations upon a recalcitrant collection of innate desires and inclinations and enforce the appropriate behavior. Through "discrimination and explanation" [*bianshuo* 辨說], the heart/mind is able to understand the Way as it is embodied in the teachings of the ancients and then to realize these teachings in action, on the analogy of an artisan who measures and cuts in accordance with the standards marked out by his tools:

> Defining and naming are the purpose of discrimination and explanation. Discrimination and explanation are the heart/mind's representation [*xiang* 象] of the Way. The heart/mind is artisan master [*gongzai* 工宰] of the Way. The Way is the classical standard and pattern [*jingli* 經理] of order. (KIII:132/W423)

This dual-aspect nature of the Xunzian heart/mind also allows him to have a fairly voluntaristic picture of the heart/mind's functioning without slipping into relativism: although the heart/mind has the capacity to actively create and choose, its receptivity allows it to see that the "classical standard" set by the sages is in fact the optimal way of harmonizing human innate nature with the demands of the environment (Ivanhoe 1991b), and this insight in turn serves as a guide for the heart/mind as it goes about the task of shaping and ordering the self.

Soteriological Scheme: Reformation through Conscious Activity and External Norms

As "artisan master of the Way," the heart/mind is what enables people to engage in conscious activity (*wei* 偽) and reform their inborn natures. The heart/mind's ability to choose (*ze* 擇)—that is, its ability to function as a ruler and be self-determining—is, in Xunzi's view, the basis of human beings' ability to think (*lü* 慮), and this in turn is the basis of what Xunzi calls conscious activity. These connections are made quite clear in the series of careful definitions offered in the "Rectification of Names" chapter:

> The way a person is from birth is what is called "nature" [*xing* 性]. What is produced by the harmony of nature—that is, out of the quintessential finding its match [*jinghe* 精合] as the senses respond [*ying* 應] to stimuli, so-of-itself and requiring no application [*bushi er ziran* 事而自 然]—is also called "nature." The feelings of liking and disliking, of delight and anger, and of sorrow and joy that come from our nature are called the "emotions" [*qing* 情]. The emotions arising and the heart/mind's choosing [*ze* 擇] between them is called "thinking" [*lü* 慮]. The heart/mind's thinking something and the abilities' [*neng* 能] putting it into action is called "conscious activity" [*wei* 偽]. When thoughts are accumulated [*ji* 積] and the abilities trained [*xi* 習] so that something is perfected, this is also called "conscious activity" [*wei* 偽]. (KIII:127/ W412)

It is no accident that the expressions Xunzi associates with nature are already familiar to us from our account of Zhuangzian wu-wei: "harmony," "matching," "responding," "so-of-itself." Xunzi's primary concern here is to distinguish such expressions and metaphors from proper human activity (*wei*). As we can see from this passage, Xunzi uses the term *wei* 偽 ("conscious activity")[35] in two related but distinct senses, based upon the two primary metaphor schemas for the heart/mind. The first sense invokes the HEART/MIND AS RULER schema, and refers to individual acts involving thought, selection, and command on the part of the heart/mind. These are actions that do not come about spontaneously from one's innate nature, but that require a certain amount of application (*shi* 事). The second invokes the HEART/MIND AS CONTAINER schema, and refers to settled dispositions that result from an accumulation (*ji* 積) of regularly repeated acts of conscious activity. Through training, this accumulation of conscious acts eventually becomes a sort of acquired, second nature.

External Reshaping: The Press Frame and Whetstone

Wei 偽 in the sense of conscious activity is intended by Xunzi to contrast with the sort of passive reliance on the desires advocated by people like Mencius and Zhuangzi, and is part of his campaign against the common wu-wei metaphors of *ying* 應 (response) and *ziran* 自然 (so-of-itself, natural).[36] As we saw in the pas-

sage, these metaphors accurately portray the manner in which the senses respond
to stimuli—"naturally and requiring no application [*bushi er ziran* 不事而自
然]"—but, in Xunzi's view, this has nothing to do with morality. Mencius is thus
completely mistaken in postulating a taste for morality analogous to one's taste
for food or sex, for morality belongs to the realm of conscious activity (involving
reflection and choice) and is fundamentally different from not only sensory
responses but even the inborn tendencies of the heart/mind:

> With regard to the eyes' love of beauty, the ears' love of music, the
> mouth's love of tastes, the heart/mind's love of profit, and the fondness
> of the bones and flesh for ease and idleness [*yuyi* 愉佚]—all these are
> produced by human beings' essential nature. When stimulated, they
> respond naturally [*ziran*]—they are not the sort of things that wait for
> application [*shi* 事] before they are produced. But what cannot be pro-
> duced in such a fashion, but rather must wait for application before it
> can be produced, is called the result of conscious activity. These are the
> characteristics that allow us to see that what is produced by conscious
> activity is not the same as what is produced by nature. (KIII:154/W438)

Even if untutored people do on occasion instinctively respond with compassion
to a child crawling toward a well or to an ox being led to slaughter, this sort of
instinctual, animal response has little or nothing to do with a truly virtuous disposition. Such reactions are attributed by Xunzi to human "original simplicity" (*pu*
樸 , Laozi's "uncarved wood") or "innate endowment" (*zi* 資) (KIII:153/W436),
which only a person like Mencius would confuse with true virtue. It is the nature
of human beings to "depart from their original simplicity and innate endowment"—these innate qualities are necessarily "lost and abandoned" (*shi er sang*
失而喪) as human beings mature (KIII:152/W436).

　　Self-cultivation thus cannot involve a naive faith in this original substance.
Against the *pu* 樸 metaphor for wu-wei that was a favorite of Laozi and employed
as well by Zhuangzi, Xunzi therefore presents the process of self-cultivation as a
metaphorical shaping or fashioning of the raw material of the Self.[37] He refers
several times to the line from ode 55—"As if cut, as if polished / As if carved, as
if ground"—quoted by Zigong in *Analects* 1.15 and approved of by the Master.
"Learning and refinement are to human beings what carving and grinding are to
jade," we read in chapter 27,

> An Ode says,
>
> "As if cut, as if polished
> As if carved, as if ground."
>
> This refers to the process of study and inquiry. (KIII:227–28/W508)[38]

　　Rather than the gentle farmer working along with the natural tendencies of
plants, then, Xunzi's sage is a craftsman who utilizes external tools and applies
outside force in order to shape a recalcitrant material. Whereas Mencius compares the process of self-cultivation to sprouts growing or water flowing downhill, Xunzi evokes images of warped wood being steamed straight, cloth being

artificially dyed, bows being bent into shape, or dull metal being sharpened.[39] The resemblance between these images and the image evoked by Gaozi in *Mencius* 6:A:1 of making morality out of human nature like carving cups and bowls out of a willow tree is not at all accidental, for Xunzi shares with Gaozi the belief that moral guidance must be imposed from the outside. Since human nature is inherently crooked, external forces must be brought to bear upon it before it can be made straight:

> A warped piece of wood must wait for the application of the pressframe and steam and be thereby forced into shape before it will be straight. A dull piece of metal must wait for the whetstone and be ground before it will be sharp. Now, since human nature is bad, it must wait for teacher and models [*shifa* 師法] before it can be made correct, and it must acquire ritual and morality before it can become orderly. (KIII:151/ W435)

The "pressframe" or "whetstone" that are to be brought to bear upon the warped material of our inborn natures are, most broadly understood, the Confucian Way as it is embodied in the practices of the ancients. I mentioned above that the Way is portrayed throughout the text as a sort of external measuring tool against which the "stuff" of the Self is to be measured. As far as the cultivation of the gentleman is concerned, the primary external rectifying force to be brought to bear upon the individual is ritual practice, which is described as the "ridgepole [*ji* 極] of the Way of human beings" and compared in its capacity as a guiding standard to the marking line, balance, compass, and square (KIII:61/W356). Just as such universal standards are required if one is to build a sturdy house, set fixed prices, or draw perfect circles and squares, ritual practice is required if the gentleman is to have a method or standard of action. Innate emotions and desires— including quite powerful and potentially destructive ones—cannot be eliminated from human nature; as Xunzi notes rather wryly, "Being with desires and being without desires belong to two categories: the living and the dead" (KIII:135/ W426). Attempting to entirely repress them would be no better than allowing them to run rampant. The sage-kings thus invented ritual forms in order to allow the orderly and proper expression of emotions and desires common to all people, such as the grief one feels upon losing a loved one (KIII:72/W377). Ritual forms are related to and based upon our inborn emotions, but in the manner that a raw material is related to the finished product—without having been cut and trimmed by conscious activity in accordance with the forms and categories (*lei* 類) provided by the ancients, raw emotions are undirected and potentially harmful. Ritually perfected emotions are thus a paradigmatic example of the transformative power that conscious activity has upon the inborn nature:

> If [innate] emotions are trimmed and stretched, broadened and narrowed, supplemented and decreased, put in their proper category and fully exhausted, brought to fruition and made beautiful—if one could cause the root and branch, end and beginning, to all flow along [*shun* 順] in their proper places and serve as a principle [*ze* 則] sufficient to

serve ten thousand generations—then you have ritual.[40] No one but the gentleman who has become obedient [*shun* 順] and has thoroughly adorned himself [*xiu* 修] through conscious activity is able to know how to do this.

Therefore I say: nature is the root and beginning, the raw material and original simplicity [*benshi caipu* 本始材樸]. Conscious activity is the refinement and patterned order, the flourishing and culmination [*wenli longsheng* 文理隆盛]. If there were no nature, there would be nothing for conscious activity to apply itself to [*jia* 加]; if there were no conscious activity, nature would have no way to beautify itself. Only after nature and conscious activity have been properly matched [*he* 合] are the name of the sage and the work of unifying the world brought to completion. (KIII:66/W366)

As in the *Analects*, ritual behavior is described as the perfect balance between form and substance. Without the form provided by ritual, one's inborn nature would cause one to behave like a wild beast, but when ritual is embodied the self becomes "classically formed" (*yasi* 雅似).[41]

Since the "substance" of ritual (the native emotions) has no proper moral direction of its own, the individual is forced to rely upon traditional norms if he is to attain the proper mean. As a result of this externalism, Xunzi is—like Confucius—a strong traditionalist. As he explains in his chapter on the "Regulations of a True King" (chapter 9), anyone wishing to rule the world as a true king would have to follow to the minutest details the ways of the "Later Kings":[42]

Clothing and dress are regulated; palaces and rooms are of fixed measurements; attendants and servants are of fixed numbers; and every ritual utensil for funerary and sacrificial rites has a form appropriate to one's social rank. With regard to music, all sounds contrary to the classical sounds should be discarded. With regard to colors, everything contrary to ancient designs should be suppressed. With regard to ritual utensils, everything contrary to the ancient forms should be destroyed. This may indeed be described as "returning to the ancients." Such are the regulations of a true King. (KII:101/W159)

Xunzi thus places an emphasis upon strict adherence to inherited forms that we find somewhat lacking in Mencius and that harken back to the original position of Confucius. He compares a person who rejects traditional standards and seeks guidance from her own moral intuitions to a blind person attempting to differentiate colors:

To oppose ritual is to be without a model. To oppose your teacher is to be without a teacher. Not to approve of your teacher and the model, but rather to prefer to rely upon your own resources [*ziyong* 自用] is like trying to use a blind person to distinguish colors or a deaf person to distinguish sounds—there is no way you will be able to avoid confusion and error. (KI:157/W34)

Traditional norms include not only ritual forms and the example of the teacher but also the knowledge embodied in the corpus of classics passed down by the sages. Although veneration of the classics is already quite evident in the *Analects*, Xunzi is credited by many scholars as being the first to establish a fixed body of canonical texts, thereby solidifying and systematizing the Confucian relationship to its textual tradition. Xunzi certainly gives the most elaborate and detailed account to be found in early Confucian writings of the role the classics are to play in forming the individual. Noting how one who lives day to day without any thought for the long-term consequences of his actions will soon be brought to dire straits, Xunzi concludes:

> How much more important, then, are the Way of the Ancient Kings, the guiding principles of benevolence and rightness, and social distinctions described in the *Odes*, *Documents*, *Rituals*, and *Music*! They certainly represent the most important thoughts in the world. . . . Their influence is eternal, their potential for being brought to life[43] is substantial, and their achievements and culminations are vast and wide. . . .
>
> The social distinctions described in the *Odes*, *Documents*, *Rituals*, and *Music* are certainly opposed to what the typical person understands . . . if you use them to bring order to your essential nature, you will benefit. (KI:194/W68–69)

Because the knowledge contained in the classics is completely beyond one's own innate understanding and is also somewhat esoteric—"certainly opposed to what the typical person understands"—it is necessary for one to rely upon the help of a teacher:

> The *Rituals* and *Music* present models but do not offer explanations; the *Odes* and *Documents* provide accounts of antiquity, but it is not always clear how they are relevant; the *Spring and Autumn Annals* are laconic, and their meaning is not immediately apparent. . . . Therefore I say: "In learning, nothing is better than to be near a person of learning." (KI:140/W14)

As opposed to Mencius's rather blithe confidence in his own hermeneutical abilities, then, Xunzi thus takes what might be characterized as a very conservative stand on the individual's relationship to the canon:[44] not only does the individual lack the resources to reform herself without traditional forms and teachings, but these standards themselves are thoroughly opaque to the individual without the interpretive aid of the teacher. A teacher is required not only when interpreting the canon, but also when training in ritual forms. The ordering principle (*li* 理) behind ritual is so profound, Xunzi warns, that someone trying to analyze it logically[45] will "soon be out of his depth," and someone trying to innovate on their own will be "brought to ruin" (KIII:61/W356). It is only the traditional authority embodied in the teacher that prevents the ritual forms themselves from going astray: "Ritual is what is used to correct the self, and the teacher is what is used to correct ritual. Without ritual, how would the individual be corrected?

Without teachers, how would you know whether or not the ritual was being performed correctly?"(KI:157/W33).[46] Mencius would see no problem with discern-
ing the true meaning of a passage from the classics or knowing whether or not a
rite was being performed correctly: the individual would merely need to look
within her own heart/mind and see whether or not it was "pleased." Xunzi
removes this guiding norm (*ze* 則) from the individual's native capacities and
locates it in an external tradition that is embodied in and properly conveyed by a
teacher, whose authoritative judgments now take the place of Mencius's "true
knowledge" (*liangzhi* 良知).[47]

Need for Gradual Effort: The Way as Long Journey

In keeping with the metaphor of self-cultivation as a kind of shaping or adornment of the Self, Xunzi often plays upon the literal sense of the common phrase
"cultural adornment" (*wenzhang* 文章), *wen* 文 referring traditionally to the
green and red emblem and *zhang* 章 to a red and white emblem of authority
(W180). In chapter 10, he explains how the ancient sage kings caused jade to be
"carved and polished" (*diaozhuo* 雕琢), wood to be carved, and metal incised,
and the *wen* and *zhang* emblems to be created in order to distinguish noble from
base, and quotes the description of the king of Zhou in ode 238:

> Carved and polished are his emblems [*zhang*]
> Of gold and jade are they made.
> Untiring is our king,
> Laying a network of norms [*gangji* 綱紀] upon the land.

Xunzi thus explicitly celebrates the artificial, "decorative" (*shi* 飾) metaphors for
Confucian self-cultivation, because in his view the forms of culture were created
by the sages in the same way that a potter creates vessels out of clay—fashioning
something entirely artificial out of undifferentiated raw material, rather than realizing some tendency or pattern rooted in their inborn nature (KIII:152/W437).

Self-cultivation thus requires not only the application of external standards
but also a great deal of effort, applied gradually over a long period of time—in
order to achieve Xunzian wu-wei, we have to try very hard indeed not to try. The
need for effort and the constraints of gradualism are conveyed not only by
Xunzi's celebration of decorative and craft metaphors for self-cultivation but also
in his targeted opposition to the *cong* 從 (following), *shun* 順 (flowing with) and
yin 因 (following, adapting) metaphors. We saw above his warning that following
or flowing along with the immediately accessible, inborn human tendencies
would lead to disaster (KIII:151/W434), as well as his belief that Mencius's failure to understand this was the result of a confusion between nature and conscious
activity. Similarly, in his criticism of Zhuangzi, Xunzi observes that Zhuangzi
"was obscured by the Heavenly and so failed to understand the human"
(KIII:102/W393). In his "Discourse on Heaven" chapter (chapter 17), Xunzi
explains that what is given by Heaven to human beings—our innate nature—is
something that needs to be domesticated and curbed. The proper vocation of
human beings is to put this order to work, to make use of it and exploit it through

human activity (*wei* 偽), not to sit back passively and wait for things to happen by themselves:

> How can glorifying Heaven and longing for it compare to raising its creatures and regulating them? How can following [*cong* 從] Heaven and singing hymns in its praise compare to regulating the Heavenly mandate and making use of it? How can watching for the seasons and awaiting what they bring compare to responding to the season and making use of it? How can passively relying upon [*yin* 因] things and waiting for them to multiply compare to employing them according to their qualities and transforming them? How can pondering things as simply another thing among them [*siwu er wuzhi* 思物而物之] compare with grasping their underlying pattern [*li* 理] and not letting go of it? How can longing for the origin of things compare with mastering that by which things are perfected?

> Thus, if you cast aside the human in order to long for the Heavenly, you will miss the essential nature [*qing* 情] of the myriad things. (KIII:20–21/W317)

We see here Xunzi rejecting the "following" (*cong*) and "adapting"/"relying" (*yin*) as unworthy of human beings. A human being is not, as Zhuangzi would have it, simply a "thing" (*wu* 物) passively flowing along among other things. "The problem with a 'way' [*dao* 道] claiming to be based upon Heaven," as Xunzi puts it in the "Dispelling Obscurations" chapter, "is that everything becomes a matter of passive reliance [*yin*]" (KIII:102/W393). Certainly it is the Way of Heaven to do nothing and say nothing and yet cause all things to be done, but this is the Way of Heaven, not humans. In fact, human beings have a unique part to play in the cosmic scheme of things: it is their task to stand outside the stream of spontaneous nature in order to grasp its underlying patterns and then master and manipulate it. To fail to see this is to miss the "essence" of the world and our proper place in it. Xunzi often invokes the social metaphor of "official task" to convey this point, as in the passage near the beginning of "Discourse on Heaven" where he associates wu-wei with Heaven:

> To bring to completion without acting; to obtain without seeking—this is what we call the official task [*zhi* 職] of Heaven. This being so, the [proper] person, however profound, does not apply any thought to the task of Heaven; however great, does not apply his abilities to it; and however perceptive, does not apply his discernment to it. This is what we call "not vying with Heaven in its task." (KIII:15/W308)[48]

The Xunzian Perfected Person (*zhiren* 至人), "understanding the proper places [*fen* 分] of the Heavenly and the human" (KIII:15/W308), thus knows that he must engage in a long process of cutting and polishing if he is to fulfill his proper duty. He does not concern himself with the mysteries of Heavenly wu-wei, or worry about the vicissitudes of fate (*ming* 命), but rather focuses upon his proper task: self-cultivation (KIII:18/W312).

When he means to target the sort of passiveness that pervades the thought of Mencius and the Daoists, we thus see Xunzi rejecting not only the *cong* (following) family but also the *an* 安 (ease) family of metaphors. Thus at the beginning of chapter 1, "An Exhortation to Learning," we see Xunzi approvingly quoting ode 207—"Oh you gentleman / Be not constantly at ease and resting [*anxi* 安息] / Diligently and respectfully assume your position / And love those who are correct and upright" (KI:136/W3)—and in chapter 17 admonishing the reader that "rightness between ruler and minister, affection between father and son, distinction between husband and wife—all of these must daily be cut and polished without rest" (*qiecuo er bushe* 切瑳而不舍) (KIII:19/W316).

The basic problem with both of the "effortless" family of metaphors that the Daoists and Mencius were so fond of is their failure to account for the *arduousness* and sheer *length* of the process of self-cultivation.[49] Human fallenness is not the result of inattention to our true moral natures, or due to an inability to get into contact with Heavenly forces that are poised to spring instantly from the depths within us. Rather, human beings are corrupt from birth, and morality involves working against a deeply ingrained set of inborn dispositions. Becoming a moral person is thus hard work, requiring great unity of will and doggedness in pursuing the Way. People are like the evil ruler Jie or Robber Zhi because they "remain uncouth [*lou* 陋]," Xunzi claims: "even Yao and Yu were not born fully equipped [*ju* 具], but rose up by changing their original selves [*biangu* 變故], perfected themselves through cultivated, conscious action [*xiuxiuzhiwei* 修修之為], and only after exhausting their efforts became complete" (KI:192/W63). Benjamin Schwartz contrasts the aspiring Mencian sage, who "like a strong swimmer swimming with the current is . . . able to draw immediate support from the deepest tendencies of human nature," with the aspiring Xunzian sage shaping, constraining, and remaking himself through concerted, sustained, long-term effort (1985: 299). Just as one wishing to become a potter must study, learn, and apply herself to the task, becoming a true Confucian gentleman requires constant, conscious effort to wrest something elegant and properly formed out of the morass of our inborn nature.

One of Xunzi's favorite metaphors for self-cultivation is familiar from the *Analects*: SELF-CULTIVATION AS LONG JOURNEY, based upon the common Warring States metaphor scheme of THE WAY AS ROAD. As in the *Analects*, this metaphor provides Xunzi with a wealth of useful entailments. Consider this passage from chapter 2, "Cultivating the Self":

> A thoroughbred can travel 1,000 *li* in a single day, but even a worn-out nag can catch up to it if given ten days to do so. Do you wish to exhaust the inexhaustible or pursue that which is without end?[50] If so, you will break your bones and exhaust your muscles for the rest of your life without ever reaching your goal. If, on the other hand, you go after that which has a stopping place [*zhi* 止], then, even though it is far, how could you not be able to complete a journey of 1,000 *li*—no matter if you travel slowly or quickly, ahead of the pack or bringing up the rear?
> . . .

This is why I say, Learning is slow-going [*chi* 遲],[51] but that stopping place awaits us. If we set out and go toward it, then—no matter that some will go more slowly and some more quickly, some will be in the fore and some will bring up the rear—how could we not all eventually arrive there together? Thus, by lifting up its feet and never resting, a lame turtle can travel 1,000 *li*...[whereas] if one is advancing and one retreating, one pulling to the left and one pulling to the right, even a team of six thoroughbreds will never get there. Certainly the talents of human beings do not vary as much as the speeds of the lame turtle and team of six thoroughbreds! Yet the fact that the lame turtle gets there and the thoroughbred team does not has no other cause than this: the one did it [*weizhi* 為之], while the other did not.

Although the Way is near, if you do not walk it [*xing* 行] you will never reach the end. Although the task is small, if you do not act, it will not be completed. One who is accustomed to spending many days in rest [*xia* 暇] will not get very far along the Way. (KI:155–56/W30–32)

Xunzi gets quite a bit of mileage (as it were) out of this metaphor. Although self-cultivation is a "long" process, anyone who displays perseverance can complete it. Unlike the heterodox ways of the logicians and seekers after supernatural powers, the Confucian Way has a destination—that is, it is worth traveling along because it actually *goes* somewhere, and there is the eventual promise of a pleasant rest at the end of the road. Innate physical skill has little to do with success: the most powerful team of horses can go nowhere without focus (*yi* 一), training, and (most importantly) the exertion of effort, while the stubborn and hard-working lame turtle can traverse 1,000 *li*. The moral: be like the turtle, do not rest, do not swerve, and eventually you will reach your destination.[52]

Other entailments of the SELF-CULTIVATION AS LONG JOURNEY metaphor include the fact that one must get an early start if one is to have any hope of reaching the final destination, which means that Xunzi (like Aristotle) emphasizes that the process of character formation must begin at an early age: "If you do not recite the classics as a child and discuss and deliberate as a youth," he warns, "then even though you may turn out alright, you will never perfect yourself" (KIII:228/W509).[53] Similarly, just as in a physical journey, point A must be traversed before point B can be reached, the Confucian soteriological path has a "beginning and an end" (*shizhong* 始終), with clearly defined steps in between. In chapter 1 Xunzi exploits this entailment of the metaphor, combining it with the SELF-CULTIVATION AS ACCUMULATION (to be discussed next) and the MORALITY AS BOUNDED SPACE schema:

Does learning have a beginning? Does it have an end? I say, its method is such that one should begin with reciting the classics and end by studying the ritual texts. Its purpose is to begin by making one into a scholar [*shi* 士], and end by making one a sage. If you genuinely accumulate your efforts over a long period of time you will be able to enter into it [*ru* 入]. Learning continues unto death and only then does it stop. Thus, though the method of learning has an end, its purpose cannot be set aside [*she* 舍] for even an instant. (KI:139/W11)[54]

We see here, as we saw above, how the WAY AS PATH metaphor can be quite easily combined with the MORALITY AS BOUNDED SPACE scheme if one pictures the path itself as a delineated space. This allows Xunzi to systematically incorporate entailments concerning the danger of going astray (that is, outside the bounds) into his SELF-CULTIVATION AS JOURNEY metaphor. We saw this combination above in the metaphor of ritual as markers delineating the boundaries of a safe ford across a dangerous river (KIII:21/W318–19 and KIII:209/W488), and it appears again in a slightly different conceptual form in one of the passages from the "Great Compendium" (chapter 27): "Rituals provide the footing upon which people walk [*renzhisuolü* 人之所履]. If you lose this footing, you will certainly stumble and fall, sink and drown" (KIII:216/W495). This variation illustrates the cognitive flexibility of the WAY AS PATH metaphor: departure from the path can involve transgressing bounded space, as with the ford metaphor, or can be cognized as losing one's metaphorical "footing."

Another of Xunzi's effort/gradualist metaphors that we saw in the chapter 1 learning passage is that of "accumulation." This metaphor appeared in the *Mencius*, of course, but Mencian accumulation (*ji* 集) is generally based upon the model of the effortless building up of water behind a dam. It is thus gradualist, but with less emphasis upon effort, because after the initial effort of building the dam the water takes care of the rest. Xunzian accumulation (*ji* 積), on the other hand, is usually portrayed metaphorically in terms of the gradual and *continually* arduous building up of a mountain or painstaking collecting of physical substances.[55] In chapter 1, for instance, the process of self-cultivation is compared to accumulating basketful by basketful enough earth to build a high hill, or—combining the metaphor of accumulation with the SELF-CULTIVATION AS LONG JOURNEY schema and invoking an EVENT OBJECT metaphor to understand actions as substances—the "accumulation" of individual steps that constitutes a completed journey of 1,000 *li* (KI:138/W7). Making the metaphorical link to self-cultivation explicit, Xunzi notes that "Through accumulating goodness Virtue is perfected, and in this way the spiritual clarity will naturally be attained [*shenming zide* 神明 自得]" (KI:138/W7). Here we thus have Zhuangzi's religious goal—spiritual clarity—attained through diametrically opposed means: accumulation rather than "fasting."

In one sense, the process of accumulation is easy, since it is not at all hard to carry a single basket of earth or take a single step. The problem is that most people lack the focus to see the process through to the end. This is the theme of the section on "Accumulating the Minute" (*jiwei* 集微) in chapter 16, which is capped with a citation from ode 260: "Virtue is light as a hair / But among the people there are few who can lift it" (KII:248/W305). Against what he no doubt perceives as the facile optimism of Mencius, Xunzi wishes to emphasize that becoming a learned and moral person is time-consuming; it takes a lifetime of steady effort, and may test the endurance of even the greatest sages. Those who are the proper "counterparts to Heaven" are described in the "Great Compendium" as "insatiable in study and inquiry and untiring in their love of scholars" (KIII:228/W508), and the heart/mind finding its true object in thinking (*lü* 慮) is compared to a person looking for a needle: he will be successful, not because his eyes have become sharper or because he has drawn upon some special talent, but because he has taken the effort to "gaze down and look more carefully for it" (KIII:222/W501). In chapter 8 ("The Teachings of the Ru"), Xunzi uses the metaphor of accumulation to deliberately contrast his picture of focused, sustained, long-term self-cultivation with that of Mencius, without actually mentioning Mencius by name:

> If a person is without a teacher or model, then he will emphasize nature [*xing* 性]; if he has a teacher and model, he will emphasize accumulation [*ji* 積]. The teacher and the model are things acquired through accumulation,[56] and are not something received from one's nature, for nature by itself is inadequate to establish good order. "Nature" is what I cannot create or make [*wei* 為] but can nonetheless transform. "Accumulation" refers to what I do not possess but can nonetheless create or make. Concentration and collection, practice and acculturation are the means by which one's nature is transformed. Unifying diversity and not becoming divided is the means by which accumulation is perfected. Practice and acculturation will eventually change [*yi* 移; lit. move] the intention [*zhi* 志], and when one dwells at ease [*an* 安] within them for a long period of time one's very substance [*zhi* 質] will be altered. (KII:81–82/W143)[57]

Both the SELF-CULTIVATION AS JOURNEY and SELF-CULTIVATION AS GRADUAL ACCUMULATION metaphors thus provide entailments that allow the reader to grasp both the necessarily gradual nature of self-cultivation and the importance of being diligent, focused, and unflagging in one's efforts.

An Externalist Virtue Ethic: Creating an Artificial "Nature"

Although a moral externalist, Xunzi nonetheless remains a self-cultivationist. That is, his purpose is not—like voluntarists such a Yizhi or Gaozi—to get the individual to rationally assent to a proposition and then immediately begin acting in accordance with its principles, but rather to have the individual submit to a process of training in external norms and forms of conduct that will eventually effect a transformation upon both the heart/mind and the emotional dispositions. This has two consequences for his moral project: 1) since training of the dispositions is involved, the process will necessarily be gradual (hence the gradualist metaphors examined above); and 2) at the end of the process, the individual will possess a completely transformed set of dispositions, desires and beliefs. Both of these aspects also characterize, as we have seen, the virtue ethical scheme proposed by Mencius. With regard to the first point, though, Xunzi takes great pains to differentiate himself from Mencius by focusing upon the arduousness of the process.

Although an externalist, where Xunzi differs from the Mohists or other voluntarist externalists is that once the process has been completed, the very character of the individual will have been transformed. To invoke the "wood straightening" metaphor, the gentleman is steamed upon the pressframe of the Way until his entire being has been permanently and irrevocably rectified:

> A piece of wood straight as a plumbline can be steamed and bent into the shape of a wheel rim, ending up as perfectly curved as a compass arc. Even after drying out in the sun, though, the wood will not return [*fu* 復] to its former straightness. This is because the process of steaming and bending has remade it. (KI:135/W1)[58]

As we recall, when one "dwells at ease [*an* 安]" in the Confucian Way for a long period of time "one's very substance [*zhi* 質] will be altered/moved [*yi* 移]" (KII:81–82/W143). The process of change effected by Confucian practice is portrayed by Xunzi according to the common EVENT LOCATION metaphor: a change involves "moving" the Self from point A to point B, and once this latter location is attained the Self will not "go back" (*fan* or *fu*). Xunzi often communicates this idea of permanent "relocation" through the metaphor of transformation (*hua* 化), perhaps most dramatically by comparing the process of learning to the transformation of a caterpillar into a butterfly in a passage from the "Great Compendium": "The gentleman going through the process of learning is like the butterfly—he is changed [*qian* 遷; lit. moved] drastically" (KIII:225/W505).

Despite the drastic nature of this transformation, the final state that is attained is quite stable. Xunzi conveys this sense of stability through the metaphors of having a "foundation" (*ji* 基), a "root" (*ben* 本) or a "source" (*yuan* 原). "If you would take the Former Kings as your source and benevolence and rightness as your root, then ritual will rectify the warp and woof, the highways and byways of your life," he notes (KI:141/W16). Xunzi shares Mencius's fondness for these "source" and "root" metaphors—indeed, these metaphors function as the distinguishing metaphorical marks setting the Warring States virtue ethicists apart from the rationalist Mohists and logicians. We noted in chapter 5 that in defending a "one-root" picture of morality against the "two-root" model championed by the neo-Mohists, Mencius was essentially defending the greater plausibility of a virtue ethical model of self-cultivation over the rationalist externalist model of moral action. Xunzi shares a similar goal, even though his "root" is located outside of the individual. An interesting contrast in the manner in which the two thinkers use the "source" metaphor is to be found in chapter 4, where Xunzi quotes a saying: "You cannot reach the source of a deep well [*shenjingzhiquan* 深井之泉] with a short rope," which he interprets to mean that "one whose knowledge is not carefully detailed [*ji* 幾] will not be able to reach up to the teachings of the sages" (KI:194/W69). Here Xunzi's source is located at the bottom of a deep well and requires the use of an external tool—a long rope —if it is to be reached, which provides a revealing contrast to Mencius's source, which comes bubbling up naturally out of the ground.

Like Mencius, however, Xunzi criticizes the Mohists for lacking a root or source for morality because their doctrines do not take into account the fixed tendencies of human nature or the proper relationship between human beings and the natural world. Were Mozi to rule over territory "as large as the whole world or as small as single state," his policies of "Denouncing music" and "Moderating Expenses"[59] would have a disastrous effect, throwing officialdom into chaos and disrupting the lives of the common people.

> With things in such a state, the myriad things lose their appropriate [*yi* 宜] places and the development of affairs loses its proper responsiveness [*ying* 應]. Above, the Heaven's timeliness [*shi* 時] is lost; below, the benefits of the Earth are lost; and in the middle human harmony is lost. Then it is as though the world was roasting, as if it were burnt or scorched. Although Mozi would have one wear sackcloth and use only a twisted rope as a belt, feed on porridge and drink only water, how could there be enough to go around? For having hacked at its roots and exhausted its source, he would have already scorched the whole world. (KII:128–29/W186)

The way of the Former Kings is otherwise. Understanding both human emotional nature and the nature of the world, they devised a standard which was designed to perfectly harmonize the two, thereby providing morality with both a root and a source:

> If your classifications are modeled upon the sage-kings, you will understand what is valuable. If you use rightness [*yi* 義] to regulate affairs, you will understand what is beneficial. If in your classifications you understand what is valuable, you will understand the means by which to cultivate things; if in your affairs you understand what is beneficial, you will understand what motivates your movements. These two things [knowing what is valuable and what is beneficial] are the root of right and wrong and the source of success and failure. (KIII:167/W452)

Although the root and source have their origin in what is external—in the model of the sage kings and their system of morality, as opposed to the heart/mind—they are designed to eventually harmonize with human dispositions and desires, and so can eventually be embodied in the self. Although he views "rightness" as something initially external to the uncultivated self, Xunzi is nonetheless just as concerned as Mencius with the mistake of trying to "ambush" it. Perfected moral action involves more than merely rigidly following an external set of rules, because it requires the kind of flexibility and responsiveness that is only possible when the "root" or "source" of these rules is (eventually, at least) found within the self. Thus Xunzi's description of the one worthy to be a "true king":

> His every adornment and movement is governed by ritual and morality. He listens to advice and makes decisions according to the proper catego-

ries. He intelligently [*ming* 明] examines everything down to the tip of the finest hair. He in inexhaustible [*buqiong* 不窮] in promoting or dismissing and in responding to every change of circumstance [*yingbian* 應變]. This may indeed be described as "possessing the source [*yuan* 原]." (KII:100/W158)

Having the "source" of morality within him, the responsiveness of the perfected person is never "exhausted."

   This accounts for Xunzi's concern with music, to which he devotes an entire chapter (chapter 20, "Discourse on Music"). Music is the traditional form that has perhaps the most immediate and powerful transformative effect on the emotions and desires, and with regard to which the ideal harmony between transformed desires and the proper mean is most clearly observed. Making use of the standard graphic pun between music (*yue* 樂) and joy (*le* 樂), Xunzi notes the essential service provided by traditional musical forms: "Music is joy. Since it represents an inescapable aspect of the human emotional essence, people cannot do without music/joy" (KIII:80/W379). Because of its intimate relationship with the powerful emotion of joy, music is the most direct way to "reform" the emotional "stuff" of human beings. Although ritual, as we have seen, eventually brings about a reformation and redirection of our emotions, it lacks the immediate and necessary link to our inner emotional state that music possesses.[60] Xunzi invokes the SELF AS CONTAINER metaphor to explain how properly balanced music is one of the most efficacious means by which the Former Kings brought harmony to the world:

> Music and sound are able to deeply enter into [*ru* 入] people and thereby transform them very quickly. This is why the Former Kings were assiduous in refining it. If music accords with the mean and is balanced, the common people will be harmonious and not given to dissipation. If it is solemn and dignified, then the common people will behave uniformly and will not be inclined to disorder. When the common people are harmonious and behave uniformly, the army is strong and the cities secure. . . .When things are so, the Hundred Clans will be at ease [*an* 安] with their dwelling places, will take joy in their villages, and will thereby be satisfied with their superiors. . . . This is the beginning of true kingship. (KIII:82/W380)

Music is so powerful because—unlike ritual—it immediately "enters into" (*ru*) the Self and is able change it from the inside. One might say that a concern with the inner transformative power of music is one of the hallmarks that separates a certain kind of virtue ethicist from a voluntarist. If one sees one's task as finished once a person has been gotten to rationally *assent* to a belief or doctrine, there is little reason to bother with such trivial issues as the type of music the person listens to. One might even be tempted, like the Mohists, to seek to do away with music altogether as a pointless extravagance. If, however, one is concerned with transforming the "inner" emotional disposition of the individual in order to put it to work in the service of morality—in other words, if one has wu-wei as a goal—

the power of music will take on a much greater significance. Xunzi is thus just as concerned as Mencius to argue for the superiority of the self-cultivationist model of morality, and therefore also in defending the viability of wu-wei as a spiritual ideal.

Xunzian Wu-wei

We have seen that Xunzian moral perfection represents the culmination of an arduous training regime, and is understood metaphorically as arriving at the end of a long journey. An individual's state of progress down the road of self-cultivation is often characterized by Xunzi by means of a classification of humanity into three "grades of people" (*renlun* 人倫):[61]

> In their intentions they do not avoid the crooked and selfish, and yet they hope that others will consider them to be public-spirited. In their conduct they do not avoid vile and deceptive, and yet they hope that others will consider them cultivated. They are stupid, uncouth, foolish, and deluded, and yet they hope that others will consider them wise. Such are the common mass of humanity [*zhongren* 眾人].

> In their intentions they repress [*ren* 忍] the selfish and only then are able to be public spirited. In their conduct, they repress their essential nature and only then are able to become cultivated. With regard to their knowledge, they are fond of inquiring of others, and only then are able to develop their talents. Public-spirited, cultivated, and talented, they may be called the "lesser Confucians" [*xiaoru* 小儒].

> In their intentions they are at ease [*an*] with what is public-spirited, in their conduct they are at ease with what is cultivated, in their knowledge they penetrate the guiding principles of proper categories—people such as this may called "great Confucians" [*daru* 大儒]. (KII:83/W145)

We find a similar tripartite hierarchy of achievement in chapter 2 ("On Self-Cultivation"), although there the hierarchy begins at a somewhat more lofty point, consisting of scholars (*shi* 士), gentlemen (*junzi* 君子), and sages (*shengren* 聖人):

> One who acts from a love of the model is a scholar. One who has a firm intention and embodies it is a gentleman. One who perceives it with even clarity and is never exhausted is a sage. A person without a model [someone below the *shi* 士] is aimlessly confused. Someone who possesses a model but lacks a recognition of its meaning [the *shi* 士] is unable to stick firmly to it. Only once one can lean upon [*yi* 依] the model and profoundly grasp its categories will one be calm and at ease [*wenwenran* 溫溫然]. (KI:156/W33)[62]

Although the characterizations of the different levels differ somewhat,[63] the general theme is quite clear. At the lowest level are those who act only upon selfish, conscious considerations of profit (*li* 利)—the common people—who must either be lured into the process of self-cultivation by consequentialist arguments or (for those who will never rise above this level) controlled by means of laws and punishments. At the middle level are those who have come to sense the inherent value of the Confucian practice—who have begun to appreciate emotionally the unique internal goods it has to offer—but who still have not succeeded in eliminating internal conflict and entirely transforming their dispositions. These are the "small Confucians," the scholars. They are certainly to be honored, but they do not approach the highest level of achievement: that of the "great Confucians" or sages, who have so completely transformed their natures that they accord with the Confucian Way in an entirely wu-wei fashion.

The final state of Xunzian wu-wei, as in many of the thinkers we have examined, includes both behavioral/physiological and cognitive aspects.

Behavioral/Physiological Aspect

Living in the post–"Inner Training" world, and no doubt having contact with medical practitioners and other "masters of techniques" at the Jixia Academy, Xunzi provides an explicit physiological grounding for a self-cultivation scheme that was already sketched out in a less precise form in the *Analects*. We have already discussed in some detail the craft metaphors of reshaping and the container metaphors of accumulation, and it is the latter that Xunzi draws upon in chapter 1 in describing learning as a kind of substance that enters the gentleman physically and takes over control of his body: "The learning of the gentleman enters [*ru* 入] through the ear, becomes firm in the heart/mind,[64] spreads out through the four limbs, and manifests itself in both activity and repose" (KI:140/ W12). Chapter 2 describes Confucian self-cultivation as the "technique" (*shu* 術) of "ordering the *qi* and cultivating the heart/mind" (*zhiqi yangxin* 治氣養心,), and portrays the human blood and *qi* (*xueqi* 血氣) as a system that can be balanced through ritual and the influence of a teacher (KI:153–54/W25–26). Similarly, in the "Discourse on Music," music and ritual are portrayed as forces that can harmonize and settle the physiological forces within the self: "When music is performed the intention is purified, and when ritual is cultivated, conduct is perfected. The ears become acute and the eyes clear, the blood and *qi* are harmonized and put into equilibrium, and manners are altered and customs changed" (KIII:84/W382).

Xunzian self-cultivation thus changes the very physiological make-up of the self. Once the blood and *qi* have been harmonized with morality, the practitioner no longer has to compel himself to accord with ritual forms or other traditional norms—they are now such an integral part of the self that they are realized in the same spontaneous and joyous fashion that uncultivated people feel in satisfying the animal desires:

The sage gives free reign to [*zong* 縱] his desires and fulfills all of his emotions, but having been regulated they accord with the ordered pattern. What need has he, then, for strength of will, endurance, or cautiousness? Thus the benevolent person practices the Way in a wu-wei fashion, and the sage practices the Way without forcing himself [*wuqiang* 無彊].The thoughts of the benevolent man are reverent, and those of the sage are joyful. (KIII:108/W404)[65]

This reads very much like *Analects* 2.4—to such an extent that Wang Xianqian suggests reading *zong* 縱 as *cong* 從 in order to make it match the description of Confucius at age 70. The metaphorical structure varies slightly—here the desires are being released to do all of the work on the part of the Subject, which is not conceptually much different from the Subject following the desires—but in any case we can find all of the original Confucian metaphors for wu-wei in the *Xunzi*. Despite his targeted criticism of the *cong* and *an* 安 family of metaphors in his diatribes against the internalists, both of these sets of metaphors are celebrated when it comes to describing the end result of Confucian self-cultivation. The description of the demeanor of the Xunzian "scholar gentleman" in chapter 6, for instance, could have been lifted from book 10 of the *Analects*:

> His cap sits high on his head, his robes are grand, and his demeanor is pleasant and relaxed; grave and correct while still comfortable and at ease, magnanimous and broad-heart/minded, enlightened and calm[66]— this is his manner as father or elder brother. His cap sits high on his head, his robes are grand, and his demeanor is assiduously respectful; humble, eager to help, honest, constantly striving, respectful, exemplary and unassuming—this is his manner as son or younger brother.

Xunzi later notes that such effortless perfection is possible because the sage relies upon "the ancestral source [*zongyuan* 宗原] to respond to changes [*yingbian* 應變], bending where appropriate so that everything attains its fit [*yi* 宜]" (KI:229/ W105).

Such perfection is often portrayed as a type of balance between inner and outer, and is linked with the "responding" (*ying* 應) or "flowing with" (*shun* 順) metaphors. In a passage from the "Great Compendium" that echoes our discussion of the rites, it is said that "refinement and appearance, emotion and offering serve as the inner and outer, surface and interior, and ritual finds its mean therein," and this aphorism is followed by the claim that "ritual represents the flowing from [*shun*] root to branch, the mutual responsiveness [*ying*] of end and beginning" (KIII:218/W497). Other examples from chapters more likely from Xunzi's own hand combine the "responsiveness" metaphor with the metaphors of "fitting" (*dang* 當) and "timeliness" (*shi* 時), for instance: "Act when the time is right [*dangshi ze dong* 當時則動], and respond [*ying*] to things as they arrive" (KIII:111/W409)(KII:179/W233). In a very interesting passage from Chapter 8 all of these metaphors are combined to liken the sage's wu-wei ease and responsiveness to the effortlessness of natural processes:

Cultivating the model of the Hundred Kings as easily as distinguishing black from white; responding to changes as they occur [*ying dang shi zhi bian*] as easily as counting from one to two; manifesting in practice the essential ritual restraint and yet being at ease [*an*] with it as if it sprang from his four limbs; skillfully welcoming occasions to establish his merit as if he were simply announcing the arrival of the four seasons; balancing, rectifying and harmonizing the goodness of the people with a comprehensiveness that makes the innumerable masses seem like a single person—only someone like this can be called a sage. (KII:76/W130; cf. KI:227/W100)

Such descriptions of the Xunzian sage and sagely ruler at times sound almost Laozian or Zhuangzian. Consider, for example, this description of the "Son of Heaven":

The Son of Heaven does not look and yet sees, does not listen and yet hears, does not contemplate and yet knows, does not act and yet is successful. Like a clod he sits alone and the whole world follows [*cong*] him like a single body, like four limbs following the heart/mind. (KII:185/W239)

Similarly, we read that the gentleman "is bright as the sun and moon, and responds [*ying*] like lightning or thunder . . . is hidden yet manifest, subtle yet bright, deferring and declining and yet, in the end, victorious" (KII:74/W129).[67] This sort of conflation of the human sage with Heaven or the cosmic forces might seem to contradict the careful demarcation Xunzi establishes between the proper roles of human beings and Heaven, and thus to represent precisely the kind of confusion between incompatible realms that he attributes to Zhuangzi and Mencius. This tension is eased when we understand such "lack of exertion" metaphors and descriptions of mysterious, cosmic ease in their proper context: as the end-results of an extremely arduous, externally applied and transformative training regime. We can see this most clearly, perhaps, in the manner in which Xunzi, like Mencius, employs the metaphor of dance to describe the wu-wei perfection of the sage:

How can we understand the meaning of dance? I say the eyes by themselves cannot perceive it and the ears by themselves cannot hear it. Rather, only when the manner in which one gazes down or looks up, bends or straightens, advances or retreats, and slows down or speeds up is so ordered that every movement is proper and regulated, when the strength of muscles and bones has been so thoroughly exhausted in according with the rhythm of the drums, bells, and orchestra that all awkward or discordant motions have been eliminated—only through such an accumulation of effort [*ji* 積] is the meaning of dance fully realized. (KIII:85/W384)

In the dance metaphor found in the *Mencius*, there is no mention of training: the hands and feet spontaneously begin moving in time to a rhythm that seems to call forth a primal response in the listener. Wu-wei perfection thus represents for Mencius merely the full realization of responses that are natural for human beings. For Xunzi, "not trying" is not so easy: the perfection of form and emotion that finds its expression in dance is a hard-won *achievement* resulting from years of difficult "accumulation" and submission to cultural forms, which serve to transform one's initially recalcitrant and ugly nature into something harmonious and beautiful.

Cognitive Aspect

Xunzian wu-wei is thus at least partially a matter of training the bones and flesh. At the same time, these physiological transformations are to be distinguished from mere habit by the fact that they are accompanied by a corresponding enhancement of the practitioner's understanding. Just as the seemingly effortless movement of the skilled pianist's fingers over the keys is a combination of physical training and increased understanding of and feeling for the principles behind the music, so the skilled Xunzian practitioner represents an ideal combination of somatic cultivation and cognitive comprehension. The Xunzian sage's perfect responsiveness to the world is thus due not only to his transformed physical dispositions, then, but also to a heightened intellectual understanding of the practices themselves. The sage, gentleman, and the "great Confucian" comprehend the constant patterned order (*li* 理) that underlies both the universe and the Confucian cultural forms that were designed to accord with it, which is what allows them to "fit" the world, both behaviorally and cognitively:

> They emulate the model of the Former Kings, keep to the guiding line of ritual and morality, unify rules and regulations, use the shallow to grasp the deep, use the past to grasp the present, and use the one to grasp the myriad. They can recognize the different categories of right and wrong as easily as distinguishing black from white, even men living among the birds and beasts. Presented with unusual things or strange alterations— things that have never been seen or heard of before—they are able to immediately pick up one corner[68] and thereby respond [*ying*] to them in accordance with the guiding principle and proper categories, without the slightest hesitation or discomfort. Extending the model to measure such things, they are all perfectly covered like two halves of a tally being joined together [*he fujie* 合符節]. Such are the great Confucians. (KII:80/W140)

We can find echoes of both Laozi and Zhuangzi in the descriptions of the cognitive powers of the Xunzian sage. Like Laozi's sage, the Xunzian sage can "sit within his room and yet perceive all within the Four Seas, live in the present and yet discourse upon far antiquity" (KIII:105/W397);[69] like the Zhuangzian sage, the understanding of Xunzi's "Great Person" (*daren* 大人) is "bright" (*ming* 明) and without limits:

Extensive and broad, who can know his limits? Massive and vast, who can know his Virtue? Roiling and multifarious, who can know his physical form? Bright like the sun and moon, his greatness filling the Eight Poles—such a person can be called a "Great Person." (KIII:105/W397)

The Xunzian sage is even able to make the same sort of flexible, situation-specific discriminations (*bian* 辩) as the Zhuangzian sage:

The discriminations of the sage involve no prior consideration and no planning beforehand, yet whatever he expresses is appropriate, perfected in form, and exactly proper to its type. In raising up issues or in setting them aside, in removing them or shifting them, he responds inexhaustibly to every change. (KI:210/W3.11b; cf. KIII:248/W525)

As with the behavioral component, however, beneath this similarity lurk profound differences. Unlike the Zhuangzian sage, for instance, Xunzi's Great Person attains this level of cognitive flexibility and power not by giving up knowledge, but by perfecting knowledge:[70]

Through penetrating inspection of the myriad things, he knows their essence. Through testing and examining the sources of order and disorder, he is able to thoroughly regulate them. By picking out the warp and woof of Heaven and Earth, he is able to properly assign offices to the myriad things. By regulating and distinguishing according to the great ordering pattern [*dali* 大理], he encompasses within himself everything in space and time. (KIII:105/W397)[71]

Xunzi's sage thus resembles Laozi's in that he responds to the "constant" (*chang* 常) principles of nature[72] in order to attain success in the world. However, whereas Laozi's sage uses this knowledge to keep his person whole and thereby bring the world to completion, the Xunzian sage is more active, using his knowledge to impose order upon and attain mastery over the world. Xunzi's type of knowledge also differs fundamentally from both Laozi's and Zhuangzi's conceptions of perfect understanding in that it is *cultural* in origin. The Xunzian sage's perfect and instant responsiveness to things arises not from some indwelling Heavenly spirit or mysterious oneness with the Way, but rather from having thoroughly internalized a culturally constructed and external code of rightness (*yi* 義). This is illustrated quite nicely in a passage where Xunzi employs the "fitting" (*yi* 宜) metaphor that is so familiar from the *Zhuangzi*, but inverts the priority of the two cognates: whereas for Zhuangzi what is right (*yi* 義) in any given situation is determined by the sage's situation-specific sense for the fitting (*yi* 宜), Xunzi's sage is able to fit (*yi* 宜) every situation because of his culturally acquired knowledge of an external standard of rightness (*yi* 義):

[The gentleman] is able to use the standard of rightness [*yi* 義] to respond to changing conditions [*bianying* 變應] because he knows how to accord [*dang* 當] with any situation, whether curved or straight. In the *Odes* we read,

> He rides to the left, to the left,
> the gentleman does it properly [*yi* 宜];
> He rides to the right, the right,
> the gentleman has the knack.
>
> This expresses the idea that the gentleman is able to employ his knowledge of what is right [*yi* 義] to bend or straighten in response to changing conditions. (KI:175–76/W42)

In a way, Xunzi is as acutely aware as Zhuangzi of the limits of the individual's capacity for knowledge. He observes along with Zhuangzi that, while the individual is limited, objects of knowledge are potentially limitless, and to pursue the limitless with the limited will surely lead to folly (KIII:110/W406). Zhuangzi's answer to this problem is to call upon the individual to surrender herself and her limited knowledge to something larger and greater: to Heaven and the mysterious promptings of the spirit. Xunzi also requires of the individual a surrender of sorts—indeed, a surrender that must be accompanied by a kind of faith. For Xunzi, though, this greater power is not Heaven but rather the Way of Human Beings, and the faith required is a faith in the traditions and institutions of the Ancient Kings. The fallenness of his contemporaries can be traced to their willful ignorance of this Way and their stubborn insistence on relying upon their own resources to determine right and wrong (KIII:111/W408–9). The answer is not, however, to abandon notions of right and wrong, but to submit oneself to the one *true* standard of right and wrong discovered by the sages. "['Right' and 'wrong'] refer, respectively, to what accords with [*he* 合] the regulations of the king and what does not" (KIII:110/W408). Once this submission is completed—once the dispositions and emotions have been thoroughly harmonized by the rites and music, and the heart/mind made unified and receptive to the ordered pattern revealed in the classics and instructions of the teacher—the result will be a state of perfect behavioral and cognitive harmony.

The Paradox of Wu-wei in the *Xunzi*

As we should come to expect by this point, Xunzi's metaphorical conception of self-cultivation and wu-wei brings with it its own new tensions. We will examine two in particular.

Problem with External Standard Metaphor

One question we might ask is how the external standards got invented in the first place. That is, if human beings are incapable of drawing a straight line without the aid of a ruler, how did the first human inventor of the ruler manage to pull it off? This first question might be viewed as something of a reverse theodicy question: if human nature is bad—meaning that human beings do not innately possess the resources to be moral, but must acquire morality from an external standard—how did the sages, who were human beings, come up with morality in the first place? This question or critique of Xunzi's position has been phrased in various ways,[73] but is summed up quite well in D. C. Lau's observation concerning Xunzi's metaphor of the sage as potter:

> For Xunzi, the sage or sage kings invented morality. They created morality out of human nature, just as the potter created a vessel out of clay. Just as the potter is able to do what he does, not *qua* man but *qua* potter, so the sage is able to do what he does, not *qua* man but *qua* sage. (Lau 1953: 562)

The problem is that before there was morality, there were no sages, only human beings. This means, Lau concludes, that "if someone invented morality, he must have done so *qua* man after all and not *qua* sage."[74] Xunzi himself recognized this problem (KIII:153–54/W438), and his answer is that morality was the product of the sages' conscious activity, not their human nature. If Xunzi were able to respond to directly Lau's criticism, he would say that a human being becoming a sage is no different from a human being becoming a potter: in either case, it is a matter of creating some new set of dispositions or skills through conscious activity, and it would be just as silly to say that morality is part of our human nature as to say that pottery is somehow built into our make-up. More contemporary scholars also point out that, for Xunzi, no *one* sage invented the ruler or pottery; these external standards or crafts emerged from the accumulation of the efforts of many sages over a long period of time.[75]

Much has been written concerning the convincingness of Xunzi's response, which is usually discussed in the context of his claims about human nature.[76] As far as the paradox of wu-wei goes, however, it is more relevant to focus upon the question of how the individual interested in embarking upon the "path" of self-cultivation is to find the markers that delineate the proper Way. Ritual, of course, serves as the "markers" (*biao* 表) of the safe ford of the Way, but we saw above that Xunzi is quite explicit about the fact that individuals cannot spot these markers on their own, but rather require the help of a teacher:

> Ritual is the means by which one rectifies [*zheng* 正] the self, and the teacher is the means by which one rectifies ritual. Without the rites, how would you rectify yourself? Without a teacher, how would you how would you know whether or not the ritual was being performed correctly?[77] . . . To oppose ritual is to be without a model. To oppose the teacher is to be without a teacher. Not to approve of your teacher and the model, but rather to prefer to rely upon your own resources [*ziyong* 自 用] is like trying to use a blind person to distinguish colors or a deaf person to distinguish sounds—there is no way you will be able to remove confusion and error. Therefore, learning involves devotion to ritual and the model. The teacher is one whom one takes as the standard of correctness [*zhengyi* 正儀] whom one values being at ease with [*zian* 自安] [i.e., at ease with following his practices].[78] (KI:157/W33–34)

So, in order to locate the ritual markers it is first necessary for the individual to find the "standard of correctness" represented by the teacher.

This is where the external standard/marker metaphor begins to unravel. When it comes to literal standards, it is fairly easy to find the "standard of correctness." A properly used plumb line, for instance, will always give one the standard of correctness of verticality, and (to use another of Xunzi's favorite metaphors) a balance-scale will always correctly tell one the relative weights of objects. When it comes to metaphorical standards, though—that is, the standard for something intangible such as virtue—things get a bit more complicated, since virtue is not *literally* a thing that we can directly see in the same way that a plumb line or scale can be seen, and it is therefore not a trivial task to distinguish "counterfeit" standards from the real things. Of course, one solution would be to stick to a literal understanding of the metaphor, holding that the social standards established by the ruler are as concrete, external, and easy to apply as physical standards. The result would be something resembling Hanfeizi's Legalism, and it is not difficult to find very Legalist-sounding passages in the *Xunzi*.[79] Despite his occasional Legalist leanings, though, Xunzi essentially remains a self-cultivationist concerned with internal, intangible, wu-wei virtue, and was therefore open to the idea that "internal" virtue might not be externally visible or that supposed virtue might be faked. Although we see no mention in the text of the "village worthy" who is so reviled by Confucius and Mencius, Xunzi was nonetheless clearly concerned with "counterfeits" of virtue. In chapter 3, for instance, he condemns people who "steal a reputation [for virtue]" (*daoming* 盗名) because this is a much more serious offense than stealing mere property (KI:181/W52).[80] In chapter 5 ("Denouncing Physiognomy"—significantly, a chapter devoted to the impossibility of judging a person's character from the outside), Xunzi criticizes the "rotten Confucians" (*furu* 腐儒) who go through the motions but do not take true joy in the Way (KI:208/W84), and in chapter 6 he criticizes "those who today are called scholars-recluses":

> They are the kind of people who lack ability but are said to have ability, who lack knowledge but are said to have knowledge. Their hearts are filled with an insatiable need for profit, but they pretend to be without desire. Their conduct is hypocritical [*wei* 偽] and secretly debauched, but they go on in a strong, loud voice about prudence and integrity. (KI:228/W101)

He was also well aware of the opposite problem: that true virtue was not necessarily recognized by society:

> The gentleman is able to make himself worthy of honor, but cannot cause other people to necessarily honor him. He can make himself trustworthy, but cannot cause other people to necessarily trust him. . . . Therefore the gentleman is ashamed of remaining uncultivated, but is not ashamed of being publicly reviled. Proceeding along the Way, unswervingly committed to rectifying himself and not allowing himself

to be deflected by external things—such a person might be called a sincere [*cheng* 誠] gentleman. (KI:228/W102)[81]

We can thus see that the external standard metaphor for the cultivation of virtue breaks down at a certain point, because virtue involves an intangible *interior* component in a way that literal standards do not, and thus is not as unproblematically visible as a concrete standard. The problem with counterfeits of virtue is that they go through the external motions of morality but lack the proper internal motivation,[82] while it is also possible that inner "sincerity" (*cheng* 誠) and rectitude will not be recognized on the "outside."

This issue of sincerity is something that will be explored further with regard to the craft metaphor, but for now let us focus on the problem of recognition. Given the possibility that metaphorical standards can be counterfeited in a way that literal standards cannot, how can the beginning student distinguish proper from improper and even get started? Xunzi's answer seems to be that the *real* student needs to already have some knowledge in order to begin the process of education. Hence an interesting passage from the "Encouraging Learning" chapter:

> Do not answer a person whose questions are uncouth, do not ask questions of a person whose answers are uncouth, do not listen to a person whose theories are uncouth, and do not debate with a person who is in an argumentative mood. Thus, it is necessary that a person have come in the proper way before you can have contact with him—if he has not come in the proper way, then avoid him. (KI:141/W17)

Up to this point, a reasonable interpretation would be that this is advice to a still fragile young student to avoid bad company, and not a general statement about the educability of human beings in general. The passage then continues:

> Therefore, a person must already be ritually proper and respectful before you can discuss the methods of the Way with him; he must already be polite and obedient [*shun* 順] before you can discuss the pattern of the Way with him; and he must already accord [*cong* 從] [with proper forms] in his countenance before you can discuss the attainment of the Way with him. (KI:141/W17)

This seems to be a more general claim, although in its context one might still understand it simply as advice to keep a beginning student out of trouble. Consider also, though, this passage from the "Great Compendium":

> When presented with [the ideal of] the gentleman, a person who loves it is the type who can actually attain it. . . . [83] When presented with an ideal contrary to that of the gentleman, a person who loves it is not the type who can actually become a gentleman. When you take a person who is not the type who can actually become a gentleman but nonetheless try to educate [*jiao* 教] him, he will become a common thief or fall in with a gang of bandits. (KIII:231/W512–13)

This passage does not rule out the possibility that one could be neutral toward the ideal of gentleman and still be educated, but—especially when read in combination with some of the more internalist passages—the strong implication is that only someone who loves the ideal when presented with it is actually able to attain it.

It would thus seem that one cannot achieve wu-wei perfection unless one is already in some way inclined toward appreciating it. As mentioned in the introduction, the paradox of wu-wei as it manifests itself here bears a resemblance to a tension identified by Alasdair MacIntyre in the Augustinian education system with regard to the relationship between the student and the foundational texts of the tradition:

> In medieval Augustinian culture the relationship between the key texts of that culture and their reader was twofold. The reader was assigned the task of interpreting the text, but also had to discover, in and through his or her reading of those texts, that they in turn interpret the reader. What the reader, as thus interpreted by the texts, has to learn about him or herself is that it is only the self as transformed through and by the reading of the texts which will be capable of reading the texts aright. So the reader, *like any learner within a craft-tradition*, encounters apparent paradox at the outset, a Christian version of the paradox of Plato's *Meno*: it seems that only by learning what the texts have to teach can he or she come to read those texts aright, but also that only by reading them aright can he or she learn what the texts have to teach. (1990:82; italics added)

It is, I think, no accident that this Augustinian paradox resembles the one faced by Xunzi of how beings entirely bereft of any innate moral sense can begin the task of self-cultivation—that is, even *recognize* it as something worth pursuing. As MacIntyre notes, the response of the Augustinian tradition to this "paradox" is to demand absolute faith in one's teacher, so that the aspiring reader can "have inculcated into him or herself certain attitudes and dispositions, certain virtues, *before* he or she can know why these are to be accounted virtues" (82). We have already noted a similar reliance in the Xunzian tradition upon the authority of the teacher, but have also seen that this only pushes the problem back one step, for there is a similar tension involved in a uncultivated student's being able to even *recognize* a true teacher—to distinguish the gentleman from the village worthy.

Xunzi's response to this tension is to smuggle in certain internalist metaphors that sit uneasily with the general metaphoric thrust of his position. In chapter 5, for instance, Xunzi notes that in order to understand ritual properly it is necessary to rely upon the models of the past—specifically, the model of the Later Kings—but that many of his contemporaries fail to recognize this fact because they are "deceived." Why is the sage not deceived as well? he asks rhetorically. The answer: "Because the sage is a person who uses himself [*ji* 己] as the standard of measurement [*du* 度]" (KI:207/W82). The "standard of measurement" metaphor is familiar, but the internal location of it certainly is not. One might argue that this is a special situation, because the sage is able to look within only because his Self has already been "straightened" by external standards. This take on the passage would still fail to explain how a beginning student could avoid being "deceived," and is at odds with other passages that suggest that certain individuals are gifted by nature. In a passage from "The Great Compendium," for instance, a line from the Old Script version of the *Book of Documents* is quoted approvingly:

> Shun said, "It is only someone such as myself who can become orderly through following my desires [*cong* 從欲]." Thus ritual was created for the sake of the worthies and others down to the rank of the common masses, not for the perfected sages. Nonetheless, it is also the means by which one perfects sageliness—without study, it will never be perfected. Yao studied with Jun Chou, Shun with Wucheng Zhao, and Yu with Xiwang Kuo. (KIII:210/W489)

Here it is claimed that the great "perfected sages" such as Shun do not really need ritual, and can become orderly merely by following their innate desires. Study and the rites are only for those less gifted by nature. The suggestion that there is something special about certain people is also found in a line in chapter 28: "whether one is worthy or unworthy is a matter of innate endowment [*cai* 材]" (KIII:249/W527). This uncharacteristic celebration of innate substance is repeated in a passage from chapter 30, where the superiority of jade is celebrated and compared favorably to serpentine: "Even if you carve and carve [*diaodiao* 雕雕] at the serpentine, it will never look as good as the [natural] markings of jade" (KIII:257/W535). Here we see natural endowment being portrayed as more crucial than "carving" or external cultivation—an inversion of the more standard Xunzian metaphors.

One might still argue that these "good endowment" passages apply only to a human elite, not to the average person, as the "Great Compendium" passage states. This is already a problematic stance for Xunzi, though, since even the great sages are supposed to have been human beings identical to us with regard to their "nature," and superior only by virtue of their ability to use external standards. As we read in the "Encouraging Learning" chapter, "The gentleman is not born different from other people. He is simply good at relying upon external things" (KI:136/W4). So even if this good endowment is characteristic of only a tiny minority of human beings, Xunzi's externalism is already rather compromised. In addition, however, we see in other parts of the text the suggestion that some sort of innate disposition toward the good allows even *ordinary* people to distinguish genuine teachers from the poseurs and respond to the transformative influence of Virtue:

> There are four techniques for [being or recognizing] [*wei* 為] a teacher, and broad acquaintance with facts is not among them. Reverent and severe, and thereby inspiring fearful respect—such a person may serve as/be considered a teacher. Aged and inspiring trust—such a person may serve as/be considered a teacher. Not arrogantly imposing his own views of transgressing tradition when reciting or explaining the classics—such

a person may serve as/be considered a teacher. Subtly knowledgeable in his discourse—such a person may serve as/be considered a teacher. (KII:209/W263–64)

How does quality X (reverence, age) inspire response Y on the part of the student? The passage goes on to explain this by invoking *nature* metaphors: "When water is deep eddies will form, and when plants drop their leaves they fertilize their roots." This passage thus answers the question we posed earlier of how a student is to even recognize a true teacher: he will *naturally respond* to a true teacher on the analogy of deep water naturally forming eddies or falling leaves bringing nourishment to the roots of a plant. Unfortunately, this is a self-cultivation *internalist* answer to the question: the student must look within to evaluate the genuineness of a potential teacher, relying upon some sort of innate emotional response—fearful respect or trust—to distinguish true reverence and trustworthiness from their counterfeits. We see a similar suggestion of an innate sense for virtue in a passage earlier in the same chapter, where the manner in which the (presumably aspiring) gentleman "returns home" (*gui* 歸) to ritual and morality is compared to the way fish and turtles return home to deep rivers or birds and beasts return to lush forests (KII:206/W260). These are not isolated metaphors: in chapter 3 we read that the gentleman attracts "kindred spirits" (*tongyanzhe* 同焉者) with the same natural ease as a neighing horse gets a response (*ying* 應) from other horses, the passage concluding with the observation that desire to remove impurities from oneself is "the essence of human beings" (*renzhiqing* 人之情) (KI:177/W45). A related passage from the "Great Compendium" claims that virtuous friends are attracted to one another "like fire being drawn [*jiu* 就] to dry kindling" or "water flowing toward [*liu* 流] dampness," concluding "things of the same category attract (lit. follow) one another [*xiangcong* 相從]" (KIII:232/W514).[84]

These natural response, spontaneous movement, and "returning home" metaphors seem more Mencian or Laozian than something from the brush of Xunzi. It thus seems that, just as Mencius was unable to keep his portrayal of an internalist morality completely free of externalist elements, the demands of the paradox of wu-wei allowed internalist metaphors to creep into the *Xunzi*.[85] Some of these metaphors could have come straight from the *Mencius*. In chapter 4, for instance, the manner in which people in a chaotic age would react when presented with moral order is compared to the way that people who had never tasted meat before would react upon being presented with this strange delicacy:

Now, imagine a person who had in his life never seen the meat of grain-fed animals, rice or millet, but knew only of beans, coarse greens, dregs and husks. He would certainly think the latter represented the height of culinary satisfaction. If he were suddenly presented with a plate of grain-fed meat and fine grains, he would be startled and say, "What are these strange things?" Upon smelling them, though, he would discover that they were not unpleasing to his nose; upon tasting them, he would find them sweet and pleasing to his palate; and upon eating them, he would find that they brought ease [*an* 安] to his body. In such a scenario, there is no one who would not discard their old foods and choose these new ones instead. (KI:192/W65)

It seems rather strange to find Xunzi speaking of a moral "taste" analogous to our taste for fine food.[86] Equally jarring is a "Great Compendium" passage (KIII:211/W490) where ritual is described as "taking as its root following along with [*shun* 順] the human heart/mind," and it is claimed that even without the *Book of Rites* it would be possible to get ritual simply by following along with this heart/mind.

Such anomalous, internalist metaphors of "taste" or natural "response" are perhaps best understood as a reaction to Xunzi's "Meno problem"—that is, the paradox of needing to somehow be able to *recognize* proper external standards before they can actually be learned. His need to fall back on such metaphors in turn is indicative of inadequacies in his family of "external standard" metaphors.

Problems with the Craft Metaphor

There are scholars who find Xunzi's portrayal of an externalist regime of self-cultivation leading to wu-wei embodiment implausible. For some, such as D. C. Lau, it is externalism itself that is perceived as the fatal flaw in Xunzi's scheme. "It is only if a man finds morality within himself," Lau claims, "that he can abide by it and draw upon its resources without the fear of its failing him" (Lau 1953: 564). Xunzi's project could do no more, Lau believes, than instill in a person a certain set of superficial habits that would be of little support in undertaking potentially difficult moral action. Although Lau overlooks the fact that Xunzi's project of self-cultivation *is* designed to eventually create a "source" of morality within the self, he certainly identifies an important tension in Xunzi's thought: the possibility that his "craft" metaphor, focusing as it does upon externally applied force, will produce nothing but a village worthy—that is, that *wei* 偽 "conscious activity" will always remain *wei* 偽 "hypocrisy."

We have seen Xunzi's metaphorical characterization of human nature as a recalcitrant material in need of external correction, an entailment of which is that human nature possesses nothing in its "raw" state that would incline it toward virtue. As we have also noted, this means that beginning students have to be lured into the process of self-cultivation with consequentialist promises of gain or driven to it out of a fear of the state of nature,[87] but that this selfish motivation eventually gives way (ideally, at least) to a genuine love for the Way. We might compare this process to MacIntyre's description of how one might lure a small child into the practice of chess by initially offering him or her the external enticement of candy. In the early stages, the child will be exclusively motivated by this "external" good (which is obtainable by means other than playing chess), but (hopefully, at least) will eventually come to see "the value of those goods specific to chess—in the achievement of a certain highly particular kind of analytical skill, strategic imagination and competitive intensity—a new set of reasons, reasons now not just for winning on a particular occasion, but for trying to excel in whatever way the game of chess demands" (MacIntyre 1981: 176). In Xunzi, progress is symbolized by the various "grades of people," and is cognized in terms of craft metaphor. For instance, in the metaphor of pressframe, there is a need in the beginning to exert external force upon the material, but once the process is complete the press can be removed and the wood will remain straight on its own.

The problem with both MacIntyre's chess analogy and Xunzi's craft metaphor, though, is that virtue is in a crucial respect quite different from a skill such as chess or the process of craft production. In the case of a skill such as chess playing, there is no problem in conceiving how externally motivated training can eventually result in an internalized, settled disposition, because there is no assumption or demand that the novice enter the training regime with any prior inclination toward the practice. That is, no one would fault a beginning chess player because she was not at first able to *feel* the beauty of the game, for it is thought that an appreciation of such goods internal to a practice are only gradually acquired after the fundamental mechanical aspects of the practice have been thoroughly mastered. It is therefore taken for granted in the acquisition of a skill such as chess playing that the novice will need simply to grind away at acquiring these new and alien skill sets—submitting against her initial inclinations to heart/ mind-numbing, repetitive practice—before there can be any hope of a truly skillful disposition to develop. More to the point, internal motivation is in the final analysis *irrelevant* with regard to a technical skill (or the types of activities that Aristotle would call "crafts"): although we might romantically suppose that a chess grand master experienced the same sublime intellectual joy in her final masterful move that the game inspired in us, we could hardly fault her if we subsequently discovered that she had, in fact, been merely thinking about how she would spend the prize money. The performance stands on its own merits, regardless of the internal state of performer.

Things are quite different with regard to the development of *moral virtue*, however. While it seems quite clear to us that forcing ourselves to play over and over again and studying the past masters—however boring or oppressive we might find it—will eventually help us to develop a degree of genuine skill in chess playing, it is somewhat less apparent that forcing ourselves to help little old ladies across the road while inwardly cursing the bother involved will make us more compassionate, or that compelling ourselves begrudgingly to give money to the poor will make us more generous. This is because moral or virtuous acts are, from the very beginning, inextricably tied up with the *internal* state of the actor. If it turns out that I gave money to the poor in order to make myself look good or merely to win a tax break for myself, this fatally tarnishes the act itself—a "generous" action performed in the absence of genuinely generous motivations is merely a semblance of generosity. This is a phenomenon that was understood and quite clearly explained by Aristotle himself in his description of the disanalogy between "craft-knowledge" (merely technical skill) and virtue:

> In any case, what is true of crafts is not true of virtues. For the products
> of a craft determine by their own character whether they have been pro-
> duced well; and so it suffices that they are in the right state when they

have been produced. But for actions expressing virtue to be done temperately or justly [and hence well] it does not suffice that they are themselves in the right state. Rather, the agent must also be in the right state when he does them. (*Nicomachean Ethics* 1105a27–31; Irwin: 39–40)

The crucial importance accorded to internal states when it comes to moral virtue leads to the conclusion that, as Aristotle puts it, "if we do what is just or temperate, we must already be just or temperate" (1105a21–22; 39). The problem, of course, is that if one must in some sense *already* be just—or at least have the beginnings of just inclinations—in order to perform a truly just act, it is somewhat difficult to see how it could be possible to train someone to acquire a virtue he or she did not already possess, at least in some incipient form.

Xunzi was not unaware of this problem. We have already seen in his characterization of the various "grades" of people the belief expressed that only unselfconscious, purely motivated acts can be considered true virtue, and we might even coordinate his grades with certain of Aristotle's categories. For instance, the three grades of "common people" (who are unable to act virtuously), "lesser Confucians" (who are able to force themselves to be virtuous), and "great Confucians" (who are spontaneously and effortlessly virtuous) (KII:83/W145) recalls Aristotle's characterization of, respectively, the incontinent, continent, and virtuous person. Xunzi even employs a technical term for the sort of internal motivation that properly accompanies any truly virtuous act, "sincerity" (*cheng* 誠):[88]

> For a gentleman wishing to cultivate his heart/mind, nothing is better than sincerity. One who can perfect sincerity need do nothing more [*wutashi* 無他事]: he will hold fast to nothing but benevolence and put into practice nothing but rightness. When benevolence is held fast to with a sincere heart/mind, it will take on physical form [*xing* 形]. Once it takes form, it will become spirit-like [*shen* 神], and once it is spirit-like it will be able to transform others. . . . This is what is called the Heavenly Virtue [*tiande* 天德].

> Heaven does not speak and yet people can infer its loftiness. Earth does not speak and yet people can infer its profound depth. The Four Seasons do not speak and yet the Hundred Clans await their arrival. All of these things possess constancy because they have perfected their sincerity. When the gentleman has perfected his Virtue, he remain silent and yet is understood, bestows no gifts and yet is beloved, displays no anger and yet is held in awe. In this way, he is able to follow along with fate because he is careful even when alone [*shenqidu* 慎其獨].[89]

> Even if a person is good at acting in accordance with the Way, if he is not sincere he will not [be careful] when alone, and if he is not careful when alone it will not take form. If it does not take form, even though it arises in his heart/mind, manifests itself in his countenance, and appears in his speech, the common people will not wish to follow him. If forced to follow, they will only do so with misgivings. (KI:177–78/W87–88)

The need for virtuous acts to be accompanied by sincerity explains Xunzi's other-wise puzzling comment that the "guiding principle" (*jing* 經) of ritual is to "man-ifest what is sincere [*cheng* 誠] and to eliminate what is hypocritical [*wei* 偽]" (KIII:84/W382).

So, even for Xunzi, then, virtue-like external behavior does not constitute true virtue unless it is done in a sincere, wu-wei fashion. This brings us back to Aristotle's paradox that one must already be just in order to perform a truly just act. Aristotle's response to this tension is to invoke the power of early accultura-tion: one can only "teach" virtue to aristocratic Athenians whose upbringing has already disposed them toward virtue. Xunzi at times employs a metaphor whose entailments suggest something similar to Aristotle's response: the metaphor of "soaking" or "infusion" (*jian* 漸).

> The root of the *huai* orchid is used to make perfume, but if it is soaked [*jian*] in urine, then the gentleman will not go near it, and the common people will not use it. This is not because its innate substance [*zhi* 質] is not fine, but rather because of what it has been soaked in. Therefore, when it comes to dwelling places the gentleman is necessarily choosy about his village, and when it comes to companions he necessarily grav-itates toward [*jiu* 就] scholars. In this way he is able to ward off what is deviant and base, and draw near to the mean of rightness [*zhongzheng* 中正]. (KI:137/W6)

In a passage from the "Great Compendium" this metaphor appears in conjunction with the craft metaphor:

> The wheel of a cart was once a tree on Tai Shan. Having been subjected to the pressframe for three or five months, it can be twisted into the wheel hub cover and will never revert back to its original shape. There-fore the gentleman cannot but take care in choosing his pressframe. Be careful! The root of the orchid and valerian are already fragrant, but if you soak them in honey or sweet liquor they will double in value. On the other hand, even a proper gentleman is open to slander if he is soaked in the reek of liquor. Therefore the gentleman cannot but be careful about what he is soaking in. (KIII:227/W507–8)

The "soaking" metaphor seems to serve as a kind of passive and unselfconscious alternate to the more active craft metaphor, and is often used in conjunction with it. Unlike the craft metaphor, the entailments of the soaking metaphor allow one to get around the problem of inner motivation. That is, at least after the initial choice of environment, the Subject is not required to make additional effort in order to be transformed, for the outside medium performs all of the work. Hence the association of habituation with unself-consciousness in chapter 23:

> Even if a person possesses a fine innate substance [*xingzhi* 性質] and a perceptive and knowledgeable heart/mind, he must still necessarily seek out a worthy teacher to serve and select excellent friends with whom to associate. Having found and entered into the service of a worthy teacher,

all that he will hear will be the Way of Yao, Shun, Yu, and Tang. Having found and begun association with excellent friends, all that he will see will be loyal, trustworthy, respectful and polite conduct. In this way his person can daily progress toward morality in a completely unselfcon-scious manner [*buzizhi* 不自知], because it is changed through habitua-tion [*mi* 靡]. Now if, on the other hand, he had fallen in with some bad associates, all that he would have heard would have been deception and hypocrisy, and all that he would have seen would have been corrupt, las-civious, and greedy conduct. In this way, his person would have daily and unconsciously become more and more criminalized, also as a result of having been changed through habituation [*mi* 靡]. As a traditional saying puts it, "If you don't know a son, look at his friends; if you don't know a ruler, look at his retainers." Everything is the result of habitua-tion! Everything is the result of habituation! (KIII:162/W449)

In this sense, "soaking" or habituation serves very similar function to Aristotle's Athenian upbringing: effortlessly and unself-consciously endowing the individ-ual with the habitual beginnings of virtue, which then only need to be refined and sharpened by the teacher.

As we might expect by now, though, Xunzi's occasional recourse to the soaking metaphor still fails to entirely resolve the paradox of wu-wei. If we take this soaking metaphor as primary, it undercuts the need for active effort (at least after the initial choice of environment), and we then fall back into the sorts of problems that plague the internalists. It also undermines the claim that anyone can become a gentleman, for only those who have been properly "soaked" are eli-gible. There is also the problem with regard to recognition: the aspiring Xunzian gentleman needs to actively choose his "soaking medium" but how is an unculti-vated person able to distinguish the "worthy teacher" or "excellent friend" from the (presumably much more numerous) imposters and hypocrites?

Switching back to the more dominant craft metaphor, we still face the prob-lem of explaining how external pressure can ever produce true virtue. Sincerity (*cheng* 誠) is essential for true, wu-wei virtue, and yet it cannot be taught. In this sense, the concept of sincerity fatally undermines the craft metaphor: in fact, no amount of external pressure can *ever* really straighten out the crooked "stuff" of an insincere person. Without sincerity, effort will eternally remain nothing more or less than effort—that is, the transition to wu-wei will never occur. Such a bleak prospect is hinted at in a rather disturbing exchange between Zigong and Con-fucius recorded in "The Great Compendium." Zigong explains that he is tired of studying and would like to rest (*xi* 息) by engaging in some other activity that might still help him along the path. He suggests several different options—resting in service to his parents, in relating to his wife, in the company of morally good friends, or even in being a farmer—but Confucius invariably responds that even these activities are difficult and afford no rest.

"Am I then never to rest?"

> Confucius replied, "Look up at the grave mound and see how lofty it is, how steep, how it resembles the *li* 鬲 tripod.[90] Only there will you finally know rest!" (KIII:230/W510)

One imagines that this was intended by the Xunzian school to serve as a goad to exertion, but it is hardly inspirational. What has happened to the ideal of the effortless and joyful sage? The bleak prospect that the exertion of effort will never cease—that the process of self-cultivation as understood by Xunzi could never result in wu-wei—no doubt accounts for the continuing appeal of internalist positions in later Chinese thought.

Conclusion

It might be helpful to review again the early Chinese responses to the paradox of wu-wei—as well as the sorts of problems these responses encountered—in order to support our claim that the ideal of wu-wei and the tension it contains can serve as a powerful lens through which to view the development of early Chinese thought. As I mentioned in the introduction, the "solutions" to the paradox can be generally be characterized in terms of an internalist-externalist split.[1]

Each response merely chooses a horn of the dilemma upon which to impale itself. The internalists answer the question of how one can try not to try to be good by gravitating toward the "not trying" horn: at some level, they claim, we already *are* good, and we merely need to allow this virtuous potential to realize itself. Zhuangzi, Laozi, and Mencius fall into this camp. The externalists, exemplified by Xunzi (and most likely including the author(s) of the *Analects* as well), maintain, on the contrary, that it is essential that we *try* not to try. That is, they claim that we do *not* possess the resources to attain wu-wei on our own and that wu-wei is a state acquired only after a long and intensive regime of training in traditional, external forms. Toward this end they formulate a rigorous training regime designed to gradually lead us from our original state of ignorance to the pinnacle of spiritual perfection. Unfortunately—as we have seen in some detail—neither of these responses to the paradox proves entirely satisfactory or even internally consistent, and both are plagued by superficial and structural difficulties.

For instance, the Confucian internalist Mencius is confronted with the superficial problem that, by placing the locus of moral authority within the individual, he has apparently undermined the need for traditional Confucian ritual practices and the classics. These cultural resources are often portrayed as merely helpful aids to moral self-cultivation, dispensable in a pinch and ultimately subordinate to the individual's own inner moral guide—the heart/mind.[2] This becomes the focus of the Xunzian critique of Mencian thought, but is less of a problem for the Daoist thinkers, who are in any case already doctrinally committed to undermining traditional Confucian institutions.

The deeper, structural problem faced by any internalist—Confucian or Daoist—is the question: if we *are* already fundamentally good, why do we not *act* like it? The fact that we are not, in our current fallen state, actually manifesting our "innate" goodness calls into question the internalist position and makes the externalist solution seem more reasonable. We apparently need to do *something* in order to eventually be able to "not-do." The result is that all early Chinese internalists feel the need to fall back occasionally into an externalist stance, making some kind of reference to the need for effort and even externalist practice regimens. We have seen that this deeper, structural tension manifesting itself in texts such as the *Mencius* in terms of a conflict between metaphor schemas for self-cultivation that possess incommensurable entailments. Mencius relies primarily upon the SELF-CULTIVATION AS AGRICULTURE schema as his dominant model for the process of education, and the entailments of this metaphor support his professed internalist position: without the need for external instructions, seedlings spontaneously tend to grow into full-grown plants at the urging of their innate telos, and all that they require to realize this internal telos is a supportive, protected environment. Unfortunately, this model does not account for the fact that following our supposed "true" innate promptings (i.e., becoming good) is in practice a real struggle for human beings—in other words, the fact that, in order to become moral, we have to try quite hard to be "spontaneous" in the way Mencius desires us to be.

I have argued that it is in response to this perceived tension that Mencius occasionally supplements his internalist metaphors with externalist schemas that possess entirely different and incompatible entailments: SELF-CULTIVATION AS CRAFT, for instance, where human behavior is portrayed as something that needs to be guided by the standards supplied by external measuring tools (4:A:1, 4:A:2).[3] Similarly, Laozi and Zhuangzi temper their faith in our spontaneous, natural tendencies— expressed by various effortless or "wild nature" metaphors— with hints of external practices and structured disciplines that are necessary if one is to actually realize wu-wei, expressed in terms of "grasping," "cultivation" or other effort-related metaphors. In this respect it is quite revealing that, regardless of whether or not such cryptic phrases as "block the openings and shut the doors" (*Laozi*) or instructions to "fast the mind" (*Zhuangzi*) originally referred to concrete, physical practices, they were certainly understood in this sense by later Daoist practitioners, and were subsequently developed into elaborate externalist systems of yogic, meditative, alchemical, and sexual regimens.

The practical difficulty of self-cultivation might thus make the externalist position seem more attractive. This position, however, is plagued by its own superficial as well as structural problems. Xunzi, for instance, is faced with the more superficial difficulty of trying to explain how, if human beings are completely bereft of innate moral resources, morality gets its start, since as a Confucian he is doctrinally committed to the position that the sage-kings who created the rites and wrote the classics were themselves human beings just like us. That this problem is superficial is indicated by the fact that Christian externalists in the West are able to circumvent it by locating the source of morality in an extra-human realm.

The deeper problem faced by externalists who are concerned with moral self-cultivation—Confucian as well as Christian—is the question of how the novice is to be *moved* from the precultivated state to the state of moral perfection when genuinely moral action seems to require some sort of preexistent (or at least coexistent) internal disposition. In chapter 7 I discussed the important *disanalogy* between a craft skill (a favorite externalist metaphor) and moral virtue; as Aristotle so concisely explains in a passage cited there, what is true of crafts is not true of virtues. For the products of a craft determine by their own character whether they have been produced well; and so it suffices that they are in the right state when they have been produced. But for actions expressing virtue to be done temperately or justly [and hence well] it does not suffice that they are themselves in the right state. Rather, the agent must also be in the right state when he does them. (*Nicomachean Ethics* 1105a27–31; Irwin: 39–40)

Genuinely moral action involves not only producing the right external "product" (behavior), but doing so while also possessing the right internal disposition. The problem of moral virtue confronting an externalist, then, is that it seems that the student must in some sense already *be* virtuous—or at least have the beginnings of virtuous inclinations—in order to act in a genuinely virtuous manner. It is precisely this difficulty that any externalist teacher of virtue must try to circumvent, the mystery being how the student is to make the transition from merely acting out morality to actually *becoming* a moral person. The common danger is that this transition will not be made and that the training regimen will thus produce nothing more than a moral hypocrite who merely goes through the motions of morality. It is this potential danger—one felt by the Confucians no less than the Daoists—that explains the perennial appeal of the internalist position.

That this was a subject of concern for both Confucius and Xunzi is evidenced by Confucius's concern about the so-called "village worthy"—the "thief of virtue," or counterfeit of the true Confucian gentleman, who observes perfectly all of the external forms of virtue but is completely lacking in the proper internal dispositions—and in Xunzi's recognition that truly moral action must be accompanied by "sincerity" (*cheng* 誠) and a genuine love for the Way. As we have seen, in both the *Analects* and the *Xunzi* this concern for proper moral dispositions results in a degree of metaphoric incommensurability, with both thinkers being motivated to supplement their dominant externalist metaphors for self-cultivation with occasional internalist ones. In the *Analects* this metaphoric tension is more pronounced, but perhaps less surprising considering the provenance of the text. Most likely cobbled together over time by different—and perhaps even rival— groups of disciples, the mixing of externalist and internalist metaphors in the *Analects* could perhaps be attributed to doctrinal conflicts with the early Confucian school. What is more revealing and significant is the appearance in the *Xunzi*—for the most part representing the writings of a single, careful thinker quite consciously and explicitly opposed to internalism—of such internalist metaphors as "natural" response or moral "taste."

My discussion has thus suggested that the early Chinese tradition was never able to formulate a fully consistent or entirely satisfying solution (whether internalist or externalist) to the tensions created by one of its central spiritual ideals. Historically, as I mentioned briefly in the introduction, the tensions inherent in the early Chinese spiritual ideal of wu-wei were subsequently transmitted to later East Asian schools of thought that inherited wu-wei as an ideal. They resurface in Chan Buddhism in the form of the sudden-gradual controversy, in Japanese Zen Buddhism in the form of the debate between the Rinzai and Soto schools, and in

East Asian neo-Confucianism in the form of the conflict between the Cheng-Zhu and Lu-Wang factions. The tenaciousness of this tension is illustrated by its resistance to being resolved by doctrinal fiat. The victory of the Southern (sudden) school of Chan Buddhism, for instance, was designed to settle the problem in an internalist/subitist fashion: all human beings originally possess pure, undefiled Buddha-nature, which means that practice and other external aids to enlightenment (scripture, etc.) are essentially superfluous. Yet the problem refuses to be so easily conjured away and simply reemerges both in Buddhism and neo-Confucianism (which also adopts the Buddhist "solution" of an originally pure nature) in the subsequent splits between the more internalist, "sudden-sudden" Rinzai and Lu-Wang schools and the more externalist, "gradual-sudden" Soto and Cheng-Zhu schools. The continued, stubborn reemergence of this split—ultimately related to a failure to produce an entirely consistent or satisfying internalist or externalist position—suggests that the paradox of wu-wei is a *genuine* paradox and that any "solution" to the problem it presents will therefore necessarily be plagued by superficial and structural difficulties.

Indeed, as I have suggested several times over the course of this discussion, the implications of the wu-wei problematic extend beyond its contribution to our understanding of Chinese or East Asian thought, because the tensions produced by the paradox of wu-wei are to be found not only in Aristotle's claim that "to become just we must first do just actions" but also in Plato's belief that to be taught one must recognize the thing taught as something to be learned—the so-called Meno problem. It seems that something resembling the paradox of wu-wei will plague the thought of any thinker who can be characterized as a virtue ethicist—that is, anyone who sees ethical life in terms of the perfection of normative dispositions.[4] We might thus be justified in seeing the "subtle dialectic of question and answer" circling about the paradox of wu-wei as having significance not only for early Chinese thinkers but also for any thinker concerned with the problem of self-cultivation—that is, with the problem of not merely winning from the individual rational assent to a system of principles but actually *transforming* them into a new type of person. Seen in this way, my discussion of the Chinese ideal of effortless action takes on a significance that goes beyond the merely sinological, for it can serve as a window through which we can gain new insight into the ideals and problematiques of our own early tradition.

Before we conclude our examination of the paradox of wu-wei, however, we should consider the question of the exact practical significance of the paradox—in other words, the degree to which this conceptual incommensurability is relevant to the actual process of self-cultivation aimed at producing a spontaneous normative state. Wu Kuang-ming, who recognizes the existence in early Confucianism of something very much like what I have been calling the paradox of wu-wei, ultimately suggests that this tension is an artifact of the language we use to *talk* about self-cultivation, rather than a feature of the process itself:

> The Confucian sages urge us to "cultivate ourselves" [*xiuji* 修己]. . . .
> This "cultivating of ourselves" is an act of cultivation, and an act of cultivation requires two people—the "cultivator" and "cultivatee." How-

ever, the process of self-cultivation obviously only involves one person—myself. So generally speaking, this sort of paradox [*maodun* 矛盾 ; alternately, "contradiction"] and difficulty arises from a conflict of language. Because language is obviously the tool we use when we are trying to understand something, every time we attempt to genuinely understand something about human existence this becomes an obvious problem, and we fall into the trap of paradox. (Wu Kuang-ming 1989: 316–17)

What Wu is touching upon here with his mention of the "cultivator" and "cultivatee" is the basic SUBJECT-SELF metaphor schema. Wu points out the contradiction between the "two people" required when we talk about self-cultivation and the fact that, literally, "only one person is involved." Put in our terms, Wu is arguing that the paradox of wu-wei is an artifact of the SUBJECT-SELF metaphor: once we realize that this schema is *only* a metaphor (there is in fact no SUBJECT-SELF split, just a single person), the problem of how this supposed Subject can act upon the Self simply dissolves.

Explaining away the tension is not quite this easy, however. Although Wu dismisses the paradox as merely a "conflict of language," we have seen that SUBJECT-SELF schema (like all metaphors) is *conceptual* as well as linguistic. That is, for whatever reason, human agents seem to perceive themselves in terms of a metaphoric split. We might reformulate Wu's position a bit, though, and argue that the paradox is a linguistic *and* conceptual one, but that it in fact dissolves in practice. In other words, we have seen that none of the metaphors proposed as models for self-cultivation—whether internalist or externalist—seem able to perfectly account for all aspects of the process, and therefore always need to be accompanied by other metaphors with supplementary (but, unfortunately, sometimes contradictory) entailments. Nonetheless, one might argue that, despite this conceptual-linguistic dilemma, moral education still somehow manages on occasion to *work*. That is, despite all of the theoretical problems that arise whenever we try to think or talk about virtue and virtue-education, society somehow seems to continue producing at least a moderate number of virtuous people. If the paradox is in fact merely an artifact of language and cognition, one might be tempted to dismiss it as unimportant or uninteresting.

This, however, would be a mistake, for the fact remains that as citizens, educators, policy makers, or simply private individuals, our actions are inevitably guided by our conceptual metaphors. I have already discussed the claim of cognitive linguistics that metaphors are not merely rhetorical window dressing, but rather the primary means by which we reason about abstract matters, and as such they have a very real and crucial influence on our practical decision making and social policy. Consider, for instance, the concrete educational techniques and policies that would be pursued by a teacher guided by the SELF-CULTIVATION AS AGRICULTURE metaphor versus one convinced of the "truth" of the SELF-CULTIVATION AS CRAFT REFORMATION schema. The former would look more like a Montessori teacher, the latter more like a strict Catholic school teacher in the Augustinian mold.[5] Of course, children are *not* sprouts or raw materials in any kind of literal sense, but this is really beside the point. If the findings of cognitive linguistics are correct, metaphor and other forms of cognitive mapping are simply not optional for creatures like us. In order to engage in or guide an abstract process such as education or self-cultivation, we must *inevitably* make reference to some sort of metaphorical schema, and the schema we invoke will have entailments that will serve as important determinants of our practical behavior. Thus, while Wu Kuang-ming may be correct in seeing that the paradox of wu-wei is an artifact of the manner in which we think and talk about self-cultivation, it is an artifact that a person concerned with the cultivation of normative dispositions cannot avoid dealing with in some manner.

Cognitive Linguistics, the Contemporary Theory of Metaphor, and Comparative Work

I would like to cap this discussion with a brief methodological observation. This project was originally conceived before I was familiar with the work of George Lakoff and Mark Johnson and others in the cognitive linguistics field, and originally took the form of more traditional intellectual history. The basic structure was the same, as were many of the fundamental points: that wu-wei serves as a spiritual ideal shared by a group of Warring States thinkers, that the concept contains within itself a basic tension, that this tension motivates the development of Warring States Chinese thought, and that it was inherited by later East Asian thinkers and bears a structural resemblance to tensions in the Western virtue ethical tradition. What this original project lacked was a coherent theoretical stance. That is, it was based upon an intuition of mine—shared by others, certainly—that Confucius at age seventy and Butcher Ding cutting up the ox and the Mencian sage giving in to the rhythm of music were all somehow representations of the "same thing," and that this "thing" was connected in some way to the ideal of spontaneous virtue celebrated in the Western virtue ethical tradition. Unfortunately, in the absence of any terminological consistency, I had no more rigorous way of demonstrating this connection than simple juxtaposition: putting the stories of "wu-wei" next to one another and arguing that they looked similar in some way. To be sure, I could argue that these stories shared certain abstract qualities—effortlessness and unself-consciousness, to name the most prominent—but the identification of these qualities as characteristic of any given story was itself already a product of interpretation. For instance, the description of Confucius's behavior at age seventy in *Analects* 2.4 seems to describe a sort of effortlessness and unself-consciousness, but these qualities are not explicitly mentioned in the text itself.

What I have found so exciting about the metaphor theory approach is that it has given me a methodology for demonstrating more concretely these previously merely intuitive connections.[6] What unifies the various stories I and others have seen as exemplifying "wu-wei" is a specific set of families of metaphors, all interrelated conceptually and neatly classifiable under the most general metaphoric rubric of "no-effort." The fact that both *Analects* 2.4 and the Cook Ding story in the *Zhuangzi* employ the metaphor of "following" (*cong* 從) and are based upon a more general SUBJECT-SELF schema allows us to connect the stories at the concrete, linguistic level. Another exciting insight revealed by the metaphor theory approach was that the tensions that I had previously sensed in the wu-wei ideal—the paradox of wu-wei—were quite neatly manifested in terms of incommensurable metaphors for self-cultivation. This gave me a new way to discuss the paradox, as well as a more powerful method for discussing its evolution over time.

What I hope to have demonstrated in this book is that the metaphor theory approach allows us to make conceptual connections between different thinkers by examining parallels in the types of metaphors that they use.

In the case of this discussion, the thinkers examined are all working in a more or less shared cultural and linguistic environment. What I would like to suggest, although there is little space to pursue the thought here, is that this same technique can be used to demonstrate conceptual parallels between thinkers more widely separated by time, language, and culture.[7] An interesting project would be to undertake a metaphor analysis of the aforementioned Chan Buddhist or neo-Confucian debates, where we might expect to find the conceptual tensions being manifested in terms of a conflict of metaphors. To take merely the first example that comes to mind, consider the doctrinal tension between Huineng (mythical founder of the "sudden" school) and Shenxiu (the fall guy representing the discredited gradualist school) as portrayed in the *Platform Sutra of the Sixth Patriarch*. As anyone familiar with this famous story will remember, the "debate" primarily takes the form of a battle of poems. Shenxiu, the smug representative of gradualism, presents his Buddha understanding in the form of the following poem:[8]

身是菩提樹	The body is a Bodhi tree
心如明鏡臺	The mind is like a bright mirror on a stand
時時勤拂拭	Always diligently wipe it clean
莫使有塵埃	And do not allow it to become dusty.

A clearer metaphorical portrayal of the need for effort could not be wished for. After having the poem read to him by a temple monk (he himself, of course, being illiterate), the future Sixth Patriarch perceives its flaws and composes the following poem in response:

菩提本無樹	The Bodhi originally has no tree
明鏡亦非臺	Similarly, the bright mirror has no stand
佛性常清淨	Buddha Nature is constantly pure and clean
何處有塵埃	Where, then, is there a place for dust to gather?

It should be clear to us by now that what we have here is a battle of metaphors for the mind, with each metaphor having important—and contradictory—entailments for self-cultivation.

Were we to systematically examine the metaphors for self, mind, and self-cultivation throughout the East Asian religious traditions, we would expect certain metaphor schemas to be repeated, but also that metaphor schemas would evolve and that new metaphors would appear as the result of (or as causes of?) new metaphysical commitments.[9] For instance, although the basic mirror metaphor for the mind found in the *Platform Sutra* passages is arguably inherited from the *Zhuangzi*, it is used in a quite novel fashion here as a result of new Buddhist metaphysical models. Another example of such change would be the appearance of the moon as a metaphor for our originally pure nature and a thatched hut as the obscurations of our material mind that we find in the writings of Zhu Xi. This metaphor is nowhere to be found in the pre-Buddhist Confucian canon, and represents the introduction of Buddhist "discovery" models of self-cultivation into Chinese religious discourse.[10]

The methods of cognitive linguistics could potentially also allow us to more rigorously link these East Asian themes to the Western virtue traditions. I have already discussed several times general similarities between these traditions with regard to end-states (spontaneous, self-activating virtue) and internal tensions. It would be interesting to explore these similarities more concretely—that is, to look at the metaphor schemas for self-cultivation and self-perfection in, say, the *Nicomachean Ethics* or the Augustinian tradition, and see how they compare to the schemas found in texts like the *Mencius* and *Xunzi*. I would venture to guess that, beneath the surface differences in conscious theological and political commitments, one would find deeper similarities between the various traditions' metaphorical models for self and self-cultivation. This is of course far beyond the scope of this study, but in this context it is helpful to recall Aristotle's discussion of the analogy between virtue and craft (*techne*). Aristotle's use of this analogy represents a conceptual link to the SELF-CULTIVATION AS CRAFT metaphor found in early Confucian texts, while at the same time his observations concerning the important *disanalogy* between crafts and virtue helps us to understand and articulate a tension that is present, but not explicitly addressed, in the Chinese texts. Identifying conceptual linkages such as this can thus enable a dialogue between culturally and linguistically dissimilar traditions that has the potential to improve our comprehension of both participants' positions.

The great potential of applying cognitive linguistic methodologies such as conceptual metaphor analysis to the humanities in general is its ability to plumb what we might call the cognitive unconscious—that is, the highly structured schemas that motivate and constrain conscious theory-formation, and that are not always directly accessible to consciousness. This represents a new, and potentially more interesting, approach to the study of intellectual history, in the sense that this conceptual "deep grammar" is in certain respects more revealing and significant than the explicit theories themselves.[11]

In addition, as suggested earlier, the metaphor analysis approach not only represents a powerful and concrete new methodology for cross-cultural comparative work but it also provides us with a convincing and coherent theoretical grounding for the comparativist project itself. That is, if the embodied realist claims of cognitive linguistics are correct—if our basic conceptual schemas arise from embodied experience—this provides an explanation for why we would expect to find a high degree of cross-cultural similarity with regard to deep conceptual structures, and thereby effectively gets us out of the postmodern "prison-house of language" Under the cognitive linguistic model, the basic schemas underlying language and other surface expressions of conceptual structure are motivated by the body and the physical environment in which it is located, which—shared in all general respects by any member of the species *homo sapien*, ancient or modern—provides us with a bridge into the experience of "the other." Metaphor, then, can serve as a linguistic "sign" of otherwise inaccessible, shared, deep conceptual structure. As Lakoff and Johnson note, "Though we have no access to the inner lives of those in radically different cultures, we do have access to their metaphor systems and the way they reason using those metaphor systems" (1999: 284). At the same time, the recognition that these structures are contingent upon bodies and physical environment, that no set of conceptual schemas provides unmediated access to the "things in themselves," and that some degree of cultural variation in schemas is to be expected allows us to address potential concerns about cultural insensitivity or rigid essentialism expressed by opponents of Enlightenment-inspired approaches to the study of thought and culture. Ideally, at least, the methods of cognitive linguistics give scholars in the humanities access to a shared conceptual grammar that allows them to engage in genuine conversation with other cultures.

Finally, we should note that cognitive linguistics is a quite young field, and is thus developing and evolving at a rapid rate. In addition, its application to the humanities is a relatively new endeavor, and—as far as I am aware—it has never before been applied to the classical Chinese context. It is therefore almost certain that my characterization of the field will be rather outdated by the time this book goes to press, and that my experiment here of applying it to Warring States Chinese thought may be found to be rough or in need of revision by my sinological colleagues. Whatever the specific limitations of this discussion, though, I hope that I have been able to at least suggest the great potential of this approach for sinologists, students of comparative religion and philosophy, and the humanities in general.

The "Many-Dao Theory"

Chad Hansen's "many dao" theory holds that the term *dao* 道 in the Inner Chapters of the *Zhuangzi* does not represent a singular metaphysical entity ("the Way"), but rather refers to an individual "discourse": "Chuang-tzu's dao is a linguistic rather than metaphysical object (roughly equivalent to prescriptive discourse), and thus his doctrine is relativistic rather than absolutist; that is, according to Chuang-tzu, there are many daos" (Hansen 1983b). Although he grants that "primitive" Daoists such as Laozi view *dao* as a metaphysical entity (the "Way"), he claims that Zhuangzi is unique among early Chinese thinkers in thinking that one can attain perfection simply by according with one's own particular "way"—the way of cutting up an ox, or the way of carving a bellstand—and that one can achieve such perfection quite literally any way. As Robert Eno (sharing Hansen's position) puts it, "the dao of butchering people might provide much the same spiritual spontaneity as the dao of butchering oxen" (Eno 1996: 142).

There are quite compelling textual reasons for rejecting this interpretation for the Inner Chapters of the *Zhuangzi* as a whole. In chapter 6, for instance, *dao* is clearly portrayed as a single, cosmogonic entity, and this would seem to be the conception of *dao* informing such stories as that of Butcher Ding in chapter 3. One might observe, for instance, that when praised for his skillful technique in cutting up the ox, Butcher Ding replies that, "What your servant cares about is *dao*, which goes beyond mere technique [*ji* 技]," and that after Ding provides an account of his spirit-guided action, Lord Wen Hui exclaims that from the words of his Butcher he has learned "the secret to caring for life." It is difficult to make sense of any of this if Butcher Ding's skill is understood as the mastery of a limited *dao*: if *dao* is simply the "way to cut up oxen," it is hard to see what it would mean to contrast mastery of it with mere "technique," and it is unclear why in this case Wen Hui would find Butcher Ding's performance so revelatory. Presumably he is not going to give up being a lord and start cutting up oxen for a living! The fact that Butcher Ding's mastery of *dao* has a general relevance that goes beyond merely the technique involved in cutting up an ox strongly suggests that we are dealing here with "the Way" and not "a way." Our uneasiness with the "many-dao" interpretation might be further heightened by the observation that no other Chinese thinker could plausibly be said to hold to the "many-dao" theory, that no traditional commentator to the *Zhuangzi* has ever thought that *dao* meant anything other than "the Way," and that the "many-dao" interpretation was promulgated by and finds adherence among only a handful of contemporary Western scholars.

Hansen himself has apparently sensed some of the difficulties with his "many-dao" theory. Although in claiming that Zhuangzi held to this theory Hansen sometimes uses "Zhuangzi" to refer to, for instance, the author of the Butcher Ding story in chapter 3, in a note in 1983b he retreats and limits the scope of this term to only the author of chapter 2. This is an extremely revealing move, because it suggests that Hansen realizes that it is really only in chapter 2 that the "many-dao" interpretation can—with enough work—be made to fit the actual Chinese text. In Hansen's defense, there is at the end of the day no way to "prove" that the term *dao* does not have a radically unique meaning in chapter 2 of the Zhuangzi (a meaning not found anywhere else in the Inner Chapters or, for that matter, *any* traditional Chinese text), but the reader is left to evaluate for herself the hermeneutical responsibility involved in basing a radical interpretation upon a single chapter that has been torn out of the context of the chapters that surround it, the religious tradition of which it is a part, and the entire commentarial tradition from ancient times to the present day.

Textual Issues Concerning the *Analects*

The earliest discussion of the *Analects*, an account in the *Hanshu*, notes the existence in the Western Han of three different versions that contained different numbers of books. Our present version of the *Analects* was compiled by He Yan (190–249 A.D.), who relied heavily upon two earlier eclectic versions, which in turn drew upon all three of the original versions mentioned in the *Hanshu*. There is no doubt among scholars that our present version is a somewhat heterogeneous collection of material from different time periods, although scholars differ in their identification of the different strata, as well as in the significance they attribute to these differences.

At one end of the spectrum of opinion are scholars such as D. C. Lau 1979, who—drawing upon the work of the Qing scholar Cui Shu (1740–1816)—separates the book into two strata (the first fifteen books and the last five) of different ages, but treats the work as more or less thematically homogenous. Steven Van Zoeren 1991 represents what was until recently the other end of the spectrum. He uses a form-critical approach to divide the work into four strata—from earliest to latest, the "core books" 3–7, books 1–2 and 8–9, books 10–15, and books 16–20—which he sees as representing not only different time periods, but also substantially different viewpoints (in the terms of his own project, significantly different hermeneutical attitudes toward the *Book of Odes*). This end of the spectrum has recently been pushed to a new extreme by Bruce and Taeko Brooks 1998, who see each individual book as representing a discrete stratum, identify vast numbers of "later interpolations" within each stratum, and claim that the work was composed over a much longer period of time than has been generally accepted—the later strata being put together as late as the third century B.C. Brooks and Brooks radically reorganize the structure of the *Analects*, and view it as an extremely heterogeneous collection of different (and in many cases competing) viewpoints. For a thorough discussion of the Brookses' approach the reader is referred to Slingerland 2000a, but my critique in brief is that their micro-periodization of the text is extremely speculative and ultimately untenable, while their macro-periodization rests on similarly shaky ground—for instance, a theory that texts (presumably on the model of redwood trees or coral reefs) "accrete" at a fairly constant rate in distinct bands precisely one-chapter thick.

Van Zoeren notes that one of the shortcomings of the form-critical approach he and the Brookses employ is its tendency to "systematically discount the continuities in a tradition, perhaps unfairly" (1991: 28). I believe that, at least in the case of the *Analects*, this systematic dismissal of continuity is indeed unfair and distorts our understanding of the text, and thus incline toward the D. C. Lau–Cui

Shu approach. Though no doubt representing different time periods and some-what different concerns, the various strata of the *Analects* display enough consis-tency in terminological use, conceptual metaphor, and general religious conception to allow us to treat the text as a whole as presenting a unified vision. The probable late date of last books in the *Analects* (especially books 15–20) should always be kept in mind. Nonetheless, the fact remains that nowhere in the *Analects* do we find even a hint of the sophisticated new conception of the heart/ mind, debates about human nature, and interschool rivalries that so permeate the *Mencius, Zhuangzi,* and *Xunzi,* and this relative lack of philosophical sophistica-tion is reflected linguistically by the absence of any of the new metaphors for the self (BODY AS CONTAINER) or *qi* (*QI* AS WATER) that become so universal in War-ring States discourse after the "Inner Training." This makes it highly unlikely that *any* stratum of the *Analects* was composed after the early fourth century B.C., which in turn means that we can safely view the text as a genuine representation of the state of the "School of Confucius" before the innovations of Mencius and Xunzi.

Textual Issues Concerning the *Laozi*

Until fairly recently, our received *Laozi* text has been the so-called Wang Bi version, after the commentary that accompanies it, composed by the brilliant scholar of the third century A.D. Although Wang Bi's commentary itself has to be dated before his death in 249, it is very likely that the received "Wang Bi" version is not the same text that Wang Bi himself had before him. As William Boltz notes, the received text itself is traceable no earlier than the compilation of the *Dao Zang* in 1445 (Boltz 1993: 277).

In 1973, two almost complete manuscripts of the text—written on silk, and referred to as versions A and B—were discovered in a tomb excavated at Mawangdui. Since the tomb is known to have been closed in 168 B.C., the so-called Mawangdui texts must have been composed before then. Use of taboo characters allows us to push this date back a bit farther. The first emperor of the Han, Liu Bang, died in 195 B.C. His personal name, *bang* 邦 "country," is used freely in version A but is systematically replaced by the synonym *guo* 國 in version B, which shows that version A must have been completed before 195 B.C., and version B between 195 and 168 B.C. This makes them the oldest complete versions of the text. Although the discovery in 1993 of the Guodian bamboo strips in a tomb that has been dated to ca. 300 B.C. has given us an even older version of the *Laozi*, these strips only constitute approximately two-fifths of the received text, although they do provide us with interesting textual variations from both the Wang Bi and Mawangdui versions.

My discussion of the *Laozi* is based upon the Mawangdui texts, because they represent the earliest complete versions of the text, although they are supplemented where appropriate with text from the Guodian fragments. For ease of reference, the chapter numbering and organization of the received Wang Bi version will be used, as this format is more or less standard in discussions of the *Laozi*. It should be noted, though, that the traditional ordering of the "Dao" and "De" sections is reversed in the Mawangdui manuscripts (the first chapter in these manuscripts is thus chapter 38 in the traditional version), while the "Dao"/"De" division is not present at all in the Guodian bamboo strips.

Composition and Relative Date of the Text

The *Laozi* or *Daodejing* is a short—at just over 5,000 words, by far the shortest of the works I have considered—and rather cryptic book. It was traditionally said to have been composed by the "Old Master" Laozi himself. The story is that as Laozi was leaving China behind for good because of the decline of the Zhou, a guard at the Western pass begged him to leave some of his teachings behind for posterity. The *Laozi* was in this way extemporaneously (and we are led to believe rather reluctantly) composed. This Laozi was also said to have been an older contemporary of Confucius, and there are several traditional stories that describe encounters in which Confucius invariably ends up being rebuked and receiving some teaching from his elder. Laozi has also been seen as the founder of the "Daoist" school of thought, with his "follower" Zhuangzi carrying on the Daoist opposition to Confucianism.

This traditional conception of the text of the *Laozi* and Laozi himself has been almost entirely discredited by modern scholarship in Asia and in the West. It has been demonstrated that the stories of the meetings between Laozi and Confucius are of quite late provenance (no earlier than the third century B.C.),[1] the existence of Laozi as an actual historical figure is now seriously doubted, and many scholars believe that the text was assembled by different authors over a period of time.[2] In addition, many modern scholars dispute the traditional placing of the *Laozi* chronologically after the *Analects* and the *Mozi* and before the *Mencius* and *Zhuangzi*. This chronology was based largely upon the fact that identifiably Confucian and Mohist ideas come under attack in the *Laozi*, and that Laozi appears as a character in many stories in the *Zhuangzi*. This of course assumes that this same Laozi was the author of the text by that name, and that both the *Laozi* and *Zhuangzi* are homogenous products of a single author—assumptions that no scholar today would care to defend. Thus liberated from the traditional chronology, many scholars have argued that the *Laozi* actually postdates at least the "Inner Chapters" of the *Zhuangzi*.[3] It is most likely that the *Laozi* is indeed an anthology of materials from various sources, smoothly edited into a more or less coherent text. The date at which this text was put together is very difficult to fix—unlike many other early texts, it nowhere makes reference to historical personages or events—but internal evidence would suggest that the text is of later origin than tradition would have it (no earlier than the fourth century B.C.), but also earlier than the *Zhuangzi* and the early collection of poems known as the *Chu Ci*.[4]

Thus, although the traditional account of the origin of the text can be dismissed as myth, the traditional ordering of the pre-Qin thinkers is probably correct in its essentials, and we might thus be justified in placing the text of the *Laozi* at least *developmentally*, and probably chronologically, between Confucius and the other thinkers we will be examining. It would appear that the author of the *Zhuangzi* "Inner Chapters," for example, had the advantage of writing in a much more intellectually developed environment than the author(s) of the *Laozi*, and had access to concepts that simply were not available to someone writing in an earlier age. For instance, the author(s) of the *Laozi* seem to share the same general, early view of the *xin* 心 ("heart/mind") that one finds in the *Analects*. If one compares, for instance, *Analects* 2.4 (Confucius's spiritual autobiography) and chapter 3 of the *Laozi*, it is clear that the *xin* is in both texts rather broadly conceived of as the locus of will, thought, emotions, ambition, and so on. This conception of the *xin* is significantly less technical than what one finds in the *Mencius* or the *Zhuangzi*.[5] At the level of linguistic metaphor, certain important new metaphors, such as *QI* AS WATER, that appear in the "Inner Training" and become standard in all later texts—employed systematically throughout the *Mencius*, *Zhuangzi*, and *Xunzi*—are absent from the *Laozi*, which is particularly strange considering how nicely they would fit in with other metaphorical schemas that are employed in the text.

Generally speaking, the new model of the self introduced in the "Inner Training" (and discussed in some detail in chapter 4) is conspicuous by its absence in the *Laozi*, a fact that argues against Harold Roth's position that the "Inward Training" precedes the *Laozi* developmentally and chronologically. Roth himself recognizes this disjunction:

> While the *Laozi* has general descriptions of the Way's activities, there is virtually nothing in the *Laozi* to parallel the concrete representation of the Way in terms of early physiological concepts of vital energy and vital essence found in *Inward Training*. Perhaps also related to this is the strong emphasis on the mind and on the practice of inner cultivation in *Inward Training*, an emphasis with few parallels in the *Laozi*. (Roth 1999: 147)

Roth also admits that the parallels between the *Zhuangzi* and "Inner Training" are much more concrete than between the "Inner Training" and the *Laozi* (153), but nonetheless remains wedded to his position that the "Inner Training" is the earliest text of Daoism. This is not the place for a detailed critique of his position, but Roth's main argument is that the political aspects of the *Laozi* are developmentally later than the sole concern with personal salvation found in "Inner Training" (see esp. 187). The argument made in chapter 4 here is, of course, quite the opposite: that the pursuit of individual, bodily salvation divorced from any political context is in fact a later development in Warring States thought. Add to this the fact that the model of the self found in "Inner Training" and the influence of the thought of Yang Zhu and the later Mohist logicians are absent from the *Analects* and the *Laozi*—while they appear as basic background assumptions in the *Mencius*, *Zhuangzi*, and *Xunzi*—and we have a strong prima facie case for the traditional chronology.

To buttess this evidence, we have other suggestions that something like our current *Laozi* text was already circulating by the time the *Mencius* and *Zhuangzi* were composed. Although Laozi himself or the text of the *Daodejing* are nowhere mentioned in the *Mencius*, I discussed in chapter 5 the fact that Mencius's criticisms of the primitivists can be seen as a rejection of Laozi-like views. Indeed, it is plausible that it is precisely in such primitivist communities that the *Daodejing* was assembled, and if Mencius was familiar with the text or fragments of the text he quite likely would have lumped them together with other primitivist teachings.

More important, on the conceptual level we can see Mencius incorporating the value of "naturalness" into Confucianism by defending Confucianism against the charge of being hypocritical or against nature, portraying it as the inevitable ful-fillment of our Heaven-given nature. This also implies that Laozi-like views were circulating in his intellectual milieu. In the *Laozi*, on the contrary, we see no indi-cations of Mencius-like views, although such views are criticized in several places in the Inner Chapters of the *Zhuangzi*. We also have Laozi himself appear-ing as an established character alongside of Confucius in the Inner Chapters of the *Zhuangzi*. This, of course, does not mean that the text that now bears Laozi's name already existed at this time. However, as Harold Roth 1991 has noted, by the time of the compilation of the *Huainanzi* (c. 139 B.C.) the *Laozi* in a form something like the received text was an already established and canonical text, whereas the *Zhuangzi* is only cited by name once, although stories that appear in the present text are often quoted without attribution. This suggests that, unlike the *Laozi*, the final text of the *Zhuangzi* as we know it was not completely set in 139 B.C., and that the *Laozi* was therefore composed in something like its received form before the *Zhuangzi*.

Specific Interpretative Issues

Considered here are more detailed discussions of particular interpretative issues that arose in the course of the discussion in chapter 3.

Laozi, Chapter 1

The grammar of the received Wang Bi version allows for two possible parsings of this sentence: 1) the way it was rendered in chapter 3 (reading *wuyu* 無欲 "with-out desires" and *youyu* 有欲 "possessing desires" together), or 2) with a pause understood after *wu* and *you*, which is how it is rendered by Feng Yulan: "Of the invariable Non-Being, we wish to see its secret essences. Of the invariable Being, we wish to see its borders" (Feng Yulan 1952: 178). Fortunately, the Mawangdui versions are grammatically unambiguous (possessing the topic-marker *ye* 也 to indicate the pause), and show that the first parsing is the correct one (at least in the view of the Mawangdui authors): 故恆無欲也以觀其妙 , and so on. This chapter is missing from the Guodian fragments.

Laozi, Chapter 21

The Wang Bi text here reads, 道之為物 , whereas the two Mawangdui manu-scripts read 道之物 (this chapter is missing from the Guodian fragments). A great deal of scholarly debate has centered on the interpretation of this phrase, espe-cially in mainland China, where it became the focus of the controversy over whether Laozi should be interpreted as an "idealist" or a "materialist." In the "materialist" interpretation 之 is taken to mean 是 ("this"), in which case the line might be rendered in modern Chinese as 道這個東西 ("This thing, the Way . . . "). This interpretation is consistent with the received Wang Bi text. In the "idealist" interpretation, 之 is taken as equivalent to 生 ("to give birth to"), based upon the *Shuowen* gloss of 之 as 出 ("to come forth"). For a brief account of the various positions, see Gao Ming 1996: 328–30. Quite wisely professing a wish to not get involved with the "materialist" versus "idealist" debate, Gao Ming believes that, based upon narrowly textual terms (the original Mawangdui wording and a comparison with similar passages in the *Laozi*), it would be most reasonable to take 之 as 生, and his position has some merit. On the other hand, it seems to me that the first reading (taking 之 as 是) is the most grammatically natural, and this reading has the further virtue of agreeing with chapter 25, where the Way is described as a very indistinct "thing." I therefore follow Lau here.

Textual Issues Concerning the *Zhuangzi*

Scholars in China have been questioning the textual integrity of the *Zhuangzi* since at least the seventh century,[1] and it is now generally agreed that the received text of the *Zhuangzi* is a heterogeneous collection of writings from different authors and different time periods. The present text is an abridgement by Guo Xiang (d. c. A.D. 312), who divided the text into the "Inner Chapters" (*nei pian* 內篇) 1–7, the "Outer Chapters" (*wai pian* 外篇) 8–22, and the "Mixed Chapters" (*za pian* 雜篇) 23–33. It is beyond the scope of this work to delve into the intricacies of the existing textual scholarship on the *Zhuangzi*;[2] the purpose of this section is merely to clarify the principles that have guided this presentation of Zhuangzi's thought, as well as to mention some of the difficulties that can be encountered if one approaches the text without having taken textual issues into account.

It is the nearly unanimous opinion of modern scholars that the seven Inner Chapters form a coherent unit, come from the hand of a single author (although it is debated whether this author is the historical Zhuangzi himself [fl. c. 320 B.C.] or merely a close and gifted disciple), and represent the earliest stratum of the text.[3] In addition, it is also quite clear that much of the Outer and most of the Miscellaneous Chapters represent works from schools of thought (variously referred to as "Yangist," "Huang-Lao," "Primitivist," or "Syncretist") only loosely related to the thought of the author of the Inner Chapters, whereas some of this material comes from writers belonging to what Graham and Liu Xiaogan term the "School of Zhuangzi"—that is, later writers who explicated or developed themes present in the Inner Chapters but did not raise important new points of their own. There is, however, a great deal of disagreement over precisely which portions of the Outer and Miscellaneous Chapters represent "School of Zhuangzi" writers. In addition, there has been some speculation concerning the amount and nature of the material that Guo Xiang eliminated in order to arrive at his thirty three-chapter version. As Livia Kohn notes (Kohn 1982), a fifty two-chapter version of the *Zhuangzi* is mentioned in the *Hanshu Yiwenzhi*, and in the Tang Dynasty Lu Deming (d. c. 630 A.D.) noted the existence of two extant versions of fifty two and twenty seven chapters each besides Guo Xiang's version. However, the differences between these various editions seem to concern only the Outer and Mixed Chapters—all three versions in Lu Deming's time contained seven Inner Chapters, which we may conclude are the same seven chapters that appear in Guo Xiang's version. Therefore, while Kohn may be correct in claiming that the text originally contained a great deal more "magical and popular material" that was eliminated when Guo Xiang "philosophically purified" it, this purge is not at all likely to have affected the seven Inner Chapters.

With all of these difficulties in mind, the textual principle I have adopted is to treat as the genuine thought of "Zhuangzi"[4] only the seven Inner Chapters, supplemented cautiously[5] with the six Outer Chapters (chapters 17–22) that both A.C. Graham and Liu Xiaogan agree represent "School of Zhuangzi" materials. In addition, material from "Syncretist" or "Primitivist" writers (along with material from other early texts, such as the "Inner Training") may be used on occasion to flesh out certain metaphysical concepts that, as it has been argued in chapter 4, help to make up a worldview that was taken for granted by intellectuals around the time that the Inner Chapters were composed.

The issue of the relationship of Zhuangzi to Laozi must also be addressed. The famous comment regarding Zhuangzi made by Sima Qian in the *Shiji* that "although there is no aspect unexamined by the range of his thought, the root of his philosophy may be traced back to the teachings of Laozi"[6]—along with his classification of both thinkers as "Daoist" (*Daojia* 道家)—represents an attitude common in China and the West that Zhuangzi and Laozi represent a more or less coherent school of thought.[7] It is clear, however, that—despite some family similarities between the two thinkers—Zhuangzi advocates a viewpoint which should be sharply distinguished from that portrayed in the *Laozi*. A factor that contributes to the conflation of Laozi and Zhuangzi's thought is the often unclear (or nonexistent) textual stance taken by many scholars toward the *Zhuangzi*, which causes them to attribute Huang-Lao or Syncretist sentiments found in the Outer and Mixed Chapters to the author of the Inner Chapters. This leads some scholars to, for instance, erroneously conclude that Zhuangzi advocates an "instrumentalist" or primarily government-oriented conception of wu-wei.[8] Zhuangzi's conception of wu-wei—as well as his thought in general—is different in many respects from what we find in the *Laozi*, and wu-wei as it is conceived of in the Inner Chapters must be distinguished from the role it plays in certain of the Outer and Mixed Chapters.

Notes

Introduction

1.   The distinction between "knowing how" and "knowing that" is one developed by Gilbert Ryle 1949.

2.   See, for instance, *Nicomachean Ethics* 1113a (Irwin 1985: 65): "The excellent person judges each sort of thing correctly, and in each case what is true appears to him . . . the excellent person is far superior because he sees what is true in each case, being a sort of standard and measure of what is fine and pleasant."

3.   Ignorance, for instance, is often analogized to not being able to distinguish black from white and compared to blindness, while (in contrast) a common metaphor for the sort of understanding that accompanies wu-wei activity is *ming* ("illumination"; "clarity"; "brightness").

4.   Hall and Ames 1987: 44. The reader is also referred to their discussion of theory versus praxis in the Western tradition and its relationship to Confucian thought (1987: 30–43), and Ames's characterization (based upon categories borrowed from Whitehead) of Chinese thought as being concerned with "aesthetic" rather than "logical" order (Ames 1985). This distinctive character of the Chinese model of knowledge has also been noted by other scholars. For instance, Herbert Fingarette urges us to overcome our Western "mentalistic" bias in approaching the teachings of Confucius and to redirect our focus from the "'interior' of the man . . . to the act of the man" (1972: 54); Wu Kuang-ming speaks of Zhuangzi's ideal as a form of "body-thinking" (1992); and the German scholar P. J. Thiel has coined the term "Tao-Erkenntnis" ("Dao knowledge") to denote the Chinese model of knowledge, which he describes as a sort of "experience of Being" (*Seins-Erfahrung*): "not irrational, but rather a deeper, entities-bound [*Wesensgebundene*] type of knowledge—one that is experienced with the entire spiritual personhood" (Thiel 1969: 85, n. 148).

5.   Fingarette 1972: 49–56; D. C. Lau 1979: 43–44; Chad Hansen 1975: 64–65; 1983a, 1983b); Robert Eno (1990: 8–10 and 1996); P. J. Ivanhoe 1993b. Hansen goes so far as to claim that the sort of "knowing how" that is exemplified in skillful action is the *only* form of knowledge in early China, and that the Chinese had no conception of propositional knowledge ("knowing that"). This is an exaggeration. Cristoph Harbsmeier 1993 has very clearly and convincingly demonstrated that not only were the early Chinese capable of entertaining propositional objects of belief but that a distinction between "knowing how" and "knowing that" is built into the very syntax of classical Chinese.

6.   This point is made by Hall and Ames in their observation that the type of praxis-knowledge emphasized by Confucius manages to avoid some of the epistemological and other problems plaguing dominant modern Western modes of thought: "Confucius pro-

vides a mode of thinking that avoids the disjunction of normative and spontaneous thought in a manner that has not been achieved in other major philosophical visions. . . . It may [then] be argued that his philosophy is directly germane to reconceptualizing one of the frustrating problems of contemporary Anglo-European speculation" (1987: 43).

7.   Throughout this work, these names will be used as convenient tags to refer to the thought expressed in various received pre-Qin texts. Problems of authorship, periodization, and similar textual problems will be treated in the individual chapters that follow.

8.   There are, of course, exceptions to this trend. In the West, Donald Munro has noted the role that wu-wei plays as a common "ideal state" for both Confucians and Daoists—a state of mental tranquility resulting from a "union" with Heaven (Munro 1969: 151, 155ff)—and Alan Fox has written on wu-wei as a spiritual ideal in the thought of Laozi and Zhuangzi (Fox 1995, 1996). The reader is referred also to Allinson 1989, Ivanhoe 1993b, and Yearley 1996. Recognition of the spiritual dimensions of wu-wei has been much more common in China and Japan (Kanaya Osamu 1965, Fukunaga Mitsuji 1965, Mori Mikisaburo 1967, Murakami Kajitsu 1969, Lin Congshun 1993, Pang Pu 1994, Liu Xiaogan 1998) and Asian scholars writing in the West (Feng Yulan 1952, Wu Guangming 1981, 1982).

9.   In the *Hanfeizi*, for instance, wu-wei refers to a technique of governing—summed up in the phrase, "those above are wu-wei, while those below act" (*shang wuwei er xia youwei*)—where the ruler is literally "not acting" because the machinery of government has been set up so efficiently that all of the ministers perform their jobs without any need for guidance or interference. Wu-wei in this sense (which we might refer to as "institutional wu-wei") is completely divorced from any connection to a personal spiritual ideal, and should be distinguished from the concept that serves as the focus of this work.

10.   For instance, Donald Munro has discussed the "apparent contradiction" involved in Daoist wu-wei (1969: 143–144), and Joel Kuppermann 1968 has struggled with the paradox in his discussion of the "problem of naturalness" in the thought of Confucius. In addition, at least two scholars—Wu Guangming and Mori Mikisaburo—have seen that this tension is endemic to both Confucian and Daoist thought (Mori 1967: 16–17, Wu 1989). Wu actually goes a step further to proclaim that the "self-contradiction" that one finds in Zhuangzi's thought is "a fundamental problem faced by all of us in cultivating ourselves" (1989: 317).

11.   In its earliest usages (as with the Latin *virtus*), de referred to the powers or qualities inherent to and characteristic of a given thing; by the time of the *Odes*, it is portrayed as a charismatic power to attract and retain followers that accrues to one who accords with the moral standards handed down by Heaven. "Virtue" or "charismatic virtue" are thus etymologically accurate renderings for *de*, as long as we are careful to avoid reading moralistic qualities into the term as it is used in the Daoist context, where it retains the more archaic sense of the vitalistic power original to and characteristic of a given creature.

12.   Nivison 1997: 31–44, "The Paradox of Virtue." See also "Can Virtue Be Self-Taught?" (45–58), "Motivation and Moral Action in Mencius" (91–120), and "Philosophical Voluntarism in Fourth-Century China" (121–32).

13.   See Gregory 1987 for an anthology of essays on this topic. As Gregory notes in his introduction to the volume, there are several aspects of religious activity to which the "sudden-gradual" distinction might refer: the nature of enlightenment, the nature of religious language, etc. (1987: 5–6). It is, I think, with regard to the third aspect he notes—the nature of ethical and religious practice—that the paradox of wu-wei is most relevant.

14.   For a discussion of this topic, see Rodney Taylor's "The Sudden/Gradual Paradigm and Neo-Confucian Mind Cultivation" in Taylor 1990: 77–92.

15. As the proposal for the conference on the sudden-gradual debate that was published as Gregory 1987 observes:

> While the controversy surrounding the sudden-gradual polarity was not without precedence in other Buddhist traditions, it assumed its greatest significance in the Chinese Buddhist tradition, where its articulation displayed a number of characteristically Chinese features linking it to non-Buddhist modes of thought. The fact that this polarity assumed its particular importance in the Chinese Buddhist tradition suggests that it resonated with, or gave form to, a similar pre-existing polarity within Chinese thought. (Gregory 1987: 1)

While the pre-Buddhist roots of the sudden-gradual controversy are mentioned in passing by some of the authors represented in this anthology, this topic is not explored in any detail there.

16. Refer to the *Nicomachean Ethics* 1105a15–25 (Aristotle 1985: 39). For Nivison's discussion of Plato and Aristotle, see Nivison 1997: 36–37 and 116–18.

17. See especially MacIntyre 1990: 62–68, 82–86.

18. *Pace* Fingarette, who claims that, in Confucius's view, once one commits oneself to the "Holy Rites," "from there onward everything 'happens'" (1972: 8). While Fingarette is careful to explain that this does not entail the individual's becoming an automaton—that "seriousness and sincerity" are necessary if one's wu-wei actions are to be "authentic"—he seems himself to move in this direction by denying to the individual any degree of interiority or ability to make choices. This is not the place for an extended critique of Fingarette's position—nor for an excursus into action theory—but suffice it to say that the Chinese ideal of wu-wei does not eliminate the need for choice or thought on the individual's part. The most obvious point is that we are not *born* into wu-wei, but need to expend great effort and make difficult choices (resisting the temptations and distractions of the fallen world around us) in order to enter this state. In addition, even once wu-wei has been achieved, it continues to require—as Fingarette himself quite perceptively observes—"seriousness and sincerity" (Fingarette 1972: 8) on the part of the agent. For a critique of Fingarette's position, see Ruskola 1992, and for a critique of Fingarette coupled with a helpful discussion of the relationship between "freedom of the will" and wu-wei in the Confucian context, refer to Schwartz 1985: 124–25.

19. For a related discussion of the difference between virtuous disposition and mere habit, see Yearley 1990: 108–10.

20. *Pace* Burton Watson's description of Zhuangzi's skillful exemplars as leading "mindless, purposeless" modes of life (1968: 6). The theme of "mindlessness" or "no mind" is something that Watson likely picked up from Fukunaga Mitsuji (see, for instance, Fukunaga 1966), and ultimately derives from Buddhist interpretations of the text.

21. I join Donald Munro in referring to the early Confucian-Daoist worldview as "mainstream" because—although it was challenged or outright rejected in the pre-Qin period by thinkers such as Mozi or Hanfeizi—its absorption into Han syncretism won for it an enduring influence on the subsequent development of religious thought in China. This mainstream Chinese worldview also had a profound effect on the adaptation of alien modes of thought—from Buddhism to Marxism—to the Chinese intellectual milieu. Refer to Munro 1969: 160–82 and Nivison 1956 for classic discussions of the influence of the ancient legacy on such contemporary Chinese modes of thought as Maoism. Nivison cites a fascinating passage from the pen of the Maoist Zhen Boda that seems to describe a communist version of self-cultivation leading to wu-wei:

> For the Communists, as for Sun [Yat-sen] and Confucianism before him, true "sincerity" gives its possessor strange powers. True communists, wrote Zhen Boda several years later, "because they devote themselves body and

mind to the party and to Communism . . . are able to develop a strength in any category of work, so that stupidity gives way to intelligence, the difficult becomes easy, and the dangerous path becomes smooth." (Nivison 1956: 57)

22. While defining "religion" has been a notoriously difficult task for scholars—with many incompatible models having been proposed over the years, and the implicit, de facto definition governing present scholarship seeming to be "I know it when I see it"—it is necessary to briefly explain what I mean by referring to wu-wei as a "religious" concept. I see at least two features of a system of thought to be crucial in marking it as "religious": 1) the postulation of an all-embracing and *normative* order to the cosmos that goes beyond any given particular individual or object (that is, a network of metaphysical claims); and 2) a program for either bringing the individual and society as a whole *back* into their proper place in this order (a soteriological project) or for preserving a realized, but constantly threatened, state of harmony with this order. I would thus characterize any concept belonging to such a system of thought as a "religious" concept (for a similar characterization of "religion," see Robert Neville's "Foreword" in Rodney Taylor 1990: ix–x). My conception of religion owes a great deal to Charles Taylor's definition of "spirituality" as involving a network of ontological claims that allow one to make "strong evaluations" (see Charles Taylor 1989: 3–5).

23. Borrowing the term from Aristotle; for a discussion of the "master craft" of living well, see *Nicomachean Ethics* I.2.

24. This translation of *ren* (often rendered "benevolence") will be discussed in chapter 2.

25. The passage in question is 15.5. While we need not (and, I think, should not) accept Brooks and Brooks's quite late and rather speculative date of circa 305 for this passage (Brooks and Brooks 1998: 234), most students of the text would now agree that chapter 15 belongs to a relatively late stratum of the *Analects*.

26. The contemporary theory of conceptual metaphor will be discussed in more detail in chapter 1. Cognitive approaches to metaphor are not entirely unknown in the study of early Chinese thought. Harold Oshima, for instance, documents (in Oshima 1983) the various metaphoric models employed to conceptualize the mind in the *Zhuangzi*. Although he somewhat understates the full conceptual function of metaphor, Oshima notes that a metaphor such as mind as mirror, "drawn from the world of common experience, tends to shape and mold the ambiguous idea it was imported originally only to describe. The metaphor goes beyond merely elaborating an idea that was already clearly understood. It functions, instead, as the model whereby the abstract idea is actually imagined and pictured" (72–73). Oshima's theoretical inspirations are Hannah Arendt and Colin Turbayne 1970, whose views on metaphor anticipate the contemporary cognitive linguistic approach. Other scholars who have noted the importance of metaphor for understanding Chinese thought include D. C. Lau 1970, who in his discussion of Mencian "analogy" notes that it is "indispensable for certain philosophical problems" (262), and Wang Jinlin 1986, who observes that "Zhuangzi's metaphors are not optional rhetorical embellishments, but are rather the direct bearers of his thought" (112). Wang Jinlin feels that Zhuangzi is the only early Chinese thinker who uses metaphor in a philosophically significant manner, however, and—as will become clear later—I would expand upon Lau by claiming that analogy or metaphor is indispensable for *all* philosophical theorizing. For a metaphor-focused approach to Song neo-Confucian thought, see Donald Munro 1985a and 1985b.

27. With the exception, perhaps, of the Legalist-style "institutional wu-wei" mentioned earlier.

28. The Subject-Self metaphor will be explained later.

29. For a cogent criticism of this sort of linguistic determinism in the sinological context, see Graham 1989: 389–428. For a more general criticism, see G. E. R. Lloyd 1990.

30. Roger Ames, for instance, concludes that "given the combination of scant data and tenuous chronology, no attempt to determine the historical origin of *wu-wei* can amount to much more than strained speculation" (1994: 216).

31. As indicated, for instance, by the fact that wu-wei was the term of art the Chinese themselves eventually adopted to denote the ideal of perfected action in texts as various as the *Analects* and the *Zhuangzi*.

32. I here qualify the type of internalism and externalism I will be talking about as "self-cultivation" internalism and externalism in order to distance my use of these labels from arguments in philosophy concerning epistemological or motivational internalism and externalism. In order to mark this distinction, T. C. Kline—a sinologist working out of a philosophy department—has coined the terms "inside-out" and "outside-in" to refer to these two types of self-cultivation strategies (Kline 2000). I find these labels rather awkward, however, and will therefore continue to use the terms "internalism" and "externalism" with all due apologies to my philosophically trained readers.

33. While there is no evidence that Mencius was aware of the *Laozi*—or even that the text of the *Laozi* existed in anything like its present form when Mencius was writing—he was clearly aware of and concerned with refuting the views of various self-preservationists (followers of Yang Zhu) and primitivists (followers of Xu Xing) whose views mirror in many ways the sentiments expressed in the *Laozi*. It is thus not unreasonable to assume that Mencius was familiar with Laozi-like soteriological strategies and metaphors.

34. Again, although neither text mentions the other by name, the author(s) of the *Zhuangzi* and *Mencius* were roughly contemporaneous, and we find clearly Mencian-like metaphors (for instance, that the heart/mind is the natural "ruler" of the self) coming under attack in the *Zhuangzi*. As I will discuss in more detail in chapter 6, it is not unreasonable to assume that the author(s) of the *Zhuangzi* were familiar with and thus responding to ·Mencian-like ideas, subsumed under the general rubric of "Confucianism."

Wu-wei as Conceptual Metaphor

1. For an introduction to the cognitive linguistic approach, as well as defense of the practice of distinguishing "cognitive" from other approaches to linguistics (such as generative), see Gibbs 1996. Gibbs cites as the distinguishing characteristics of the cognitive linguistic approach "(a) the way that it incorporates empirical findings from other disciplines into linguistic theory, and (b) [the fact that] it seeks to examine the specific contents, and not just the architecture, of human conceptual knowledge" (29).

2. See Wolf 1994: 38–41 for a discussion of the link between phenomenology and the work of Lakoff and Johnson. For a basic introduction to contemporary metaphor theory, see Lakoff and Johnson 1980 and 1999, Lakoff and Turner 1989, Johnson 1987 and 1981, Sweetser 1990, Kövecses 1986 and 1990, and Turner 1991. Lakoff 1993 is perhaps the best article-length, general introduction to the cognitive theory of metaphor, and Ortony 1993 is a helpful resource that provides a variety of theoretical perspectives on metaphor. For the more general theory of mental spaces and conceptual mapping, see Fauconnier 1997 and Fauconnier and Sweetser 1996.

3.   See Fauconnier 1997: 1–5 for a brief discussion of how this treatment of language as mere "signals" connected to a deeper, nonlinguistic structure differs from structural or generative linguistic approaches.

4.   See especially Johnson 1987 for a discussion of this phenomenon.

5.   A standard convention in the field of cognitive linguistics is to indicate metaphor schemas by means of small caps.

6.   Cf. Paivio and Walsh 1993 and Miller 1993 for views that see metaphor as based upon similarity between source and target domains. According to the cognitive theory of metaphor, metaphor cannot be understood as a device that merely highlights previously existing similarities, because the source domain actively shapes the taget domain, "provid[ing] structures and attributes not inherent in the target domain" (Lakoff and Turner 1989: 123). Another basic argument against the similarity theory is that the "similarity" we see in metaphor is not symmetrical, as genuine similarity should be; that is, we might say that billboards are like warts in the sense that "Billboards are warts upon the landscape," but this metaphor does not involve the symmetrical idea that warts are like billboards. See Ortony 1993:345–348 for an argument against literal similarity as being central to metaphor.

7.   See Lakoff and Johnson 1999: 122–27 for criticisms of the views that metaphors are linguistic, not conceptual; that metaphor has to do with unusual (poetic) or otherwise "deviant" usages; or that conventional metaphors are "dead" (i.e., fixed literary expressions).

8.   Mark Turner and Gilles Fauconnier have pointed out that, in addition to direct source-target mappings, metaphor often involves the construction of more complex "blended spaces" that are composed of elements drawn from multiple domains (see Fauconnier 1997:168–71). The metaphors I will discuss rely mostly upon the more basic source-target mapping, and even more complex metaphors will be reduced to a source-target mapping for the sake of simplicity. The "skeleton-flesh" metaphor for characterizing source-target mappings is George Lakoff's personal communication to Gregory Murphy (reported and characterized in Murphy 1996: 187). We should also note that different— and in many cases incompatible—metaphor schemas or blends may be called upon to help conceptualize a single abstract concept, depending upon what aspect of the target domain is being addressed. This phenomenon will be discussed further.

9.   I say "most" aspects, because the skeletal structure of the target domain that is directly represented in consciousness not only serves to constrain what source domains can be mapped onto it but also which aspects of the source domain can be successfully mapped and which ignored as irrelevant (see Lakoff 1993: 228–35 and 1990: 67–73).

10.   By "folk belief" or "folk theory," Lakoff and Johnson refer to everyday, intuitive, taken-for-granted, "common sense" assumptions shared by a given culture. "Folk" is not intended as a derogatory term (Lakoff and Johnson 1999: 352). For a discussion of the relationship between "folk beliefs" and "expert theories," see Lakoff and Johnson 1981: 205 and (for a more extended discussion) Wolf 1994, chapter 4.

11.   Of course, even seeing life as an entity already involves the basic OBJECT-EVENT STRUCTURE metaphor schema, whereby events are conceptualized as physical "things." See Lakoff and Johnson 1999: 196–97 for a discussion of the OBJECT-EVENT schema.

12.   Another argument against the similarity theory of metaphor is the asymmetry between source and target domains. We invariably draw upon structures from more concrete domains such as physical journeys to conceptualize and reason about abstract domains such as life, but the converse is not true: while it seems natural to say of a newborn that she has "begun her journey of life" or for a villain to say to the person he is about to gun down that he has "reached the end of the road," it would be very strange to say that

a person just starting out on a journey from Los Angeles to San Francisco is being "born," or that once they reach San Francisco they are "dead." This sort of asymmetry between conceptual metaphor source and target domains is systematic.

13. See Gibbs 1994 for a survey of such evidence.

14. See Sereno 1991 and Damasio 1994. Various theoretical models have been proposed to explain exactly *how* bodily patterns become instantiated in cognitive image schemas; see Lakoff and Johnson 1999: 39–44.

15. Lakoff and Johnson claim that *all* metaphors for self are based upon this schema, but we will see many cases in Warring States texts where we have a unitary subject interacting metaphorically with an external entity, such as the world.

16. See Pulleyblank 1995: 76–77 for a discussion of the *wu/wo* distinction.

17. Conceptually speaking, forgetting and losing are structurally identical processes, as is indicated even more clearly in Warring States Chinese than in English. To simply choose a few examples from the *Zhuangzi*, "forgetting" (*wang* 忘) and "losing" (*shi* 失 or *yi* 遺) are used interchangeably in parallel clauses such as "I forgot [*wang*] my answer because I lost/forgot [*shi*] the question" (W251/G781), and are also combined in compounds such as *yiwang* 遺忘 (to forget) (W337/G1012). Of course, this conceptual connection is reflected as well in modern Chinese compounds such as *wangdiao* 忘掉 (to forget; lit. forgetting by letting it fall away).

18. The basic SELF AS CONTAINER schema is described by Lakoff and Johnson (275), but is mapped in a different manner because they connect it with a rather different metaphor.

19. Just in passing, it is worth noting the cross-cultural metaphor of straight=self-determined, proper behavior; crooked=accomodating, improper behavior.

20. E.g., "The chaos in Eastern Europe *emerged from* the end of the Cold War." It would seem that this metaphor is simply an extension of the container + essence schemas: that is, the end of the Cold War is being conceptualized as a container with an internal essence (chaos) that then emerges in the way a plant emerges from a seed or a child from the womb. Arguably, this NATURAL CAUSATION IS MOTION OUT metaphor arises from our experience with mammalian birth and the germination of seeds.

21. See especially 1980: 92–94 for an example of overlap between the ARGUMENT AS JOURNEY and ARGUMENT AS CONTAINER metaphors.

22. This explains why all of the various and sometimes literally inconsistent metaphor schemas used to portray a given concept must be considered together if we are to arrive at a full understanding of it. For instance, in the *Zhuangzi* the metaphors of "emptying" or "losing" the self, taken by themselves, might suggest a kind of no-self picture. As we shall see in chapter 6, however, when these metaphors are understood in conjunction with the INNER SELF AS ESSENTIAL SELF schema, it becomes clear that the "self" being targeting by these metaphors is merely the "false" or "external" self, not the "true" self. Michael LaFargue makes a similar point in observing that many of the statements made in the *Laozi* are "aphorisms" rather than elements of a systematical philosophical position, and as such their meaning "seems to be exhausted in making a point against their particular target," which means that "I am not necessarily contradicting myself if I use [literally inconsistent aphorisms] on different occasions" (1998: 265). LaFargue also notes that "while the various sayings . . . have different targets and offer different images, there is a plausible unity to their stance and its motivation" (271), which is similar to my point about the conceptual coherence of literally inconsistent metaphors.

23. Lakoff and Turner 1989:53 note the existence in English of metaphors for life that have mutually contradictory entailments (LIFE IS A PRECIOUS POSSESSION and LIFE IS BONDAGE), but believe that these metaphors work together coherently because they pro-

vide "very different perspectives on life." On the contrary, I would argue that, although these two schemas are both found in the English language, they are conceptually incompatible and could *not* be used consistently by a single thinker endeavoring to present a coherent view of "life."

24. I will focus almost exclusively upon the *Odes*, both because the pre-Confucian status of the majority of the *Odes* is the least disputed among scholars and because it serves as the richest source of metaphors for wu-wei. Occasional references to the "New Text" chapters of the *Book of History* (considered by most scholars to represent genuinely pre-Confucian material; see Loewe 1993: 376–80) will also be made.

25. Wu-wei as a compound term appears twice in the received Mao version of the *Odes*—in odes 70 and 145—but never in our full technical sense. Ode 70 is a marginal case:

> Gingerly walked the hare;
> But the pheasant was caught in the snare.
> At the beginning of my life
> I did nothing / kept out of trouble / refrained from acting (wu-wei);
> In my latter days
> I have met these hundred woes.
> Would that I might sleep and never stir! (Following Waley 1960, p. 307)

One could perhaps see in this ode a proto-Laozian view of wu-wei. In ode 145, however, "wu-wei" is used in the completely nontechnical sense of being at a loss as to what to do (following Karlgren 1950, p. 92).

26. *Junzi* means literally "son of a lord/ruler," and in pre-Confucian times referred to a member of the feudal aristocracy. Confucius later moralized the term, using it to refer to anyone who merely *acted* like the aristocracy: that is, demonstrated the virtues proper to a true human being. Although there has been some debate recently as to how to render *junzi*, the traditional translation of "gentleman" seems the most felicitous, as this English word parallels quite closely both the original and extended meanings of *junzi*.

27. Following Karlgren; Waley renders *si* 似 as "to continue."

28. Lit. "He counts [*xuan* 選] [the beat]."

29. Lit. "revert [to the same place]" (*fan* 反) (following Mao).

30. Cf. the descriptions of the gentleman in odes 143, 173, 174, and 189. For other examples of metaphors from the "fitting" family, see odes 235, 243, and 249, and see ode 255 for an example of the related metaphor of "timeliness" (*shi* 時).

31. Karlgren remarks that according with principles "without knowledge or wisdom" signifies doing it "by nature, without effort" (1950: 196).

32. This is a clear instance of a metaphor found throughout the *Odes* that will become central to later Chinese thought (especially Confucianism): MORALITY AS BOUNDED SPACE, in terms of which immorality is understood as a kind of "transgression" (*yue* 越 or *guo* 過) of the boundaries of the proper "Way" (*dao*).

33. After Karlgren 1950: 265 and Waley 1960: 277–78.

34. See, for example, odes 209, 240, and 299.

35. See also ode 249.

36. See, for instance, odes 157, 161, 191, 209, 223, 242, 256, and 299.

37. See Nivison 1997: 17–30, "'Virtue' in Bronze and Bone."

38. Following Karlgren 1950: 228.

At Ease in Virtue: Wu-wei in the *Analects*

1. The *Analects* (*lunyu* 論語 or "classified sayings") is a collection of the sayings of Confucius and his disciples that was no doubt put together after his death. Although there is considerable disagreement concerning the integrity of the received text—which clearly consists of various strata from different time periods—it is my belief that no portion of the *Analects* was composed after the early fourth century B.C., which means that we can safely view the text as representative of the state of the "School of Confucius" before the innovations of Mencius and Xunzi. For a brief discussion of textual issues concerning the *Analects*, see appendix 2.

2. The conception of Heaven as a ruler is metaphorical because, even if Confucius or other early Chinese consciously believed in Heaven as an anthropomorphic deity who issues orders, could be angered or appeased, etc., Heaven nonetheless was *not* literally a person able to speak or feel emotions, and the structuring of this unseen, metaphysical entity was entirely derived from the concrete domain of social relations. Conceptual metaphors (unconscious cross-domain mappings of the type discussed in chapter 1) are often taken literally at a conscious level, but this does not diminish their metaphoric quality.

3. As I noted earlier, although the suspicion of language is usually associated with Daoist thinkers such as Laozi and Zhuangzi, excessive or glib speech also serves as a very prominent symbol of non-wu-wei action throughout the *Analects*, and will be discussed in greater detail later (see especially n. 14).

4. Many traditional commentators claim that this border official was a sage person who deliberately took up such a remote and lowly post because of the corruptness of his contemporaries, and that this accounts for his perceptive and appreciative assessment of Confucius.

5. This loss of office is presumably the reason that Confucius and his disciples are leaving the state.

6. See, for instance, the *Book of History*, Book of Xia, "Punitive Expedition of Yin," section 3 (Legge 1991b: 164).

7. A similar metaphorical structure is suggested in the concept of the "Heavenly Mandate" (*tianming* 天命): things that are beyond the immediate control of the individual (wealth, fame, health, life span) are portrayed as being metaphorically "commanded" or "mandated" by the Heavenly ruler, and thus the true gentleman—understood in the metaphor as a loyal minister—submits to these "decisions" without anxiety or complaint (see 12.4 and 12.5; for further discussion of the conception of *ming* in early Confucian thought, see Slingerland 1996). This metaphorical conception of Heaven as an anthropomorphic being with intentions and loyalties is also a great source of reassurance for the dedicated "minister." Confucius, for instance, is possessed of a deep faith that he is on a mission to fulfill the Mandate of Heaven, and it is this faith that sustains him through periods of doubt and crisis (see especially 9.5 and 7.23)

8. See chapter 4.

9. As is discussed in appendix 1, this suggests that the very last stratum of the *Analects* (books 15–20) might have been composed around the time that the ethical life was beginning to be linked to psycho-physiological factors, a theme that we find much more highly developed and systematized in the "Inner Training" and the *Mencius*.

10. This saying is repeated in 15.13.

11. Literally, people are "close" by nature and become "far away" as a result of practice—an instance of the familiar metaphor SIMILARITY IS CLOSENESS.

12. Herbert Fingarette 1972 has famously argued that the concept of interiority is entirely alien to the *Analects*, claiming that distinctions between inner virtue and outward appearance and such images as "examining oneself inwardly" (*neixing*) are merely "ad hoc metaphors" revealing nothing about Confucius's true views of the self. The findings of cognitive science should make us very leery about dismissing *any* metaphor as merely *ad hoc*, and in any case the manner in which the inner-outer container metaphor is coordinated with the self-other dichotomy in the *Analects* should make it clear that we are dealing here with a coherent conceptual structure—one that is systematically employed throughout Warring States thought in conceptualizing the self.

13. Vermillion—the color of the Zhou—being the traditional and proper color for ceremonial clothing, and purple a more "modern" and increasingly popular variant.

14. Throughout the *Analects* we see a suspicion of those who are too glib. In 1.3 Confucius declares "a glib tongue and an ingratiating manner—such people are rarely *ren*" (this saying is repeated in 17.7; cf. 5.25, 12.3), and in 15.11 the danger presented by "glib people" (*ningren* 佞人) is compared to the derangement of morals brought about by the music of Zheng. David Nivison (1999: 751) has made a very interesting observation that may explain Confucius's hatred for these "plausible men" (see also 5.5, 11.25, 16.4): in archaic Chinese, *ning* was pronounced **nieng* and is actually a graphic modification of its cognate *ren* 仁 (AC **nien*). As I shall discuss later, the original meaning of *ren* was something like "noble in form," and it would appear that *ning* was its counterpart in the verbal realm: "attractive or noble in speech." In giving *ning* a negative meaning in the *Analects*, Confucius drives a wedge between the two qualities: *ren* now becomes "true" (i.e., inner) nobleness or Virtue, whereas *ning* represents the false, external counterfeit of *ren*. This is no doubt the sentiment behind such passages as 12.3 ("The *ren* person is sparing of speech") and 13.27 ("reticence is close to *ren*"), as well as Confucius's general suspicion of language.

15. The radical (or meaning component) for *xiu* is *shan* 彡, which the *Shuowen* dictionary defines as "to draw or write with a hair-brush." Other meanings for *xiu* include "to sweep" (i.e., with a broom), and the *Shuowen* defines *xiu* itself as *shi* 飾 , "to adorn," "to brush or sweep," or "to clean" (the radical of *shi* is *jin* 巾 , meaning "canvas," "napkin," "cloth"). While it is possible to read too much into the radical chosen for a given character, it seems that the basic meaning of *xiu* is to adorn or paint a surface with a brush or to burnish or clean a surface with a cloth.

16. The importance of model emulation for Confucian self-cultivation has been noted by many scholars (see, for example, Creel 1960: 77; Munro 1969: 96–112; and Hall and Ames 1987: 97), and Herbert Fingarette has emphasized the contrast between "natural law theories" in the West—which teach "an ideal, non-personal authority in the form of moral law, or natural law, or an abstract, rational principle" (Fingarette 1981: 29)—with the Confucian ideal of "authority as model." A similar point is made by Hall and Ames, who note that the principles of action contained in ritual are not general, deontological maxims for action, but are meaningful only when embodied in specific persons in specific situations (Hall and Ames 1987: 180). For Confucius, then, the "form" of moral knowledge is to be found not in abstract principles but in the concrete institutions, cultural forms, and exemplary deeds of the ancients. Characterizing this feature of Confucian self-cultivation in terms of a stark East-West contrast is, however, a bit of an oversimplification, since the "virtue ethic" tradition in the West (represented most prominently by Aristotle) certainly makes use of role models in much the same way as the Confucian tradition, and offers up ideals that cannot be reduced to general principles but rather must be conveyed through embodiment in specific virtuous people. Scholars such as Fingarette and Hall and Ames can thus perhaps best be seen as responding to the primacy given to deon-

tological or consequentialist theories of ethics in recent Western history rather than (as they sometimes seem to imply) to some sort of essential gulf between "Western" and "Chinese" worldviews and modes of reasoning.

17. Most traditional commentators gloss *xing* as *qi* 起 (to begin, start), with the extended meaning of "give rise to." Although it is interpreted by many commentators as referring to the early stages of one's course of study (and thus taken in the sense of "to begin"), I follow Lau and Van Zoeren in taking it to mean "inspired" (taking *qi* in the sense of "giving rise to"). As Van Zoeren notes, *xing* later becomes a technical term of art in the Mao Commentary on the *Odes*, where it refers to one of the characteristic tropes of the *Odes*, and it may even have this technical meaning in *Analects* 17.9. In 8.8 however, it is best to understand *xing* in the sense in which it is used in 8.2, where the gentleman's affection for his parents is said to "inspire" (*xing*) *ren* in the common people. Refer to Van Zoeren 1991: 36–37.

18. The questioner is curious to see if, because of his special relationship to the Master, he has obtained any sort of esoteric learning not shared with the other disciples.

19. These are the first two sections of the *Book of Odes*, and are used here as a synecdoche for the *Odes* as a whole.

20. In the opinion of some scholars, the *Odes* did not actually serve as a source of normativity for Confucius, but was rather simply a linguistic resource that he used for his own purposes. Holzmann 1978 argues for this interpretation, but a more plausible and sophisticated case is made by Van Zoeren 1991. Van Zoeren admits that in what he views as the latest stratum of the *Analects* the *Odes* possesses for Confucius a certain normative value, but argues that in the "second and third strata" (chs. 1–2, 8–9 and 10–15) the words of the *Odes* were employed merely as "pretexts" in didactic situations, and were not seen as being invested with stable meanings or moral significance (see esp. 35). In holding to this interpretation, Van Zoeren is forced to overlook or give forced readings to certain passages in the second and third strata, and to discount the continuity in the Confucian tradition. To give just one example of a passage from the strata in question that cannot be accounted for by the "pretext" interpretation, in 9.27 a couplet from the *Odes* is described by Confucius as either containing a teaching (*dao* 道) that is not by itself able to make one a good person, or (depending on how it is interpreted) as expressing the Way, but which has to be actually put into practice before it will enable one to become a good person. No matter how 9.27 is interpreted, it is clear that Confucius is concerned with the meaning of the words in the ode, which he believes contains some sort of teaching. Other passages from early strata that seem to contradict the "pretext" interpretation include 3.2, 9.15, and 9.31.

21. According to P. J. Ivanhoe, *si* refers not to ratiocination or abstract, theoretical reasoning, but has the basic meaning of keeping "one's attention focused, often upon a goal or ideal which one intends to achieve." This is certainly the meaning of *si* in the now-lost ode quoted by Confucius in 9.30, where a lover is described as "thinking" of the departed object of his or her affections (for similar meanings, Ivanhoe refers the reader to 4.17, 14.12, 14.26, 16.10, and 19.1). At the same time, Ivanhoe adds, "*si* does appear to include relating such goals and ideals to one's attitudes and particular situation and hence includes a certain level of practical reasoning" and refers to the reader to 2.15, 15.31, 19.6 and perhaps 5.20 as examples of this usage. See Ivanhoe 1993:12–13. It would seem that *si* includes both what we would call concentration and practical reasoning. Benjamin Schwartz 1985 remarks that "The *Analects* . . . abounds in abstract terms and even in propositions which directly relate abstract terms to each other as well as to concrete illustrations" and thus concludes that "much of the 'extension' of the word *si* corresponds well to

298   *Effortless Action*

much of the extension of the word 'thought' in Western languages" (89). *Si* will thus be rendered as "thought" or "thinking" throughout this discussion.

22. Cf. 7.17 ("If I were given a few more years, so that by the age of fifty I could complete my studies of the Changes, this might enable me to be free of major faults") and 7.28.

23. See also 9.10 and 12.15.

24. Cf. 17.8, where the restraining force is a love of learning.

25. See also 5.7, where Zilu is criticized for not having "worked his material" (*qucai* 取材).

26. See 13.18 and 15.7 for the more specific and 12.20 and 15.25 for the more general sense of "straight." A similar and even more common metaphor is that of "rightness" (*zheng* 正), which refers to straightness in the sense of being "square."

27. Perhaps best conceived as a subschema of the basic LIFE AS JOURNEY metaphor discussed in chapter 1.

28. The first two lines appear in the present version of ode 57, while the third does not.

29. Cf. 19.14: Mourning should fully express grief and then stop at that. "

30. For music as a metaphor for self-perfection in pre-Qin thought, see Cook 1995.

31. *Nicomachean Ethics* 1127a-b.

32. The ideal of the mean also becomes a very common theme in later commentaries. In the *Lunyu Bijie*, for example, Han Yu writes, "I take the rites as representing holding to the mean. If there is a deficiency, one will 'wear oneself out' or become 'timid.' If there is an excess, then one will become 'unruly' or 'intolerant.'" Li Ao adds, "In the application of ritual, it is harmony (*he*) that is to be valued' . . . this indicates that what is meant by 'harmony' is when [the emotions] come forth and hit upon (*zhong* 中) the proper regulation" (Cheng Shude: 514–15).

33. Incidentally, the fact that specific terms representing "transgression" or the "boundaries" can vary serves as a nice illustration of the fact that we are dealing here with a conceptual structure rather than merely a fixed idiomatic expression.

34. Although Confucius often concerns himself only with the text of the *Odes*, it would seem that in this case he refers both to the lyrics and to the music that accompanied them. Zhu Xi's commentary reads in part: "[Confucius] wanted his students to savor the lyrics, to appreciate the music, and in this way gain an understanding of rectitude with regard to the emotions."

35. A. C. Graham, among others (such as Xu Fuguan, Lin Yusheng, and Arthur Waley; see Shun 1993: 476 for references) notes that in pre-Confucian texts such as the *Book of Odes*, *ren* is an adjective referring to the appearance of an aristocratic man, and thus means something like "manly" or "handsome." Graham believes that this is how *ren* should be understood in the *Analects* as well, and that it is not until Mencius that it begins to take on a more specifically moral meaning (Graham 1989: 18). Scholars operating in the neo-Confucian tradition such as Wing-tsit Chan, Tu Weiming, and Tang Junyi argue that *ren* even in pre-Confucian times referred to the kindness shown by the ruler to his subjects, and thus should be translated as something like "benevolence" (See Chan 1969: 2, and the works referenced in Shun 1993: 476). It is clear that some of the occurrences of *ren* in the *Book of Odes* have to be understood as Graham would have it: as simply the appearance of a nobleman. At the same time, it is equally clear that by the time of the *Analects* this concept has been thoroughly ethicized. The most balanced account of *ren* is presented by Benjamin Schwartz, who sees Confucius as taking the aristocratic virtue of "manliness" or "virility" and giving it a moral meaning: "true manhood" or "perfect virtue," the perfection of all of the lesser virtues (Schwartz: 75).

36. The issue of whether or not Confucius believed in the unity of the virtues in the strong sense is not entirely clear, but it would seem that he held at the very least a weaker (and more plausible) version of this doctrine. The doctrine of the unity of the virtues in its strongest sense holds that a truly virtuous person must possess all of the virtues in full and in their proper proportion, and that no virtue can exist in isolation. As Lee Yearley has argued with respect to Aquinas's doctrine of the unity of the virtues (Yearley 1990: 34–35), such belief in the strong unity of the virtues is not entirely plausible. A weaker version would hold that a particular virtuous exemplar might possess more of one virtue (say, courage) than another (say, wisdom), and could nonetheless be accounted a virtuous person, but that courage *entirely* uninformed by wisdom would be mere recklessness—a semblance of the true virtue. In this sense, a truly virtuous person would have to possess all of the virtues to some degree, but could excel in some rather than others.

While Confucius sometimes describes certain disciples as possessing some virtues but not others (5.7, 11.3, 11.18) in a guardedly approving manner, he also echoes Aristotle's opinion that a potential virtue like courage is dangerous, and merely a semblance of true courage, if it exists in isolation. This, I would argue, is the proper way to read such passages as 8.10 and 17.23 ("A gentleman who possessed courage but lacked a sense of rightness would create great disorder, while a petty person who possessed courage but lacked a sense of rightness would become a thief or robber."). In 17.24, he criticizes imbalances in the virtues, and discusses as well the issue of semblances of virtue, which for him seem to be virtue-like behavior without the guidance provided by the unifying virtue of *ren*.

37. Zang Wuzhong and Meng Gongzhuo were both respected officials in Lu, and Zhuangzi of Bian (not to be confused with the thinker Zhuangzi to be discussed in chapter 6) was an official in the state of Bian who was legendary for his courage.

38. The link between these two stages—being without doubts and understanding the Mandate of Heaven—is also suggested by the line from 9.29, "One who understands does not doubt."

39. Cheng Shude: 78.

40. This is the interpretation of Zheng Xuan and Wang Bi (Cheng Shude: 75).

41. This ideal of being free from doubt and perplexity, of course, only makes sense in contrast to some alternative state of moral doubt or indecision. The fact that an early Confucian was even capable of feeling such perplexity is disputed by Herbert Fingarette 1972, who claims—voicing an opinion which is seconded by scholars such as Chad Hansen 1975, A. C. Graham 1989, and Hall and Ames 1987—that Confucius did not have at his disposal a conception of "choice" or "decision," and that actions for him did not involve mental struggle. The Confucian practitioner "simply decides" he says (49), guiding these actions on the basis of "classification" (e.g., ritual/nonritual). Hall and Ames make a similar argument in describing Confucius as an "ontology of events" (1987: 15) rather than as a moral agent who struggles over choices and ethical options. The basis for Fingarette's argument is that the Confucian Way is a "Way without crossroads": a Confucian does not face a choice between different sets of equally viable values, but only the option of being on the Way or off it. The implication is that without the possibility of choosing between equally viable alternatives, there is no such thing as "choice" or "freedom of the will." It seems to me that Fingarette and Hall and Ames have confused the issue by making the sort of "existential choice" purportedly faced by postmodern Westerners the paradigm of choice in general, and that they make the state of anxiety characteristic of an age without foundations the model of what it means to have "freedom of will." As Benjamin Schwartz 1985 and Teemu Ruskola 1992 have argued quite cogently, self-doubt, perplexity, deliberation, and inner struggle are entirely possible in situations where the

only problem is choosing a means to a known end; indeed, this is the situation in which most (if not all) traditional religious and ethical thinkers have found themselves. As Schwartz notes of the Jewish tradition, "the question of 'moral choice' does not involve choosing among 'value systems' or creating one's own values. It means *choosing between the known good and evil*. . . . This is in no way different from Confucius's choice between following the Way and straying from it" (79).

42. It would seem that a similar point is made in 6.2, where a certain ruler is described as trying so hard to embody the virtue of simplicity that he "takes simplicity too far."

43. Cf. 7.37 and 7.38.

44. 7.14; "I never imagined that music could be so sublime" was his only comment.7.14; "I never imagined that music could be so sublime" was his only comment.

45. In modern Mandarin, pronounced *le* for "joy" and *yue* for "music"; Karlgren's reconstructed ancient pronunciations are **lak* and **ngâk*, respectively.

46. I.e., the Confucian Way.

47. This is an elaborated version of 5.26.

48. According to traditional commentators, the Yi River was near Confucius's home, and the Rain Altar was located just above the river.

49. As D. C. Lau notes, this is in contrast to the man who "pretends to have it when he has in fact lost it, pretends to be full when he is in fact empty" (7.26).

50. Traditionally identified as Yan Hui.

51. Cf. 15.37; "The gentleman is true and correct, but is not rigid when it comes to fulfilling the details of his promises." Both Kwong-loi Shun (Shun 1993: 474) and Benjamin Schwartz (Schwartz 1985: 79) describe the role of *yi* as a standard for a judgment of "rightness" that counterbalances the demands of the rites.

52. We should note that the change Confucius accedes to is a rather minor one, and that he does not actually propose changing the rite, but simply goes along with the popular practice (with possibly a hint of reluctance).

53. It is significant that Confucius's response ("Zigong! That is something quite beyond you") indicates that shu is a virtuous state which is difficult to obtain and presently beyond Zigong's grasp.

54. See Nivison 1996: 59–76, "Golden Rule Arguments in Chinese Moral Philosophy," and Ivanhoe 1990 for the details of these positions. Ivanhoe's article also includes a review of previous interpretations by Feng Yulan, D. C. Lau, and Herbert Fingarette.

55. It is important to see that *shu* represents a virtuous *disposition*, not a *rule*. Arguing against interpretations that have presented *shu* as the Chinese version of the Golden Rule, Nivison notes that "it is not really a "rule" at all, but a maxim to guide one in shaping and cultivating a character of ideal human kindliness in oneself. That is, it describes a virtue in persons rather than a quality of correctness in *acts*" (1996: 75).

56. Personal communication.

57. For instance, Ivanhoe 1990 notes that in 5.18 the disciple Zigong asks about a certain prime minister, whom Confucius then pronounces to be *zhong* but not *ren*. "What was missing?" Ivanhoe asks. "It was the other strand of Confucius's 'one thread'—the moral sensitivity of *shu*." The put-down of the prime minister is no doubt also a message intended by Confucius for Zigong himself, who seems to be the disciple designated throughout the *Analects* to illustrate the shortcomings of *zhong* uninformed by *shu*: his fastidious adherence to the rites leads Confucius to dub him a "sacrificial vessel" of limited capacity (5.3); in 14.31 he is criticized by Confucius for being too strict with others (i.e., for not moderating his *zhong*-demands upon others with *shu*); and, of course, in 5.11 his claim to be *shu* is sharply dismissed by the Master.

58. D. C. Lau's translation.

59. Chinese commentators throughout history have been puzzled as to *why* exactly the pheasant should be praised by Confucius as being timely (even the resourceful Zhu Xi admits to being stumped, and suggests that some explanatory text has been lost), but for our purposes it is sufficient to note that "timeliness" is being praised.

60. The most prominent example in the West is Roger Ames's *The Art of Rulership* (Ames 1994). See also Duyvendak 1947, Jia Dongcheng 1989, Li Shenglong 1986, 1987b, Pang Pu 1994, Yang Darong 1994, Zhao Jihui 1986, and Zhou Daoji 1968.

61. Barbarians outside of the Chinese cultural sphere—and therefore lacking the proper ritual practices—are described as living a somewhat less than human life, although they too have the potential to become "true people" if properly educated (see *Analects* 3.5 and 13.19). Although Confucius shared the patriarchal orientation of his day, and apparently never considered the idea that women could become sages, stories from the later Confucian tradition (e.g., the *Lienü Zhuan* or "Biographies of Exemplary Women") make it clear that women have the capacity to reason in the same moral terms as men, and they are often portrayed as upbraiding their husbands or sons for ritually incorrect or morally questionable behavior. Nonetheless, it is clear that the term *ren* 人 ("person") refers almost exclusively to men in most Confucian writings up to the present day. See Raphals 1998 for a discussion of the place of women in traditional Confucianism.

62. As one of the Cheng brothers notes, "If we were to take this to mean that the sage does not allow the people to understand, then this would be something like the kind of 'four in the morning, three in the afternoon' technique advocated in later generations. How could this adequately describe the mind of the sage?" (Cheng Shude: 532). "Four in the morning, three in the afternoon" is, of course, a reference to the technique employed by the monkey-keeper in chapter 2 of the *Zhuangzi*, which has been perceived by some as being rather cynical.

63. As Zhang Ping (a Jin commentator) explains, "It means that the most appropriate way of governing is through Virtue, which the people will simply follow" (Cheng Shude: 432).

64. Cf. 3.11 (cited earlier), where Confucius claims that someone who has mastered the *di* 禘 sacrifice could manage the world as if he had it in the palm of his hand.

65. See also *Analects* 2.20 and *Mencius* 3:A:4.

66. That is, let everyone concentrate on fulfilling their role-specific duties and order will result naturally—there is no need for some special technique or theory of "governing." Cf. 13.3.

67. It is important to make this point clear, because when we read of the charismatic power of Virtue, perhaps the first image that comes to mind is that of a charismatic figure in the Weberian sense, drawing flocks of people to his or her person and leading them off to forge a revolutionary new path. This is not the Confucian conception. The Virtue of the Confucian gentleman draws people into an ordered system within which he himself has a proper and predetermined place. This is the theme of 12.11 cited earlier, as well as the "correction of names" (*zhengming* 正名) passage (13.3), where properly ordered names create a bounded space within which the people are allowed to move.

68. In 2.3, Confucius notes that if you try to keep the people in order by means of laws it may keep them out of trouble temporarily, but they will have no sense of shame. The only way to get the people to truly *reform* themselves is to "guide them with Virtue." Similarly, in 12.18 Confucius's advice to a ruler worried about the prevalence of thieves in his state is not to pass harsher laws, but to look to his own conduct. "If you could just get rid of your own excessive desires," he rather sharply remarks, "the people would not steal even if you rewarded them for it."

69. See 15.1, where in response to a ruler who asks him about military formations Confucius replies, "I have heard something about the use of ceremonial stands and dishes for ritual offerings, but I have never learned about the use of battalions and divisions." He departed on the next day, presumably out of distaste for the ruler.

70. The idea is that the influence of Yao's Virtue was so subtle and pervasive that the people were transformed naturally, without being aware of what was happening. Compare this to Heaven's manner of ruling "without the need for words," as described in 17.19, and to the *Laozi*, chapter 17.

71. 12.17: "To govern [*zheng* 政] is to be correct [*zheng* 正]. If you set an example by being correct, who would dare to remain incorrect?" It should be noted that this advice is given to the same misguided ruler, Ji Kangzi, who is so worried about thieves in 12.18 and who proposes enforcing the Way through capital punishment in 12.19.

72. The reference is to Confucius's lack of an official position.

73. Kupperman 1968: 177. Scott Cook 1995 makes a similar point when he notes that, with regard to musical perfection in the Confucian scheme, there is "a fundamental paradox between the hardship and incessant discipline of constrained practice leading up to it and the spontaneous freedom of performance or the perfect embodiment of artistry marked by its complete attainment" (131).

74. Plato, *Meno* 80d ff. This link between the paradox of wu-wei and the so-called Meno problem will be discussed in more detail in the conclusion.

75. Seeing this passage in terms of the *zhi-wen* dichotomy goes back at least as far as the Jin dynasty and Fan Ning's commentary (Zhu Xi: 18).

76. As Yang Liang comments, "The ability to hit the bullseye is something that a person can learn, whereas strength is not something that one can achieve through effort" (Zhu Xi: 17).

77. And, in the case of Xunzi, against "heretical" Confucians such as Mencius.

So-of-Itself: Wu-wei in the *Laozi*

1. The translation here will follow the silk manuscript versions of the Laozi, which were discovered in a tomb at Mawangdui in 1973. One of these texts has been dated to 194–188 B.C. and the other to 195 B.C., making them the oldest complete versions of the text. When appropriate, the Mawangdui versions will be supplemented with text from the even older Guodian bamboo strips (ca. 300 B.C.) that were discovered in 1993. For a discussion of textual issues surrounding the *Laozi*, refer to appendix 3.

For ease of reference, the chapter numbering and organization of the received Wang Bi version will be used, as this format is more or less standard in discussions of the *Laozi*. It should be noted, though, that the traditional ordering of the "Dao" and "De" sections is reversed in the silk manuscripts (chapter 1 in these manuscripts is thus chapter 38 in the received version), while the "Dao"/"De" division is not present at all in the Guodian bamboo fragments.

2. As mentioned earlier, for the sake of convenience I will be referring to "Laozi," "Zhuangzi," etc. as a convenient shorthand for the author(s) of the texts that bear these names.

3. Consider also the contrast with the portrayal of the self in *Analects* 3.8 as "the unadorned (*su*) upon which to paint."

4.   The word *wei* 為 pronounced in a rising tone can mean either (a) "to do" (full verb) or (b) "to be" (copula); pronounced in a falling tone, it means (c) "for the sake of." When used in sense (b) in conjunction with the particle *yi* 以 ("to take, use"), it means (d) "to take [something] to be [something else]" or (less literally) "to regard [something] as [something]." The fact that Laozi, by celebrating "wu-wei," is often targeting sense (b/d) as well as sense (a) has been obscured in the received text of the *Laozi*. For instance, the famous phrase *wuwei er wu buwei* 無為而無不為 ("do nothing and nothing will be left undone") appears nowhere in the Mawangdui texts, and in chapters 38 and 48 of all three archeological versions (Mawangdui A and B and Guodian) it is replaced by the phrase, *wuwei er wu yiwei* 無為而無以為 (lit. "do nothing and do not have anything that you regard [as something]," rendered in my translation as "not acting (wu-wei) and not holding anything in regard." The Chinese will be provided in translations in order to indicate when *wei* in sense (b/d) is coming under attack from Laozi, although *wei* (b/d) will of necessity be translated differently in different contexts.

5.   Because of its rather sympathetic treatment of Laozi's thought and its emphasis on self-cultivation (which is something pointedly rejected in most of the other chapters in the *Hanfeizi*), some scholars doubt that the "Jielao" chapter was actually written by Hanfeizi himself.

6.   Guodian version: "having excessive desires."

7.   The "Explicating the *Laozi*" author—who is one of the more perceptive commentators on the text—certainly has something like this in mind when he links the greed of the ruling class to the "embellishment of knowledge" in the comment cited earlier.

8.   Cf. the account in *Laozi*, chapter 32 of the creation of names.

9.   In order to convey the element of self-conscious action, it would seem that in the *Laozi* it is best to render *ren* in its later sense of "benevolence" rather than in the sense of "true humanness" that it has in the *Analects*.

10.   Reading 安 as 焉.

11.   See, for instance, Liu Xiaogan 1999.

12.   Jia is following the Wang Bi text, which reads 以其智多 rather than 以其智也.

13.   It is interesting that the Guodian version of chapter 19 does not employ specifically Confucian references, the "three teachings" criticized being knowledge and disputation (*bian* 辯), cleverness and profit, and artifice and reflection.

14.   Guodian: "preserve" or "guard" (*bao* 保).

15.   As is the case with Confucius's soteriological vision, it is not entirely clear whether or not the potential catalyst of universal salvation being addressed must *already* be a ruler. It is certain that the transformation of the world through the suasive influence of Virtue is to be effected by a ruler, but it is conceivable that the potential audience for this message includes people who are not already in a position of power, since the personal Virtue which they would acquire through following the text's advice would presumably allow them to *become* a ruler if they were not one already. In any case, it is clear that the "sage" whom this text is designed to produce is a ruler of people, and not merely a private individual seeking personal salvation (this issue will be discussed in further detail later). It is also important to note, along with Roger Ames, that in the Laozian worldview, "as in Confucian political theory, the ruler and his position in society are taken as natural conditions" (Ames 1994: 41). That is, a monarchical/feudal political structure is not considered a human artifact but is seen as part of the natural structure of the universe.

16.   See appendix 3 for a discussion of this rendering.

17.   Certain commentators have expended a great deal of effort trying to establish the metaphysical identities of the "one," the "two," and the "three" mentioned here, arguing that, for instance, they correspond to "Heaven," "Earth," and "Humans" or to the

"Supreme Ultimate," "Heaven and Earth," and "the Harmonious *qi* of Heaven and Earth." I thoroughly agree with Jiang Xichang that the progression from one to two to three is intended merely as a poetic metaphor describing a process of gradual increase, and that to attempt to identify these numbers with specific metaphysical concepts amounts to forced overinterpretation. See Jiang's comment in Gao Ming: 30.

18. These terms were customarily used by rulers as polite first-person pronouns, something like "I, this humble orphan," etc.

19. In chapter 32, we read that "the Way is enduringly nameless"; and in chapter 25 we read of a "thing, confusedly formed" that lacks a name, and that is therefore styled "the Way."

20. See appendix 3 for a discussion of this rendering.

21. See, for example, Ren Jiyu (cited in Gao Ming: 29) and Liu Xuezhi 1986: 70–71.

22. Feng Yulan 1952: 178. Feng's use of the *ti/yong* 體用 ("essence/function") distinction to interpret chapter 1 can be traced to Wang Bi.

23. For details on this vessel, see D. C. Lau 1968. This is presumably the same vessel that is referred to by the metaphor of the "goblet words" (*zhiyan* 卮言) in chapter 27 of the *Zhuangzi* (see Wu Guangming 1988 and Watson 1968: 303, n. 1).

24. In which case it will overturn itself as soon as it is released.

25. Guodian: "Within it he finds that which he is able to diligently put into practice."

26. Munro 1969: 141. Kanaya Osamu has described Laozian wu-wei as the culmination of a process of cultivating the Way (Kanaya 1964: 2–3), and Roger Ames makes a similar point in noting that "the project of human consummation as conceived of by the Daoists is for people to emulate the natural Dao as a means of achieving integration and ultimate identity with the constant Dao" (Ames 1994: 39). The intimate relationship between the Way and wu-wei in Laozi's thought is also noted by Li Shenglong, who claims that "the basic content of the Way is 'wu-wei'" (Li 1987: 18).

27. Some scholars have distinguished even more finely than this. Roger Ames lists a total of eight qualities possessed by the Way that the sage ruler is to emulate: 1) wu-wei; 2) sparing of speech; 3) tenuous (*xu* 虛) or still (*jing* 靜); 4) soft and weak; 5) non-contentious; 6) taking the lower position; 7) naturally genuine; 8) non-appropriating (Ames 1994: 39ff). Donald Munro, who also notes the role that emulation of the Way plays in Laozi's scheme, lists the qualities to be emulated as two: 1) wu-wei and 2) tenuousness ("emptiness") or "Non-Being." In addition, he remarks that it is difficult to separate these two qualities: "Actually, the two attributes of the Way (emptiness and wu-wei) are interrelated . . . 'emptiness' (the absence of evaluations made by an evaluating mind) is a necessary condition for wu-wei (the absence of end-directed conduct)" (Munro 1969: 142). I agree with Munro that the qualities of the Way can be essentially reduced to two interrelated attributes, although I think that "non-evaluating" quality is expressed most basically by the term *wuyiwei*, which is (as we have seen) in several places coupled with wu-wei in the phrase 無為而無以為. This clear pairing of two attributes is, of course, obscured in the received Wang Bi version (the only version to which Munro had access in 1969).

28. The description of these two aspects as "behavioral" and "cognitive" is derived from Alan Fox 1995.

29. The term *de* is here literally to be understood in its more original sense of the "kindness" or benefit done for another than in the sense of "charismatic power," although Laozi is most likely playing with both senses of the word in order to highlight his conception of Virtue-power. By calling upon the sage to repay injury with (kindness)-*de* / (power)-*de*, Laozi is emphasizing the therapeutic ability of Virtue to disarm and subtly win over those acting in a manner contrary to the Way.

30. It should be kept in mind that Confucianism as portrayed in the *Laozi* is something of a caricature. For instance, a true Confucian gentleman would not "demand" recognition for his kindness or contributions. As we have seen in chapter 2, virtuous action in Confucius's view is only truly virtuous when done for its own sake. Of course it is expected that honor and recognition will follow, but in the same sort of non-coerced, wu-wei fashion that the Way (in Laozi's view) is honored and recognized. One might say that the target of Laozi's criticism resembles more the "village worthy" condemned by Confucius than the Confucian gentleman himself. I will continue to refer to the way of being that Laozi criticizes as "Confucianism," however, because I believe that one of Laozi's implicit beliefs is that "true" Confucianism is not in fact possible: because it is based upon "doing" and "regarding," the Confucian Way can never lead to wu-wei perfection, but will inevitably degenerate into the sort of hypocrisy represented by the village worthy.

31. Both very festive occasions, the *tailao* being the most elaborate kind of feast.

32. Cf. Feng Yulan's description of *ming* 明 as an understanding of the general, invariable (*chang* 常) laws of the universe, the greatest of which is reversion (Feng 1952: 181–82).

33. Maspero 1971: 201–22. For a discussion of traditional Chinese "technical" or "inner alchemical" readings of the text, see Robinet 1984. The most prominent contemporary proponent of this view is Harold Roth (see Roth 1991a, 1999a and b).

34. Heshang Gong was traditionally said to have lived during the time of Emperor Wen (179–156 B.C.), but there are no stories concerning his existence from before the 3rd c. A.D., and recent scholarly opinion is that the commentary as it has come down to us goes back to only the 5th c. A.D. See Kohn 1992: 62–69 for a brief introduction to the Heshang Gong commentary and the problems of dating it, and Alan Chan 1991 and 1998 for a more extended account of the commentary and additional references on the subject.

35. For Heshang Gong's commentary on this passage, see Gao Ming: 264.

36. This is somewhat obscured by the fact that the Wang Bi version reads 無為 in place of 毋以知 in the last line.

37. See, for example, Feng Yulan 1952: 180ff; Alan Fox 1995: 8; and Benjamin Schwartz 1986: 193.

38. Munro 1969: 158. The issue of physical practice will be returned to later.

39. As Gao Ming puts it, "The infant is pure, genuine and free of desires, and in this way represents the root-origin of human beings, while the unhewn, uncarved wood represents the root-origin of wood" (Gao Ming: 375).

40. Cf. chapter 61, where the female's lower position in sexual intercourse allows her to "win out" over the male.

41. Following the Wang Bi version here in reading: 不遠徙.

42. As Roger Ames observes, "Contrary to the *Analects*, the *Laozi* literature idealizes antiquity not because of its culture but rather because of the lack of it" (Ames 1994: 8).

43. Cf. chapter 45. Both Mawangdui versions, some stone versions of the text, and many extant versions read *zizheng* 自正 here, while the Guodian, Wang Bi, and many other extant versions read *ziding* (Gao Ming: 427–28). *Ding* 定 and *zheng* 正 have similar meanings, and are etymologically related, graphically quite similar, and easily confused by scribes. I have gone with *ding* because it better fits with the sense of stillness.

44. In other words, the wheel itself is made up primarily of what is "not there"—the space between the spokes.

45. Cf. *Mencius* 1:A:7 for this rendering.

46. Version A of the Mawangdui texts reverses this phrase: "My teaching have a ruler / My actions have an ancestor."

47. In the context of the controversy concerning the relative dating of the *Laozi* vis-à-vis texts such as the "Inner Training," it is revealing that the *Laozi* employs no consistent metaphorical model for Virtue. As we shall see, in the "Inner Training" and the texts that follow it, Virtue is quite consistently conceptualized as a liquid substance (related to the *qi*) and understood in terms of water metaphors. This would suggest that the text of the *Laozi* was assembled before the psycho-physiological theories that inform the "Inner Training," *Mencius*, and *Zhuangzi* were widely known and accepted.

48. Several scholars have noted this relationship between wu-wei as a negative praxis and naturalness as a positive force. Liu Xiaogan, for instance, distinguishes between the two terms by noting that wu-wei is a negative term that places restrictions upon human activity, whereas naturalness is a positive term used to describe the progression of a state of affairs (Liu 1999: 211), and this idea of negative restrictions upon ordinary human perception and activity unleashing the positive forces of nature (both internal and external) is also expressed by Jia Dongcheng, who notes that it is only by "shutting off the senses, gazing upon the mysterious in silent contemplation—devoid of selfishness and free of desires—that simple and pure human nature can be naturally brought into harmony with the original substance of the myriad things. It is only once this state has been reached that one can grasp the root of affairs and events and attain the ideal spiritual state" (Jia 1989: 91).

49. It is also hinted at by the admonition in chapter 7 to "put the self on the outside."

50. Note the metaphoric conceptualization of Virtue as a liquid. As we will see later, this is a standard convention in post–"Inner Training" writings that is not regularly observed in the text of the *Laozi* itself.

51. See also Zhang Qin 1995: 61 and Donald Munro 1969: 141.

52. Cf. chapter 57 (quoted earlier) and chapter 65.

53. Reprinted in Creel 1970: 1–24.

54. As I also noted in the introduction, Creel believes that the concept of wu-wei itself originated with Shen Buhai, and that the *Laozi* merely represents a later development of this essentially Legalist doctrine.

55. See Feng Yulan 1953: 175; Waley 1945: 92; Duyvendak 1947 and 1954: 12; Kanaya Osamu 1964; and LaFargue 1994.

56. Li Shenglong believes that the "objectivist" flavor of Laozian wu-wei is what made it attractive to the Legalists, whereas the more "subjectivist" versions of wu-wei found in the Confucians or in Zhuangzi made these thinkers less attractive (Li 1987b).

57. See Zhao Jihui's opinion that the thought of Laozi is in no way as systematic as that of Huang-Lao or Legalist thought, and is in fact essentially opposed to this sort of systematization (Zhao Jihui 1986: 64).

58. Refer to the introduction for a brief explanation of the term "religious" as used here.

59. That is, the problem of explaining the existence of evil in a supposedly good cosmic order. See Harvey 1964: 236–39 for a discussion of the theodicy problem and attempted solutions in the Judeo-Christian tradition.

60. Consider, e.g., chapter 29, where both terms are condemned.

61. See especially Graham 1983 and 1985.

62. See appendix 3 for a discussion of this rendering.

63. Harold Roth has long argued that the meditative techniques described in the *Guanzi*—particularly in the "Inward Training" chapter—represent the earliest stage of what has come to be viewed as the "Daoist" school, and that at least "Inward Training" is both chronologically and developmentally prior to both the *Laozi* and *Zhuangzi* (see Roth 1999 for the most recent statement of this position). For reasons hinted at earlier and are

discussed in more detail in chapter 4 and appendix 3, I continue to feel that the traditional placement of the *Laozi* as the earliest "Daoist" text remains the most reasonable.

64. See Roth 1999, Harper 1998, and Li Ling 1993.

New Technologies of the Self: Wu-wei in the "Inner Training" and the Mohist Rejection of Wu-wei

1. As noted by many commentators, this is almost certainly a distortion of Yang Zhu's position, which was that it was not worth harming a hair on one's head in order to *possess* the world—i.e., that one should put one's personal safety above attaining any kind of official post.

2. The classic discussion of the background to Mencius's conception of human nature is to be found in Graham 1967.

3. With whom, it should be noted, Mencius also had several audiences.

4. See Graham 1989: 54–55.

5. This is not the place for a detailed discussion of Emerson's thesis, but I find his position that the Chinese prior to Yang Zhu had no conception of the physical "person"—understanding the self as being disembodied, "made up of parts shared by others"—somewhat bizarre. Although the early Chinese certainly did not have developed theories of the physical self or "personhood," I will only note that I strongly concur with Bernard Williams's observation that "the absence of a theory is not a theory of absence" (Williams 1993: 27). Williams's criticism of the classical scholar Bruno Snell—who argues that Homeric Greeks had no grasp of their bodies as units—might serve as a model for those concerned with the occasional interpretative excesses of sinologists such as Emerson or Herbert Fingarette (whose argument concerning the lack of interiority in the *Analects* I discussed briefly in chapter 2). See Williams 1993: 21ff.

6. Xu Fuguan 1969 and Benjamin Schwartz have noted that "the history of an idea may be more than the history of the term with which the idea ultimately comes to be identified" (Schwartz 1985:176)—which is, of course, an observation that informs our present study of wu-wei—and argue that Mencian-like views of human nature can be traced back as early as the *Book of Odes* (see especially Xu Fuguan 1969, chapter 1). I have similarly argued that we can see implicit but nonetheless fairly clear pictures of human nature operating in the thought of both Confucius and Laozi, and the same can be said of Mozi as well. Indeed, arguably *any* religious thinker is inevitably operating on the basis of some at least implicit picture of human nature. On the other hand, it is hard to deny that having a word for an idea not only forces one to sharpen the outlines of that idea but also gives it a prominence it would not otherwise enjoy. Technical terms serve to clarify thought and sharpen and focus debate. Yang Zhu's contribution to Chinese thought was to force thinkers hoping to defend their religious ideals to bring to the forefront and explicitly formulate the conception of human nature that formerly merely lurked in the background, and to defend these formulations against others.

7. Harper 1998: 125; for the Chinese text, refer to Li Ling 1993: 322.

8. See Thiel 1968, 1969; Graham 1989: 100ff; Schipper 1993, esp. p. 6; Robinet 1997: 35ff; and Paper 1995, chapters 3–5, but esp. pp. 132–40 (tracing shamanistic roots of Zhuangzian "transformation").

9.   For instance, the occupant of the tomb from which the Mawangdui medical manuscripts were recovered was not a physician, but had a lay interest in medicine, astrology, and philosophy (Harper 1998: 8).

10.   We will also find most of its elements—the focus on the *qi*, the new sophisticated conception of the *xin* as locus of self-cultivation, and an unambiguously physiological approach—glaringly absent from both the *Analects* and the *Laozi*, which supports the traditional placement of these texts as earlier than the *Mencius*, *Zhuangzi*, and *Xunzi*. See appendices 2 and 3 for more details.

11.   As established by Roth 1999. All references to the "Inner Training" will be keyed to Roth's text.

12.   A trend of course also marked in the very titles of the "Techniques of the Heart/ Mind" chapters of the *Guanzi*.

13.   As Roth notes, this idea of a "heart/mind within the heart/mind" indicates a strong tendency toward internalism in the "Inner Training" (151–52).

14.   Many scholars have noted this and other links between the Mencius and "Inner Training." For instance, the phrase in "Inner Training," "Concentrate the *qi* like a spirit / And the myriad things will be completely preserved" strongly echoes the phrase in *Mencius* 7:A:4, "The myriad things are all complete in me." For other discussions of the links between the *Mencius* and "Inner Training," see Jeffrey Riegel 1980; Graham 1989: 105; Yang Rur-bin 1990, 1993; Scott Cook 1995: 299–301; and Kwong-loi Shun 1997: 121. Riegel suggests that by the time of Mencius it had become a common philosophical practice to rely upon "Inner Training" language when discussing the *qi*.

15.   Roth takes *ren* in its medical sense of "sensitive," citing Ma Feibai and the *Huangdi Neijing Suowen* for support (Roth 1999: 227, n. 112). This seems most likely, although—considering the presence of other Confucian references in the text (e.g., 89)— the Confucian sense cannot be ruled out.

16.   It is not clear whether or not Mozi believed *all* persons had the capacity to adopt proper beliefs in this way. In some passages he implies that only certain exceptional individuals possess this capacity, and that the mass of common people must then be compelled to proper action by use of laws and punishments.

17.   Lit. "using this, go a bit further with our explanation".

18.   Throughout this passage Mozi is invoking a common metaphor schema, ARGUMENT AS JOURNEY: we can "go along" (*wang*) with an argument, note where we are at some given point along the way (*dangci*), and finally "arrive at" (*zhi*) a conclusion.

Cultivating the Sprouts: Wu-wei in the *Mencius*

1.   The text of the Mencius, although often traditionally said to be the work of Mencius himself, was almost certainly compiled by his disciples or disciples of disciples, and in its extant form was edited and shortened in the 2nd c. A.D. by Zhao Qi, who also wrote the first commentary to the text. Although several minor textual corruptions have been noted, there are remarkably few textual controversies concerning the Mencius. It is (especially when compared to other extant pre-Qin texts) an intact and rather well-organized textual account of the teachings of Mencius.

2.   We saw the "root" metaphor in the *Analects*, but Mencius is quite revolutionary in connecting this metaphor with a whole system of metaphors for moral cultivation having to do with plants and agricultural cultivation.

3.   3:B:9. In this context, we can understand the two abilities that Mencius lays claim to in 2:A:2—understanding doctrines and being good as cultivating the floodlike *qi*—as complementary: understanding doctrines serving as a more negative technique to defeat heresies and "unblock the path of morality" (3:B:9) and cultivating the floodlike *qi* as the positive process of becoming a true gentleman.

4.   That is, whether or not these material desires and inclinations find satisfaction is a matter of fate.

5.   Cf. 6:A:3 on the contrast between senses (a) and (b).

6.   For a discussion of *gu* in this sense, see Graham 1989: 124–25.

7.   Gaozi's philosophical affiliation has been the subject of some debate, a very detailed summary of which is to be found in Shun 1997: 119–26. Several scholars have noted that another Gaozi is mentioned several times in the Mozi, and on the basis of this many have concluded that the Gaozi who appears in the *Mencius* should be identified as a Mohist. As Shun points out, however, not only is it not at all clear that the Gaozi who appears in the Mencius is the same person who appears in the Mozi, it is also not at all certain that the Gaozi in the Mozi is himself a Mohist. After reviewing the claims of various scholars, Shun concludes that it is impossible to establish without doubt the affiliation or identity of the Gaozi who appears in the *Mencius*. This granted, I think there are some significant similarities between the views of the Gaozi of the *Mencius* and a certain Yi Zhi who appears in 3:A:5, and who is there explicitly identified as a Mohist. My argument for a parallel between passages such as 6:A:4 and 3:A:5 will be presented later; for now it suffices to note that I view Gaozi and Yi Zhi as sharing certain views that I will refer to as "neo-Mohist" to distinguish them from classical Mohism.

8.   In a note, Shun credits this observation to Irene Bloom.

9.   As Kwong-loi Shun explains, "For Mencius, *keyi* 可以 in the ethical context . . . involves not just a mere capacity but emotional dispositions in the appropriate direction" (Shun 1997: 219). This is an important distinction, because the difference between people having an active tendency toward good and having merely an empty capacity marks the most important difference between the thought of Mencius and Xunzi. Shun (216ff) notes in this context that Mencius uses the two Chinese terms for "to be able to," *keyi* and *neng* 能, in a more or less interchangeable fashion, and in Xunzi's opinion this is one of the main sources of error in Mencius's thought. For Xunzi, *keyi* refers only to an empty capacity for action, whereas *neng* adds to this capacity the proper emotional dispositions. It is only by conflating these two terms, Xunzi argues in chapter 23 ("Human Nature is Bad"), that Mencius comes to the erroneous conclusion that human nature is good. This critique of Mencius will be discussed further in chapter 6.

10.   Compare 6:A:8 with, for instance, 1:A:3, where King Hui of Liang is urged to do more to provide for his people, with one of the measures being mentioned to "allow the woodcutters to enter the mountain forests only during the proper season, so that the timber [*caimu* 材木] will not be entirely used up." This reading of the Ox Mountain story is confirmed by traditional commentaries. For instance, Zhao Qi's "passage summary" (*zhangzhi* 章指) for 6:A:8 reads, "Unifying the mind and holding fast to rectitude, and causing evil to not interfere—like stopping the woodcutters from cutting down trees on Ox Mountain—will cause the mountain to have luxuriant growth and the people to exalt benevolence" (Jiao Xun 1996: 778). Similarly, Jiao Xun sees the message of 6:A:8 to be that the sage needs to "establish teachings" (*shejiao* 設教) in order to protect and encourage the moral tendencies of the people (778).

11.   At least within the context of traditional Chinese medicine.

12.   See, for instance, 1:A:6, 2:A:6, and 4:B:18.

13. In my discussion of the *Analects*, I noted that—although he occasionally uses *ren* 仁 in the sense of "benevolence" or affective concern for the well-being of another—Confucius more commonly uses it as a general term for overall human moral excellence ("true humanness"). The practice in the *Mencius* is somewhat different. Here, *ren* is used almost exclusively in the sense of the specific virtue of "benevolence" (Shun 1997: 49 cites 7:B:16 as an exception), while it is *yi* that is often appropriated to stand for morality in general.

14. As will be discussed, Mencius uses the term *xin* to refer to both the organ (the heart/mind) and the moral feelings that arise from the heart/mind. I will translate this latter sense as "heart," mainly for stylistic reasons ("the four heart/minds" sounds a bit awkward), but the reader should keep in mind that this distinction is not made in the original Chinese.

15. The relationship of the four hearts to their corresponding virtues is formulated here in terms of the A B 也 pattern, which could signify identity (A is B), an undefined relationship (A pertains to B), or class membership (A is part of B or the class of Bs). As the relationship will be clarified later, I will follow Lau in leaving it undefined here.

16. See Porkert 1974 regarding the claim that Chinese "organs" such as the *xin* were understood more as "orbs" of energy than actual physical organs in the Western sense. Seeing the *xin* as a kind of "orb of energy" could help us understand why Mencius could use the term in such a flexible fashion: as a specific term referring to either the seat of conscious agency (that is, the commander of the *qi*) or the four hearts, or as a general term referring to our hearts in general (as in the term, "good heart" *liangxin* in 6:A:8 or "benevolence is the heart of man" in 6:A:11).

17. Refer to David Wong 1991. Wong claims, however, that such feelings provide one with justifying reasons for action, but this seems too strong (for cogent criticisms of this claim, the reader is referred to Ihara 1991 and Van Norden 1991). The motivational force imparted by the "hearts" is affective, not rational; to claim otherwise would, I think, involve attributing a "two root" model of moral action to Mencius (the subject of "one root" versus "two root" models of morality will be discussed later).

18. Shun 1997: 71. See also D. C. Lau 1953: 548.

19. The former are valuable species of trees, whereas the latter is a noxious weed that—if allowed to grow unchecked—would form an impenetrable thicket and choke out the trees.

20. I.e., focusing so much attention on the finger that he fails to notice that the disease has spread to the main body.

21. Cf. the similar agricultural analogy in 6:A:13.

22. That is, it was to be sacrificed and its blood used in a ceremony to consecrate the new bell.

23. Lit. "What (or which) heart/feeling (*xin*) was this really [that motivated my action]?"

24. This adoption of the term *shu* may be a conscious or unconscious response to the popularity of "practitioners of techniques" (*fangshu* 方術) at the courts that Mencius frequented.

25. Incidentally, this belief no doubt contributed to the low social status accorded butchers in Chinese society: being constantly exposed to their cries and seeing them die, one might argue that the butcher is gradually desensitized to his "heart of compassion," and it would thus be very difficult for such a one to become a sage. In light of this, it is tempting to see the story of Butcher Ding in chapter 3 of the Zhuangzi as at least in part a satire of this passage in the *Mencius*.

26. P. J. Ivanhoe has noted that Mencius's claims about human nature are generic claims—that is, they are claims about normal, healthy representatives of the group X in a "natural" environment (see Ivanhoe 1993a). Therefore, the existence of "bestial" human beings or "inhuman" behavior does not invalidate Mencius's claims any more than the existence of people with missing limbs invalidates the claim that people have four limbs— the fact that some people are born with birth defects or lose their legs in battle does not change the fact that it is "normal" for people to have four limbs. The MORAL FEELING AS LIMB metaphor informs the metaphor I will discuss of being "robbed" or "injured" (*zei*), which is why D. C. Lau translates *zei* as "crippled."

27. A hundred *jun* is approximately equal to seven hundred kilograms.

28. As Zhu Xi explains:

When it comes to human beings' relationships to other humans, they are all of the same ilk and thus drawn emotionally to one another. Therefore the arising of the heart of compassion is more urgent when it comes to [the suffering of] the common people, and less urgent when it comes to [the suffering of] animals. Extending this to the method of benevolence, we would expect that being benevolent toward the common people would be easy, whereas caring for animal*μ*s would be difficult. Now as for the king, his heart of compassion is able to extend all the way to the animals. This means that, when it comes to protecting the people and being a true king, it is not that he is not able, but rather that he is simply unwilling to do it. (Zhu Xi 1987, Mencius commentary, p. 10)

29. This aspect of Mencius's voluntarism will be considered later, with particular reference to King Xuan of Qi.

30. As I noted in chapter 4, the use of "extension" as a technical term originated with the Mohists. The difference between Mencian and Mohist extension will be discussed later.

31. The other locution employed in the passage above, to "reach" (*ji*), is more ambiguous, but in the latter portion of the passage it seems to be used in the causative sense ("to cause to reach from A to B"), in which case it also has the sense of forced movement.

32. Ivanhoe (n.d.).

33. See Shun 1989 and Wong 1991. For a criticism of these interpretations, refer to Ivanhoe n.d., Ihara 1991, and Van Norden 1991.

34. A chef of legendary talents, whose food was acclaimed throughout the world.

35. A famous musician.

36. A legendarily handsome man.

37. As we shall see, this seems to correspond the Gaozi's belief that benevolence (i.e., the positive force of affection) is internal whereas rightness (i.e., the negative strictures on how this affection is to be manifested) is external.

38. The metaphor of "welling up" will be discussed in more detail later.

39. See chapter 4 and also my later discussion of water metaphors.

40. Reading *yue* 悅 as *shuo* 説.

41. To my knowledge, this was first suggested by David Nivison (Nivison 1996, chapter 8).

42. The most comprehensive survey of the scholarship on these passages is provided by Shun 1997: 87–199.

43. See Shun 1997: 113ff for a discussion of this controversy, and p. 118 for his proffered solution. Cf. Nivison 1997: 125.

44. Van Norden 1992: 172.

45. See Schwartz 1985: 277. Schwartz notes that the "main arena" in which the mind can lose control of the *qi* is in "the realm of man's transactions with the outer world through the channel of the senses."

46. The influence here of the medical theories discussed in chapter 4 is quite clear.

47. Lit., "to the left and to the right".

48. If we think back to our discussion of the "Inner Training" material in chapter 4, we will recall a link established there between the *qi* and Virtue. This link seems to have become an item of general background agreement, because from Mencius onward water metaphors become standard for conceptualizing Virtue as well as *qi*. This link allows Mencius to use the QI AS HYDRAULIC FORCE metaphor as a model for understanding the influence of Virtue: VIRTUE AS HYDRAULIC FORCE. In 2:A:1, although the spread of Virtue is conceptualized by means of a social metaphor ("faster than an order passed from one posting station to another"), it is said to "flow out" (*liuxing* 流行) like water. In 4:A:6, after explaining how easy it is to govern the state by winning the admiration of its various classes, Mencius concludes: "Thus, the instructive influence of Virtue inundates [*yi* 溢] all within the Four Seas with the force of a heavy rain [*peiran* 沛然]." The primal force of Virtue is also conveyed in passages such as 4:A:9, where we are told that the people "come home" (*gui*) to benevolence "like water flowing downhill or wild beasts running toward the open fields." All of these metaphorical expressions provide us with very concrete models in terms of which we can conceptualize the workings of this quite abstract force.

49. Which are less productive and tasty, but at least grow easily and produce a consistent crop.

50. Cf. 7:A:29.

51. Ivanhoe (n.d.). Cf. Nivison's comment (Nivison 1997: 106) concerning Mencian self-cultivation, "the natural enjoyability of morality is what makes it possible."

52. For instance, "who could restrain [*yu* 禦] it" or "none could constrain it" [*mo zhi neng yu*].

53. For instance, from an inferior, or in other situations where an informal address would constitute social humiliation.

54. Cf., for instance, 2:A:1, where the sounds of chickens and dogs are said to "spread out" to the borders of a state.

55. Not coincidentally, in language that strongly echoes that of the "Inner Training"; cf. Roth 1999: 81.

56. Glossed by Zhao Qi as a "glossy and moist [*runze* 潤澤] appearance."

57. Cf. 6:B:6, 6:B:15

58. *Goufeiqiren* 苟非其人; i.e., if this is not really part of his character.

59. 沛然莫之能禦也.

60. Literally referring to a vessel being full of liquid, another instance of the VIRTUE AS WATER metaphor.

61. For the most part, at least. Kwong-loi Shun has noted that a motivational tension structurally similar to what we found in the *Analects* still appears from time to time in the Mencius. For instance, in trying to convince rulers such as King Xuan of Qi to begin trying to act like true kings, Mencius sometimes slips into a utilitarian argument: yes, you enjoy hunting and women and wealth; well, you will enjoy them even more if you share this enjoyment with the people, and if you share with the people no one will try to take these things away from you (see, for instance, 1:A:1 and 1:A:2). In essence, he argues that by not being so focused on gain (*li* 利) the king will in the end gain everything (Shun 1997: 167–68). We can also find echoes of this tension in passage such as 6:A:16, where it is said that it is precisely by not pursuing worldly honors that the gentleman in the end is able to enjoy them (see also 2:A:3, 3:B:5 and 4:B:19). These sorts of arguments are really quite

secondary in Mencius's scheme, however, and his theory of human nature arguably resolves the questions of motivation that they raise.

62. The analogy with Plato is not exact, of course, because "recollection" implies the discovery of some lost or forgotten but nonetheless fully intact capacity, whereas in the Mencian scheme what one is discovering is a mere potential form of the full capacity, which once discovered still needs to be developed. As I have noted, later thinkers in the neo-Confucian tradition came to espouse more "discovery"-oriented views of human nature. Also, for Plato what we are discovering is knowledge—knowledge that gives rise to motivation—whereas for Mencius we are discovering mainly sources of motivation, and it is unclear to what extent Mencius thinks that this involves knowledge per se (Eric Hutton, personal communication).

63. See, for instance, *Analects* 7.15.

64. For this rendering of *si* as "concentration," see Van Norden 1992: 169.

65. As Benjamin Schwartz puts it, our moral potentialities are not programmed into our DNA in the same way that the development of our limbs and organs is, and human beings thus possess the "supernatural" power to stray from their "natural" course of moral development (Schwartz 1985: 289). Consider, for instance, 2:A:6, where the four sprouts of virtue were compared to the four limbs: it is there said that these four sprouts need to be "filled" (*chong*), whereas the four limbs presumably develop without requiring any such effort or process.

66. Who, interestingly enough, is from the state of Chu, said also to have been the native state of Laozi.

67. Cf. 3:B:9.

68. Or, perhaps more accurately, a caricature of the primitivist position, since neither Xu Xing nor Laozi advocated abandoning agricultural or settled village life.

69. See 2:A:2 and 5:B:1

70. There is one instance—related in *Analects* 9.3 and discussed here in chapter 2—in which Confucius acceded to such a modification.

71. See 3:B:10, 4:A:17, 4:A:26, and 5:A:2; cf. 2:B:3, 2:B:7, 6:B:1, and 7:B:6.

72. I have noted in my discussion of Confucius that *Analects* 9.3 indicates the presence of something like Aristotle's "good person" criterion (the "good" being indicated by what the "good" person would do) in Confucius's thought, but—as 4:B:6 demonstrates—this criterion (which as formulated there might be called the "great person" criterion) becomes even more prominent in the Mencius. As Lee Yearley notes of Mencius's thought, "Except for those few actions covered by injunctions, the ultimate standard of evaluation is that the sage would do that particular action in that particular situation" (Yearley 1990: 71).

73. 5:A:4. Mencius's rationale for rejecting the literal meaning of certain odes is that "one who is interpreting an Ode should not allow the words to obscure the sentence, nor the sentence to obscure the intention (*zhi*). The way to get it right is to use your own understanding to trace your way back to the intention of the poet."

74. 7:B:3. Kwong-loi Shun downplays the radicalness involved in this act by arguing that, in Mencius's time, the *Book of History* was not yet completely established as a canonical text (Shun 1997). This may well be the case, but the interpretative approach evinced toward the *Book of History* in 7:B:3 is not inconsistent with the hermeneutical stance toward the *Book of Odes* (which even Shun admits was an established part of the canon by this time) that is described in 5:A:4. That the *Book of History* might at this time have been less sacrosanct than the *Odes* would thus seem to do little to mitigate the radical implications inherent in Mencius's attitude toward the classics.

75. It should be noted that Roger Ames (Ames 1991) has claimed that Mencius actually has a culturally specific conception of *xing*, which in fact involves more of an "ongoing poetic process" characterized by "radical changeability" than any kind of universally shared human nature. This position is an excellent example of the problems encountered when one fails to appreciate the cognitive importance of metaphor—deliberately overlooking or dismissing as it does Mencius's systematic use of agricultural and other nature metaphors—and there is thus little textual support for it. For some other critiques of Ames's position, see Graham 1991 and Bloom 1994.

76. See, for instance, the observation by Graham 1967 that *xing* for Mencius is both a factual and normative concept. Cf. Bloom 1994: 33 and Munro 1969: 44.

77. Cf. 7:B:38.

78. Consider how strange it is to hear Mencius speaking of the need to instruct people how to love their father or son.

79. Cf. 4:A:2, 4:A:15, 6:A:20, and 7:A:41.

80. Zhu Xi 1987, Mencius commentary: 196.

81. As Yearley explains the distinction between preservative and inclinational virtues, "Preservative virtues protect the inclinational virtues by resisting desires that impede their actualization. Inclinational virtues, in turn, often produce the goals for which preservative virtues strive" (1990: 14). Preservative virtues involve dealing with emotions that contend with or oppose proper action.

82. This is the point at which, Yearley argues, normal courage passes into religious courage. See Yearley 1990: 142–43.

83. This, of course, is a quite recent innovation in the institution of marriage, and even today is limited primarily to Western Europe, North America, and those isolated cultural spheres in other regions of the world that take their cue from modern Western Europe and North America. Arguably, the traditional institution of marriage is constructed more along Xunzian lines than Mencian, involving as it does no initial component of inclination.

84. Cf. 6:A:8 and 6:A:9.

85. To take just a sampling of passages to contrast here, consider 7:A:15 ("What a person is able to do without having studied is their 'proper [*liang* 良] ability'; what they are able to know without having deliberated is their 'proper knowledge' [*liangzhi*]") or 4:A:11 ("Proper action lies in what it easy, and yet people look for it in what is difficult").

The Tenuous Self: Wu-wei in the *Zhuangzi*

1.   See appendix 4 for a discussion of textual issues surrounding the *Zhuangzi*. Here I will merely note that my discussion of the text will be based primarily upon the seven so-called Inner Chapters and elaborations of Inner Chapter themes in other chapters identified as "School of Zhuangzi" writings. As usual, the name "Zhuangzi" is intended as a convenient shorthand to refer to the author(s) of the texts involved.

2.   名止於實. Both *ming* and *shi* are terms of art in early Chinese logic: "name" and "object" (see Graham 1978).

3.   In archaic Chinese the two words were homophonous (Karlgren's reconstruction: **ngjie*), and in early texts the two graphs were not sharply distinguished, with *yi* 宜 often being used as a loan character for *yi* 義.

4.   Recall also the association of *yi* 宜 with wu-wei "rightness" in the odes discussed in chapter 1.

5. This is, of course, one of the main themes of the Laozi, as we have seen in chapter 3.

6. *Weishi* has been identified by A. C. Graham as a philosophical term of art (rendered by him as the "contrived 'it is'"), and means literally "deeming that 'it is.'" This term will be discussed at greater length later, where it will be contrasted with the "adaptive" or "responsive 'it is'" (*yinshi* 因是).

7. Or "the discriminations that are not formulated into doctrine."

8. P. J. Thiel notes that the *tianfu* is in the *Zhouli* the name of a particular officer, who was charged with guarding the state treasures. It is also the name of a constellation, which is said to correspond in the human body with the vein of the *dayin* 大陰 (the sexual organs). Although Thiel rejects this as a possible meaning in this context (Thiel 1969a: 46, n. 71), the reference to the vein may indicate a link to physical praxis.

9. Graham renders *bian* 辯 as "disputation", to distinguish it from its cognate *bian* 辨 ("discrimination"), which lacks the "word" or "speech" radical. "Disputation," however, seems to me to carry too strong a negative connotation, since Zhuangzi clearly does not disapprove of a certain type of *bian*: the "great" *bian* that does not speak. "Discrimination" seems to convey better the potentially nonverbal character of *bian*. I will render *bian* 辨 as "distinguishing."

10. These two terms will be translated variously as their context demands, but will always be identified.

11. It is interesting to note along with A. C. Graham that in the later Mohist canons *sheng* serves as a technical term referring to winning a case of competitive discrimination (*bian*); he quotes a passage from the later Moists canons: "In discrimination, one person says 'it is' (*shi*) and the other that 'it is not' (*fei*), and the one who fits the facts is the winner" (Graham 1978: 35).

12. The issue of how precisely to render *cheng*—which has a wide range of meanings in archaic Chinese—will be discussed later with regard to the term *chengxin* 成心.

13. Although Mencius and Zhuangzi were roughly contemporaries, neither figure mentions the other by name. It is clear, however, that Zhuangzi was reacting against certain beliefs that we now associate with Mencius (e.g., that the heart/mind is the natural lord of the body, or that "right" and "wrong" are discovered by the heart/mind based upon qualities inherent in things), and certain passages in the *Zhuangzi* (as I will note later) seem actually to be making fun of stories from the *Mencius*. Feng Yulan 1952 believes that the two were aware of each other's existence, and that Zhuangzi includes Mencius in his criticism of "Confucians," while Mencius includes Zhuangzi in his criticism of "Yangists" (Zhuangzi being perceived by him as a disciple of Yang Zhu). This is not entirely implausible, but for my purposes it is merely important to note that many of the main doctrines we associate now with Mencius were known to and criticized by Zhuangzi.

14. 順物之自然.

15. Tattooing and the cutting off of the nose were common punishments in ancient China.

16. As in the *Mencius*, *qing* should be understood in the *Zhuangzi* in its technical Mohist sense (see chapter 4), and not—as it is often rendered—as "feelings."

17. Note the characteristic contrast between "physical form" (*xing* 形) and "essence" (*qing* 情) mentioned by Graham and noted here in chapter 4. This contrast recurs frequently throughout the Inner Chapters (see, for example, the later discussion of the "True Master"), which is further evidence that *qing* should be understood in the Mohist technical sense.

18.   Although, as we shall see, Zhuangzi often advocates losing or forgetting the self, the *shen* (literally, "trunk of the body") is always described positively as something to be protected or nurtured, and therefore enjoys a status distinct from that of the more generic pronouns for the self such as *wo* 我 or *ji* 己. This special status will be indicated throughout by translating *shen* as the "true self."

19.   獨成其天.

20.   It is clear that Huizi is arguing (as usual) on strictly logical grounds: how can you call something X if it lacks that which characterizes it as X? This is further evidence that *qing* must be taken as the characteristic "essence," since there is of course no a priori reason why a person could not be without feelings.

21.   Here Huizi uses *shen* in its literal sense of the physical body: if a person does not actively pursue life, how can he or she manage to stay alive? Some readers might tend to be rather more sympathetic to Huizi's position in this and other dialogues with Zhuangzi, as Huizi's position is actually quite reasonable: if it is the "essence" of human beings to make distinctions and engage in activities (to "help life along"), one might conclude that the highest spiritual state would be attainable through the cultivation of precisely these capacities. This, of course, is going to be Xunzi's objection to Zhuangzi, as I shall show in chapter 7.

22.   Literally, "'hard' and 'white'" (*jianbai* 堅白), a general term of art for distinct but mutually pervasive properties, of which hardness and whiteness are taken as typical examples. Ancient Chinese logicians debated the nature of these sorts of compound qualities and how they might inhere in objects, and the term *jianbai* thus became a metaphor for logical hair-splitting, especially in the *Zhuangzi* (see also W42/G75). The definitive discussion of this term can be found in Graham 1978: 170–76.

23.   Both of these terms will be treated in greater detail later, when the link between *jing* and the *qi* will also be explored.

24.   P. J. Ivanhoe has noted (personal communication) the parallelism between this exchange and *Mencius* 6:B:4, where Mencius encounters a certain Song Keng who is going off to dissuade a king from engaging in war by pointing out the unprofitability of war for all involved. It is interesting to note that Mencius's response is to urge him to replace one set of rigid values (*li* 利; "profit") with another set (*yi* 義 ; "rightness" or "morality").

25.   Following the emendation of the Zhang Junfang edition and commentary (G146).

26.   *Fu* literally refers to the matching up of two halves of a jade tally. Thus, when it is being used correctly, the heart/mind stops merely matching up words with things (cf. the passage quoted earlier in this chapter, where it is said that names (i.e., words), when properly used, "stop at simply picking out objects").

27.   Watson and Graham both read this line in the active voice, taking it to mean that the Way "gathers tenuousness." This unfortunately does not make much sense; it would thus seem better to read this sentence with an implied *yu* 於. Wang Shumin 1976: 34 cites a passage from the "Interpreting Doctrines" chapter of the *Huainanzi* to support this reading: "Tenuousness is where the Way takes up its abode."

28.   Discussions of this parallel are also to be found in David Nivison 1996: 128–30, and Scott Cook 1997: 534–36.

29.   Regarding the Zi Qi of Southwall passage, for instance, Wu Kuang-ming 1990 and David Hall 1994 see it as evidence of two different types of self in the Zhuangzi: the wu-self and the wo-self, and P. J. Thiel seems to have something similar in heart/mind when he speaks of "doing away with of the empirical self (*das empirisches Ich*)" (Thiel 1969: 50). As Paul Kjellberg has noted, however, the phrase *wu sang wo* is simply proper

classical Chinese, *wu* being the subject first-person pronoun and *wo* being the object first-person pronoun. In this sense, the sense of *wu sang wo* could have equally been expressed with other, interchangeable reflexive or first-person object pronouns (as *wu sang ji* 吾喪己 or *wu zisang* 吾自喪), and the phrase itself is thus neither more nor less freighted with philosophical significance than the English phrase, "I lost myself" (Kjellberg 1993b). As we have seen, even this English expression is significant in that it gives expression to the SUBJECT-SELF conceptual metaphor schema, and this is true as well of classical Chinese. Since it is a mostly unconscious metaphor, however, use of the SUBJECT-SELF schema does not commit the speaker to the conscious belief in literally distinct "types" of the self.

30. See Lakoff and Johnson 1999: 272–73.

31. As Watson notes, Zhuangzi probably intends this as a humorous reference to the words of Confucius in *Analects* 6.9: "The Master said, "What a worthy man was Hui!'"

32. See, for instance, the comment in chapter 2 that "If benevolence is constant, it cannot be universal" (W44/G83). This is to say that the sort of codifying of the scope of benevolence that one finds in a system of morality (whether Confucian or Mohist) makes it rigid and ultimately hypocritical: true benevolence flows forth spontaneously and unself-consciously ("Great benevolence is not benevolent," W44/G83), and so reaches everywhere.

33. And that, as discussed in chapter 1, is found in English as well and seems to represent some commonality in human experience.

34. The link between the normative order and a kind of internal "true" self will be documented more fully later.

35. Cf. W96/G301: "fame and results cannot get in."

36. Cf. W50/G115

37. 定乎內外之分，辯乎榮辱之境.

38. *Diaozhuo* 彫琢; probably a reference to Confucian metaphors for self-cultivation (see *Analects* 1.15).

39. To see things *in the light* of Heaven is not equivalent to seeing things *from the perspective* of Heaven. Many scholars have confused the two. The position that Zhuangzi wants us to see things *from* Heaven's perspective—that is, the perspective from which "everything is one"—is held most prominently by Feng Yulan, Fukunaga Mitsuji, and Chad Hansen. This position is problematic for several reasons. Textually, Zhuangzi's exemplars are constantly engaging in some form of discrimination, choosing one course of action over another, etc. This is also logically a difficult position to advocate: "everything is one" is, as A. C. Graham notes, "a proposition which immediately distinguishes itself from the world which is other than it" (Graham 1969/70). Indeed, Zhuangzi himself makes fun of the idea of a human being taking up such a position (W43/G79). The skepticism about right and wrong for which Zhuangzi is famous—which arises when things are seen from the perspective of Heaven—thus has only a therapeutic value for the sage: by undermining the apparent objectivity of human categories, it loosens the hold of these categories on the him. The belief that Zhuangzi is a thorough-going skeptical relativist is of fairly recent provenance, and—significantly—seems to be limited to a few modern Western scholars (most prominently Chad Hansen, Robert Eno, and Lee Yearley). This is an opinion that does not appear anywhere in the entire Chinese commentarial tradition, from Guo Xiang to the present, and it would seem that a majority of modern Western scholars (Wu Kuang-ming, A. C. Graham, Benjamin Schwartz, P. J. Ivanhoe, Robert Allinson, P. J. Thiel, Jean-François Billeter, Paul Kjellberg, Alan Fox, et al.) also agree that Zhuangzi's skepticism only extends so far (to the power of language to adequately represent reality, for instance) and is intended as a sort of therapy. For general discussions of this issue, refer to Kjellberg 1993 and Ivanhoe 1993 and 1996.

40. P. J. Thiel 1969a interprets the sort of knowing involved in Zhuangzian clarity as akin to William James's conception of mystical experience (which Thiel refers to as the *"Alleins-Erlebnis"* ["Absolute Experience" or "Pure Experience"]). This mystical experience gives the sage immediate access to reality: "Sensory as well as rational knowledge requires intermediaries (sensory impressions, concepts, ideas, images) the way a bird requires wings in order to fly. In *Alleins-Erlebnis*, however, "Being is experienced in an 'unmediated' fashion—the person touches raw Being (*das nackte Sein*)" (50).

41. A legendary beauty.

42. Following Graham 1981.

43. For a discussion of the "fitting" metaphor in the *Zhuangzi*, see Fox 1995 and 1996.

44. With regard to my discussion of externalist elements in the *Mencius* and of the *Xunzi* below, it is significant that Artisan Chui rejects external tools because he has no need for them. Again, whether or not this is a direct response to the *Mencius* is difficult to say, but it is clear that the compass and carpenter's square were conventional metaphors for external standards by this time.

45. *Shi* can also be translated as "according with" or even "feeling comfortable"; all of these meanings are intended in this passage.

46. *Weishi* thus roughly corresponds to what Laozi refers to as "regarding [something as something else]"/"holding [something] in regard" (*youyiwei* 有以為).

47. See also the discussion by A. C. Graham 1989: 201 of *yuyan* 寓言: "saying from a lodging place."

48. As Wu Kuang-ming 1990: 203 puts it, *yinshi* 因是 is an "affirmation of the as-is in *each* case, from *its* perspective."

49. Lit., "go against the current."

50. This phrase appears again in chapter 6 (W84/G260), where it is similarly associated with timeliness and submission to the flow of the normative order.

51. Cf. W46/G96, W87/G268, W93/G293.

52. Following the gloss of Cheng Xuanying (Guo Qingfan: 270).

53. Cf. W69/G191: "he lets his heart/mind wander in the harmony of Virtue."

54. Cheng Xuanying's gloss (Guo Qingfan: 163).

55. The "no-self" interpretation of the Zhuangzian sage is—as one would expect—particularly common among commentators with Buddhist sympathies (see, for instance, Mori Mikisaburo 1967 or David Loy 1996). I would include under this rubric also those scholars who believe that, in achieving tenuousness, the Zhuangzian sage in is effect eliminating everything human within himself and becoming a mere conduit through which Heaven now acts—in Alan Fox's metaphor, becoming a "human superconductor" for the Dao (Fox 1996: 64). For other accounts of the Zhuangzian sage being "possessed" by the alien force of the spirit or becoming a mere passive conduit of the Dao, refer to Graham 1983, Yearley 1996, Forke 1927, Thiel 1969a, and Chang Weichun 1993.

56. Especially because *xu* was appropriated by Buddhist translators to render *sunyata*: "emptiness" or "unreality." In pre-Buddhist China, *xu*—unlike *kong* 空, the other common term for *sunyata*—encompassed both "empty" and "rarefied"/"diffuse"/"scarce" (*xi* 稀 or *shao* 少); see, for instance, "The Debaters" chapter of the *Lüshichunqiu*, where we read, "[They] were not aware of the poverty/desolateness (*xu*) of its agricultural and residential land"; or chapter 4 of the *Zhuangzi*, where we read that the "state was depopulated and made desolate [*xuli* 虛厲]" (W56/G139). *Xu* thus signifies a relative absence of something rather than an absolute void.

57. Again, whether or not these metaphor schemas were explicitly associated by him with Mencius is a question that would be difficult to answer definitively.

58. Cf. Zhuangzi's rejection of the related metaphor of the heart/mind as ruler or teacher (W38–39/G56 and W57/G145).

59. The presence of the lord suggests that this is a ceremonial sacrifice.

60. As Watson notes, "the Mulberry Grove is identified as a rain dance from the time of King Tang of the Shang dynasty, and the Jingshou music as part of a longer composition from the time of Yao." We are thus to understand that Cook Ding's actions are in perfect harmony with the way of the ancients—that is, they are free from the corruption of the current fallen age.

61. 無非牛 (rejecting the textual emendation of the Zhao Jianyi edition, which interpolates a 全); Guo Qingfan: 124, textual note 1.

62. 未嘗見全牛.

63. 官知止而神欲行.

64. Lit. "gotten [de 得] [the secret or method of] cultivating life from it." This verb *de* ("to get") is the same as is used in *Mencius* 2:A:2 in the discussions of where one should "get it": from doctrine, from the heart/mind, or from the *qi*. The significance of this parallel will be discussed later. Billeter 1984 emphasizes that this remark by Lord Wen Hui shows the paradigmatic nature of Cook Ding's activity. As we noted above in chapter 1, this fact—understood along with Cook Ding's contrast of the Way with mere "technique"—would seem to argue against the theories of Hansen and Eno that Cook Ding's Way is a limited "dao."

65. For instance, this portrayal of the ideal Daoist sage hacking up an ox before an admiring ruler may very well be a jab at the story of King Xuan of Qi sparing the sacrificial ox in *Mencius* 1:A:7. Chang Tsung-tung 1982: 496 notes that Cook Ding's peace and equanimity in cutting up the ox contrasts quite sharply with Mencius's fastidious observation at the close of 1:A:7 that "the gentleman keeps his distance from the kitchen."

66. Cf. Rickett 1965: 154; Roth 1999: 47.

67. A causal connection of some sort between *qi* and spirit is implied in chapter 15 (identified as "Syncretist" by Graham and as "Huang-Lao" by Liu Xiaogan), where we read that the sage is able to possess "complete Virtue and undamaged spirit" because cares and worries cannot get inside and "the noxious *qi* cannot assault him" (W168/G538). The parallelism of the passage suggests that it is cares and worries that affect Virtue and noxious *qi* that affects the spirit.

68. For a detailed and excellent account of the relationship between spirit, the "quintessential," and the *qi* in early "Daoistic" texts such as the "Inner Training," refer to Roth 1990, 1991, and 1999: 101–10

69. The parallelism between these two passages was brought to my attention by Pang Pu 1994.

70. Notice the connection between embracing the spirit and protecting one's *jing*, which echoes the language in the "Inner Training" passage cited earlier.

71. Graham identifies this passage as the beginning of an authentic section of "School of Zhuangzi" writing after the "Primitivist" essay that begins the chapter. However, the concern with long life, the appearance of the Yellow Emperor, and the highly developed metaphysical language of this second half of the chapter make me inclined to agree with Liu Xiaogan that this is the work of a "Huang-Lao" author (Graham's "Syncretist"). The similarity to the advice given to Yan Hui in chapter 4 is nonetheless illuminating.

72. It is significant that the verb for "focusing" the spirit, *ning* 凝, refers literally to a congealing liquid, such as freezing water. The phrase, "concentrated in spirit" (*ningshen* 凝神) also appears in chapter 1, where the Spiritual Man (*shenren* 神人) living in Gushe Mountain is described as being able to concentrate his spirit and thus protect creatures

from sickness and assure a plentiful harvest (W33/G28). The fact that spirit is here and in many other places characterized metaphorically as a liquid substance reinforces its connection to both the *qi* and Virtue.

73. *Ling* is a common synonym for *shen*; Sima Biao glosses *lingtai* as "the heart/ mind made into a spiritual/noumenous tower" (quoted in Wang Shumin 1988: 713). Another significant use of *ling* occurs in chapter 5, where it is explained that the key to "keeping your endowment whole" is to keep external things from disturbing your harmony or "entering the Spirit Storehouse (*lingfu* 靈府)" (W74/G212).

74. 動而以天行.

75. Note the water imagery again. While chapter 15 ("Constrained in Will") is almost certainly a late Syncretist work, we can find some of the themes expressed in this passage in "School of Zhuangzi" chapters as well. In chapter 21, for instance, we read that the spirit of the ancient "True Person" could soar throughout the world and "completely fill [*chongman*充滿] Heaven and earth" (W232/G727). Spirit is also paired again with the "quintessential" in the term *jingshen* ("quintessential and the spirit") in chapter 22, where it is linked with wu-wei and the workings of Heaven and described as being "born out of the Way" (W236–37/G735 and W238/G741).

76. It now seems to be the opinion of a majority of scholars that Zhuangzi has an at least implicit picture that human nature is benign, in the sense that Zhuangzian sages (who are in touch with their true natures) continue to act spontaneously in a manner not inconsistent with conventional morality. At one extreme are scholars (Chang Weichun 1993, P. J. Thiel 1969a and—arguably—Wu Kuang-ming 1982 and Allinson 1989) who feel that Zhuangzi has a picture of human nature very similar to that of Mencius, and is merely advocating a different method for getting in touch with that nature. More cautious are scholars such as Kupperman 1996 or Ivanhoe 1993, 1996, who note that there is simply no evidence that "forgetting morality" necessarily implies *transgressing* morality, or that all of the available exemplars in the text seem to be engaged in activities that are benign at worst, and at times actively benevolent. Moving toward the other extreme, Mori Mikisaburo 1967 and A.C. Graham 1989 feel that there is no evidence that Zhuangzi believes that we have any inborn inclinations or natures, but that in opening themselves up to the Way of Heaven, Zhuangzian sages will spontaneously act in a nonselfish, essentially "ethical" manner. Finally, scholars such a Robert Eno 1996 and Lee Yearley 1996 feel that the "spiritual desires" that guide the Zhuangzian sage are entirely amoral, and that, for instance, "the Way of butchering people might provide much the same spiritual spontaneity as the Way of butchering oxen" (Eno 1996: 142). This extreme amoralist position appears textually unfounded, and is primarily motivated by the "many dao" theory of Chad Hansen discussed (and rejected) in appendix 1.

77. Literally, "put on the outside."

78. Feng Yulan 1952, for instance, describes Zhuangzi as an advocate of "complete liberty," and Fukunaga Mitsuji 1969: 10 sees Zhuangzi's ideal as the possession by humans of a "free self in no way subject to the dictates of the surroundings." Lin Congshun 1993 believes that in addition to "incomplete wu-wei"—which involves passively going along with the negative external constraints imposed by "what cannot be avoided" (*budeyi*)—Zhuangzi also advocates a deeper level of "thorough-going wu-wei" that transcends all constraints and limitations.

79. "Spontaneity" in this sense should, as Graham emphasizes, be distinguished from Western Romantic notions of emotionally based spontaneity. He explains that "The Daoist ideal is a spontaneity disciplined by an awareness of the objective," and notes that whereas Western Romanticism distinguishes between rationality (which is objective) and spontaneity (which is emotional and subjective), "The Daoist is somewhere where this

dichotomy does not apply. He wants to remain inside nature, to behave as spontaneously as an animal, to be caused rather than to choose; on the other hand, he has contempt for emotions and subjectivity, a respect for things as they objectively are, as cool and lucid as a scientist's" (Graham 1983: 10–11). Billeter 1993 agrees with Graham on this point, but believes that we should desist from using the term "spontaneity" to describe Zhuangzi's ideal state, since (for instance) the skill displayed by Butcher Ding is not irrational or "mysterious" at all, but is rather "perfectly rational" (i.e., it accord with the objective structure of reality).

While I agree with the substance of both of these scholars' positions, to describe the Zhuangzian sage as "perfectly rational" or as functioning like a scientist seems to me a bit misleading. It glosses over the fact that the movements of the spirit and of Heaven *are* essentially mysterious and not amenable to rational explanation (which is why they transcend the limits of the human mind), and ignores the important element of submission and abnegation of the everyday self that is involved in entering into a state of wu-wei.

80. Graham 1983: 9. I would quibble with Graham's analogy of a "physical reflex," since the sort of responsiveness involved in Zhuangzi's ideal is much more flexible and aware than a mere physical reflex, but I believe his general point—that this responsiveness is a kind of "body knowing"—is quite valid (regarding the idea of "body knowledge," refer to Wu Guangming 1992).

"Spontaneity" in this sense should, as Graham emphasizes, be distinguished from Western Romantic notions of emotionally based spontaneity. He explains that "The Daoist ideal is a spontaneity disciplined by an awareness of the objective," and notes that whereas Western Romanticism distinguishes between rationality (which is objective) and spontaneity (which is emotional and subjective), "The Daoist is somewhere where this dichotomy does not apply. He wants to remain inside nature, to behave as spontaneously as an animal, to be caused rather than to choose; on the other hand, he has contempt for emotions and subjectivity, a respect for things as they objectively are, as cool and lucid as a scientist's" (Graham 1983: 10–11). Billeter 1993 agrees with Graham on this point, but believes that we should desist from using the term "spontaneity" to describe Zhuangzi's ideal state, since (for instance) the skill displayed by Butcher Ding is not irrational or "mysterious" at all, but is rather "perfectly rational" (i.e., it accord with the objective structure of reality).

While I agree with the substance of both of these scholars's positions, to describe the Zhuangzian sage as "perfectly rational" or as functioning like a scientist seems to me a bit misleading. It glosses over the fact that the movements of the spirit and of Heaven *are* essentially mysterious and not amenable to rational explanation (which is why they transcend the limits of the human heart/mind), and ignores the important element of submission and abnegation of the everyday self that is involves in entering into a state of wu-wei.

81. See, for instance, Maspero 1971, Creel 1970: 4, Zhuan Xianchun 1993, and Lee Yearley's 1996 "radical Zhuangzi."

82. Where, for instance, we read of the sage "abandoning the world" and being "free of entanglements" (W197/G632).

83. Indeed, many scholars (beginning with Henri Maspero) have seen a story in chapter 20 as a "conversion" experience in which the young Zhuangzi encounters a rude shock and realizes that acceptance of his place in the universe is a prerequisite for the preservation of his "true self" (W219/G695–98). Graham 1985 sees this story as indicative of Zhuangzi's advance over Yang Zhu, involving the realization that "it is inherent in things that they have ties to one another"; Nivison 1991 similarly see this story as an account of Zhuangzi being shocked out of his earlier Yang Zhu-like belief in withdrawal from the world. See Ivanhoe 1991 for a review of these interpretations (as well as for perhaps the

most cogent take on the passage), and also Epstein 1998 for a general discussion of the
theme of "conversion" in the Zhuangzi.

84. 乘物以遊心託不得已以養中.

85. Watson notes that in this context *zhiming* could be interpreted as either "carrying
out one's orders" or "obeying fate," and that both meanings are almost certainly intended.
He also notes, quite correctly, that "throughout this passage Confucius, while appearing to
give advice on how to carry out a diplomatic mission, is in fact enunciating Zhuangzi's
code for successful behavior in general." Watson notes that in this context *zhiming* could
be interpreted as either "carrying out one's orders" or "obeying fate," and that both meanings are almost certainly intended. He also notes, quite correctly, that "throughout this passage Confucius, while appearing to give advice on how to carry out a diplomatic mission,
is in fact enunciating Zhuangzi's code for successful behavior in general."

86. Much of the current literature in mainland China presents Zhuangzi as being resolutely opposed to all forms of culture, morality, or social participation (see, for instance,
Lin Congshun 1993, Chang Weichun 1995, and Lu Qin 1962), and even a sophisticated
scholar such as Mori Mikisaburo has written that the Zhuangzi of the Inner Chapters
agrees with Laozi in rejecting all forms of active social participation and culture (see Mori
1967). However, in addition to the passage concerning the "Great Constraints," we find
explicit accounts of the Zhuangzian sage acting as a ruler in chapter 6 (W79/G232) and in
the "School of Zhuangzi" chapter 21 (W227-28/G718; W229–30/G720–22; and W231–
32/G726–28). Paul Kjellberg (personal communication) has noted that Zhuangzi's two
most famous exemplars, Butcher Ding and Woodcarver Qing, are harmonizing with the
Way by engaging in essentially Confucian activities (ceremonial sacrifice and the creation
of elaborate ceremonial bellstands). When this is considered along with the fact that in
chapter 4, for instance, Confucius does not tell Yan Hui *not* to go and advise the unruly
king, but only to do it the *right* way, it would seem to indicate that we should not draw the
line between Confucianism and Zhuangzi's vision of the ideal life too starkly.

87. Following my translation above; Billeter actually translates this line somewhat
differently: "Rien n'importe davantage que d'agir selon la necéssité." His translation of
ming as "necessity" follows from his general tendency to "demystify" or rationalize the
Zhuangzi. He apparently wishes to dissociate *ming* from the social metaphor of Heaven as
an "order giver" and all of the cosmological associations it carries, and thereby obscures
the an important aspect of Zhuangzi's religious vision.

88. In chapter 33 we even find a phrase that could loosely be translated, "The Way
of being Caesar with the heart of Christ" (lit. "the Way of being a sage within and a true
king without"; *neisheng waiwang zhi Way* 乘物以遊心託不得已以養中).

89. One might contrast this sort of flexible nonattachment with the legendary (and
apocryphal?) monkey traps reportedly used in certain cultures where food is placed inside
of a container with a narrow opening that is secured to the ground. The opening is
designed so that the monkey can reach its empty hand inside the container and grasp the
food, but is unable to extract both its hand *and* the food. As the villagers close in upon it,
the monkey (trapped by its rigid valuation that food is *good*) is unable to let go and so is
captured. Zhuangzi would no doubt have loved this parable.

90. This phrase echoes the title of chapter 4, "In the Human World," which of course
is largely devoted to descriptions of how to keep one's virtue intact while moving about in
the world.

91. See also the description of the "Great Person" who "sticks to his lot in life," harmonizing with Heaven without antagonizing or despising the human (W178–79/G574).

92. The incongruousness of someone like a tax-collector being a perfected person is,
interestingly enough, also exploited by Kierkegaard in *Fear and Trembling*. In comment-

ing upon the mystery that "every second man" might be a "knight of faith," he says that were he to encounter such a perfect person he would no doubt be incredulous, exclaiming, "Good Lord, is this the man? Is it really he? Why, he looks like a tax collector!" (Kierkegaard 1954: 49).

93. This refers to the story of Liezi returning to his home in chapter 7 (W97/G300). "Carving and polishing," of course, refer metaphorically to Confucian self-cultivation.

94. *Xunzi*, "Dispelling Obsessions" (KIII:102/W393).

95. A metaphor that should be familiar from the *Analects*!

96. As I have mentioned in the introduction, when Buddhism was sinified under the strong influence of Zhuangzian thought, the spiritual ideal of wu-wei—sometimes used as a translation of *nirvana*—was inherited by Chinese forms of Buddhism, particular the Chan 禪 (J. Zen) tradition. As we have seen, this spiritual ideal brings with it its own baggage, most significantly the paradox of wu-wei. The particular tension that we have been tracing here in the *Zhuangzi* was taken over into the Chan school and there it played itself out in terms of the perennial controversy over the relationship of practice to the attainment of enlightenment, manifested institutionally and doctrinally in the split between the "gradual" and "sudden" enlightenment schools. To greatly simplify a complex debate with a long history, the basic battle lines were these: the advocates of "sudden" enlightenment argued that the setting up of practices inevitably contaminated the quest for enlightenment, whereas the "gradual" advocates point out that, since we are currently mired in an unenlightened state, it is hard to see how we could attain enlightenment without some sort of practice to get us there. The fact that this debate was "won" by the sudden school with the triumph of the *Platform Sutra* and the Hui Neng line of transmission and yet refused to go away—arguably reappearing in the split between the "sudden-sudden" Rinzai and "gradual-sudden" Soto schools in Japanese Zen—gives some indication of the tenacity of this problem and perhaps the impossibility of resolving it, at least intellectually or doctrinally.

97. This "faith" should be understood more in the sense of *fiducia* (confidence, trust) than *assensus* (mental assent to some truth). For a brief discussion of *fiducia* versus *assensus* in the Christian tradition, see Harvey 1964: 95–98.

98. What these scholars are sensing might be better termed a distinction between a religious vision with specific social and political goals and one which refuses to formulate such goals, rather than a distinction between "secular" and "religious" formulations of wu-wei.

99. This division seems to reflect a universal religious problem—one that is an issue not only in the *Jodo Shu* vs. *Jodo Shinshu* split but also in the debate concerning the relative importance of faith vs. good works in the Christian tradition.

Straightening the Warped Wood: Wu-wei in the *Xunzi*

1. We actually know a fair amount about Xunzi's life compared to most other pre-Qin Chinese thinkers, career, and intellectual development (see Knoblock I:1–35 for an introduction). In this discussion it will be assumed that chapters 1–26 of the text are actually Xunzi's work, while chapters 27–32 represent a mixture of Xunzi's own writings with the writings of disciples, and include as well older materials used by the Xunzian school in pedagogy.

2.   There is a chapter each in the Xunzi devoted to "Strengthening the State" and "Enriching the State." See KII:113, 121 and 236 for a discussion of the "non-Confucian" aspects of these chapters.

3.   See, for instance, KII:94ff.

4.   Xunzi's long tenure at the Jixia Academy in the state of Qi brought him in contact with the cutting edge of new theories about the state and the self, and no doubt had a great deal of influence upon his thought. At the time Xunzi arrived in Qi, the Academy was filled with the followers of the Legalists Tian Pian and Shen Dao and under the influence of many Daoist and neo-Mohist ideas (see KI:11–16).

5.   For examples of the Mohist influence, see the emphasis on honoring the worthy (KII:94ff) or moderating the use of goods (KII:121); examples of the influence of Laozi (or Laozi-like thought) can be found in the Laozi-like military strategies found in "Regulations of a King" chapter (KII:108–109). The influence of Legalism is pervasive throughout the Xunzi, especially chapters 9–16, and the influence of Zhuangzi will be discussed later with regard to Xunzi's theory of the heart-heart/mind.For examples of the Mohist influence, see the emphasis on honoring the worthy (KII:94ff) or moderating the use of goods (KII:121); examples of the influence of Laozi (or Laozi-like thought) can be found in the Laozi-like military strategies found in "Regulations of a King" chapter (KII:108–109). The influence of Legalism is pervasive throughout the Xunzi, especially chapters 9–16, and the influence of Zhuangzi will be discussed later with regard to Xunzi's theory of the heart-heart/mind.

6.   For instance, in "Strengthening the State" Xunzi discusses goals and concerns normally associated with Legalism or military science, while at the same time arguing that Virtue and not punishments or laws is the only way to obtain the true allegiance of the people (KII:236–240; other defenses of the Virtue-ideal can be found in KI:225; KII:70 and 208; and KIII:36 and 265). Similarly, despite his discussion of the need for clear laws and punishments, he continually emphasizes that a system of law does not apply itself (as the Legalists claimed), but rather requires a Confucian gentleman to function properly (KII:176–177); while deigning to discuss subjects such as military techniques that were rejected out of hand by Confucius himself, Xunzi follows in the spirit of Confucius by refusing to discuss anything but the broad principles of a military strategy built upon moral correctness and based upon the fundamental principles of benevolence and ritual propriety (KII:211–234). As Benjamin Schwartz notes, "In arguing that no techniques of war will work without a basis in troop morale, and that no system of penal laws and incentives will work without a basic attitude of trust, what [Xunzi] is defending is the very notion and relevance of Confucian moral self-cultivation" (Schwartz 1985: 320)

7.   Although Mencius is Xunzi's most common target, Knoblock (KI:52–53) explains that Mencius's thought was viewed by Xunzi as only one example of a variety of heterodox pseudo-Confucian doctrines and lineages current in his age. Only the lineage descended from the otherwise unknown disciple "Zigong" 子弓 (tentatively identified by scholars as the disciple Ran Yong mentioned in our extant *Analects*; KI:53 and passim) was considered by Xunzi to be orthodox.

8.   See especially KI:174–75/W39–40.

9.   Cf. KI:135/W2.

10.   We see here that the metaphor of the senses as human officials with specific tasks to perform was conceptually active in the Warring States period, allowing Xunzi to speak of them as "registering" sense data, etc.

11.   Xunzi sometimes also invokes a social metaphor to convey the idea of an ordered reality, with each thing in the world having its proper "official task" (*zhi* 職)

(KIII:46/W343; KIII:15/W308), "government office" (*guan* 官) (KIII:105/W400), or "position" (*wei* 位) (KIII:105/W397).

12. The fact that Mencius is nonetheless concerned with the health of traditional forms points to the tension between internalism and externalism that we identified in chapter 4.

13. For just a few examples, see KI:179/W49, KII1:55/W209–10, and KIII:36/W325.

14. Knoblock, Watson, and many other Western translators and commentators have rendered *e* as "evil," and Homer Dubs has even gone so far as to identify it with the Augustinian view of original sin (Dubs 1956: 216). As P. J. Ivanhoe has pointed out (1993: 39–40), since the word "evil" possesses the connotation of a positive force opposing the good, and the early Chinese conceived of vice or badness in terms of a "lack" (of goodness, of proper upbringing, etc.) rather than as a positive force in its own right, it would seem better to render *e* as "bad" rather than "evil." Similarly, the early Chinese (or at least the early Confucians) have always been relatively optimistic about human beings' abilities to improve themselves, and never felt the need to rely upon a transcendent power for salvation. Even in Xunzi's scheme, human beings ultimately have the ability to redeem their "bad" nature through conscious human activity—a possibility that is denied by Augustine. To Dubs's credit, however, Xunzi's theory that human nature is "bad" arguably serves a similar structural purpose in Xunzi's thought as the doctrine of original sin does in that of Augustine: shifting the emphasis from the individual's own resources and abilities to the importance of relying upon tradition. This is a theme that will be explored throughout this chapter.

15. Cf. *Analects* 15.30.

16. See, for instance, Antonio Cua 1977, 1978 and Donald Munro 1969: 80–81.

17. A. C. Graham 1989: 250 and D. C. Lau 1953, 1970.

18. Graham 1989: 250.

19. See also Van Norden 1992 and Ivanhoe 1994 for critiques of "assimilationist" views of the Mencius-Xunzi relationship.

20. Following Wang Niansun in reading *li* 離 in place of *sui* 雖 (W387).

21. Following Yu Yue in reading *bi* 蔽 for *shi* 使 (W387).

22. Yearley 1980: 473. Yearley actually describes the second view as the heart/mind as "spectator," but—as we shall see later—the heart/mind as "receptor" might be a more apt description.

23. We also see the metaphor of HEART/MIND AS HUMAN AGENT here in the description of the heart/mind "wandering off on its own," but this metaphor is less prominent in the passage.

24. That is, one's intention represents the "accumulation" of a lifetime of acquired knowledge or awareness.

25. Following Yang Liang in understanding *xu* 須 as *dai* 待 and following Wang Yinzhi in reading *ren* 人 as *ru* 入 (W396). There is a fair amount of disagreement concerning how to read and even where to punctuate this passage; see KIII:330, n. 41–43 for suggestions from Japanese scholars.

26. Consider, for instance, the contrast between Xunzi's confidence in the sageking's ability to "fix names" (*dingming* 定名) as described in the "Rectification of Names" chapter and Zhuangzi's belief that names have no set referents.

27. A type of edible green.

28. Cf. KIII:176/W461: "Water is perfectly level / Its correctness does not tilt/ When the techniques of the heart/mind are like this one is like unto the sage."

29. See Oshima 1983: 74–76.

30. Cf. KIII:108/W404: "As a general rule, when observing things about which one is in doubt, if on the inside one's heart/mind is not settled (*ding*), then external things will not be clear (*qing* 清)."

31. See Van Norden 1992.

32. Following Van Norden 1992: 174.

33. Following Knoblock's suggested textual emendation (KIII:330–31 n. 49).

34. In the early stages of self-cultivation, that is. These standards are of course eventually internalized by the sage or gentleman.

35. Lit. "human activity." "Conscious activity" is in most cases a more felicitous rendering, but—especially when the Heavenly and the human are being contrasted—the literal meaning is perhaps best.

36. Again, we are speaking here of aspiring sages. As we shall see, Xunzi makes recourse to concepts such as "response" to describe his wu-wei ideal, but does not believe that such passive concepts have anything to do with self-cultivation.

37. Also see Jonathan Schofer 1993: 72 on Xunzian ritual "reformation" and his use of craft metaphors.

38. See also KIII:19/W316, and cf. the metaphor of "sharpening with the whetstone" (KII:238–39/W291).

39. See KI:135/W1, KIII:150–51/W435, and KIII:161–62/W449.

40. Cf. the description of the rites as "trimming that which is too long and adding to that which is too short, taking away from that which is excessive and supplementing that which is insufficient" (KIII:65/W363) and the rites and morality as "straightening out and adorning" human beings' essential nature (KIII:151/W435).

41. KIII:195/W473 (from one of the "Fu—Rhyme-Prose Poems"). The term *ya* means both elegant and in accordance with ancient standards; hence the rendering "classical" (cf. *Analects* 7.18, "What the Master used the classical (*ya*) pronunciation for: the Odes, the History and the performance of the rites. In all these cases, the Master used the classical pronunciation.")

42. As Knoblock notes, the "doctrine of the Way of the Later Kings (*houwang* 後王) is unique to Xunzi" (KII:28). Other thinkers generally refer to the "Former Kings" or "Ancient Kings" (*xianwang* 先王), as did Xunzi in his earlier writings. As Knoblock describes, however, Xunzi gradually began to wish to distinguish his traditional appeals from those of other thinkers, such as Mozi and the Daoists, who used the term *xianwang* to refer to figures in high antiquity. Xunzi, following Confucius, notes that we know too little about high antiquity to use them as a model, and that we should therefore follow the "Later Kings"—which embraces the Three Dynasties, but refers primarily to the Zhou. Even when he refers to the "Ancient Kings," then, Xunzi has in heart/mind the Three Dynasties. Refer to Knoblock II: 28–31, for a discussion of this issue.

43. Lit. "warmed up" (wen 溫); cf. *Analects* 2.11 ("A true teacher is one who, keeping the past alive (*wen*), is also able to understand the present.")

44. In this respect, Homer Dubs is not too far off the mark when he notes that Xunzi's "Augustinian" view of human nature serves to emphasize the "authoritarian" aspect of Confucianism, which is somewhat undermined by the more individualist Mencian strand (Dubs 1965: 216).

45. Lit., "with the kind of discernment that distinguishes 'hard and white' and 'identity and difference.'"

46. 禮之為是 ; alternately, "which ritual to use (lit., "that [this] ritual is the right one") or (as Knoblock renders it) "which ritual is correct."

47. In this context, it is very revealing to note the different manners in which Mencius and Xunzi use an identical passage from the *Odes*, Mao 260:

Heaven produced the teeming masses,
And where there is a thing there is a norm [*ze* 則].
If the people held to their constant nature,
They would be drawn to superior Virtue.

In *Mencius* 6:A:6 this ode is cited as evidence that its sage author had a Mencian picture of human nature: the norm is an internal principle with which people are born that draws them naturally toward the good. In chapter 4 of the *Xunzi* ("Of Honor and Disgrace"), only the first line of the ode is cited directly and the second line paraphrased: "As 'Heaven produced the teeming masses,' so there exists a means by which they can be won" (KI:189/W2.2a). The passage goes on to describe the external model—consisting of rites, rules and laws, weights and measures, and other cultural norms—that the Son of Heaven employs to win the world. It is clear that Xunzi takes the "norm" (*ze*) of Mao 260 to be an external, cultural standard designed to take advantage of a fixed but morally neutral "nature" possessed by the common people, whereas Mencius sees it as a morally charged native disposition granted by Heaven.

48. The roots of this human-centered orientation are clearly to be found in the *Analects* (consider, for instance, *Analects* 11.12: "You are not even able to serve your fellow humans, how can you worry about serving the spirits? . . . You do not even understand life, how can you understand death?") See also Xunzi's diatribe against those who superstitiously live in fear of such "Heavenly monstrosities" as falling stars or eclipses and so neglect their human duties (KIII:18/W312–13).

49. In his criticism of these wu-wei metaphors, then, Xunzi is essentially targeting any "inclinational" account of perfected action. As Jonathan Schofer has noted (1993: 126ff) Xunzi's model of virtue is fundamentally preservative.

50. Later in the passage Xunzi makes it clear that by "pursuing that which has no end" he is referring to the endless quibbling of the logicians or the pursuit of supernatural powers.

51. Following Knoblock in adopting Momoi Hakuroku's emendation of the word order (KI:278, n. 60).

52. Cf. KI:138/W8, KIII:228/W509, and KII:248/W526.

53. Cf. KIII:258/W537: "If the gentleman does not study as a child, when he matures he will be without ability."

54. Cf. KIII:62/W356–57.

55. One example of Xunzi using accumulation in the liquid sense is found in a saying from the "Great Compendium" chapter that combines the accumulation metaphor with the metaphor of Virtue as Water to describe the formation of the sage: "That which exhaustively collects the small becomes large; that which accumulates the minute becomes visible. When a person has perfected Virtue it gathers like water in a marsh and suffuses (*zexia* 澤治) his countenance" (KIII:226/W506).

56. Reading 情 as a scribal error for 積 throughout.

57. Cf. KI:192/W63 (discussed earlier) and KIII:59/W351.

58. Cf. KIII:227/W507: "This chariot wheel was once a tree of Mount Tai. Having been subjected to the pressframe for three to five months, though, it . . . will never return (*fan* 反) to its original form."

59. Both titles of chapters in the Mozi.

60. Knoblock has something like this distinction in mind when he claims that "music is more profound than ritual since it affects our inner states rather than our external conduct. One can force a man to smile, but not feel joy. Ritual may cause us to act in a certain way, but it cannot cause us to feel in a way consonant with what we do" (KIII:79). This, of course, is not entirely accurate, since ritual is in fact designed to ultimately work

upon our emotions. Music's more direct link with the emotions does nonetheless make it, in the sense of transformative efficacy at least, more "profound."

61. Following Wang Niansun in reading 論 as 倫 (W145).

62. Cf. KII:73/W125 ("One who learns and puts it into practice is a scholar. one who is enthusiastic about it is a gentleman, and one who comprehends it is a sage") and KII:75–76/W129–30.

63. In one of the chapters that is probably not from Xunzi's own hand, chapter 31 ("Duke Ai"), we find the hierarchy broken down into five grades of people: the average person (*yongren* 庸人), the scholar, the gentleman, the "worthy" (*xianren* 賢人) and the "great sage" (KIII:259–61/W539–42). The progression to an increasing level of effortlessness and a decreasing level of self-consciousness is the same, however.

64. This may very well be deliberately intended to contrast with the "fasting of the heart/mind" passage in chapter 4 of the *Zhuangzi*, where Yan Hui is warned not to listen with the ear or the heart/mind.

65. Cf. KI:142/W19. It should be noted that the passage cited here is actually part of a criticism of Mencius, whom Xunzi portrays as someone who cultivated an iron will but who never really understood and embodied the Way. In essence, Xunzi is criticizing Mencius because he fell short of the wu-wei ideal.

66. There is a great deal of commentarial debate and confusion over how to render the strings of adjectives here and in later passages, and in several places I am following Knoblock.

67. See also KII:105/W165, KII:232/W287, KIII:106/W400, and KIII:261/W251–52.

68. An oblique reference to *Analects* 7.8, where Confucius praises Yan Hui because, when given one corner of the Way, he can come back with the other three.

69. Cf. KI:179/W49: "The gentleman does not descend from his dais, and yet the essence of all within the seas is accumulated there."

70. As Donald Munro observes of Xunzi's conception of "unity" (*yi* 一) or "union," "It is obvious that this 'union,' for Xunzi, is not mystical but intellectual; the sage sees how each thing is interrelated with certain other things to form an ordered whole." (Munro 1969: 157–58)

71. See also the explanations of how the "ordering pattern" (*li*) encompasses every occasion and situation in the world (KIII:220/W500), not only in the present world but throughout time (KI:207/W82). See also KII:103/W163, "By using proper categories (*lei*), one is able to deal with diversity; by using unity, one is able to deal with the myriad."

72. See, for instance, the opening line of the "Discourse on Heaven" (KIII:14/W306–7), where it is said that "The course of Heaven is constant (*chang*): it is not preserved by Yao and is not lost because of a Jie."

73. Fu Sinian claims that human beings' ability to undertake conscious activity contradicts the claim that human nature is bad; Lao Siguang argues that the sage's ability to create the rites and morality shows that human nature is not bad. Refer to Shun 1997: 227–28 for a summary of some of these criticisms.

74. *Ibid.*

75. Originally suggested by Zhang Xuecheng, as reported and developed by David Nivison 1996: 205. See also Ivanhoe 1994: 168.

76. See Van Norden 1992, Munro 1996, Kline 2000, Wong 2000, and Hutton 2000.

77. As noted earlier, alternately, "which ritual to use (lit., "that [this] ritual is the right one") or (as Knoblock renders it) "which ritual is correct."

78. Translation following Eric Hutton (personal communication).

79.   Consider, for instance, Xunzi's discussions concerning job performance matching job descriptions and the ruler being able to be literally wu-wei (without action)
because the machinery of government runs so smoothly (KII:157/W214, KII:176–77/
W230–31, KII:186–87/W241, KII:189/W243, KII:191/W246, KIII:185–88/W468–72,
KIII:224/W504). See also Knoblock's discussion of the Legalist elements in Xunzi's
thought (KI:103).

80.   Eric Hutton (personal communication).

81.   Cf KIII:231/W511 regarding the "state on the verge of decline."

82.   See, for instance, the descriptions of the false Confucians who "are straight and
established but are not recognized because they are only interested in success" (KI:187/
W54) or the "lowly Confucians" of the Zixia School who "wear their robes and caps in
perfectly proper/right (*zheng* 正) form, keep their facial expressions perfectly uniform and
orderly, and are so satisfied with themselves that they go the entire day without speaking"
(KI:229/W104).

83.   君子也者而好之其人也.

84.   See also KI:139/W10 and KII:243/W298.

85.   Donald Munro 1996 has made a similar claim about inconsistencies in Xunzi's
picture of human nature, one of his assertions being that the famous "ladder of life" passage in chapter 9 (KII:104/W164) describes the existence of an inherent human moral
"sense." Eric Hutton 2000 has quite convincingly argued against this position, claiming,
for instance, that *yi* 義 in the "ladder of life" passage should be understood as an external
cultural artifact rather than an innate sense. Hutton's arguments are still, however, not
enough to entirely explain away the presence of the internalist metaphors documented
here. See also Nivison's discussion (1997: 210) of Xunzi and Pascal and the structural
need for a certain kind of inborn "sense of duty."

86.   Cf. KII:235/W518, where the universal acceptance of the Way of the Three
Kings is compared to human beings' common taste for the cooking of the famous cook
Yiya—an analogy also found in Mencius 6:A:7.

87.   See especially Xunzi's observation that the regulations of the true king allow
everyone to ultimately satisfy their desires (KII:156/W210–11; KII:160–61/W216–17);
that restraining one's desires with the rites and morality is actually the only way to satisfy
them in the end, since merely focusing upon gain alone will result in one's getting nothing
(KII:244/W299–300; KIII:136/W429); and that choosing the Confucian Way is a simple
matter of calculation—by following the Way, you are getting "two for one" (realizing both
personal ends and public ends), and thus anyone who rejects the Way simply "does not
know how to count" (KIII:137/W430).

88.   There is one passage in which *cheng* is characterized in an externalist fashion,
KIII:61/W356, where it is used to describe the proper orientation or adjustment of external
standards such as the plumb line or ruler, but even this externalist characterization is
immediately undercut in the next line by an emphasis on the importance of the sage "loving" ritual. For an alternate interpretation of *cheng* in the Xunzi as something closer to
"constancy," as well as a quite different translation of the passage, see Hutton 2001.

89.   That is, his carefulness permeates every aspect of his life, and is not merely put
on display for others. Cf. *Analects* 2.9.

90.   As Knoblock notes, how to render these few lines has long troubled commentators. I follow Hao Yixing.

Conclusion

1.   When we pick up the debate in the early Chan tradition, we find that self-cultivation internalism has become the unquestioned orthodoxy, and the tension is therefore formulated in terms of a "sudden-gradual" split. It is interesting to note, though, that although internalism becomes a theological commitment, we can still see the paradox as creating an internalist-externalist split with regard to soteriological strategies. That is to say, the gradualist school of Chan Buddhism also endorses what look like more externalist soteriological techniques, and the Cheng-Zhu versus Lu-Wang debate can arguably also be characterized along self-cultivationist externalist-internalist lines, even though both schools were theologically committed to internalism.

2.   Consider the discretion displayed by the Mencian gentleman in adapting or even violating the dictates of the rites if they fail to accord with what is "right" for the situation (3:B:10, 4:A:17, 4:A:26, 5:A:2) or following his intuition in reinterpreting or even rejecting portions of the classics (5:A:4, 7:B:3).

3.   See also 3:A:4 and 6:A:20.

4.   In this respect, it is revealing that the significance of Aristotle's paradox and Plato's Meno problem have been "rediscovered" by Alasdair MacIntyre in the course of his retrieval of our own lost virtue ethical tradition.

5.   Cf. George Lakoff's observations concerning the tension between the STRICT FATHER (conservative) and NURTURING PARENT (liberal) schemas in American political discourse (Lakoff 1996).

6.   Of course, the technique of metaphor analysis also requires a certain amount of interpretation—interpretation is involved in simply reading the texts, parsing lines, dealing with textual problems, deciding what constitutes a metaphorical versus a literal statement, etc.—but the ability to use particular linguistic signs to trace deeper conceptual structures allows us to stay in closer contact with the primary texts themselves.

7.   See Slingerland 2000b for an example of how this might be done with respect to modern Western and early Chinese conceptions of the "self."

8.   Following the Dunhuang version of the text. See Yampolsky 1967.

9.   See Boyd 1993 and Kuhn 1993 for discussions of the role of metaphor in the conceptual evolution of the sciences.

10.   See Ivanhoe 1993: 68–69 for a discussion of "discovery" versus "developmental" models of self-cultivation.

11.   For just a sampling of how cognitive linguistic approaches have been applied to the humanities in general, see Turner 1991 and Lakoff and Turner 1989 (literature), Winter 1989 (legal reasoning), and Lakoff 1996 (American political discourse).

Textual Issues Concerning the *Laozi*

1.   D. C. Lau places the origin of these stories between 286 and 240 B.C. (1963: 147–62). A. C. Graham 1986b finds evidence of the existence of myths concerning a meeting between Confucius and a figure named Lao Dan as early as the fourth century B.C., but believes that it was only much later that this Lao Dan was eventually associated with the Laozi who supposedly composed the *Dao De Jing*. Also see Kohn 1998 for discussions of some of the early Laozi myths.

2. See Czikszentmihalyi and Ivanhoe 1999: 4, for references.

3. This argument has been made by A. C. Graham, Feng Yu-lan, Arthur Waley, Herrlee Creel, Takeuchi Yoshio, and Ku Chieh-kang, among others. See Graham 1989: 217–18 and Creel 1970: 47 (n. 41) for references. Qian Mu believes that the *Laozi* was put together by a certain Zhan He, whose dates he gives as 350–270 B.C. (Qian Mu 1956: 223–26 and 448–49).

4. For instance, the use of the compound *renyi* 仁義 is a fairly late development (Zhang Dainian in Gao Ming 1996: 2), but the phonological characteristics of the text place it after Confucius but before the *Zhuangzi* and *Chu Ci* (Baxter 1998).

5. In this respect, it is quite revealing that a scholar as careful as Benjamin Schwartz would make use of what is essentially a Zhuangzian notion of the *xin* as "mind" in his explication of the *Laozi* (see Schwartz 1985: 207). He apparently allows himself this anachronism because of a (most likely unconscious) belief that the author(s) of the *Laozi* would have explained themselves with this sort of language had it been available to them. It is, in fact, the case that Zhuangzian conceptions of the "mind" and its discriminating function allow us to more precisely and economically express certain themes in the *Laozi*, such as the critique of Confucianism and "regarding."

Textual Issues Concerning the *Zhuangzi*

1. Roth 1991: 80.

2. The reader is referred to Graham 1986, 1989, Roth 1991, Liu Xiaogan 1994, and the works referenced therein.

3. A.C. Graham believes, however, that they require emendation: the order and placement of several passages must be altered, he claims, and the text needs to be supple-·mented with fragments from the Outer and Mixed Chapters that he believes have been misplaced (see Graham 1981, 1982, 1989). He is, however, in the minority in this regard, and most scholars (see, for example, Liu Xiaogan 1994) argue for the textual integrity of the Inner Chapters.

4. The author of the Inner Chapters is clearly from the higher, educated class, and is a brilliant thinker and gifted writer, intimately familiar with the philosophical trends and jargon of the time. I consider the question of whether or not he (and there is little doubt that he was a man, as women of that period had little or no access to classical education) was the historical Zhuangzi himself to be ultimately unimportant.

5. Outer Chapter material will be used only to further explicate themes that can be firmly located within the Inner Chapters themselves; I treat them with the same level of caution with which I approach other "commentaries" on early Chinese texts (see my note regarding commentaries in the section on conventions, p. viii).

6. *Shiji*, "Biographies of Laozi and Hanfeizi," Sima Qian 1964: 2143.

7. Indeed, in modern Chinese "Daoism" is often referred to as "Lao-Zhuang" thought.

8. See, for example, Lin Congshu 1993 and Chen Shuide 1995.

Bibliography

Allinson, Robert. 1989. *Chuang-tzu for Spiritual Transformation*. Albany, NY: State University of New York Press.

Ames, Roger. 1981. "Wu-wei in 'The Art of Rulership' Chapter of the *Huai Nan-tzu*: Its Sources and Philosophical Orientation." *Philosophy East & West* 31.2: 193–213.

———. 1985. "The Common Ground of Self-Cultivation in Classical Taoism and Confucianism." *Tsing Hua Journal of Chinese Studies* 17.1–2: 65–97.

———. 1991. "The Mencian Conception of *Ren xing*: Does It Mean Human Nature?" In *Chinese Texts and Philosophical Contexts*, ed. Henry Rosemont, 143–175. La Salle, IL.: Open Court.

———. 1994. *The Art of Rulership: A Study of Ancient Chinese Political Thought*. Albany, NY: State University of New York Press.

Anazawa Tatsuo 穴澤辰雄. 1967. "Soshi ni okeru shizen (mui) teki ten no kannen" 莊子 における 自然（無為）的天 の 觀念. *Nihon Chugoku Gakkaiho* 日本中國學會報 19: 109–117.

Aristotle. 1985. *Nicomachean Ethics*. Trans. Terence Irwin. Indianapolis: Hackett.

Baxter, William. 1998. "Situating the Language of the *Lao-tzu*: The Probable Date of the *Tao-te-ching*." In *Lao-tzu and the Tao-te-ching*, ed. Livia Kohn and Michael LaFargue, 231–253. Albany, NY: State University of New York Press.

Billeter, Jean François. 1984. "Pensée occidentale et pensée chinoise: le regard et l'acte." In *Différances, valeurs, hiérarchie*, 25–51. Paris: Ecole des Hautes Etudes en Sciences Sociales.

———. 1993. "La phénoménologie de l'activité dans le *Zhuangzi*." *Asiatische Studien* 47.4: 545–558.

———. 1994. "Arrêt, vision et langage: essai d'interprétation du *Ts'i Wou-Louen* de Tchouang-Tseu." *Philosophie* 44: 12–51.

———. 1995. "Seven Dialogues from the Zhuangzi." Trans. Mark Elvin. *East Asian History* 9: 23–46.

———. 1996. "Non-pouvoir et non-vouloir dans le *Zhuangzi*—un paradigme." *Etudes Asiatiques* 4: 853–880.

Bloom, Irene. 1994. "Mencian Arguments on Human Nature (*Jen-hsing*)." *Philosophy East & West* 44.1: 19–54.

Bodde, D. 1953. "Harmony and Conflict in Chinese Philosophy." *Studies in Chinese Thought*: 19–80.

Boltz, William. 1993. "*Lao tzu Tao te ching*." In *Early Chinese Texts*, ed. Michael Loewe, 269–292. Berkeley, CA: The Society for the Study of Early China.

Boyd, Richard. 1993. "Metaphor and Theory Change: What Is 'Metaphor' a Metaphor For?" In *Metaphor and Thought* (2nd edition), ed. Andrew Ortony, 481–532. Cambridge: Cambridge University Press.

Brooks, E. Bruce, and A. Taeko Brooks. 1998. *The Original Analects: Sayings of Confucius and His Successors*. New York: Columbia University Press.

Campany, Robert. 1992. "Xunzi and Durkheim and Theories of Ritual Practice." In *Discourse and Practice*, ed. Frank Reynolds and David Tracy, 197–231. Albany, NY: State University of New York Press.

Chan, Alan. 1991. *Two Visions of the Way: A Study of the Wang Pi and Ho-Shang-Kung Commentaries on the* Lao-tzu. Albany, NY: State University of New York Press.

_____. 1998. "A Tale of Two Commentaries: Ho-Shang-Kung and Wang Pi on the *Lao-tzu*." In *Lao-tzu and the* Tao-te-ching, ed. Livia Kohn and Michael LaFargue, 89–117. Albany, NY: State University of New York Press.

Ch'an, Wing-tsit. 1955. "The Evolution of the Confucian Concept Jen." *Philosophy East & West* 4.1: 295–319.

Chao, Y. R. 1955. "Notes on Chinese Grammar and Logic." *Philosophy East & West* 5.1: 31–41.

Chang Tsung-tung. 1982. *Metaphysik, Erkenntnis und Praktische Philosophie im Chuang-tzu—Zur Neu-Interpretation und Systematische Darstellung der Klassischen Chinesischen Philosophie*. Frankfurt am Main: Vittorio Klosterman.

Chang Weiqun 常為群. 1995. "Mengzi, Zhuangzi bijiao yanjiu santi" 孟子, 莊子比較研究三題. Nanjing Shida Xuebao 南京師大學報: 84–86, 105.

Chen Shuide 陳水德. 1995. "Qiansi Zhuangzi wuwei zhengzhi sixiang de shehuixing" 淺析莊子無為政治思想的社會性. *Anhui Shixue* 安徽史學 12.3: 6–7.

Cheng Shude 程樹德. 1996. *Lunyu Jishi* 論語集釋. Beijing: Zhonghua Shuju.

Chen Zizhan 陳子展. 1991. *Shijing Zhijie* 詩經直解. Shanghai: Fudan Daxue Chubanshe.

Cikoski, John S. 1975. "On Standards of Analogical Reasoning in the Late Chou." *Journal of Chinese Philosophy* 2: 325–357.

_____. 1978. "Three Essays on Classical Chinese Grammar." *Computational Analyses of Asian and African Languages* 8: 77–208.

Cook, Scott. 1995. *Unity and Diversity in the Musical Thought of Warring States China*. Ph.D. dissertation, University of Michigan.

_____. 1997. "Zhuangzi and His Carving of the Confucian Ox." *Philosophy East & West* 47: 521–553.

Crandall, Michael Mark. 1983. "On Walking Without Touching the Ground: 'Play' in the *Inner Chapters* of the *Chuang-tzu*." In *Experimental Essays on Chuang-tzu*, ed. Victor Mair, 101–124. Honolulu: University of Hawaii Press.

Creel, Herrlee. 1960. *Confucius and the Chinese Way*. New York: Harper Torchbooks.

_____. 1970. *What Is Taoism and Other Studies in Chinese Cultural History*. Chicago: University of Chicago Press.

Cua, A. S. 1977a. "The Conceptual Aspect of Hsün Tzu's Philosophy of Human Nature." *Philosophy East & West* 27: 373–389.

_____. 1977b. "Forgetting Morality: Reflections on a Theme in Chuang-tzu." *Journal of Chinese Philosophy* 4: 305–328.

_____. 1978. "The Quasi-Empirical Aspect of Hsün Tzu's Philosophy of Human Nature." *Philosophy East & West* 28: 3–19.

_____. 1985a. *Ethical Argumentation: A Study in Hsün-tzu's Moral Epistemology*. Honolulu: University of Hawaii Press.

_____. 1985b. "Ethical Uses of the Past in Early Confucianism: The Case of Hsün Tzu." *Philosophy East & West* 35: 133–156.

Czikszentmihalyi, Mark, and Philip J. Ivanhoe, eds. 1999. *Religious and Philosophical Aspects of the Laozi*. Albany, NY: State University of New York Press.

Damasio, Antonio. 1994. *Descartes' Error: Emotion, Reason, and the Human Brain*. New York: G. P. Putnam.

Dan Weihua 單維華 . 1992. "Lun *Laozi* de 'wuwei er zhi'" 論老子的無為而治 . *Qiushi Xuekan* 求是學刊: 25–26.

Dubs, Homer. 1965. "Mencius and Sun-dz on Human Nature." *Philosophy East & West* 6: 213–222.

Duyvendak, J. J. L. 1947. "The Philosophy of Wu-wei." *Asien Studien* 3.4: 81–102.

_____ trans. 1954. *Tao Te Ching*, London.

Emerson, John. 1996. "Yang Chu's Discovery of the Body." *Philosophy East & West* 46.4: 533-566.

Eno, Robert. 1990. *The Confucian Creation of Heaven*. Albany, NY: State University of New York Press.

_____. 1996. "Cook Ding's Dao and the Limits of Philosophy." In *Essays on Skepticism, Relativism, and Ethics in the* Zhuangzi, ed. Paul Kjellberg and P. J. Ivanhoe, 127–151. Albany, NY: State University of New York Press.

Epstein, Shari. 1998. "Conversion Narratives in the *Zhuangzi*." Paper delivered at the third Annual Conference of the Society for Asian and Comparative Philosophy.

Fauconnier, Gilles. 1997. *Mappings in Thought and Language*. Cambridge: Cambridge University Press.

Fauconnier, Gilles, and Eve Sweetser, eds. 1996. *Spaces, Worlds, and Grammar*. Chicago: University of Chicago Press.

Feng Yulan. 1952. *History of Chinese Philosophy*. Princeton: Princeton University Press.

Fesmire, Steven. 1994. "What is 'Cognitive' About Cognitive Linguistics?" *Metaphor and Symbolic Activity* 9: 149–154.

Fingarette, Herbert. 1972. *Confucius: Secular as Sacred*. New York: Harper Torchbooks.

_____. 1981. "How the *Analects* Portrays the Ideal of Efficacious Authority." *Journal of Chinese Philosophy* 8.1: 29–49.

_____. 1983. "The Music of Humanity in the *Conversations* of Confucius." *Journal of Chinese Philosophy* 10: 331–356.

_____. 1991. "Reason, Spontaneity, and the Li—A Confucian Critique of Graham's Solution to the Problem of Fact and Value." In *Chinese Texts and Philosophical Contexts*, ed. Henry Rosemont, 209–225. La Salle, IL.: Open Court.

Forke, Alfred. 1927. *Geschichte der Alten Chinesichen Philosophie*. Hamburg: L. Friederichsen.

Fox, Alan. 1995. "*Wu-wei* in Early Philosophical Daoism." Paper delivered at the Eastern Division Meeting of the American Philosophical Association, December 18.

_____. 1996. "Reflex and Reflexivity: *Wuwei* in the *Zhuangzi*." *Asian Philosophy* 6.1: 59–72.

Fukunaga Mitsuji 福永光司 . 1965. "Mui o toku hitobito" 無為を説く人人 . *Shiso no Rekishi* 思想の歷史 2: 209–257.

_____. 1966. *Soshi* 莊子. Tokyo: Asahi shin bun sha.

_____. 1969. " 'No-mind' in Chuang-tzu and Ch'an Buddhism." *Zinbun* 12: 9–41.

Gao Ming 高明. 1996. *Boshu Laozi Jiaozhu* 帛書老子校注. Beijing: Zhonghua Shuju.

Gao Xiuchang 高秀昌. 1995. "Laozi 'wuwei er zhi' sixiang guanshi" 老子無為而治思想闡釋. *Shehui Kexue Yanjiu* 社會科學研究 1: 70–73.

Gibbs, Raymond. 1994. *The Poetics of Mind: Figurative Thought, Language, and Understanding*. Cambridge: Cambridge University Press.

_____. 1996. "What's Cognitive About Cognitive Linguistics?" In *Cognitive Linguistics in the Redwoods: The Expansion of a New Paradigm in Linguistics*, ed. Eugene Casad, 27–53. Berlin: Mouton de Gruyter.

Gibbs, Raymond, and Herbert Colston. 1995. "The Cognitive Psychological Reality of Image Schemas and Their Transformations." *Cognitive Linguistics* 6: 347–378.

Goldin, Paul Rakita. 1999. *Rituals of the Way: The Philosophy of Xunzi.* Chicago: Open Court.

Goodman, Russell. 1985. "Skepticism and Realism in the *Chuang-tzu.*" *Philosophy East & West* 35.3: 231–37.

Grady, Joe. 1997. *Foundations of Meaning: Primary Metaphors and Primary Scenes.* Ph.D. dissertation, University of California, Berkeley.

Graham, A.C. 1967. "The Background of the Mencian Theory of Human Nature." *Tsing Hua Journal of Chinese Studies* 1–2: 215–271.

———. 1969. "Chuang-tzu's Essays on Seeing Things as Equal." *History of Religions* 9: 137–159.

———. 1978. *Later Moist Logic, Ethics, and Science.* Hong Kong: Chinese University Press.

———. 1981. *Chuang Tzu: The Inner Chapters.* Boston: Unwin Paperbacks.

———. 1982. *Chuang-tzu: Textual Notes to a Partial Translation.* London: School of Oriental and African Studies.

———. 1983. "Taoist Spontaneity and the Dichotomy of 'Is' and 'Ought.'" In *Experimental Essays on the Chuang-tzu*, ed. Victor Mair, 2–23. Honolulu: University of Hawaii Press.

———. 1985a. *Reason and Spontaneity.* London: Curzon Press.

———. 1985b. "The Right to Selfishness: Yangism, Later Mohism, Chuang Tzu." In *Individualism and Holism: Studies in Confucian and Taoist Values* ed. Donald Munro, 73–84. Ann Arbor: Center for Chinese Studies, University of Michigan.

———. 1986a. "How Much of *Chuang-tzu* Did Chuang-tzu Write?" In *Studies in Chinese Philosophy and Philosophical Literature.* Singapore: Institute of East Asian Philosophies.

———. 1986b. "The Origins of the Legend of Lao Tan." In *Studies in Chinese Philosophy and Philosophical Literature.* Singapore: Institute of East Asian Philosophies; reprinted in *Lao-tzu and the* Tao-Te-Ching, ed. Livia Kohn and Michael LaFargue, 23–40. Albany, NY: State University of New York Press.

———. 1989. *Disputers of the Tao.* La Salle, Ill.: Open Court.

———. 1991. "Reflections and Replies." In *Chinese Texts and Philosophical Contexts*, ed. Henry Rosemont, 267–322. La Salle, IL: Open Court.

Gregory, Peter, ed. 1987. *Sudden and Gradual Approaches to Enlightenment in Chinese Thought.* Honolulu: University of Hawaii Press.

Guodian Chumu Zhujian 郭符店楚墓竹簡 . 1998. Jingmenshi Bowuguan 荊門市博物館 (ed.). Beijing: Wenwu Chubanshe.

Guo Qingfan 郭慶藩. 1961. *Zhuangzi Jishi* 莊子集釋. Beijing: Zhonghua Shuju.

Hall, David. 1994. "To Be or Not To Be: The Postmodern Self and the *Wu*-Forms of Taoism." In *Self as Person in Asian Theory and Practice*, ed. Roger Ames, Wimal Dissanayake, and Thomas Kasulis, 213–234. Albany, NY: State University of New York Press.

Hall, David, and Roger Ames. 1987. *Thinking Through Confucius.* Albany, NY: State University of New York Press.

Hansen, Chad. 1975. "Ancient Chinese Theories of Language." *Journal of Chinese Philosophy* 2: 245–283.

———. 1983a. *Language and Logic in Ancient China.* Ann Arbor: University of Michigan Press.

———. 1983b. "A *Tao* of *Tao* in Chuang-tzu." In *Experimental Essays on Chuang-tzu*, ed. Victor Mair, 24–55. Honolulu: University of Hawaii Press.

_____. 1991. "Should the Ancient Masters Value Reason?" In *Chinese Texts and Philosophical Contexts*, ed. Henry Rosemont, 179–208. La Salle, IL.: Open Court.

Harbsmeier, Cristoph. 1991. "The Mass Noun Hypothesis and the Part-Whole Analysis of the White Horse Dialogue." In *Chinese Texts and Philosophical Contexts*, ed. Henry Rosemont, 49–66. La Salle, IL.: Open Court.

_____. 1993. "Conceptions of Knowledge in Ancient China." In *Epistemological Issues in Classical Chinese Philosophy*, ed. Hans Lenk and Gregor Paul, 11–30. Albany, NY: State University of New York Press.

Harper, Donald. 1995. "The Bellows Analogy in *Laozi* V and Warring States Macrobiotic Hygiene." *Early China* 20: 381–392.

_____. 1998. *Early Chinese Medical Literature: The Mawangdui Medical Manuscripts*. London: Kegan Paul International, Sire Henry Wellcome Asian Series.

_____. 1999. "Warring States Natural Philosophy and Occult Thought." In *The Cambridge History of Ancient China*, ed. Michael Loewe and Edward Shaughnessy, 813–884. Cambridge: Cambridge University Press.

Holzman, Donald. 1978. "Confucius and Ancient Chinese Literary Criticism." In *Chinese Approaches to Literature from Confucius to Liang Ch'i-ch'ao*, ed. Adele Rickett, 21–41. Princeton: Princeton University Press.

Hong Liangji 洪亮吉, ed. 1987. *Chunqiu Zuozhuan Gu* 春秋左傳詁. Beijing: Zhonghua Shuju.

Hsieh, Shen-yüan. 1979. "Hsün Tzu's Political Philosophy." *Journal of Chinese Philosophy* 6: 69–90.

Hummel, A. W. 1925. "The Case Against Force in Chinese Philosophy." *Chinese Social and Political Science Review* 9: 334–350.

Hutton, Eric. 1996. "On the Meaning of *Yi* 義 for Xunzi." Unpublished M.A. thesis, Department of East Asian Languages and Civilizations, Harvard University.

_____. 2000. "Does Xunzi Have a Consistent Theory of Human Nature?" In *Virtue, Nature, and Moral Agency in the* Xunzi, ed. T. C. Kline and P. J. Ivanhoe, 220–236. Indianapolis: Hackett Publishing Company.

_____. 2001. "A Study of *Xunzi* HYIS 7/3/26–8/3/34." Unpublished manuscript.

Ihara, Craig. 1991. "David Wong on Emotions in Mencius." *Philosophy East & West* 41.1: 45–53.

Ivanhoe, P. J. 1990a. *Ethics in the Confucian Tradition*, Atlanta: Scholar's Press.

_____. 1990b. "Reweaving the 'One Thread' of the *Analects*." *Philosophy East & West* 40.1: 17–33.

_____. 1991a. "Zhuangzi's Conversion Experience." *Journal of Chinese Religions* 19: 13–25.

_____. 1991b. "A Happy Symmetry: Xunzi's Ethical Philosophy." *Journal of the American Academy of Religion* 59.2: 309–322.

_____. 1993a. *Confucian Moral Self Cultivation*. New York: Peter Lang Publishing.

_____. 1993b. "Zhuangzi on Skepticism, Skill, and the Ineffable Dao." *Journal of the American Academy of Religion* 61.4: 639–654.

_____. 1994. "Human Nature and Moral Understanding in Xunzi." *International Philosophical Quarterly* 34.2: 167–175.

_____. 1996a. "Was Zhuangzi a Relativist?" In *Essays on Skepticism, Relativism, and Ethics in the* Zhuangzi, ed. Paul Kjellberg and P. J. Ivanhoe, 196–214. Albany, NY: State University of New York Press.

_____, ed. 1996b. *Chinese Language, Thought, and Culture: Nivison and His Critics*. La Salle, IL: Open Court.

_____. 1998."The Concept of De in the *Dao De Jing*." In *Essays on Religious and Philosophical Aspects of the Laozi*, ed. Mark Csikszentmihalyi and P. J. Ivanhoe, 239–258. Albany, NY: State University of New York Press.

_____. n.d. "Chinese Moral Self Cultivation and Mencian Extension."

Jia Dongcheng 賈東城. 1989. "Ye tan 'wuwei'" 也談無為. *Hebei Shifandaxue Xuebao* 河北師範大學學報 45.2: 88–92.

Jiang Guanghui 姜廣輝. 1984. "Laozi de bukezhilun jiqi wuwei zhengzhiguan" 老子的不可知論及其無為政治觀. *Zhongguo Zhexue* 中國哲學 11: 36–48.

Jiao Xun 焦循. 1996. *Mengzi Zhengyi* 孟子正義. Beijing: Zhonghua Shuju.

Johnson, Mark. 1987. *The Body in the Mind: The Bodily Basis of Meaning, Imagination, and Reason*. Chicago: University of Chicago Press.

Kanaya Osamu 金谷治. 1964. "Mui to injun" 無為と因循. *Toho Shukyo* 東方宗教 23: 1–14.

_____. 1996. "The Mean in Original Confucianism." In *Chinese Language, Thought, and Culture*, ed. P. J. Ivanhoe, 83–93. La Salle, IL: Open Court.

Karlgren, Bernhard. 1923. *Analytic Dictionary of Chinese and Sino-Japanese*. Paris: P. Guethner.

_____. 1950. *The Book of Odes*. Stockholm: The Museum of Far Eastern Antiquities.

Keightley, David. 1978. "The Religious Commitment: Shang Theology and Generation of Chinese Political Culture." *History of Religions*. 17: 3–4, 211–215.

Kierkegaard, Soren. 1954. *Fear and Trembling* and *The Sickness Unto Death*. Trans. by Walter Lowrie. Princeton: Princeton University Press.

Kjellberg, Paul. 1993a. Zhuangzi and Skepticism. Ph.D. diss., Stanford University.

_____. 1993b. Review of *Butterfly as Companion*, *Philosophy East & West* 43.1: 127–135.

Kjellberg, Paul, and P.J. Ivanhoe, eds. 1996. *Essays on Skepticism, Relativism, and Ethics in the* Zhuangzi. Albany, NY: State University of New York Press.

Kline, T.C. 2000. "Moral Agency and Motivation in the *Xunzi*." In *Virtue, Nature, and Moral Agency in the* Xunzi, ed. T. C. Kline and P. J. Ivanhoe, 155–175. Indianapolis: Hackett Publishing Company.

Kline, T. C. and Ivanhoe, P. J., eds. 2000. *Virtue, Nature, and Moral Agency in the* Xunzi. Indianapolis: Hackett.

Knoblock, John. 1988–1994. *Xunzi: A Translation and Study of the Complete Works*. 3 vols. Stanford: Stanford University Press.

Kohn (Knaul), Livia. 1982. "Lost *Chuang-tzu* Passages." *Journal of Chinese Religions* 10: 53–79.

_____. 1986. "Chuang-tzu and the Chinese Ancestry of Ch'an Buddhism." *Journal of Chinese Philosophy* 12: 411–428.

_____. 1998. "The Lao-tzu Myth." In *Lao-tzu and the* Tao-Te-Ching, ed. Livia Kohn and Michael LaFargue, 41–62. Albany, NY: State University of New York Press.

Kohn, Livia, and Michael LaFargue, eds. 1998. *Lao-tzu and the* Tao-Te-Ching. Albany, NY: State University of New York Press.

Kövecses, Zoltán. 1986. *Metaphors of Anger, Pride, and Love: A Lexical Approach to the Structure of Concepts*. Philadelphia: John Benjamins.

_____. 1990. *Emotional Concepts*. New York: Springer-Verlag.

Kramers, R. P. 1966. "Die Eigenart der chinesischen Gedankernwelt, über die Bedeutung der alten chinesischen Philosophie für die modernen Chineschen." *Sinologia* 9. 1: 1–13.

Kuhn, Thomas. 1993. "Metaphor in Science." In *Metaphor and Thought* (2nd edition), ed. Andrew Ortony, 533–542. Cambridge: Cambridge University Press.

Kupperman, Joel. 1968. "Confucius and the Problem of Naturalness." *Philosophy East & West* 18: 175–185.

_____. 1996. "Spontaneity and the Education of the Emotions in the *Zhuangzi*." In *Essays on Skepticism, Relativism, and Ethics in the* Zhuangzi, ed. Paul Kjellberg and P. J. Ivanhoe, 183–195. Albany, NY: State University of New York Press.

LaFargue, Michael. 1994. *Tao and Method: A Reasoned Approach to the* Tao Te Ching. Albany, NY: State University of New York Press.

_____. 1998. "Recovering the *Tao-te-ching*'s Original Meaning: Some Remarks on Historical Hermeneutics." In *Lao-tzu and the* Tao-Te-Ching, ed. Livia Kohn and Michael LaFargue, 255–275. Albany, NY: State University of New York Press.

Lakoff, Andrew, and Miles Becker. 1992. *Me, Myself, and I*. Manuscript. University of California, Berkeley.

Lakoff, George. 1987. *Women, Fire, and Dangerous Things: What Categories Reveal About the Mind*. Chicago: University of Chicago Press.

_____. 1990. "The Invariance Hypothesis: Is Abstract Reasoning Based Upon Image-Schemas?" *Cognitive Linguistics* 1: 39–74.

_____. 1993. "The Contemporary Theory of Metaphor." In *Metaphor and Thought* (2nd edition), ed. Andrew Ortony, 202–251. Cambridge: Cambridge University Press.

_____. 1996. *Moral Politics: What Conservatives Know That Liberals Don't*. Chicago: University of Chicago Press.

Lakoff, George, and Mark Johnson. 1980. *Metaphors We Live By*. Chicago: University of Chicago Press.

_____. 1981. "The Metaphorical Structure of the Human Conceptual System." In *Perspectives on Cognitive Science*, ed. Donald Norman, 193–206. Norwood, N.J.: Ablex Publishing Corporation.

_____. 1999. *Philosophy in the Flesh: The Embodied Mind and Its Challenge to Western Thought*. New York: Basic Books.

Lakoff, George, and Mark Turner. 1989. *More Than Cool Reason: A Field Guide to Poetic Metaphor*. Chicago: University of Chicago Press.

Lan Kaixiang 藍開祥. 1990. "Zhuangzi yuyan zhexueli ji yishu tese" 莊子寓言哲理及藝術特色. *Xibei Shida Xuebao* 西北師大學報 65: 33–36.

Lau, D. C. 1953. "Theories of Human Nature in *Mencius* and *Shyuntzyy*." *Bulletin of the School of Oriental and African Studies* 15: 3: 541–565. Reprinted in *Virtue, Nature, and Moral Agency in the Xunzi*, ed. T. C. Kline III and Philip J. Ivanhoe, 188–219. Albany, NY: State University of New York Press, 2000.

_____. 1963. *Lao Tzu: Tao Te Ching*, New York: Penguin Books.

_____. 1968. "On the Term '*ch'ih ying*' and the Story Concerning the So-Called 'Tilting Vessel.'" *Symposium on Chinese Studies Commemorating the Golden Jubilee of the University of Hong Kong, 1911–1961*, no. 3. Hong Kong.

_____. 1970. *Mencius*. New York: Penguin Books.

_____. 1979. *Confucius: The Analects*. New York: Penguin Books.

Lau, D. C. and Fong Ching Chen, eds. 1992. *Liji Suizi Suoyin* 禮記逐字索引 (*A Concordance to the Liji*). Hong Kong: Commercial Press.

Legge, James. 1991a. *The She King (The Chinese Classics, Vol. 4)*. Taipei: SMC Publishing.

_____. 1991b. *The Shoo King (The Chinese Classics, Vol. 3)*. Taipei: SMC Publishing.

Li Caiyuan 李才遠. 1992. "Mengzi de 'yang haoranzhiqi' shuo." 孟子的 養浩然之氣説. *Xinan Shidaixue Xuebao* 西南師範大學學報: 17–23.

Lin Congshun 林聰舜. 1993."Zhuangzi wu-wei zhengzhi sixiang de jiceng yiyi" 莊子無為政治思想的幾層意義. *Hanxue Yanjiu* 漢學研究 21: 1–14.

Li Ling 李零. 1993. *Zhongguo fangshu kao* 中國方術考. Beijing: Renmin zhongguo chu-banshe.

Li Sheng-long 李生龍. 1986."Xianqin 'wu-wei' sixiang jianlun" 先秦無為思想簡論. *Hunan Shifan Daxue Shehuikexue Xuebao* 湖南師範大學社會科學學報 52.2: 7–13, 96.

_____. 1987a. "Handai 'wu-wei' sixiang jianlun" 漢代無為思想簡論. *Hunan Shifan Daxue Shehuikexue Xuebao* 湖南師範大學社會科學學報 61.5: 56–61.

_____. 1987b. "Kongzi, Laozi de 'wu-wei' sixiang zhi yitong ji qi yinxiang" 孔子老子的無為思   想之異同及其影響. *Zhongguo Zhexueshi Yanjiu* 中國哲學史研究 29.4: 18–22.

Lin Yu-sheng. 1924. "The Evolution of the Pre-Confucian Meaning of Jen and the Confu-cian Concept of Moral Autonomy." *Monumenta Serica* 31: 172–204.

Liu Gang 劉剛. 1987."'Bao Ding' bian" 庖丁辯. *Fanyang Shifan Xueyuan Xuebao* 藩陽師範學院學報 43.3: 19–21.

Liu Xiaogan 劉肖干. 1994. *Classifying the Chuang-tzu Chapters*. Ann Arbor : Center for Chinese Studies, University of Michigan.

_____. 1999. "Shilun laozi zhexue de zhongxin jiazhi" 試論老子哲學的中心價值. Trans. by Edward Slingerland as "An Inquiry Into the Central Value in Laozi's Phi-losophy." In *Essays on Religious and Philosophical Aspects of the Laozi*, ed. Mark Csikszentmihalyi and Philip J. Ivanhoe, 211–238. Albany, NY: State University of New York Press.

Liu Xuezhi 劉學智. 1986. "*Laozi* de daode fanchou xilie" 老子的道德範疇系列. *Shaanxi Shifan Daxue Xuebao* 陝西師範大學學報 53: 68–73.

Liu Zhanglin 劉長林. 1991. "'Qi' gainian de xingcheng ji zhexue jiazhi" 氣概念的形成及哲學價值. *Zhexue Yanjiu* 哲學研究 10: 56–64.

Lloyd, G. E. R. 1990. *Demystifying Mentalities*. New York: Cambridge University Press.

Loewe, Michael, ed. 1994. *Early Chinese Texts: A Bibliographical Guide*. Berkeley, CA: Institute of East Asian Studies.

Łoewe, Michael, and Edward Shaughnessy, eds. 1999. *The Cambridge History of Ancient China: From the Origins of Civilization to 221 B.C.* Cambridge: University of Cam-bridge Press.

Loy, David. 1985. "Wei wu-wei: Nondual Action." *Philosophy East & West* 35.1: 73–86.

Lu Qin 陸欽. 1962. "Zhuangzi 'wu-wei' shijie" 莊子無為試解. *Guangming Ribao* 光明日報. August 10.

Machle, Edward. 1976. "Hsun-tzu as a Religious Philosopher." *Philosophy East & West* 26: 443–461.

MacIntyre, Alasdair. 1981. *After Virtue*. Notre Dame: University of Notre Dame Press.

_____. 1990. *Three Rival Versions of Moral Inquiry*. Notre Dame: University of Notre Dame Press.

Mair, Victor, ed. 1983. *Experimental Essays on Chuang-tzu*. Honolulu: University of Hawaii Press.

Maspero, Henri. 1981. *Le Taoisme et les religions chinoises*, Paris: Gallimard, 1971. Trans. by Fran A. Kerman as *Taoism and Chinese Religion*. Amherst: University of Massachusetts Press.

Metzger, Thomas. 1977. *Escape from Predicament*. New York: Columbia University Press.

_____. 1987."Some Ancient Roots of Modern Chinese Thought: This Worldliness, Epis-temological Optimism, Doctrinality, and the Emergence of Reflexivity in the Eastern Chou." *Early China:* 11–12, 61–117.

Miller, George. 1993. "Images and Models, Similes and Metaphors." In *Metaphor and Thought* (2nd edition), ed. Andrew Ortony, 357–400. Cambridge: Cambridge University Press.

Mori Mikisaburo 森三樹三郎. 1967. "Shizen to jin-i" 自然と人為. *Tetsugaku Renkyu* 哲學研究 43.10: 1–21.

_____. 1972. "Chuang-tzu and Buddhism." *The Eastern Buddhist* 2: 44–69.

Moritz, Ralf. 1985. "Der Chinesische Philosoph Zhuang-zi im Licht Neuer Forschungen." *Orientalistische Lituraturzeitung* 80.2: 119–127.

Munro, Donald. 1969. *The Concept of Man in Early China*. Stanford, CA: Stanford University Press.

_____. 1985a. "The Family Network, the Stream of Water, and the Plant: Picturing Persons in Sung Confucianism." In *Individualism and Holism: Studies in Confucian and Taoist Values*, ed. Donald Munro, 259–291. Ann Arbor: Center for Chinese Studies.

_____. 1985b. "The Mirror and the Body: Values Within Chu Hsi's Theory of Knowledge." *Tsing Hua Journal of Chinese Studies* 1–2: 99–125.

_____. 1996. "A Villain in the *Xunzi*." In *Chinese Thought, Language, and Culture*, ed. P. J. Ivanhoe, 193–201. La Salle, IL: Open Court.

Murakami Yoshimi 村上嘉實. 1969."Gijutsu (jin-i) to shizen" 技術(人為)と自然. *Fukui Hakase Shoju Kinen Toyo Bunka Ronshu* 福井博士頌壽記念東洋文化論集 : 1051–1066.

Murakami Tokumi 村上德美 . 1966."Mui shizen ni tsuite" 無為自然について . *Kochi Daigaku Gakujutsu Renkyuho* 高知大學學術研究報: 169–172.

Murphy, Gregory. 1996. "On Metaphoric Representation." *Cognition* 60: 173–204.

Nivison, David. 1956. "Communist Ethics and the Confucian Tradition." *Journal of Asian Studies* 16.1: 51–74.

_____. 1978. "Royal 'Virtue' in Shang Oracle Inscriptions." *Early China* (Berkeley) 4: 52–55.

_____. 1991. "Hsun tzu and Chuang tzu." In *Chinese Texts and Philosophical Contexts*, ed. Henry Rosemont, 129–142. La Salle, IL.: Open Court. Reprinted in *Virtue, Nature, and Moral Agency in the Xunzi*, ed. T. C. Kline III and Philip J. Ivanhoe, 176–187. Albany, NY: State University of New York Press, 2000.

_____. 1996. "Replies and Comments." In *Chinese Language, Thought, and Culture: Nivison and His Critics*, ed. P. J. Ivanhoe, 267–341. La Salle, IL.: Open Court.

_____. 1997. *The Ways of Confucianism*, ed. Bryan Van Norden. La Salle, IL.: Open Court.

_____. 1999. "The Classical Philosophical Writings." In *The Cambridge History of Ancient China*, ed. Michael Loewe and Edward Shaughnessy, 754–812. Cambridge: Cambridge University Press.

Ortony, Andrew, ed. 1993. "The Role of Similarity in Similes and Metaphors." In *Metaphor and Thought* (2nd edition), ed. Andrew Ortony, 342–356. Cambridge: Cambridge University Press.

Oshima, Harold. 1983. "A Metaphorical Analysis of the Concept of Mind in the *Chuangtzu*." In *Experimental Essays on Chuang-tzu*, ed. Victor Mair, 63–84. Honolulu: University of Hawaii Press.

Paivio, Allan, and Mary Walsh. 1993. "Psychological Processes in Metaphor Comprehension and Memory." In *Metaphor and Thought* (2nd edition), ed. Andrew Ortony, 307–328. Cambridge: Cambridge University Press.

Pang Pu 龐朴. 1994. "Jie niu zhi jie" 解牛之解. *Xueshu Yuekan* 學術月刊 3: 11–20.

Paper, Jordan. 1995. *The Spirits Are Drunk: Comparative Approaches to Chinese Religion*. Albany, NY: State University of New York Press.

_____. 1997. "Dating the *Chuang-tzu* by Analysis of Philosophical Terms." *Chinese Culture* 18.4: 33–40.

Pinker, Steven. 1994. *The Language Instinct*. New York: HarperCollins.

Polanyi, Michael. 1966. *The Tacit Dimension*. New York: Doubleday.

Porkert, Manfred. 1974. *The Theoretical Foundations of Chinese Medicine*. Cambridge: MIT Press.

Pulleyblank, Edwin. 1995. *Outline of Classical Chinese Grammar*. Vancouver: University of British Columbia Press.

Qian Mu 錢穆 . 1951. *Zhuangzi Cuanjian* 莊子纂箋 . Hong Kong: Dongnan Yinwu Chubanshe.

_____. 1956. *Xianqin Zhuzi Xinian* 先秦諸子繫年. Hong Kong: Xianggang Daxue Chubanshe.

Raphals, Lisa. 1995. *Knowing Words*. Ithaca: Cornell University Press.

_____. 1998. *Sharing the Light: Representations of Women and Virtue in Early China*. Albany, NY: State University of New York Press.

Rickett, Allyn W. 1965. *Kuan-tzu (Volume 1)*. Hong Kong: Hong Kong University Press.

_____. 1998. *Guanzi: Political, Economic, and Philosophical Essays from Early China (Volume 2)*. Princeton, NJ: Princeton University Press.

Riegel, Jeffrey. 1980. "Reflections on an Unmoved Mind: An Analysis of *Mencius* 2:A:2." *Journal of the American Academy of Religion* 47.4: 433–457.

Robinet, Isabelle. 1984. "Polysémisme du texte canonique et syncrétisme des interprétations: Étude taxinomique des commentaires du *Daode jing* au sein de la tradition chinoise." *Extrême Orient—Extrême Occident* 5: 27–47. Trans. by Livia Kohn and reprinted in *Lao-tzu and the Tao-Te-Ching*, ed. Livia Kohn and Michael LaFargue, 119–142. Albany, NY: State University of New York Press.

_____. 1997. *Taoism: Growth of a Religion*. Trans. Phyllis Brooks. Stanford, CA: Stanford University Press.

Roetz, Heiner. 1993. *Confucian Ethics of the Axial Age*. Albany, NY: State University of New York Press.

Rosemont, Henry. 1970. "State and Society in the *Hsun Tzu*: A Philosophical Commentary." *Monumenta Serica* 29: 38–78.

_____. 1974. "On Representing Abstractions in Archaic Chinese." *Philosophy East & West* 24.1: 71–88.

_____, ed. 1991a. *Chinese Texts and Philosophical Contexts*. La Salle, IL.: Open Court.

_____. 1991b. "Who Chooses?" In *Chinese Texts and Philosophical Contexts*, ed. Henry Rosemont, 227–266. La Salle, IL.: Open Court.

Roth, Harold. 1990. "The Early Taoist Concept of *Shen*: A Ghost in the Machine?" In *Sagehood and Systematizing Thought in Warring States and Han China*, ed. Kidder Smith, 11–32. Asian Studies Program, Brunswick, Maine: Bowdoin College.

_____. 1991a. "Psychology and Self-Cultivation in Early Taoistic Thought." *Harvard Journal of Asiatic Studies* 51.2: 599–651.

_____. 1991b. "Who Compiled the Chuang-tzu?" In *Chinese Texts and Philosophical Contexts*, ed. Henry Rosemont, 79–128. La Salle, IL.: Open Court.

_____. 1999a. *Original Tao: Inward Training (Nei Yeh) and the Foundations of Taoist Mysticism*. New York: Columbia University Press.

_____. 1999b. "The *Laozi* in the Context of Early Chinese Mystical Praxis." In *Essays on Religious and Philosophical Aspects of the Laozi*, ed. Mark Csikszentmihalyi and P. J. Ivanhoe, 59–96. Albany, NY: State University of New York Press.

Ruskola, Teemu. 1992. "Moral Choice in the *Analects*: A Way Without Crossroads?" *Journal of Chinese Philosophy* 19: 285–296.

Ryle, Gilbert. 1949. *The Concept of Mind*. New York: Barnes and Noble.

Schipper, Kristofer. 1993. *The Taoist Body*. Trans. Karen Duval. Berkeley: University of California Press.

Schofer, John. 1993. "Virtues in Xunzi's Thought." *The Journal of Religious Ethics* 21.1: 117–136. Reprinted in *Virtue, Nature, and Moral Agency in the Xunzi*, ed. T. C. Kline III and Philip J. Ivanhoe, 69–88. Albany, NY: State University of New York Press, 2000.

Schwartz, Benjamin. 1973. "On the Absence of Reductionism in Chinese Thought." *Journal of Chinese Philosophy* 1.1: 27–43.

_____. 1985. *The World of Thought in Ancient China*. Cambridge: Harvard University Press.

Sereno, M. 1991. "Four Analogies Between Biological and Cultural/Linguistic Evolution." *Journal of Theoretical Biology* 151: 467–507.

Shun, Kwong-loi. 1989. "Moral Reasons in Confucian Ethics." *Journal of Chinese Philosophy* 16: 317–343.

_____. 1993. "Jen and Li in the Analects." *Philosophy East & West* 43.3: 457–479.

_____. 1997. *Mencius and Early Chinese Thought*. Stanford: Stanford University Press.

Sima, Qian 司馬遷. 1964. *Shiji* 史記. Shanghai: Zhonghua Shuju.

Slingerland, Edward. 1996. "The Conception of *Ming* in Early Chinese Thought." *Philosophy East & West* 46.4: 567–581.

_____. 2000a. "Why Philosophy Is Not 'Extra.'" In Understanding the *Analects*, a review of Brooks and Brooks, *The Original Analects.*" *Philosophy East and West* 50.1: 137–141, 146–147.

_____. 2000b. "Conceptions of the Self in the *Zhuangzi*: Conceptual Metaphor Analysis and Comparative Thought." Manuscript. Forthcoming in *Philosophy East & West* 54:3 (July, 2004).

_____. 2001. "Virtue Ethics, the *Analects*, and the Problem of Commensurability." *Journal of Religious Ethics* 29.1: 97–125.

Smith, Jonathan. 1970. "The Influence of Symbols on Social Change: A Place on Which to Stand." *Worship* 44: 457–474.

Smith, M. P. 1924. "Chinese Optimism." *Asia* 24: 622–626, 654.

Sweetser, Eve. 1990. *From Etymology to Pragmatics: Metaphorical and Cultural Aspects of Semantic Structure*. Cambridge: Cambridge University Press.

Tao Tiesheng 陶鐵勝. 1994. "'Dao fa ziran' shijie yu 'ziran wuwei' feng guxi" 道法自然 視解與自然無為風骨析. *Huadong Ligong Daxue Xuebao* 華東理工大學 學報: 29–33.

Taylor, Charles. 1989. *Sources of the Self*. Cambridge, MA: Harvard University Press.

Taylor, Rodney. 1990. *The Religious Dimensions of Confucianism*. Albany, NY: State University of New York Press.

Thiel, P. J. 1968. "Shamanismus in Alten China." *Sinologia* 10: 149–204.

_____. 1969. "Das Erkenntnis Problem bei Chuang-tzu." *Sinologia* 11: 1–89.

Thomas, Léon. 1987. "Les États de Conscience Inhabituels dans le *Zhuang Zi*." *Revue de l'Histoire des Religion*.

Turbayne, Colin. 1970. *The Myth of Metaphor*. Columbia, SC: University of South Carolina Press.

Turner, Mark. 1991. *Reading Minds: The Study of English in the Age of Cognitive Science*. Princeton: Princeton University Press.

Van Houten, Richard. 1988. "Nature and *Tzu-jan* in Early Chinese Philosophical Literature." *Journal of Chinese Philosophy* 15: 35–49.

Van Norden, Bryan. 1991. "Shun on Moral Reasons." *Journal of Chinese Philosophy* 18: 355.

_____. 1992. "Mencius and Xunzi: Two Views of Human Agency." *International Philosophical Quarterly* 32.2: 161–184. Reprinted in *Virtue, Nature, and Moral Agency in the Xunzi*, ed. T. C. Kline III and Philip J. Ivanhoe, 103–134. Albany, NY: State University of New York Press, 2000.

Van Zoeren, Steven. 1991. *Poetry and Personality*. Stanford: Stanford University Press.

Waley, Arthur. 1960. *The Book of Songs*. New York: Grove Press.

Wang Bangxiong 王邦雄. 1991. "Zhuangzi sixiang jiqi xiuyang gongfu" 莊子思想及其修養工夫. *Ehu Yuekan* 鵝湖月刊 7: 1.

Wang Fuzhi 王夫之. 1961. *Zhuangzi Jie* 莊子解. Beijing: Zhonghua Shuju.

_____. 1975. *Du Sishu Daquanshuo* 讀四書大全説. Beijing: Zhonghua Shuju.

Wang Jinlin 王景琳. 1986. "Zhuangzi dui yuyan yishu de gongxian." 莊子對寓言藝術的貢獻. *Beijing Daxue Xuebao* 北京大學學報 113: 110–115, 118.

Wang Shumin 王叔岷. 1988. *Zhuangzi Jiaoquan* 莊子校詮. Taibei: Zhongyang Yanjiuyuan Lishi Yuyan Yanjiusuo zhuankan zhi 88.

_____. 1976. "Huainanzi yu Zhuangzi" 淮南子與莊子. In *Huainanzi Lunwenji* 淮南子論文集, ed. Chen Xinyong 陳新雄 and Yu Dacheng 于大成, 27–39. Taibei: Mutuo Chubanshe.

Wang Xianqian 王先謙. 1988. *Xunzi Jijie* 荀子集釋. Beijing: Zhonghua Shuju.

Watson, Burton. 1963. *Hsun-tzu*. New York: Columbia University Press.

_____. 1968. *The Complete Works of Chuang Tzu*. New York: Columbia University Press.

Wei Jiaqi 魏家齊. 1992. "Shilun Laozi 'Wuwei er zhi' de zhengzhi sixiang" 試論老子無為而治的政治思想. *Guizhou Shehuike Xuebao* 貴州社會科學報 117: 9.

Williams, Bernard. 1993. *Shame and Necessity*, Berkeley: University of California Press.

Wilson, Steven. 1995. "Conformity, Individuality, and the Nature of Virtue." *Journal of Religious Ethics* 23.2: 263–289.

Winter, Steven. 1989. "Transcendental Nonsense, Metaphoric Reasoning, and the Cognitive Stakes for Law." *University of Pennsylvania Law Review* 137.

Wolf, Hans-Georg. 1994. *A Folk Model of the "Internal Self" in Light of the Contemporary Theory of Metaphor: The Self as Subject and Object*. Frankfurt: Peter Lang.

Wollheim, Richard. 1993. "The Sheep and the Ceremony." In *The Mind and Its Depths*, 1–21. Cambridge: Harvard University Press, 1–21.

Wong, David. 1991. "Is There a Distinction Between Reason and Emotion in Mencius?" *Philosophy East & West* 41: 31–44.

_____. 2000. "Xunzi on Moral Motivation." In *Virtue, Nature, and Moral Agency in the Xunzi*, ed. T. C. Kline and P. J. Ivanhoe, 135–154. Indianapolis: Hackett.

Wu, Kuang-ming. 1981. "Trying Without Trying: Toward a Taoist Phenomenology of Truth." *Journal of Chinese Philosophy* 8:1, 143–167.

_____. 1982. *Chuang-tzu: World Philosopher at Play*. New York: Crossroad.

_____. 1987. "Counterfactuals, Universals, and Chinese Thinking." *Philosophy East & West* 37.1: 84–94.

_____. 1988. "Goblet Words, Dwelling Words, Opalescent Words—Philosophical Methodology of Chuang-tzu." *Journal of Chinese Philosophy* 15: 1–8.

_____. 1989. "Zhuangzi de zixiang maodun" 莊子的自相矛盾. *Taida Zhexue Lunping* 臺大哲學論評 12: 313–323.

_____. 1990. *Butterfly as Companion*. Albany, NY: State University of New York Press.

_____. 1992. "Body Thinking in the Chuang-tzu." *Guoli Zhongzheng Daxue Xuebao* 國立中正大學學報 3.1: 193–213.

Wu Yujiang 吳毓江. 1993. *Mozi Jiaozhu* 墨子校注. Beijing: Zhonghua Shuju.

Xiang Xi 向熹, ed. 1987. *Shijing Cidian* 詩經詞典. Chengdu: Sichuan Renmin Chuban-she.

Xu Fuguan 徐復觀. 1966. *Zhongguo Yishu Jingshen* 中國藝術精神. Taibei: Xuesheng Chubanshe.

_____. 1969. *Zhongguo Renxing Lunshi* 中國人性論史. Taibei: Shangwu Chubanshe.

Yampolsky, Philip. 1967. *The Platform Sutra of the Sixth Patriarch*. New York: Columbia University Press.

Yang Darong 楊達榮. 1994. "'Wuwei er zhi de beijing, hanyi he zuoyong" 無為而治的背景涵義和作用. *Hainan Daxue Xuebao* 海南大學學報 3: 51–57.

Yang Rur-bin (Yang Ru-bin) 楊儒賓. 1990. "Lun Mengzi de guan: yi chizhi yangqi wei zhongxin zhankai de gongfu lunmianxiang" 論孟子的觀以持志養氣為中心展開的工夫論面相. *Qinghua Xuebao* 清華學報 20.1: 83–123.

_____. 1993. "Zhiyan jianxing yu shengren" 知言踐形與聖人. *Qinghua Xuebao* 清華學報 23.4: 401–428.

Yang Qi 楊琦. 1992. "Shi Mengzi de 'yang haoranzhiqi'" 釋孟子的 養浩然之氣. *Shanxi Shida Xuebao* 陝西師大學報: 111–114.

Yearley, Lee. 1980. "Hsun Tzu on the Mind." *Journal of Asian Studies* 39.3: 465–480.

_____. 1983. "The Perfected Person in the Radical Chuang-tzu." In *Experimental Essays on the Chuang-tzu*, ed. Victor Mair, 125–139. Honolulu: University of Hawaii Press.

_____. 1990. *Mencius and Aquinas*. Albany, NY: State University of New York Press.

_____. 1996. "Zhuangzi's Understanding of Skillfulnes and the Ultimate Spiritual State." In *Essays on Skepticism, Relativism, and Ethics in the* Zhuangzi, ed. Paul Kjellberg and P. J. Ivanhoe, 152–182. Albany, NY: State University of New York Press.

Yin Zhenhuan 尹振環. 1993. "Daojia de wuwei lun." 道家的無為論. *Zhongguo shi yanjiu* 中國史研究: 75–81.

_____. 1991. "Wuwei Zhexue: xi Laozi de yiwuweiweiwei, yi buzhengzheng deng six-iang." 無為哲學析老子的以無為為，以不爭爭等思想. *Fudan Xuebao* 復旦學報: 51–53.

Zhang Qin 張欽. 1995. "Lun Laodan zhi 'dao' yu 'ziran wuwei'" 論老聃之道與自然無為. *Zongjiaoxue Yanjiu* 宗教學研究: 59–62.

Zhang Wei 張偉. 1986. "'Ziran wuwei' yu 'sangji yu wu'" 自然無為與喪己於物. *Liaoning Daxue Xuebao* 遼寧大學學報 80.4: 30–32.

Zhao Jihui 趙吉惠. 1986. "'Wuwei er zhi' de zhengzhi sixiang jiqi lishi yanbian" 無為而治的政治思想及其歷史演變. *Shaanxi Shidaxue Xuebao* 陝西師大學學報 53.4: 63–67.

Zhou Daoji 周道濟. 1968. "Dao ru fa sanjia zhi junzhu wuwei sixiang" 道儒法三家之君主無為思想. *Dalu Zazhi* 大陸雜志 37.7: 15–17.

Zhu Xi 朱熹. 1987. *Sishu Zhangju Jizhu* 四書章句集注. Shanghai: Shanghai Shudian.

Zhuan Xianqun 傳獻群. 1993. "Shixi Laozi de 'wuwei er zhi'" 試析老子的無為而治. *Fuzhou Daxue Xuebao* 福州大學學報: 7.3: 39–42.

Index

347